The World through Children's Books

Edited by
Susan Stan

The Scarecrow Press, Inc.
Lanham, Maryland, and London
2002

SCARECROW PRESS, INC.

Published in the United States of America
by Scarecrow Press, Inc.
4720 Boston Way, Lanham, Maryland 20706
www.scarecrowpress.com

4 Pleydell Gardens, Folkestone
Kent CT20 2DN, England

British Library Cataloguing-in-Publication Information Available

Library of Congress Cataloging-in-Publication Data

The world through children's books / edited by Susan Stan.
 p. cm.
 Includes bibliographical references and indexes.
 ISBN 0-8108-4198-3 (pbk. : alk. paper)
  1. Children's literature—Bibliography. 2. Children's literature—History and criticism. I. Stan, Susan.
Z1037 .W954 2002
[PN1009.A1]
011.62—dc21   2001045863

♾™ The paper used in this publication meets the minimum requirements of American National Standard for Information Sciences—Permanence of Paper for Printed Library Materials, ANSI/NISO Z39.48-1992.
Manufactured in the United States of America.

Contents

Foreword   *vii*

Preface   *ix*

Part 1: International Children's Literature

1. An Overview of International Children's Literature   3
   Carl M. Tomlinson

2. Books as Bridges   *Susan Stan*   27

Part 2: Bibliography

About the Bibliography   41

3. Latin America and the Caribbean   43
   - Argentina   43
   - Bolivia   43
   - Brazil   43
   - Chile   45
   - Colombia   46
   - Cuba   46
   - Dominican Republic   47
   - Ecuador (Galapago Islands)   47
   - El Salvador   48
   - Guatemala   48
   - Haiti   51
   - Jamaica   52
   - Mexico   53
   - Nicaragua   61
   - Peru   62
   - Puerto Rico   62
   - Trinidad   63
   - Venezuela   64
   - Latin America—Mixed or Unspecified Settings   64

4. Canada and the Far North   69

5. Asia   95
   Afghanistan   95
   Cambodia   95
   China   97
   India   100
   Indonesia (Bali)   104
   Japan   104
   North Korea and South Korea   109
   Laos   111
   Pakistan   112
   Philippines   112
   Thailand   113
   Tibet   114
   Vietnam   115
   Asia—Regional   116

6. North Africa and the Middle East   117
   Egypt   117
   Iraq   118
   Israel & Palestine   118
   Lebanon   122
   Morocco   122
   North Africa—Regional   123

7. Africa South of the Sahara   124
   Cameroon   124
   Democratic Republic of Congo   124
   Ethiopia   125
   Ghana   126
   Kenya   126
   Liberia   128
   Nigeria   128
   Sierra Leone   129
   South Africa   129
   Sudan   133
   Tanzania   133
   Zimbabwe   134
   Africa—Regional   135

8. Australia and New Zealand   138

Australia 138
New Zealand 157

9. Europe 160
   Austria 160
   Belgium 163
   Czech Republic 164
   Denmark 166
   Finland 168
   France 168
   Germany 179
   Greece 191
   Hungary 195
   Republic of Ireland 195
   Italy 199
   Lithuania 202
   The Netherlands 202
   Norway 209
   Poland 212
   Russia 214
   Slovak Republic 216
   Spain 216
   Sweden 218
   Switzerland 223
   United Kingdom 225
   Yugoslavia 269

10. Global 272
    Multinational Books 272
    Geography Series 277

Part 3: Resources
11. Children's Book Awards 285
12. Organizations 292
13. Publishers 294
14. Sources for Foreign-Language and Bilingual Books 298

Author/Illustrator/Translator Index 303
Title Index 313
Subject Guide 322
About the Editor 325

Foreword

The world of childhood is a space we all share: the earliest sense of comfort and pain and wonder, the first word, the first step, the need for a circle of loving support that allows us to look beyond the place where we live. The experiences of each individual vary according to circumstance, culture, community, and locality. Yet our journeys through time are lined with stories that can bind us together if we share them along the way. Stories allow us to feel another's experience as if it were our own. It is no accident that the doorway through which Alice enters Wonderland is a looking glass, ordinarily used for self-reflection. Encountering others helps us take the full measure of ourselves.

The World through Children's Books is a looking-glass through which children can find others along with themselves. It represents the practical ideal of the United States Board on Books for Young People (USBBY)—that stories help us understand our differences and at the same time reveal our common humanity. The dedicated USBBY members who volunteered their time and energy to compile and annotate this bibliography, as well as to contextualize the information with background on the development of international work with children's literature, have opened a doorway of stories into the universe of childhood. Now all the rest of us can help young readers step through that doorway by opening and using this book to its fullest extent.

Betsy Hearne
President, 2001
USBBY

Preface

The World through Children's Books is the second volume to be sponsored by the United States Board on Books for Young People. The first, *Children's Books from Other Countries,* edited by Carl M.Tomlinson (Scarecrow, 1998), was a long overdue compendium of international children's literature. Like this volume, it included a historical overview and a guide to best practices, along with a bibliography listing over seven hundred titles from countries other than the United States. This selection included both in-print and out-of-print books published between 1950 and 1996.

Because *The World through Children's Books* is intended for use along-side *Children's Books from Other Countries,* it begins where the first volume left off, listing international books published in the United States from 1996 through 2000. In addition, it includes a selection of books written by authors residing in the United States but set in other countries. A number of these books have been written by newcomers to America, whose memories of their homelands have shaped their work. While there is little duplication between the first and second volumes, one exception is Carl M. Tomlinson's comprehensive introduction to international children's literature, which has been reprinted in updated form in this volume.

Part 1, therefore, offers an introduction to the field of international children's literature and a current look at its status in the United States, as well as provides suggestions for sharing international books with children and resources that can help foster an international perspective. Part 2 presents listings of quality international and domestic books organized by region of the world and country. Part 3 lists resources to help readers find these and other books with an international focus.

Gratitude is due to numerous people whose ideas, insights, and energy at varying stages went into creating this book. An advisory board, whose members are listed opposite the foreword, helped determine what form this volume would take. The work of thirty-three annotators, whose names are listed at the beginning of Part 2, forms the core of the book; without them, it would not exist. Special recognition goes to Doris Gebel, researcher extraordinaire, who not only annotated the greatest number of titles but also combed databases to be sure relevant books would be included. All of these people volunteered their time and energy because they believe in the importance of international literature for children. The fine staff at Scarecrow Press, including editors Jessica McCleary and Melissa Ray, helped both to shape the book and to refine its contents.

Central Michigan University (CMU) supported this project at many levels. Contributions from the Faculty Research and Creative Endeavors program at CMU helped to fund attendance at IBBY and USBBY conferences, including the 27th World IBBY Congress in Cartagena de Indias, where I first saw Aleko's art, which was created for that event and now appears on the cover of this book. Administrating this project required technical expertise beyond mine, and so I am grateful to Jeffrey McDowell of CMU's Office of Information Technology for his help in setting up a database, to Cheryl Dusty-Delauro of CMU's Graphic Production Department for her tutelage in computer design, and to Larry McDonald and Elizabeth Vogel of CMU's College of Human Sciences and Behavioral Sciences for their ongoing technical support to maintain the project website. Dr. Robert Aron of CMU's Geography Department was an invaluable resource when it came to organizing the bibliography into regions. The English Department, chaired by Dr. Stephen Holder, lent much needed support in the form of equipment use and student labor. Thanks go to Karen Sanborn and Linda Bearss for database entry and to Carole Pasch, department secretary, for being so accommodating.

A final word of thanks is owed to Carl M. Tomlinson, who as editor of *Children's Books from Other Countries* set the standard for me to follow, and who as friend and fellow USBBY member encouraged me to take on its sequel.

Part 1

International Children's Literature

1
An Overview of
International Children's Literature
Carl M. Tomlinson

It is through literature that we most intimately enter the hearts and minds
and spirits of other people. And what we value in this is the *difference*
as well as the human similarities of others: that way, as C. S. Lewis put
it, we become a thousand different people and yet remain ourselves.

—*Aidan Chambers*

What Is International Children's Literature?

In 1998, the appearance of *Harry Potter and the Sorcerer's Stone* thrust
children's literature into the limelight. Further, J. K. Rowling's series
about the boy wizard made apparent a fact that most of the general reading public in America had never considered—that not all books published for American children originate in the United States. Because of
the publicity surrounding this series, some readers became aware for the
first time that the book they were reading was written in another country
and being enjoyed simultaneously by children in many different countries. Harry Potter takes his place alongside Heidi, Pinocchio, Bambi,
Peter Pan, Pippi Longstocking, Peter Rabbit, and Winnie-the-Pooh as a
story character that is an important part of childhood. In fact, many of
our classic children's stories and most memorable literary characters are
international. We claim them as part of our literary heritage.

International children's literature, for those who live in the United
States, is that body of books originally published for children in a country other than the United States in a language of that country and later
published in this country. It includes all types of literature—prose and
poetry, fiction and nonfiction. These books can be subdivided into (1)
books that were originally written in a language other than English and

subsequently translated into English (e.g., *Heidi* by Johanna Spyri, originally published in Switzerland in German); (2) books that were originally written in English, but in a country other than the United States (e.g., *Peter Pan* by Sir James Barrie, originally published in England); and (3) books that were originally published in a country other than the United States in a language other than English and subsequently published in the United States in the original language (e.g., *Le Petit Prince* by Antoine de Saint Exupéry, originally published in France in French). *The World through Children's Books* includes the first two types.

In addition, this book includes selected *domestic* children's books—books originally published in the United States for children of this country but whose characters or settings are foreign (e.g., *Red Scarf Girl* by Ji-Li Jiang). Some of these books have been written by recent immigrants whose stories are set in the countries where they grew up, while others have been written by Americans who have lived in, adopted, or otherwise come to know the culture of another country. In some cases, we have more domestic books about a country or culture than we have international books. That is because some countries currently lack well-developed publishing programs for children and have no books for American publishers to reprint.

Ideally, American children will learn about other countries of the world through a combination of international and domestic books. International books have much to offer American children, as they allow readers to see a country through the eyes of someone who lives there. The entire next section enumerates the many positive results that can come from reading these books. Domestic books, too, have much to offer, as there are times when a writer who knows how the intended reader sees the world can best explain how others see it differently.

Is International Literature for Children Necessary?

With the thousands of children's books written and published in this country annually, why do we also need children's books from other countries? Here are some excellent answers to that question:

- Good stories from other countries bridge geographical and cultural gaps. Hearing stories enjoyed by children in other nations establishes in American children a foundation for international understanding. These stories connect us to the rest of the world.

- Some of the best works of children's literature are international. It would be a shame to miss such classics as Jules Verne's *Twenty Thousand Leagues Under the Sea* (France), and the folktales of the Brothers Grimm (Germany), as illustrated by Lisbeth Zwerger (Austria), or such modern favorites as Phillip Pullman's *The Golden Compass* (originally published as *Northern Lights* in the United Kingdom), Anne Frank's *The Diary of a Young Girl* (The Netherlands), or Mitsumasa Anno's intriguing wordless picture book, *Anno's Journey* (Japan).

- International stories teach children about their peers in other lands, since they bring the people, history, and traditions of these countries to life and counteract stereotypes. The beauty of reading a good story from another country is that living, breathing *individuals* emerge, not a faceless mass of people, all with a common stamp (Rochman 1993).

- Both the emotional and the cognitive aspects of reading international literature make clear to young readers that they have much to gain from knowing about their peers in other lands. Adversely, having no exposure to books from other countries might give children the impression that there is little worth knowing outside the United States.

- By interpreting events in the everyday lives of their characters and by depicting long-term changes in the characters' lives, international authors of contemporary realistic fiction present truer and more understandable pictures of life in other countries than does the sensation-prone, narrow coverage of television and newspapers.

- Compelling stories build students' interest in the people and places they are reading about and pave the way to a deeper understanding and appreciation of the geographical and historical content encountered in textbooks.

- Literature written by natives of a country or region or those who have lived there and studied the country or region gives accuracy, authenticity, and an international perspective to classroom materials. Those who have taken the time to become thoroughly familiar with a culture write *from* the culture, based on their experience, rather than *about* the culture (Italiano 1995).

- International authors often confront issues that U.S. authors are reticent to discuss, but that children and young people benefit from knowing about. Examples include alienation, living with disabilities, human sexuality, interracial marriage, and poverty. Morris Gleitzman's humorous novel *Blabber Mouth*, about a teenage girl who is congenitally mute, is such a book.

• International picture book art is often fresh and distinctive.

• International literature reflects the cultural and language diversity found in our classrooms. By reading international books, students can learn to respect the heritage of others and to take pride in their own. Children who only read about characters just like themselves, on the other hand, limit their knowledge of others and, more important, of themselves.

• International and U.S. books work well together. Selecting a good mix of U.S. and international books for units of instruction, reading aloud, or independent reading is a daily reminder to students that similarities outweigh differences between cultures.

A corollary to the value of international books in translation is the value of having foreign-language books in our libraries and classrooms. Frazier (1981) points out that lack of exposure to foreign-language books gives our students the false notion that all that is worth knowing is written in English. Regardless of whether students have facility in languages other than English, they benefit from seeing original versions of translated literature and seeing what other languages look like in print. Wherever available, sources for foreign-language editions are included at the end of the country listings in Part 2, and further sources can be found in the listings that follow the bibliography.

International Children's Literature, Past and Present

Some background knowledge of the field of international children's literature may add interest to your reading of these books or initiate further inquiry. The following summary presents only the highlights of the interesting history and features of this field:

Early International Literature

Surely, the first international stories were the traditional tales—myths, legends, and folktales—that originated long ago and followed humans as they populated the globe. Some anthropologists believe that this explains why many cultures share similar folktales. At any rate, such ancient stories as these and *Aesop's Fables* tend to be accepted as our own, since they were already present when the first books were published (Meigs et. al. 1953). Such early works from other lands laid the groundwork for the children's book field. Chief among these are the *Gesta Romanorum* of the Middle Ages, which provided many of the beginnings and basic situations for later stories, and Comenius's Renaissance masterpiece, *Orbis Pictus* [The World Illustrated], which appeared in 1657. *Orbis Pictus* is thought to be the first picture book for children, since it coupled for the first time the notions of books and joyful learning.

Formal international exchange of children's stories began several centuries ago. *Histoires du Temps Passés* [Stories of Times Past] (1698), which we know as *Tales of Mother Goose*, written down by Charles Perrault in France at the end of the seventeenth century, and *Robinson Crusoe,* written by Daniel Defoe in England and published in 1719, are examples of early books enjoyed by children in many countries and in many different languages. Prior to this century the relative percentage of imported children's books to the total available was higher than today. The publishing industry was small compared to today's standards, and imported books helped to satisfy the demand.

International Children's Literature Today

Australia, Canada, the European nations, Great Britain, Japan, New Zealand, and the United States have well-developed bodies of children's literature. Most children's books originate in these countries. *Children's Books in Print 2000-2001* lists over 188,900 children's books available in the United States alone. While many of these titles are duplicates—the same title published in different editions or bindings—that number is still astounding.

Venezuela, Russia, China, South Africa, and India also actively publish children's books, though not in the variety produced in the developed countries mentioned above. In some cases, social, political, and economic difficulties in these countries have spawned powerful works of protest literature that have attained international prominence, such as *The Streets Are Free* (Toronto: Annick, 1995) by the Venezuelan, Kurusa, or *Journey to Jo'burg* and *Chain of Fire* (New York: Lippincott, 1986, 1990) by the South African émigré, Beverley Naidoo. In China and India, while the numbers of children's books published are impressive, the quality and content of these books are less so. In these countries, where illiteracy is widespread, children's books are still primarily for the purpose of instruction, and so the lion's share of resources is devoted to textbook production. Legends, folktales, and myths are also widely published in order to convey cultural values. The few works of contemporary fiction that emerge are, with rare exceptions, didactic and obviously intended to teach moral values or to mold young readers' characters (Khorana 1993; Louie 1996). We must remember that publishing in a country such as India, with its 17 languages and 1,652 dialects, presents challenges unimagined by publishers in the United States. Since the breakup of the Soviet Union, Russia has been making valiant efforts to establish a new, private publishing industry despite an unstable economy, huge inflation, and lack of booksellers. Independent Russian publishers, some devoted exclusively to children's books, have many problems, but relish the fact that, at long last, there is no censorship and no interference from government agencies (Frenkel 1994).

Many developing countries have yet to establish a children's book publishing industry, primarily due to economic constraints. In some countries of Africa, for instance, there are virtually no books for children. The notable exception is Zimbabwe and its capital, Harare, known as the "book capital of Africa," where the annual Zimbabwe International Book Fair is held. In most developing countries the publishing obstacles are formidable: numerous major language groups, requiring multiple translations and unprofitably small print runs of each title; few bookstores; no sales network; and few parents who can afford books for their children. The oral tradition prevails in these countries, with ancient stories, rich in history and culture, passed along by word of mouth from generation to generation. As young people abandon their villages for large cities, however, there is a danger that these oral histories will die out. Grass-roots efforts to bring literacy to children in these countries are often inspiring. In Kenya, for example, women print letters, numbers, proverbs, and pictorial messages on bright *kanga cloths*, the traditional all-purpose cloth used for clothing, curtains, tablecloths, and other household purposes. These "primers" are economical, practical, versatile, and visible.

From time to time, authors who have visited or lived in developing countries have written stories set in these countries. Sometimes the author's intent is to help create a body of literature for the children of the country, and the books have been first published there. Such is the case with *I'm José and I'm Okay: Three Stories from Bolivia*, an international collaboration between Werner Holzwarth of Germany and Yatiyawi Studios, a nonprofit organization founded in Bolivia to encourage literacy through stories based on actual experiences. In other cases, the authors want to spotlight the conditions in which some children are forced to grow up. A recent example is the 2000 Batchelder Honor Book *Asphalt Angels*, by the Dutch writer Ineke Holtwijk, set in Rio de Janeiro, Brazil. Both books feature orphans as their main characters.

The International Children's Literature Movement

The international children's literature movement was founded primarily through the efforts of Jella Lepman, a German Jew who fled the Nazi Holocaust of World War II but who returned to her devastated homeland  immediately after the war. Determined to do something to prevent the recurrence of such destruction, Lepman convinced publishers from all over Europe to donate children's books for a traveling exhibit. These books, Lepman believed, would build bridges of understanding between the children who read them. For years this exhibit drew great crowds all over Europe, and in 1949 it became the foundation of the Internationale Jugendbibliothek, or International Youth Library (IYL). Today, the first of Lepman's great accomplishments, the International Youth Library, is housed in Schloss

Blutenburg, a former castle, in Munich, Germany. It is the only institution in the world that systematically collects the world's literature for children. With more than 500,000 volumes in over 130 languages, the IYL is the world's largest collection of children's literature. Its publications include the quarterly *IJB Report,* the annual *IJB Bulletin*, and *The White Ravens*, an annual selection of recent international children's books recommended for translation. The IYL maintains a German-language website that provides current information about these activities.

Encouraged by the success of the international book exhibit and the fledgling IYL, Lepman and others founded in 1953 the International Board on Books for Young People, or IBBY. This nonprofit organization provides an international forum for those committed to bringing children and books together and is the centerpiece of the international children's literature movement. Its general mission is to promote international understanding and world peace through children's books. More specifically, IBBY strives to give children everywhere the opportunity to have access to books with high literary and artistic standards; encourage the publication and distribution of high-quality children's books, especially in developing countries; provide support and training for those involved with children and children's books; and stimulate research and scholarly works in the field of children's literature.

All countries are eligible to join IBBY. Currently, there are sixty-five member nations, each of which has a national organization affiliated with IBBY. The organization has its headquarters in Basel, Switzerland, and is supported through dues from the national sections and donations. Individuals join the organization through their national section, if there is one. If not, individual membership in IBBY is possible. In the United States one joins the United States Board on Books for Young People (USBBY). IBBY furthers its missions through these main activities:

• The Hans Christian Andersen Medals. The best-known way in which IBBY and its member nations promote international children's literature is through sponsorship of the Hans Christian Andersen Medal program. The Hans Christian Andersen Medal is the most prestigious children's book award in the world. Every two years each IBBY member nation is eligible to nominate a living children's author and illustrator from that country to compete for the medals. An international panel of jurists selects from the nominees an author and an illustrator whose complete works, in the jury's opinion, have made the most important international contributions to children's literature. In 2001 the jury that will select the 2002 medalists will be divided for the first time into two sections, an author section (five jurists) and an illustrator section (five jurists). Both sections will be led by the overall chair of the jury. Her Majesty Queen Margrethe II of Denmark is the patron of these awards, an appropriate link to Denmark's famous storyteller and award namesake, Hans Christian Andersen.

The Hans Christian Andersen Medal program was founded in 1956. Originally, only one medal was conferred every two years, but beginning in 1966 the committee gave separate medals for writing and for illustration. To date, five authors from the United States have won the medal: Meindert DeJong (1962); Scott O'Dell (1972); Paula Fox

(1978); Virginia Hamilton (1992), and Katherine Paterson (1998). Maurice Sendak is the only U.S. winner for illustration (1970). See Chapter 11 for a complete listing of Hans Christian Andersen medalists.

- The IBBY Honor List. Every two years, IBBY produces a catalog of outstanding, recently published books, recommended by IBBY member nations as suitable for publication in other languages. Each national section may submit three entries, one each for excellence in writing, illustration, and translation. The catalog, available in English, French, German, and Spanish, is distributed throughout the world. Five traveling exhibitions of current Honor List books are always on view, and past collections 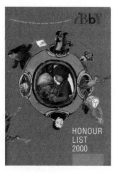 are kept permanently in some of the world's leading book institutions. The Honor List is credited with increasing the number of translations and foreign editions of excellent children's books (Raecke and Maissen 1994). For a copy of the Honor List, write to the executive director, IBBY secretariat (see Chapter 12 for contact information).

- *Bookbird.* Members of IBBY and its affiliate national organizations keep in touch through their journal, *Bookbird: The Journal of International Children's Literature,* and their 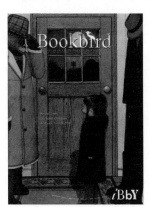 biennial world congresses. *Bookbird* was founded in 1966 and, since 1993, has been published in the United States. Each issue of this outstanding quarterly contains articles and shorter opinion pieces focused on a single theme, as well as letters from readers in response to earlier articles, a calendar of events, national book award listings, and important new trade and resource literature. A network of associate editors from IBBY member nations assists the editors in producing the journal. Part of the task of producing this handsome international journal is providing translation services in many languages. This service encourages submissions from many nations, helping to ensure the global perspective that distinguishes *Bookbird* from most other children's literature journals.

- IBBY Biennial Congresses. IBBY holds an international conference every two years in a cultural and historic world center. The atmosphere at these gatherings is both exciting and inspiring. Language is not a problem for registrants from the United States, since many sessions are conducted in English and since translation services are provided. In 1990 the United States hosted the twentieth IBBY Congress in Williamsburg, Virginia. Cartagena de Indias, Colombia, was the site of the 27th Congress (2000), and congresses are scheduled for Basel, Switzerland (2002), Cape Town, South Africa (2004), and Beijing, China (2006).

- IBBY-UNESCO Workshops and Seminars for Developing Countries. The IBBY-UNESCO workshops focus on the writing, illustrating, production, publishing, promotion, and distribution of children's books in countries that publish few books. To date, workshops have been held in Costa Rica, Kenya, Argentina, Mexico, Ghana, Colombia, Mali (for Francophone Africa), Thailand, Egypt, Bulgaria, Slovak Republic, and Austria (for Central and Eastern Europe). The most recent IBBY-UNESCO workshop, for Latin American and Canadian publishers, was held in Toronto in March 1998. One of the pioneers of the IBBY-UNESCO Workshop Project is Anne Pellowski, former director of the UNICEF Information Center on Children's Cultures and renowned teller of stories from around the world.

- The IBBY-Asahi Reading Promotion Award. This competitive award, cosponsored and endowed by the Japanese newspaper company, Asahi Shimbun, is presented annually to a group or institution for making a lasting contribution to book promotion programs for children and young people. Recent winners have included the Fureai Bunko Braille Library in Japan, the Library on Wheels for Nonviolence and Peace in Palestine and Israel, Tambogrande—Sowing a Reading Field in Peru, and the Children's Reading Development Programme in the Pechenga District, a program spanning the decade of 1992 to 2002 in Russia.

- The IBBY Documentation Centre of Books for Disabled Young People. This center, with headquarters at the Norwegian Institute of Special Education in Oslo, Norway, promotes international exhibits, seminars, and bibliographic surveys of books for and about disabled young people. Some of its projects, cosponsored by UNESCO, have been exhibited by IBBY worldwide.

• IBBY's International Children's Book Day. On or around Hans Christian Andersen's birthday, April 2, the International Children's Book Day (ICBD) is celebrated to call attention to children's books. Each national section of IBBY is invited to sponsor ICBD for one year. Often the national sponsor commissions a poster to commemorate the day.

• Janusz Korczak Literary Prize. This international children's book prize commemorates the Polish humanitarian who established orphanages in Jewish ghettoes in Poland during World War II. It is sponsored by the Polish National Section of IBBY and is given biennially to living writers whose books are distinguished for their human and artistic values and for their promotion of understanding and friendship among children worldwide. Two awards are conferred: one for a book *for* children, and one for a book *about* children. The winners of this prize are listed in Chapter 11.

Those interested in a more personal account of the early days of IBBY should read Jella Lepman's *A Bridge of Children's Books* (1969) in which she tells the story of the establishment of an international children's book field. A current overview of the organization is available at its online website in French, German, Spanish, or English; printed brochures are also available from the IBBY secretariat. All addresses and websites are listed in Chapter 12.

Several other international organizations focus on children's literature from the unique perspectives of their own professions. The International Research Society for Children's Literature (IRSCL) was founded in 1970 in Europe to promote research and scholarship in children's literature and now has about 300 members from forty countries, including the United States. The International Reading Association (IRA) has seventy affiliates worldwide that work toward literacy for all by improving the quality of reading instruction. Both IRSCL and IRA have biennial world congresses held in various locations around the globe. The International Federation of Library Associations and Institutions (IFLA), founded in Scotland in 1927, has a section of Libraries for Children and Young Adults, whose major purpose is to support the provision of library service and reading promotion to children and young adults throughout the world. IFLA holds an annual conference, each year in a different location.

International Literature in the United States

Today in the United States relatively fewer children's books are imported than in the eighteenth and nineteenth centuries. This is due largely to the rapid growth in this century of U.S. children's book production. It is due also to the additional costs of translation and to the difficulty of selling many of these books in this country.

Reporting on the status of imported books in the United States is hampered by the fact that no U.S. agency officially tracks such information. We must rely on the estimates of children's book experts. Bamberger, in 1978, placed the number of children's book translations in the United States, compared to total annual book production, at "no more than 1%" (20). This estimate would seem to be borne out by more recent reports. In 1992, White found 572 translated books out of 58,000 children's books listed in *Children's Books in Print 1989-1990*, or less than 1 percent.

In 1993, the selection committee for the best translated children's book of the year (see discussion of the Batchelder Award on page 15 decided not to confer an award, due to the weak field of submissions. Almost ten years later, the number of titles eligible for the award has not grown significantly. An overview of books received at the Cooperative Children's Book Center in Madison, Wisconsin, in 2000 shows that out of an estimated 5,000 new books received that year, only 46 were translated books. Moreover, only 7 of these were translations of books of substantial enough length to be considered for the Batchelder Award. This paltry number has decreased in the last five years from 1.2 percent in 1995 to less than 1 percent annually. The number of translated children's books brought to this country has always been a mere trickle, but now the trickle is becoming even slower.

A similar situation prevails in the United Kingdom, where, during the past decade, only 3 percent of the sizeable number of children's books published annually are translations (Flugge, 1994). It might be tempting for consumers to conclude that they have no part in the decision to publish imported books, that publishers alone make these decisions, or that a large native book production precludes a need for imported books. The truth is that we, the reading public, *are* responsible, in part, for the degree to which our publishers look beyond our borders for the books they publish. Klaus Flugge, a British publisher of children's books, states that the reason for the paltry number of translations in his country is "simply a lack of interest . . . in anything foreign" (Flugge 1994). Could the same thing be said about us? Are we provincial? Books originally written in English in other English-speaking countries and then published in the United States are more numerous than translations. Again, however, there are no exact figures for how many of these books are imported each year. Estimating these figures is further complicated by copublication arrangements (discussed later in this chapter), which sometime make a book's country of origin difficult to determine. It is safe to say, however, that the great majority of imported English-language books comes from Great Britain, Canada, and Australia. Children's magazines are an important reading resource. Notable in this field for its inclusion of international literature is *Cricket* magazine and its sister publications. Founder and editor Marianne Carus (1980) insists on having in *Cricket* "translated stories from as many countries as possible and about as many different cultures as possible" (174).

The Mildred L. Batchelder Book Award

In 1966 the Children's Services Division (now Association for Library Service to Children), a division of the American Library Association, founded the Mildred L. Batchelder Award Program to encourage international exchange of high-quality children's books. This annual award is made to an American publisher for a book considered to be the most outstanding of those books originally published in a foreign language in a foreign country and subsequently translated into English and published in the United States during the previous calendar year. The award program recognizes publishers of such books in translation in the United States and honors its namesake, Mildred Batchelder, who devoted her entire career to children's librarianship and who was outspoken on the need for greater exchange of children's books around the world. In a 1966 publication Batchelder wrote, "To know the classic stories of a country creates a climate, an attitude for understanding the people for whom that literature is a heritage. When children know they are reading in translation the same stories that children in another country are reading, a sense of nearness grows and expands. Interchange of children's books between countries, through translation, influences communication between the peoples of these countries, and if the books chosen for traveling from language to language are worthy books, the resulting communication may be deeper, richer, more sympathetic, more enduring. I accept and believe in these assumptions" (Wheeler 1967, 180). The children's literature community is indebted to those who proposed this award program and to Mildred Batchelder, whose work inspired it, for giving international children's literature an enduring presence in this country.

Winners of the Batchelder Award are selected by a five-person committee (four members and a chair) appointed each year by the president-elect of the Association for Library Service to Children. The winner is announced each year at the Midwinter Meeting of the American Library Association. Since 1990 the committee has been authorized to name an honor book or books in addition to the winner. Among other selection criteria are the provisions that the book retain enough of its original flavor that the reader can sense that it comes from another country, that folk literature is ineligible, and that the original illustrations are retained.

Some well-known titles that first came to the attention of librarians and teachers as a result of winning the Batchelder Award include *Konrad* by Christine Nöstlinger from Austria, *Hiroshima No Pika* by Toshi Maruki from Japan, and *The Island on Bird Street* by Uri Orlev from Israel. If you want to become familiar with the best translated international children's books available in this country, the Mildred L. Batchelder Award list is a good place to begin. A complete listing of the Batchelder winners is included in Chapter 11. Winners in 1996 and prior years are annotated in *Children's Books from Other Countries*; winners from 1997 through 2001 are annotated in Part 2 of this book.

The United States Board on Books for Young People (USBBY)

USBBY is the United States National Section of IBBY. USBBY's purposes are to explore and promote excellent children's reading materials that have been created throughout the world; to cooperate with IBBY and with other groups whose goals are comparable to those of USBBY; to facilitate exchange of information about books of international interest; and to promote access to and reading of these books by children and young adults in the United States and elsewhere. It provides support for, and disseminates information to, those involved with children and children's literature, and it stimulates research and scholarship in the field of children's literature. In addition, USBBY has several important projects, which are described below.

• IBBY Regional Conferences. Not everyone can make it to the far-flung IBBY Congresses, and so the U.S. Regional IBBY Conferences are a welcomed addition to USBBY's activities. The first IBBY Regional Conference was held at Callaway Gardens, Georgia, in 1995. Since then, conferences have been held in Albuquerque, New Mexico (1997), Madison, Wisconsin (1999), and San Francisco (2001).

- The Bridge to Understanding Award promotes, through reading, sensitivity to our global environment. It was established in 1994 in memory of a devoted internationalist, Arlene Pillar. Schools, libraries, scout troops, clubs, and bookstores are eligible for this award for one-time events or ongoing programs that serve children in grades K-10. The award carries a $500 prize and a certificate.

- Discovery Project. The goal of this project is to promote writing for children among those groups of people who have little or no support for such endeavors. Two writing workshops, one in New York and one in California, were funded in 1996. USBBY oversees the Discovery Project and, in conjunction with it, has developed the brochure, *10 Tips for Becoming a Children's Writer.*

- *USBBY Newsletter.* Members of USBBY receive the *USBBY Newsletter* twice a year. This informative bulletin contains news reports, brief articles, a calendar of events, and book reviews related to national and international children's literature.

- USBBY Liaisons to IBBY Activities. USBBY oversees U.S. participation in the Hans Christian Andersen Medal competition, the IBBY Honor List project, the IBBY-Asahi Award competition, the Janusz Korczak Literary Prize competition, the Outstanding Books for Young People with Disabilities Project, and selection of the U.S. associate editor of *Bookbird.*

USBBY holds board of directors and general membership meetings and presents literature-related programs at the annual conferences of the American Library Association (ALA), the International Reading Association (IRA), and the National Council of Teachers of English (NCTE). These organizations and the Children's Book Council are patrons of USBBY. Like IBBY, USBBY has a website to keep its members up to date on all events and activities, including information about the annual programs presented at the conferences of ALA, IRA, and NCTE. The USBBY home page contains information about IBBY and USBBY, contact information for becoming a member, and excerpts from the *USBBY Newsletter.*

How International Books Come to the United States

International Book Fairs

For most international books the journey to American bookshelves is long and challenging. It usually begins at the annual international book fairs in Frankfurt, Germany, and Bologna, Italy, and, to a lesser extent, Harare, Zimbabwe, where publishers, editors, and literary agents from all over the world meet to negotiate publishing and licensing rights for foreign publication.

The Frankfurt Book Fair exhibits books for all ages, but the Bologna Fair is devoted to children's books exclusively. At these vast fairs, publishers arrange extensive displays of their wares to encourage reading and browsing in hopes of selling the right to publish their books in other countries. Negotiations are begun, deals are struck, and in some instances where limited text is involved (e.g., concept books, nearly wordless books), on-the-spot translations are made. International children's book publishing is now a serious consideration for publishers (Beneduce 1991).

Another international event that attracts the attention of children's book publishers is the Biennale of Illustrations Bratislava, or BIB. This juried competition for excellence in picture book illustration has been held in Bratislava, the capital of the Slovak Republic, every two years since 1967. A Grand Prix winner and up to five recipients of Golden Apple awards are selected by an international jury, whose selection criteria emphasize artistic creativity. During its more than thirty years of existence, BIB has presented 40,000 illustrations by 4,487 illustrators from 90 countries of all continents.

Selection

Many considerations precede the decision to publish an international book in the United States. Publishers must first ask themselves, Will this book appeal to American children? Fully aware of this, foreign authors and editors who hope to sell their books in the United States are often influenced by their perceptions of what will and will not be accepted here. There is much truth in New Zealander Margaret Mooney's statement (1987), "A good book is a good book anywhere," but literary tastes can differ from culture to culture and from country to country. Clear evidence of this fact is the absence of works of many Hans Christian Andersen Medal and BIB Grand Prix winners in the United States.

For example, are you familiar with the works of Bohumil Riha (Czechoslovakia), Tormod Haugen (Norway), or Michio Mado (Japan), Hans Christian Andersen Medal winners in 1980, 1990, and 1994, or John Rowe, winner of the BIB Grand Prix in 1995?

There is also the issue of whether aspects of foreign books must be changed or "Americanized" to make them more marketable in this country (Whitehead 1996, 1997). Some editors believe that all children want to read about their peers in other lands, however different. Others believe that children in this country only want to read about people who are just like themselves. Ideally, in the process of editing a foreign book for the U.S. audience, a balance is achieved between the book's integrity and its marketability so that the flavor of the book's origins is apparent, and yet the story is easily understood by the new audience. Luckily, many foreign stories over the years have transcended national borders with ease. Their themes are universal, and their content is relevant to the needs and interests of all children. These are the stories sought after by publishers today.

Tastes in illustration also vary from culture to culture. Publishers have found that the stylistically sophisticated and symbol-rich picture books of some European artists, such as Dušan Kalláy's *December's Travels* (Czechoslovakia) and Jörg Müller's *The Animals' Rebellion* (Switzerland), have not proved successful with young American audiences. The trend toward increased use of picture books for older readers in U.S. middle and high school grades may change this situation, since many of these works are artistically inspiring and thought provoking.

Publishers must sometimes consider potential for censorship of international children's books in this country. Foreign authors and illustrators of children's books are often more straightforward than their U.S. counterparts in discussing topics such as sexuality and religion and in depicting nudity. Thankfully, some publishers have not been hampered by this concern, and so those who choose to can enjoy such books as Jenni Overend's *Welcome with Love*, an Australian picture book that depicts a home birth.

Publishers must consider the extra expense of publishing an international book. First, there is the cost of buying publication rights. Then, there is the cost of translation, which varies by length of the book and difficulty of the project, but in the case of a novel could cost several thousand dollars. To recoup these extra expenses, the publisher must either charge more for the book or generate extra sales. This is problematic, since international books traditionally have a limited audience in the United States (Batchelder 1988). This situation helps to explain why publishers market more international picture books than novels (they are cheaper to translate), and more international classics and folk literature than contemporary works (older works are in the public domain; classics have a surer market).

Translation

Many of the children's books imported to this country come from other countries where English is a major language: Canada, the United Kingdom, Australia, New Zealand, and South Africa. American publishers or editors can base their decisions to buy the rights to these books on personal readings, since the books are written in English. If a book is written in a language unknown to the publisher or editor, however, he or she must then rely on secondhand information—a synopsis or book review or the opinion of a literary agent or professional reader—a risky basis for what could be an expensive publishing venture.

When rights to a foreign-language book have been purchased, the publisher must then arrange for the book to be translated. A good translation is critical to a book's success. Some people think of translation as a mechanical, word-for-word process of exchange that can be accomplished by anyone with the requisite bilingualism. Not so. Word-for-word translations are, at best, awkward and, at worst, unintelligible. To translate successfully is

- to rewrite the original text while remaining true to the original story and to the author's tone, voice, and emotion;

- to make the book appealing to children of one culture while retaining the flavor of another;

- to know to what extent foreign terms and place names will intrigue child readers without confusing them;

- to know the idioms of both languages, both contemporary and historical, so that appropriate idiomatic substitutes retain the original linguistic verve and cultural authenticity;

- to understand the complementary nature of text and illustrations and to consider the illustrations when translating.

Translators must be skillful writers as well as skillful linguists, and they must be attuned to authors' and readers' sensibilities. Stephen Croall (1990), translator of the Swedish picture book *The Cat Hat*, suggests that translators also consult the author, if possible, take time for multiple drafts, and read the final draft to children.

Copublication

To reduce costs, publishers sometimes enter into copublication agreements. The nature of these agreements varies, but copublishing a book generally means that two or more publishers share initial production costs. In this way, publishers can afford to publish more books or to issue larger print runs than they could manage independently, and they can procure publishing rights to foreign books less expensively or avoid them altogether. Sometimes publishers in different countries agree to publish a number of one another's books in translation every year, as is the case with the American publisher Farrar, Straus & Giroux and the Swedish publisher Rabén and Sjögren. On occasion, many publishers participate in a project, as is the case in The Creative Company's copublication of Hoffmann's *Nutcracker*, illustrated by Roberto Innocenti, with eleven foreign publishers. One of the most outstanding examples of copublication is UNESCO's Asian-Pacific Copublication Program, which, since its inception in 1973, has published twenty children's titles, involving thirty Asian countries and forty languages (including English), and has disseminated 4.5 million copies of these books (Tajima 1995). Also noteworthy in this regard are bilingual picture books, which are naturally suitable for copublication in countries that do not share a language, since one printing can be marketed in both countries.

Copublication agreements allow publishers to bring together far-flung authors, illustrators, and editors. In this way a child in Kansas can read a book written by an author from Austria, illustrated by an artist from Indonesia, and first published by a small company in Switzerland, as is the case with *Andrew's Angry Words* (1995) by Dorothea Lachner and illustrated by Thé Tjong-Khing (born in Indonesia, now living in Holland) and copublished by North-South Books. Of concern to some observers (Jobe 1996) is that, to make books acceptable to several cultures for the purposes of copublication, their creators will omit most culture-specific features, producing books that will neither offend nor excite anyone.

Many cooperative publishing ventures have been enormously successful. Such international best-sellers as Pfister's *The Rainbow Fish* (Switzerland), Wild's *The Very Best of Friends* (Australia), and Browne's *Gorilla* (England) have gained publishers' attention. Cooperative publishing is a definite wave of the future.

Identifying and Locating International Children's Books

Knowing how to identify a children's book as international and where to find information about these books is a necessary first step in establishing an international children's literature information network. There is no single, surefire way to ascertain that a book at hand is international, particularly since copublishing agreements sometimes mask a book's country of origin. Nonetheless, one or more of the following clues may provide the answer:

* The listing of a translator on the title page.
* Foreign award medallions on the cover.
* Copyright information on the reverse side of the title page (in some recent picture books, this information is found on the last page). There, the listing of an original publisher, original date of publication, and original title indicates that the book is international. In the French picture book *Star of Fear, Star of Hope*, by Jo Hoestlandt with illustrations by Johanna Kang, the catalog page includes the following lines, both of which indicate that the book is international:

Copyright ©1993 by Editions Syros
Originally published in Paris in 1993 as *La grande peur sous les étoiles*

Not all international books include all of this information, but most include some piece of this information. If you think that a title may be international, and original publication information is not provided, numerous indices may be consulted for more complete bibliographic information. *Children's Books in Print* and electronic databases such as the Library of Congress or WorldCat, available on OCLC Online Computer Library Center's FirstSearch collection, are good references with which to begin.

For obtaining copies of international titles that your local library does not own, the interlibrary loan system is a godsend. Even the remotest libraries are linked electronically to larger systems so that locating almost any title is possible. Ideally, the search continues in ever-widening circles until the desired title is located. Usually, the books themselves can be procured in about a week.

The following sources of information about international children's books are worth investigating:

* Annual notable book lists and bibliographies often flag international books, although a book's international origins are not always noted.

• Recommended international titles can be found in the appropriate section of survey-type children's literature textbooks.

• Former IBBY President Ronald Jobe has written *Cultural Connections* (Jobe 1993), which offers suggestions of books, most from Canada and the United States, that help children explore world cultures, and has coauthored *Canadian Connections* (Jobe & Hart 1991), which lists key Canadian children's books.

• Complete lists of winners of major book awards in other English-language countries can be found in the Children's Book Council's *Children's Books: Awards & Prizes* (1996) and *Children's Book Prizes: An Evaluation and History of Major Awards for Children's Books in the English-speaking World* by Ruth Allen (1998).

• *International Companion Encyclopedia of Children's Literature* (Hunt & Ray 1996) contains over thirty essays on the literature of individual countries and regions.

• Booklists developed by the International Relations Committee of ALA's Association for Library Service to Children are occasionally published in *The Journal of Youth Services in Libraries*.

• "News from Down Under" and "News from the North" columns in *The Horn Book Magazine* feature notable books from Australia and Canada, respectively. The "Hunt Breakfast" column lists winners of the major book awards in the English-speaking countries.

• The International Reading Association's IRA Children's Book Awards in three categories (younger readers, older readers, informational book) for an author's first or second published book often recognize international works.

• The Michael L. Printz Award for Excellence in Young Adult Literature, sponsored by the ALA's Young Adult Library Services Association, does not stipulate that nominated books originate in the United States, and international books have been named as medal and honor books.

• Publishers' catalogs are another excellent source of both recent and backlisted international titles. In most catalogs, imports are well marked or can be determined by noting translation and publishing histories or author information. Determined internationalists soon learn which publishers specialize in international books, and make sure that they receive these catalogs. A list of American publishers known for their support of international children's literature is included in Chapter 13.

- Some professional library and education journals regularly include annotated lists of recent children's books around themes or topics, and occasionally this will include international books. *Bookbird: A Journal of International Children's Literature* and *USBBY Newsletter* list global literature of note in every issue, and *Book Links*, *The Horn Book Magazine*, *The Journal of Children's Literature*, *Language Arts*, *The New Advocate*, and *The Reading Teacher* all feature reviews of international books from time to time.

The Internet has transformed the world of international children's literature. We are now able to access websites in other countries where children's books are published. These include publisher's websites, author and illustrator websites, sites of organizations that promote children's books and provide current news relàting to children's literature, and online bookstores.

Journals published in other countries offer a different perspective on the international book scene and are easily subscribed to via mail or the Internet. Their cost is nominal, relative to their worth. Descriptions and addresses for available websites, organizations, and journals are included with the appropriate country listings in Part 2.

References

Allen, Ruth. *Children's Book Prizes: An Evaluation and History of Major Awards for Children's Books in the English-speaking World*. Brookfield, VT: Ashgate, 1998.

Association for Library Service to Children. *Mildred L. Batchelder Award Selection Committee Manual*. Chicago: ALA, 1995.

Bamberger, Richard. "The Influence of Translation on the Development of National Children's Literature." In *Children's Books in Translation: The Situation and the Problems*, ed. G. Klingberg, M. Ørvig, and S. Amor. Stockholm: Almqvist & Wiksell International, 1978.

Batchelder, Mildred. "Children's Books in Translation." *The Five Owls* 2.5 (May/June 1988): 65-67.

Beneduce, Ann. "Children's Publishing in a Shrinking World." *Publishers Weekly*, 8 November 1991, 30-34.

Carus, Marianne. "Translation and Internationalism in Children's Literature." *Children's Literature in Education* 11.4 (1980): 171-79.

Chambers, Aidan. Personal corrrespondence quoted in "Crossing the Divide: Publishing Children's Books in the European Context," by Klaus Flugge.

Signal 75 (September 1994): 210.

Children's Book Council. *Children's Books: Awards & Prizes*. New York: Children's Book Council, 1996.

Croall, Stephen. "Infallible Guide to a Successful Translation." Paper presented at the World Congress on Reading, Stockholm, June 1990.

Flugge, Klaus. "Crossing the Divide." *The Bookseller*, 8 April 1994, 18-19.

Frazier, J. H. "'Internationalism' and the Children's Literature Community in the United States: A Second Look." *Library Quarterly* 51.1 (1981): 54-67.

Frenkel, Pavel. "Russia, an Equation with Many, Many Unknowns." *Bookbird* 32.1 (Spring 1994): 11-15.

Horning, Kathleen T., Ginny Moore Kruse, and Megan Schleisman. *CCBC Choices 2001*. Madison, WI: Friends of the CCBC, 2001.

Hunt, Peter, and Sheila Ray, eds. *International Companion Encyclopedia of Children's Literature*. New York: Routledge, 1996.

Italiano, Graciela. "Can Cultural Authenticity Be Identified?" Paper presented at IBBY Regional Conference, Callaway Gardens, GA. October 1995.

Jobe, Ron. *Cultural Connections*. Markham, Ontario: Pembroke Publishers, 1993.

Jobe, Ron. "Translation." In *International Companion Encyclopedia of Children's Literature*, ed. Peter Hunt and Sheila Ray. New York: Routledge, 1996, 519-29.

Jobe, Ron, and Paula Hart. *Canadian Connections*. Markham, Ontario: Pembroke Publishers, 1991.

Khorana, Meena. *The Indian Subcontinent in Literature for Children and Young Adults*. New York: Greenwood Press, 1993.

Lepman, Jella. *A Bridge of Children's Books*. Chicago: American Library Association, 1969.

Louie, Belinda Yun-Ying. "Children's Literature in the People's Republic of China." *The Reading Teacher* 49.6 (1996): 494-96.

Meigs, Cornelia, et al. *A Critical History of Children's Literature*. New York: Macmillan, 1953.

Mooney, Margaret. "A Good Book Is a Good Book Anywhere." *Teachers Networking*, unpaginated. December 1987.

Raecke, Renate, and Leena Maissen. *What Is IBBY?* Basel: International Board on Books for Young People, 1994.

Rochman, Hazel. *Against Borders*. Chicago: ALA Books, 1993.

Subject Guide to Children's Books in Print. New Providence, NJ: R. R. Bowker, 2000.

Tajima, Shinji. "Hope in Numbers: Cooperative Book Development in Asia." *Bookbird* 33.2 (Summer 1995): 28-33.

Wheeler, S. H. "The Mildred L. Batchelder Award." *Top of the News* 23.2 (Winter 1967): 180-81.

White, Maureen. "Children's Books from Other Languages: A Study of Successful Translations." *Journal of Youth Services in Libraries* 5.3 (Spring 1992): 261-75.

Whitehead, Jane. "This is NOT what I wrote!: The Americanization of British Children's Books," part 1. *Horn Book*, November/December 1996, 687-93.

Whitehead, Jane. "This is NOT what I wrote!: The Americanization of British Children's Books," part 2. *Horn Book*, January/February 1997, 27-34.

2
Books as Bridges
Susan Stan

There has never been a more important time for children to be able to
read books from other areas of the world.

—*Penni Cotton* (2000)

Connecting International Books and Children

Bridges are links connecting bodies of land, groups of people, and cultural systems that are often disparate. They work in two ways: to bring others to us, and to take us to other places. That is why books are perfect bridges—the act of reading an international book accomplishes both of these tasks at once. The book comes to us from another country, bringing along the culture of its creators, and at the same time it transports us there or elsewhere.

The information in this chapter addresses practices that foster traffic in both directions. First are techniques for sharing with children the books that come from other places, each book a bridge on which a new idea, fictional friend, or exciting adventure travels to an American reader. Next are resources for helping children move in the other direction, traveling out of their own familiar surroundings to explore what might lie at the other end of the bridge.

In *Children's Books from Other Countries*, Carl Tomlinson (1998, p. 31) emphasizes that "the same good practices work well with domestic and international books alike." Sharing international books with children relies on skills that most of us already possess or are working to develop: presenting engaging book talks, reading aloud with animation, creating eye-catching book displays, generating extension activities where appropriate, and, if in a classroom situation, integrating literature into the curriculum.

Unfamiliar Words and Names

Tomlinson offers many excellent ideas for activities that can extend and add meaning to the reading of a book from another country. Unfamiliar place and character names are sometimes difficult to remember or keep straight, and if you are reading a book aloud in a classroom setting, he suggests listing these names on posterboard with an identifying line. That way, children can glance at the board while they are listening to the story, should they forget who a character is. The same technique can be used to translate foreign words scattered throughout a text. Not all children will grasp their meaning from context, and those who do will not always catch on simultaneously.

A related suggestion for those reading individually is to encourage them to jot down the characters' names and pertinent information on an index card, along with any words that may need translation. They can add the meanings as they learn them, either through context or by asking someone.

Filling in Background Information

Tomlinson also recommends contextualizing an international book by providing background information about the country or culture in which the book originated. Locate it on a world map and discuss its location in relation to the United States as well as the children's home state and hometown. Americans in general—even educated adults—are geographically ignorant when compared to citizens of other countries. Our country's position as a world power has precluded the need to work interdependently with other countries, and therefore learning about other countries and cultures has not been an educational priority in our school systems.

Depending on their age and the resources available in their schools or public libraries, children can be encouraged to search for informational books that supply the context needed to understand a story more fully. Writers write within the context of their own countries and cultures, which they share with readers from those countries. Readers from other countries, whether the United States or elsewhere, do not bring the same prior knowledge to a book that a native reader does, nor do they have the same resources—such as knowledgeable adults—to answer their questions. While this lack doesn't interfere with their enjoyment of a good international book, filling in missing gaps can extend the meaning and enrich the reading experience.

In *My Friend the Painter* (1991), for example, Lygia Bojunga uses a daily journal format to present the thoughts of a boy trying to make sense of his upstairs neighbor's suicide and his own feelings of loss. The spare writing style, reminiscent of an impressionist painting, suits the subject matter, as Claudio, the boy, reflects on the new ways his neighbor, a painter, taught him to see color. Bojunga, winner of the 1982 Hans Christian Andersen Medal for Writing, is from Brazil, where the book was published in 1987. Non-Brazilian readers will have no trouble identifying with the boy's confusion over suicide and can appreciate the artistic insights as Claudio revisits conversations he had with the artist. They may, however, skip over parts that make no sense to them, especially when they are not an integral part of the plot. In this book, the artist's passion for politics, which landed him in prison for a while, comes up several times in peripheral ways. Knowing that Brazil was governed by a military dictatorship between 1964 and 1985—and finding out more about what that meant for the lives of ordinary Brazilians—gives this story added resonance. Certain passages, such as the hushed conversations of Claudio's parents, are read differently by those who have an appreciation of what it means to live in a country where one cannot speak freely.

Incidentally, the conventional wisdom for matching book to reader in the United States is that children do not want to read about characters younger than they are. This book is slight in number of pages and written in straightforward, short sentences. The publisher has suggested eight to twelve as the target age level for this book, perhaps basing this suggestion on Claudio's age, which is somewhere between ten and eleven. Yet this quiet book lacks the sort of action that most readers in that age group require and instead addresses philosophical issues of identity and meaning more in keeping with the interests of adolescents.

Author and Illustrator Studies

One of the rationales for international children's literature noted in Part 1 is that it brings to American children some of the world's best books. Some of these authors and illustrators are represented by a large enough body of work available in the United States to warrant individual study.

Illustrators Lisbeth Zwerger (Austria) and Anthony Browne (England), both Hans Christian Andersen Medal winners, are prime candidates for such a study. Dozens of books illustrated by Zwerger, ranging from work done in the late 1970s through the present, are in print and readily available to American children. Young readers can trace the way her style has evolved from early illustrations such as those found in *The Legend of Rosepetal* (1977), which show the influence of the nineteenth-century British illustrator Arthur Rackham, to a more original and abstract form, such as that found in *Dwarf Nose* (1994), in which she plays more freely with proportions and color.

Anthony Browne's numerous picture books, including the Willie series, *Voices in the Park, Zoo*, and *Changes*, offer opportunities for a study in intertextuality. His hallmark chimps and gorillas appear throughout his work, often calling to mind images from other Browne books. In *Willie the Champ* (1985), for instance, Willie takes a walk in the park with his friend, Millie. Those children who have read *Voices in the Park* (1998) are sure to notice the compositional similarities between the Willie illustration and one from the first story in *Voices*. The details may differ, but the position of the bench in the foreground, anchored by a person at either end, with trees in the background, gives the same effect. Certain images present in this 1985 book (e.g., bananas, Santa) reoccur in later books.

Browne's work is also a good starting point for introducing the work of fine artists. The bedroom in *Changes* echoes Van Gogh's painting, "The Bedroom," and pictures in *Willy the Dreamer* pay homage to Dali, Rousseau, and Degas, among others. In *Willy's Pictures*, Browne is explicit about these connections, including a fold-out section at the end of the book that reproduces the original works of art he plays with in the book. In addition, Browne's surrealistic style offers readers a way of looking at human nature in *Piggybook* (1986) and *Zoo* (1992) that, once recognized, can be used to help children explore some of the underlying themes in his other books as well.

Mem Fox, from Australia, is an example of a writer whose picture book texts have been illustrated by artists from Australia, the United Kingdom, and the United States. Reading a number of books by one writer can lead to a discussion of what is distinctive in an author's writing style, even as the books reflect a wide range of artistic styles. Some of Fox's picture books, such as *Possum Magic* (1990) and *Koala Lou* (1989), have a strong Australian setting, while others, such as *Wherever You Are* (1999), are deliberately international in scope; all speak directly to children's interests. Like many other authors and illustrators today, Mem Fox has a website where young readers involved in an author study can learn more about her and her books (www. MemFox.net).

Comparing Original Editions with American Editions

The American editions of books that originated in other countries frequently differ from the original editions. As Tomlinson has noted in Part 1, books for younger readers are often "Americanized," with vocabulary changes made to ensure comprehension. They also differ simply in appearance—perhaps the trim size has been slightly altered, the cover redesigned, or the paper stock changed—so that the book the American child holds is not exactly the same as that read by the child in the country where the book originated. Margaret McElderry has said that when she was a child receiving books from her relatives in Ireland, "their very awayness" attracted her (Stan 1988). Most American children will not have that sensation; very likely, they will not even know that the book they are reading is international unless it is pointed out to them. Often it is only avid readers of jacket flaps and miniscule copyright type who are privy to such knowledge.

Unless the children in question have some facility with another language, it is most useful to compare books from English-language countries, such as the United Kingdom and Australia, with their American counterparts. The Harry Potter books are a prime example, both in terms of their different cover images and changes made to the texts. The advent of the Internet has made it both possible and relatively easy to purchase the original editions through online bookstores (web addresses are supplied in Part 2 as available, and further listings are included in Part 14.) Such a comparison can lead to a discussion of why such changes have been made, in the case of content, and the different feelings evoked by the physical appearance of each edition. In picture books, even small changes (*mummy* to *mommy* in Martin Waddell's *Owl Babies*, for instance) are sure to be noticed by young readers.

Books on Tape

More and more children's books, both picture books and novels, are being issued as books on tape, and international books read by the author provide a wonderful chance to hear different forms of the English language. The characters in Brian Jacques's Redwall series, recorded by the author along with a cast of readers, speak in different voices that draw on the variety of accents found in the United Kingdom. The three books in Philip Pullman's His Dark Materials trilogy are all available in unabridged editions from Listening Library, with Pullman narrating the story and London stage actors in the roles of the main characters.

For books that haven't been commercially recorded, one way of supplying the same listening experience is to ask a native speaker to read the story—or part of it—into a tape recorder. Once children have heard the voice in the story, they will continue to hear it as they read silently.

Building on the Familiar

It is always a challenge when children discover a book they like and ask for "another one just like it," since there are so many aspects in which books are potentially similar. Does the child want a book that's funny, or one with the same kind of setting, or one in which the protagonist encounters the same kind of situation? Scaffolding, or using one book that children already know and enjoy as the basis for introducing another book, works well to promote international literature. The child who loves *There's a Nightmare in My Closet* by Mercer Mayer (1968) may enjoy the French book *Papa!* (Corentin 1997) about a human boy and a child monster who are equally afraid of each other at bedtime. The advent of a new sibling causes jealousy in *Julius, the Baby of the World* (1990) by American picture book artist Kevin Henkes and evokes similar responses from Andrew in *This Baby* (McClellend 1992), published in Australia, and Tommy in *Tommy's New Sister* (Unzner 1999), published in Switzerland. In each story, the author takes a different path to arrive at the same happy resolution.

Middle school readers who laugh out loud at *Heads or Tails* and other stories by Jack Gantos will probably have the same reaction to the novels of the popular Australian writer Morris Gleitzman, who has a knack for creating larger-than-life characters and situations that reveal the essence of preadolescent life. American children will have no problem identifying with the feelings of the Australian kids who populate his books. Family stories, survival stories, historical fiction, mysteries—all these and other reading tastes are represented by the books listed in Part 2.

The boxes on the next two pages contain examples of how an international book can be introduced on the heels of a familiar American book. These examples can be taken as a starting point for beginning to use the bibliography in Part 2. The subject index at the back of the book will be useful for linking books by theme or topic across national borders. It is often the adult, not the child, who is wary of the unfamiliar. Whether we are teachers, librarians, parents, university educators, or consultants, the very first step for all of us is to become intentional about including

If someone you know likes
Charlotte's Web

you might suggest *Ned Kelly & the City of the Bees*
by Thomas Keneally (Australia).

Keneally, author of *Schindler's List* and other books for adults, grew up in Australia in a rural town in the mid-twentieth century. This is his only children's book. Like *Charlotte's Web*, this story uses realistic details of natural science combined with deft characterization to make readers believe something they ordinarily would not accept as true. In both books readers learn why some creatures behave as they do. Charlotte, the most likeable of spiders, traps other insects for their blood. Just so, the queen of this hive, who can be friendly or hostile, has achieved her position by killing all her siblings as they emerged from their cells. Keneally lets Ned narrate this story and maintains the child's point of view while offering some observations about adult life and the world at large. His sure tone and well-honed language make this ideal for reading aloud, and the book contains so much of interest that each successive reading brings new enjoyment.

Grounded in a very specific time and place, this is an adventure story with broad appeal. In a note for the American edition, Keneally explains some of the differences between life in Australia and the United States (e.g., the reversal of seasons) that are pertinent to the story.

If someone you know likes
The Giver

you might suggest *Off the Road* by Nina Bawden (England).

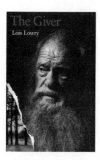

Like *The Giver*, *Off the Road* is set in a future that resembles the present in enough ways to be uncomfortable. Eleven-year-old Tom, his parents, and his grandfather, Gandy, live in an enclosed community surrounded by a wall. Their environment is engineered, and they are earmarked for jobs as soon as they are born. Tom has learned in school that outside the wall live barbarians and cannibals, and he considers himself lucky to be on the inside. He has also been taught that Oldies such as his grandfather, who has just turned sixty-five, rapidly lose their mental competence; that is the reason his parents have been instructed to take Gandy to the nearest Memory Theme Park to be "permanently cared for." So when Gandy escapes through a space in the wall, Tom follows, thinking he is saving his crazy grandfather. Actually, Gandy is opting for life on the outside, and what Tom

finds there shatters his blindly held beliefs. Both *The Giver* and *Off the Road* challenge readers to think about what makes a meaningful society. In Jonas's world, people have been relieved of their memories: Jonas says, " I thought there was only us. I thought there was only now." Lowry's book ends without giving readers a chance to see any community but Jonas's; Bawden takes us from Tom's planned community into what Gandy calls "the real world," enabling readers, through Tom's eyes, to view their own world anew.

international books in our everyday work with children and books. When we do not, these books go out of print and become unavailable because they are not being bought, borrowed, and used. Worse yet, a track record of poor sales can readily influence publishers not to acquire future books from other countries, thus shrinking even more the choices for young people.

Connecting Children with Children Worldwide

Reading international books opens young people's eyes to other parts of the world at a time when they are most receptive. Very young children wonder about children in other countries: What do they eat and wear? What are their houses like? What kinds of pets do they have? (Monson, Howe, and Greenlee, 1989). As they get a bit older and learn about the lives of children who seem to be suffering from what they consider deprivation—children in war-torn countries, for instance—many children are called to action. With guidance, this newfound interest and curiosity can be nurtured and channeled into activities that will further enrich their understanding.

Penpals

The Internet provides opportunities for child-to-child as well as classroom-to-classroom connections. The programs below are only a sample of what was offered at the time of this writing, but bear in mind that websites change, and not all of these web addresses may be active by the time you check. Letter-writing penpal programs have not been totally supplanted by e-mail and are particularly important for children in countries where Internet access is rare or impossible. Some of these sites contain alternative "snail mail" programs.

- Penpals for Kids offers an entire section of international programs, some country specific. The site also includes netiquette tips and guidelines for staying safe online. (kidspenpals.about.com/kids/kidspenpals)

- Intercultural E-Mail Classroom Connections is a free service to help teachers link with partners in other countries and cultures for e-mail classroom penpal and project exchanges. The K-12 list has several thousand subscribers from fifty-eight countries. (www.iecc.org)

- Kidlink is a nonprofit grass-roots organization working to involve children through the secondary school level in a global dialogue. Would-be paraticipants must answer four questions when they enroll: Who am I? What do I want to be when I grow up? How do I want the world to be better when I grow up? What can I do now to make this happen? (www.kidlink.org)
- Pitara for Kids is an Indian website that invites children from all around the world to become epals and lets them search for others by age. It also offers a forum for expressing opinions on issues and contains news briefs relating to India. (www.pitara.com)

Learning Sites

More action-oriented lists exist for children who want to express their opinions (and learn from others) about humanitarian and social justice issues.

- UNICEF's website contains information about children's and women's rights, along with a special section of interest to children. An identity puzzle game introduces them to the plight of children whose birth is never officially recognized and who therefore will never be able to attend school, vote, own land, or partake in many of the life events American children take for granted. (www.unicef.org)

- Natural disasters, such as floods, earthquakes, and droughts, lead to mass starvation and death in countries where people are dependent on the land for food and shelter. The American Red Cross offers current worldwide disaster information and includes quizzes about the relative effects of global disasters. Interaction is available in the form of a forum where children can have their questions answered. (www.disasterrelief.org)

Action Programs

- Kids to Kids International is a program in which American school children create handmade books to send to children in areas of the world where few children's books are available. The children put their own pictures on the back, along with brief biographies, and they send along disposable cameras and art supplies, which the recipients often use to create books to send in return. To learn how to become part of this program, write to Kids to Kids International,

1961 Commerce Street, Yorktown Heights, NY 10598 or see their website (www.kidstokidsintl.org).

• Reader-to-Reader is a program that provides books to children in need, either locally or in a number of worldwide sites. Current locations include Kenya, Tanzania, South Africa, Ghana, Puerto Rico, and the Caribbean. Participating in a Reader-to-Reader collection involves raising money or collecting books and can be an excellent community service activity for a small organization or group, whether adults or children. (www.childrensliterature.org/home.html)

References

Bojunga-Nunes, Lygia. *My Friend the Painter*. New York: Puffin, 1991.
Brentano, Clemens. *The Legend of Rosepetal*. Illustrated by Lisbeth Zwerger. Somerville, MA: Picture Book Studio, 1988. Reissued by North-South in 1995.
Browne, Anthony. *Piggybook*. New York: Knopf, 1986.
Browne, Anthony. *Willy the Champ*. New York: Knopf, 1998.
Browne, Anthony. *Changes*. New York: Knopf, 1990.
Browne, Anthony. *Zoo*. New York: Knopf, 1992.
Browne, Anthony. *Voices in the Park*. New York: DK Ink, 1998.
Browne, Anthony. *Willy the Dreamer*. New York: Candlewick, 1998.
Browne, Anthony. *Willy's Pictures*. New York: Candlewick, 2000.
Corentin, Philipe. *Papa!* San Francisco: Chronicle Books, 1997.
Cotton, Penni. *Picture Books sans Frontières*. Stoke on Trent, England: Trentham, 2000.
Gantos, Jack. *Heads or Tails*. New York: Farrar, Straus & Giroux, 1994.
Gleitzman, Morris. *Blabber Mouth*. San Diego: Harcourt Brace, 1995.
Hauff, Wilhelm. *Dwarf Nose*. Illustrated by Lisbeth Zwerger. New York: North-South, 1994.
Henkes, Kevin. *Julius, the Baby of the World*. New York: Greenwillow, 1990.
Jacques, Brian. *Redwall*. New York: Putnam, 1987.
Mayer, Mercer.. *There's a Nightmare in My Closet*. New York: Dial, 1984.
McClelland, Julia. *This Baby*. Illustrated by Ron Brooks. Boston: Houghton Mifflin, 1994.
Monson, Dianne L., Kathy Howe, and Adele Greenlee. "Helping Children Develop Cross-Cultural Understanding with Children's Books." *Early Child Development and Care* 48 (1989): 3-8.
Pullman, Phillip. *The Golden Compass*. His Dark Materials I. New York: Knopf, 1996.
Scheidl, Gerda. *Tommy's New Sister*. New York: North-South, 1999.
Stan, Susan. "Conversations: Margaret McElderry." *Five Owls* 2 (1988): 73.
Tomlinson, Carl, ed. *Children's Books from Other Countries*. Lanham, MD: Scarecrow, 1998.

Part 2

Bibliography

About the Bibliography

Two factors have influenced the decisions regarding where to place books within these country listings: (1) the original country of publication, and (2) the country in which an author and/or illustrator lives. Often these two factors coincide, with the author and illustrator's work first being published in their home countries. Increasingly, though, publishers are working with authors and illustrators across national borders, often pairing people from different countries. The Swiss publisher Nord-Süd Verlag, for instance, many of whose books are published by North-South Books in the United States, works with authors and illustrators from throughout Europe. As more and more American editors develop ties with authors and illustrators from other countries, they, too, have begun to pair writers and artists from different countries. This situation has made it impossible to develop a hard-and-fast rule for categorizing these listings and has required individual judgment calls along the way. In general, books have been listed under the author's home country and cross-listed, as appropriate, elsewhere in the bibliography.

In the same way that many American writers choose to set their books in places other than their own countries, so do writers everywhere. Thus you will find a South African author writing a book set in Italy, a German author writing about children in Bolivia, and British authors setting stories in Caribbean countries. Within the listing of each country you will find books by authors from that country (though they may not have been first published there) and cross-references to related books by authors from other countries. Because this is primarily a collection of books from other countries, books by American authors have been included sparingly and are identified by the line, "Author from the United States." For many countries listed here, the only books available are those by American authors.

In parts of the world, national entities are changing, some because of war and others through peaceful negotiation. By the time you read this book, some of the countries listed may no longer have the same names, and new countries may exist that were once part of other countries. That process in itself should remind us that national borders are arbitrary distinctions and that it is our cultures—customs, traditions, beliefs, behaviors—that distinguish communities of people from one another.

Each entry includes author, title, and publication information, as well as the number of pages followed by the age range of the target reader in parentheses. Awards received by the book or the author are noted at the end of the annotation, as are the initials of the annotator in italic.

Annotators

Robert Ackland
Plattsburgh State University, New York

Carolyn Angus
Claremont Graduate University, California

Maggie Bokelman
Mechanicsburg, Pennsylvania

Elizabeth B. Brockman
Central Michigan University

Peg Ciszek
Niles Public Library, Illinois

Hilary Crew
Kean University, New Jersey

Charlotte Cubbage
Northwestern University Library, Evanston, Illinois

Frances Ann Day
Sebastopol, California

Doris J. Gebel
Northport Public Library, New York

Susan Golden
Appalachian State University, North Carolina

Linnea Hendrickson
University of New Mexico, Albuquerque

Rose Henninge
Mentor, Ohio

Amy Kellman
Carnegie Library of Pittsburgh

Barbara J. Killian
Webster, New York

Fawn Knight
Kentucky Christian College, Grayson

Ronald L. Kooi
Central Michigan University

Cindy Lombardo
Orrville Public Library, Ohio

Susan Dove Lempke
Niles Public Library, Illinois

Maureen Maloney
Duluth Public Library, Minnesota

Kenneth Marantz
Columbus, Ohio

Sylvia Marantz
Columbus, Ohio

Janelle B. Mathis
University of North Texas, Denton

Paula Morrow
Cricket Magazine Group, Peru, Illinois

Robert Morrow
Princeton, Illinois

Marianne Newman
San Gabriel, California

Heather Raabe
Madison Country Day School, Waunakee, Wisconsin

Martha Rasmussen
Martha's Kidlit Newsletter, Ames, Iowa

Dominique E. Sandis
University of the Aegean, Rhodes, Greece

Dean Schneider
The Ensworth School, Nashville, Tennessee

Carol H. Sibley
Moorhead State University, Minnesota

Phyllis A. Sigmond
Lake Country School, Hartland, Wisconsin

Susan Stan
Central Michigan University

Barbara Tobin
University of Pennsylvania, Philadelphia

Carl M. Tomlinson
Northern Illinois University, DeKalb

3
Latin America and the Caribbean

Argentina

1. Brusca, María Cristina. **On the Pampas.** Illustrated by María Cristina Brusca. New York: Holt, 1991. (Paperback: Holt, 1995). ISBN 0-8050-1548-5. 32p. (6-10). Picture book.

Based on her experiences as a child, María Cristina Brusca reminisces about one of the summers she spent at her grandparents' ranch on the pampas in Argentina. She and her spirited cousin, Susanita, ride and groom horses, help with the cattle, search for ñandú eggs, and listen to the gauchos spin tall tales. Both girls embrace ranch life wholeheartedly, never missing an opportunity for an adventure. This lively book is noteworthy for its depiction of two courageous young Latinas who take risks, solve problems, and live each day with enthusiasm. Endpapers feature an illustrated glossary of terms. A *1992 Notable Trade Book in the Field of Social Studies; 1992 Parents' Choice Picture Book Award. fd*
Author from the United States

Bolivia

2. Holzwarth, Werner. **I'm José and I'm Okay: Three Stories from Bolivia.** Translated by Laura McKenna. Illustrated by Yatiyawi Studios (Erlini Tola, Freddy Oporto, and Carlos Llanque). New York: Kane/Miller, 1999. Originally published as *Ich Heibe Jose und bin Zeimlich Okay!* by Peter Hammer Verlag, in 1996. ISBN 0-916291-90-1. 36p. (7-12). Picture book.

See Europe/Germany for description.

Brazil

3. Ancona, George. **Carnaval.** Illustrated by the author. New York: Harcourt Brace, 1999. ISBN 0-15-201793-3. 32p. (7-12). Picture book.

The folklore and cultural traditions of Brazil's predominant groups—

indigenous, European, and African—combine to create the joyous festivities during Carnaval, the five-day celebration before Lent. Ancona's photographs of Olinda vividly share the many weeks of preparation as well as the parades, parties, dances, and performances in which all participate. The author's use of Spanish words in addition to his notes provide further insight into the significance of this northeastern town's unique and popular celebration. *jbm*
Author from the United States

4. Holtwijk, Ineke. **Asphalt Angels**. Translated by Wanda Boeke. Asheville, NC: Front Street/Lemniscaat, 1999. Originally published as *Engelen van het Asfalt* by Lemniscaat in 1995. ISBN 1-886910-24-3. 184p. (14 up). Novel.
See Europe/Netherlands for description.

5. Lewington, Anna. **Antonio's Rain Forest**. Photographs by Edward Parker. Minneapolis: Carolrhoda, 1993. Originally published by Wayland in 1992. ISBN 0-87614-749-X. 48p. (7-9). Informational book.
See Europe/United Kingdom for description.

6. Machado, Ana. **Nina Bonita**. Translated by Elena Iribarren. Illustrated by Rosana Faría. New York: Kane/Miller, 1996. This edition originally published as *Nina Bonita* by Ediciones Ekaré in 1994. ISBN 0-916291-63-4. 28p. (4-6). Picture book.
Nina Bonita is so lovely a girl that an admiring white rabbit wishes that he could have "a daughter as black and as pretty as she." The rabbit asks Nina Bonita why her skin is "so dark and so pretty." Nina Bonita, who does not know, offers various suggestions (using black ink, drinking coffee, eating blackberries). Finally, Nina Bonita's mother explains that skin color is inherited from parents. At last the rabbit finds a wife and has the multicolored family he envisioned. Some readers will embrace this effort to explain inherited differences in skin color for young children, while others may find the approach unsettling. Machado: *2000 Hans Christian Andersen Medal for Writing. fk*

7. Munduruku, Daniel. **Tales of the Amazon: How the Munduruku Indians Live**. Translated by Jane Springer. Ilustrated by Laurabeatriz. Toronto: Groundwood, 2000. Originally published as *Historias de indio* by Companhia das Letrinhas in 1996. ISBN 0-88899-392-7. 56p. (10 up). Informational book.

This book is designed to teach readers about an indigenous people of Brazil called the Munduruki. The tribe is comprised of approximately 5,500 people living in eighty-six villages in Para, a Brazilian state bordered by the Rapajos River and its estuaries. A key theme is cultural pride—and even survival—in modern times. The book provides information in three different, but overlapping, modes: a folktale called "The Tale of the Boy Who Didn't Know How to Dream," an informational report called "The Indigenous Peoples of Brazil," and an autobiographical account by the author called "Chronicles and Testimonies." Three kinds of illustrations (photographs, childlike sketches, and an award-winning artist's beautiful, color paintings) depict and even celebrate daily village life. The book concludes with a glossary, a reading list, and a subject index. *ebb*

8. Schwartz, David M. **Yanomami: People of the Amazon**. Photographs by Victor Englebert. New York: Lothrop, 1995. ISBN 0-688-11157-2. 48p. (7-14). Informational book.

This riveting photo essay eloquently tells the story of an indigenous people along the Brazil-Venezuela border who not only take care of their basic needs by living off the land but do it in such a caring way that their environment suffers no harm. However, as government decisions allow mining, ranching, and logging to infringe on the Yanomami land and culture, their very future is at stake. Our differences are noticeable, yet author and photographer make sure the reader will respond to how we are so alike, particularly the children doing things all children do: playing, teasing, doing chores, learning from adults, and the like. Includes a map and suggestions of helpful actions to take (addresses of organizations that aid indigenous people are listed), reaffirming the belief that children can make a difference and empowering them to do so. *bjk*
Author from the United States

Chile

9. Skármeta, Antonio. **The Composition**. Illustrated by Alfonso Ruano. Translated by Elisa Amado. Toronto: Groundwood, 2000. Simultaneously published as *La composicion* by Ediciones Ekaré. ISBN 0-88899-390-0. 36p. (8-12). Picture book.

In this powerful, understated story set in an unnamed country, young Pedro knows something is wrong when his neighborhood fills with soldiers and the father of one of his friends is dragged away from his grocery store because he opposes the dictatorship. Pedro's parents quietly listen to the radio at night, but are reluctant to tell him what is happening and what they think. When soldiers come to Pedro's school, asking the children to write compositions about what their families do at night, Pedro makes up a story about how his parents play chess every evening while he does his homework. Pedro's composition does not win a prize, but it may have saved his parents' lives. *2000 Américas Award. lh*

Colombia

10. Jenkins, Lyll Becerra de. **The Honorable Prison**. New York: Dutton, 1988. (Paperback: Puffin, 1989). ISBN 0-525-67238-9. 199p. (11 up). Novel.

Marta's father is a journalist who refuses to back down from his stand against the Colombian dictatorship during the 1950s. As a result, the family is sent to a remote village and put under house arrest, where her father's physical condition deteriorates daily without the medicine he needs. Even the smallest infraction of the rules—talking to someone at the weekly market—can mean death. This is a vivid portrait of not only how military dictatorships operated fifty years ago but also how they continue to operate today. *1989 Scott O'Dell Award Winner. ss*

Author from the United States

11. Torres, Leyla. **Saturday Sancocho**. New York: Farrar, Straus & Giroux, 1995. ISBN 0-374-36418-4. 32p. (5-8). Picture book.

Every Saturday, Maria Lili looks forward to making chicken sancocho with her grandparents Mama Ana and Papa Angelino. But this Saturday, there is not enough money to buy the chicken. So Mama takes Maria Lili to the market, to barter their eggs for the chicken and vegetables they will need to make the delicious stew. Soft watercolor illustrations portray a Colombian marketplace, and a recipe for this dish, enjoyed in Central and South America, is appended. *djg*

Author from the United States

Cuba

12. Ada, Alma Flor. **Under the Royal Palms: A Childhood in Cuba.** New York: Atheneum, 1998. ISBN 0-689-80631-0. 88p. (8-12). Informational book.

In this companion book to *Where the Flame Trees Bloom*, Cuban American author Alma Flor Ada offers another inspiring collection of reminiscences drawn from her childhood in Cuba in the 1940s.

Heartwarming, poignant, and often humorous, this accessible collection paints a loving portrait of Ada's vibrant extended family and provides insight into the experiences that shaped the prolific author's life and writing. Black-and-white family photographs add to the richness of this eloquently written book. *2000 Pura Belpré Award Winner. fd*
Author from the United States

13. Ancona, George. **Cuban Kids**. New York: Marshall Cavendish, 2000. ISBN 0-7614-5077-7. 40p. (8-12). Informational book.

Written by a highly regarded American photojournalist, this book provides a window into daily Cuban life through a collage of colored photographs depicting happy-looking rural and urban children in various settings: school, work, home, and play. The author enhances these photographs with one- or two-paragraph explanations in which he often refers to the photographed children by name. The author's purpose in creating the book is to document changes in Cuban life since an earlier visit in 1957 when Fidel Castro first came into power and to celebrate both differences from and similarities with American children. *2000 Américas Commended List. ebb*
Author from the United States

Dominican Republic

14. Joseph, Lynn. **The Color of My Words**. New York: HarperCollins, 2000. ISBN 0-06-028232-0. 138p. (8-12). Novel.

Narrated by twelve-year-old Ana Rosa, this is the story of a young Dominican girl whose desire is to be a writer in a place where words are often feared. She struggles to find her place within her family and community, to find her voice and to write it all down. Painfully she learns that her words have the power to transform the world around her, celebrating what is most beautiful on her island and transcending even the most unthinkable tragedies. *2000 Américas Award. djg*
Author from the United States

Ecuador (Galapagos Islands)

15. Johnston, Tony. **An Old Shell: Poems of the Galapagos**. Pictures by Tom Pohrt. New York: Farrar, Straus & Giroux, 1999. ISBN 0-374-35649-1. 54p. (7-12). Poetry.

Hold this place gently like an old shell. Hold it to your ear. Hear the

song that sings inside. Each of the thirty-four poems in this collection resonate with the marvels of animal and plant life found in this archipelago. Painted locust, flamingo, cormorant, gull, and green turtle are among the creatures celebrated in poems and in accompanying pencil drawings, which tell of the wonder of nature while reminding us of its fragility. *djg*
Author from the United States

16. Lewin, Ted. **Nilo and the Tortoise**. Illustrated by the author. New York: Scholastic, 1999. ISBN 0-590-96004-0. 40p. (4-9). Picture book.

A little boy becomes separated from his fisherman father and is stranded overnight on a tiny island in the Galapagos. After an initial scary encounter with an angry sea lion, Nilo feels at home with the island's other natural inhabitants, namely, the birds and a friendly giant tortoise. Nilo has such confidence that his father will return for him the next day that young readers will not be distracted with worry and can concentrate on the realistic watercolor illustrations. Lewin shows his "true colors" here as a conservationist and environmentalist by including a brief factual description of five animals indigenous to the Galapagos; also included is a map. *bjk*
Author from the United States

El Salvador

17. Temple, Frances. **Grab Hands and Run.** New York: Orchard, 1993. ISBN 0-531-05480-2. 165p. (10-12). Novel.

In El Salvador, twelve-year-old Felipe and his sister, Romy, are staying on their grandparent's farm when the military arrives to round up boys for the army. Felipe is able to hide but his mother arrives to take him and Romy back home. Back in San Tecla, Felipe becomes aware that his father, Jacinto, is involved in subversive activities against the government. When Jacinto disappears, Felipe, Romy, and their mother, Palome, leave their home in fear of their lives and journey north, crossing the borders of Guatemala and Mexico into the United States, where they eventually obtain permission to enter Canada. *American Library Association Best Books for Young Adults, 1994. hc*
Author from the United States

Guatemala

18. Amado, Elisa. **Barrilete: A Kite for the Day of the Dead**. Photographs by Joya Hairs. Toronto: Groundwood, 1999. ISBN 0-88899-366-8. 32p. (5-9). Informational book.

In a small village in Guatemala the people make and fly some of the biggest kites in the world. They do this on *El Dia de los Muetos*, the Day of the Dead, which is also know as *los barriletes*, the day of the kites. This year is 1970, the year the photographs were taken, and Juan and his brothers must carry on the tradition without the help of their grandfather, who has recently died. Beautiful black-and-white and color photographs show us the village of Santiago and how Juan and his brothers gather the materials, build the kite and finally, with his friends' help, fly it. *djg*

19. Cameron, Ann. **The Most Beautiful Place in the World**. Illustrated by Thomas B. Allen. New York: Knopf, 1988. (Paperback: Bullseye, 1993). ISBN 0-394-89463-4. 64p. (6-9). Transitional book.

Juan, seven, introduces readers to his life in San Pablo, Guatemala. Although he has never been elsewhere, he knows it is the most beautiful place in the world, just as the sign says at the tourist office. Juan shines shoes near that corner, and he has taught himself to read by asking his customers questions. The dollar he earns goes to his grandmother, in whose house he lives. His father has gone off, and his mother has married a man who doesn't want Juan. When Juan asks to go to school, his grandmother not only agrees but also shows that she is proud of him. Then Juan realizes that the most beautiful place in the world in anywhere you love someone and know that person loves you back. *ss*
Author from the United States

20. Carling, Amelie Lau. **Mama and Papa Have a Store**. New York: Dial, 1998. ISBN: 0-8037-2044-0. 32p. (4-7). Picture book.

Carling grew up in Guatemala, the daughter of Chinese storekeepers who emigrated from China in 1938, part of a small group of Chinese expatriates living in Guatemala City. Her parents opened a store that sold notions, a little bit of everything, including a wide selection of buttons, ribbons, thread, and cloth. The title page illustration offers an enticing aerial view of the store in context of the neighborhood and the distant mountains, and subsequent illustrations offer detailed pictures of the inside and outside of the building, which also houses an open courtyard and their living quarters. On the particular day that Carling chose to chronicle, a Mayan couple have traveled into the city from a village to purchase thread for their embroidery, a fellow Chinese immigrant visits, and it rains so hard that the lights go out. *2000 Pura Belpré Honor Book Award for Illustration; 1998 Américas Award. ss*
Author from the United States

21. Castañeda, Omar S. **Abuela's Weave**. Illustrated by Enrique O. Sanchez. New York: Lee & Low, 1993. (Paperback: Lee & Low, 1995). ISBN 1-880000-00-8. 32p. (4-10). Picture book.

In this exquisitely illustrated intergenerational story, a wise elder teaches her granddaughter an important lesson about creating from the heart and believing in herself. Young Esperanza and her beloved abuela work tirelessly as they create beautiful handwoven goods to sell at the Fiesta de Pueblos in Guate. As they work together, Esperanza discovers the magic of her abuela's artistry as well as her own hidden strengths. The rich text and brilliantly colored paintings present a wealth of cultural detail, authentically portraying images of rural Guatemala. *1993 Parents' Choice Honor Award; 1994 Consortium of Latin American Studies Programs Award. fd*
    Author from the United States

22. Castañeda, Omar S. **Among the Volcanoes**. New York: Dutton, 1991. (Paperback: Dell, 1993). ISBN 0-525-67332-6. 183p. (11 up). Novel.

Isabel Picay lives in one of the small Mayan villages dotting the slopes of volcanoes above Lake Atitlán in Guatemala. She is torn between the expectations of the village—to quit school and marry—and her desire to be a teacher. Her will is to do both, and by book's end, readers believe that to be possible. The customs, beliefs, and behaviors of the villagers are deftly woven into the telling, as are political issues (presence of both military and guerrilla forces) that affect the lives of these people. Sequel: *Imagining Isabel* (Dutton, 1994). *ss*
    Author from the United States

23. Franklin, Kristine L., and Nancy McGirr, editors. **Out of the Dump: Writings and Photographs by Children from Guatamala**. New York: Lothrop, 1995. ISBN 0-688-13923-X. 56p. (10 up). Informational book.

Living near the dump in the heart of Guatemala City are families whose livelihood comes from picking through the dump, scavenging items to use and to sell. McGirr, a photographer, started a project to help the children of some of these families, giving them cameras so they could photograph their own community and disseminating these photos worldwide. All proceeds from exhibits, notecards, and the like return to the children to support them in school and to give more children the chance to participate. Here their work offers a searing portrait of hard work, poverty, and irrepressible spirit. Children invent diversions out of their findings (an old bedspring covered by cardboard becomes a trampoline) and adults look old before their time. These young photographers and writers give readers much to see and consider. *ss*
    Editors from the United States

Haiti

24. Lauture, Denizé. **Running the Road to ABC.** Illustrated by Reynold Ruffins. New York: Simon & Schuster, 1996. ISBN 0-689-80507-1. 32p. (5-8). Picture book.

A Haitian village comes to life as six schoolchildren rise before dawn, eat breakfast, and begin their long run to school, up and down hills, carrying their raffia bookbags and lunches. Their route, wonderfully captured in stylized paintings full of details, takes them past sellers going to market on foot, across the countryside, through a town bustling with morning traffic, past houses busy with early morning chores, until they arrive in daylight at their open-air school, eager to learn. *1997 Coretta Scott King Honor Book. ss*
Author from the United States

25. Temple, Frances. **Taste of Salt: A Story of Modern Haiti.** New York: Orchard, 1992. (Paperback: HarperTrophy, 1994). ISBN 0-531-05459-4. 179p. (12-14). Novel.

In Port-au-Prince in 1991, seventeen-year-old Djo lies in the hospital recovering from the "Macoute" firebombing of Father Aristide's shelter for boys. Jeremie records Djo's moving story about his poverty and political education; his teaching reading (the "taste of salt" that brings understanding); his abduction to the Dominican Republic where he slaved on a sugar plantation, and his escape. Jeremie, in turn, tells about her protected life and education at the convent and her political awakening after her narrow escape when voters are gunned down. Their narratives document the Haitian fight for democracy during the 1980s and 1990s. Glossary and map included. *1993 Jane Addams Book Award; 1993 Child Study Association Book of the Year; NCTE Notable Trade Book. hc*
Author from the United States

26. Temple, Frances. **Tonight by Sea.** New York: Orchard, 1995. ISBN 0-531-06899-4. 152p. (12-14). Novel.

Paulie lives with her grandmother and uncle in Belle Fleuve, where life is hard. In 1993 it is dangerous to express dissent against the military dictatorship that has ousted President Aristide. When Paulie's friend, Jean-Desir, is murdered after speaking the truth to journalist Anton Bertis, Paulie, determined that the truth be known, goes to Port-au-Prince. When she finds Bertis, she is apprehended by the military police but escapes. After being driven home by Bertis, Paulie, with family and friends, makes the difficult voyage in her uncle's boat to Miami to seek a better life. Historical note, glossary, and map provided. *hc*
Author from the United States

27. Williams, Karen Lynn. **Painted Dreams.** Illustrated by Catherine Stock. New York: Lothrop, 1998. ISBN 0-688-13901-9. 32p. (4-8). Picture book.

Ti Marie's Haitian family cannot afford art supplies for her. She uses stones, bricks, and charcoal to color with, until one day she finds some used paint tubes in the trash behind the home of a local priest who is also a talented artist. Ti Marie paints a mural on the wall behind her parent's stand at the marketplace, and the whole village admires her work—including the priest, who tells her she has a gift. Includes glossary of Creole words. *mb*
Author from the United States

Jamaica

28. Belafonte, Harry, and Lord Burgess. **Island in the Sun.** Illustrated by Alex Ayliffe. New York: Dial, 1999. (Paperback: Puffin, 2001). ISBN 0-8037-2387-3. 32p. (7-9). Picture book.

Belafonte's popular paean to his Caribbean island home is extended through vibrant collage illustrations that capture the natural beauty, the rhythms of daily work, the fierce heat, and the joy of carnival described by the words of the calypso song. Musical score is included. *sp*
Author from the United States

29. Bloom, Valerie. **Fruits: A Caribbean Counting Poem.** Illustrated by David Axtell. New York: Holt, 1997. First published by Macmillan (U.K.) in 1997. ISBN 0-8050-5171-6. 24 p. (4-9). Poetry.

See Europe/United Kingdom for description.

30. Hanson, Regina. **The Tangerine Tree.** Illustrated by Harvey Stevenson. New York: Clarion, 1995. ISBN 0-395-68963-5. 32p. (5-8). Picture book.

Ida's father is going to work in New York and he won't return to his West Indies home for a long time. Mama explains that they want a better life for Ida and her brother and sister and that the money papa will send home will help pay for the rent, school uniforms, and a cow. Papa gives Ida a book and assures her that by the time she can read it, he will be home. Ida gives papa a bottle of tangerine juice from their tree so that he can bring a bit of sunshine with him. This bittersweet story, which simply tells of the anguish a family experiences when a parent must leave the family to support it, is perfect to read with Rachel Isodora's *At the Crossroads. djg*
Author from the United States

Mexico

31. Alarcón, Francisco X. **From the Bellybutton of the Moon and Other Summer Poems/Del Ombligo de la Luna y Otros Poemas de Verano.** Illustrated by Maya Christina Gonzales. San Francisco: Children's Book Press, 1998. ISBN 0-89239-153-7. 31p. (4-8). Picture book.

In this joyous collection of bilingual poetry, Francis Alarcón tells about his childhood summers in Atoyac, Mexico. In free verse he celebrates his grandmother, his auntie Reginalda, who serves "little yellow suns smiling in our plates," his uncle, Vicente, a farmer, and his grandfather, who teaches the children the Spanish alphabet. Fresh bright paintings depict Alarcón's smiling family and the lithe, dancing figures of children enjoying the green grass, the sun, and the sea whose "waves burst out laughing." The title of the book, Alarcón explains, refers to the Aztec name for the city, Mexico-Tenochtitlan. *1998 Américas Award for Children's and Young Adult Literature; 2000 Pura Belpré Award Honor Book. hc*
Author from the United States

32. Ancona, George. **Charro: The Mexican Cowboy.** San Diego: Harcourt Brace, 1999 (Paperback: Harcourt, 1999). ISBN 0-15-201047-5. 48p. (4-8). Informational book.

Ancona's photo essay celebrates the history, traditions, and skills of the Mexican *charros.* After a visit to Don Pablo's ranch in Guadalajara where the ranch hands spin the lariat, Ancona documents the main events of the national sport, *la charrería. Charros* and young boys compete in rodeo-like competitions while women and girls perform an equestrian ballet (*escaramuza charra*). Brilliant colored photographs capture details of the elaborate costumes, the drama of roping and riding bulls and wild horses, the skill of the women and girls riding side-saddle, and the musicians. The text includes Spanish vocabulary gathered together in "A Charro's Glossary." *hc*
Author from the United States

33. Ancona, George. **Fiesta Fireworks.** Illustrated by the author. New York: Lothrop, 1998. ISBN 0-688-14818-2. 32p. (4-9). Picture book.

Karen lives in the town of Tultepec, famous for its fireworks, and her grandfather is one of the master pyrotechnists who live there. As the town gets ready for a fiesta honoring its patron saint, Karen's family helps in the preparation as well as participates in the celebration. Bright photographs share both family life in this town as well as the colorful festivities. Spanish words that highlight the story's focus are explained within the text as well as in a glossary. *jbm*

Author from the United States

34. Ancona, George. **Mayeros: A Yucatec Maya Family.** Illustrated by the author. New York: Lothrop, 1997. ISBN 0-688-13456-3. 40p. (7-9). Picture book.

An American author of Mayan descent, Ancona describes contemporary life in a Mayan village on the Yucatan Peninsula. He focuses on the daily activities of one family within a village to illustrate how Mayan culture has absorbed western ideas from Spanish conquerors but maintains many native traditions as well. Photographs combined with occasional line drawings add vivid detail to the text. *cc*

Author from the United States

35. Ancona, George. **Pablo Remembers: The Fiesta of the Day of the Dead.** Illustrated by the author. New York: Lothrop, 1993. ISBN 0-688-11249-8. 48p. (7-9). Picture book.

The Mexican fiesta of the Day of the Dead is also celebrated in many communities in the United States. Ancona follows the preparations for, and celebration of, the holiday by a family in a small Mexican village. He focuses on the family's four children to illustrate the fiesta's multiple purposes. Publicly the community treats death as a joke, but privately people honor the memories of their ancestors. Ancona's photographs show off the many traditions and fanciful artwork that have grown out of the celebration. *cc*

Author from the United States

36. Burr, Claudia, Krystyna Libura, and Maria Cristina Urrutia. **Broken Shields.** Illustrated with images from the *Historia de las Indias* by Diego Duran. Toronto: Groundwood, 1997. Originally published as *Escudos rotos* by Ediciones Tecolote in 1994. ISBN 0-88899-303-X. 32p. (8-12). Informational book.

The Spanish text of this account of the conquest of Mexico is based on *Historia general de las cosas de Nueva Espana* [A general history of the things of New Spain], book 12 of the Florentine Codex by Fray Bernardino de Sahagun originally published in the sixteenth century. Based on conversations with Mexicans who were present at the time of the conquest, the text takes the form of a lament. This is a powerful presentation of the conquest from the perspective of the Aztecs, effectively illustrated by arrangements from very old pictures. *lh*

37. Burr, Claudia, Krystyna Libura, and Maria Cristina Urrutia. **When the Viceroy Came**. Illustrated by Krystyna Libura with designs from a historic painting. Toronto: Groundwood, 1999. Originally published as *La llegada del virrey* by Ediciones Tecolote in 1993. ISBN 0-88899-354-4. 32p. (8-12). Informational book.

This unusual book relates the arrival of the Viceroy of Albuquerque from Spain to Chapultepec Palace in Mexico City in 1702. The narrative is based on historic accounts but is told in the voice of young Luis Guzman, a page, who guides the reader through the event, pointing out such details as the carriages, costumed revelers, and onlookers crowded onto balconies. The narrative is illustrated with pictures taken from a painted screen depicting the event. The screen is reproduced at the end of the book along with a note providing historical context and a note on sources, although unfortunately there is nothing about the screen or its location. *lh*

38. Castillo, Ana. **My Daughter, My Son, the Eagle, the Dove**. Illustrated by S. Guevara. New York: Dutton, 2000. ISBN 0-525-45856-5. 48p. (all ages). Picture book.

Castillo has adapted Aztec chants, recited as rites of passage, into this volume tracing the growth of first a girl child, then a boy child, to adulthood. At each significant moment in the child's life, the parent offers appropriate advice and wisdom. Guevara has illustrated the lives of these two young people using the medium of the traditional bark painting, supplemented by images from the precolonial period rife with symbolism and explained in an illustrator's note. The result is a small gem of a book that bears repeated viewing and telling. *2000 Américas Commended List. ss*
Author from the United States

39. Corpi, Lucha. **Where Fireflies Dance/*Ahí, donde bailan las luciérnagas***. Illustrated by Mira Reisberg. San Francisco: Children's Book Press, 1997. ISBN 0-89239-145-6. 32p. (5-10). Picture book.

This is the author's gift to her national and familial culture, for she writes lovingly of her local folk hero, Juan Sebastián, her adventures with her brother, and memories of the songs and stories sung and told in their home. That a person in the past can be a driving force in achieving a goal is a message added in an autobiographical touch as she compares her own leaving of home and country to find her destiny with Juan Sebastián's journey years earlier to find his purpose in life. Bright, bold, colorful illustrations reflect the joyful recollections, which are in bilingual text on each page. *fd*
Author from the United States

40. deMariscal, Blanca Lopez. **The Harvest Birds**. Illustrated by Enrique Flores. San Francisco: Children's Book Press, 1995. ISBN 0-89239-131-6. 32p. (4-9). Picture book.

Third and youngest brother redeems himself by following his dream to become a farmer against all odds. Juan tends a plot of land given him by an elderly villager, the only one who believes in him. He listens to the advice of the *zanate* (harvest) birds when the other farmers tease him and do not support him. Juan's plentiful harvest of the traditional trio of corn, squash, and beans amazes the farmers who had previously laughed at him, proving once again the power of motivation, encouragement, and hard work. Vibrant colors showcase Juan's determination and plodding endurance, with the birds always attentive to and protective of this determined young man. *bjk*

Author from the United States

41. Fine, Edith Hope. **Under the Lemon Moon**. Illustrated by Rene King Moreno. New York: Lee & Low, 1999. ISBN 1-880000-69-5. 32p. (4-8). Picture book.

Deep in the night, Rosalinda heard noises. Creeping into the garden with her hen, Blanca, she sees a night man stealing all the lemons from her tree. Struggling to understand why someone would steal from her and damage her tree, she visits friends and finally her abuela to find out what to do. It is La Anciana, the Old One, who helps her understand and ultimately share the gift of forgiveness under the Lemon Moon. *1999 Smithsonian Notable Book; 1999 Parents' Choice Silver Honor Book; 2000 Notable Social Studies Trade Book. djg*

Author from the United States

42. Geeslin, Campbell. **On Ramón's Farm**. Illustrated by Petra Mathers. New York: Atheneum, 1998. ISBN 0-689-81134-9. 48p. (4-8). Picture book.

As Ramón tends the animals on his family's farm in Mexico, each one makes a unique sound and brings its own funny story. Includes Spanish words with pronunciation. *jr*

Author from the United States

43. Johnston, Tony. **The Magic Maguey**. Illustrated by Elisa Kleven. San Diego: Harcourt Brace, 1996. ISBN 0-15-250988-7. 32p. (5-8). Picture book.

Miguel learns many of the important uses of the giant maguey plant while his family is preparing for the Christmas celebration in his Mexican pueblo. But on the way to buy tortillas from Dona Josefa, he overhears Don

Cesar talking about chopping down the maguey. Miguel rounds up his friends and comes up with a way to save the plant. *djg*
Author from the United States

44. Johnston, Tony. **My Mexico/*Mexico mio*.** Illustrated by F. John Sierra. New York: Putnam, 1996. 36p. (6-9). Poetry.

Eighteen short poems written in Spanish and English present a variety of subjects and scenes designed to introduce the culture of Mexico. Small houses, adobe houses, corn, iguanas on the Taxco road, street dogs, trucks, and women weaving are some of the topics briefly introduced and portrayed in soft illustrations of pastel pencil over watercolor. *djg*
Author from the United States

45. Lasky, Kathryn. **Days of the Dead**. Photographs by Christopher G. Knight. New York: Hyperion, 1994. (Paperback: Hyperion, 1996). ISBN 0-7868-0022-4. 48p. (7-9). Informational book.

During *los Días de Muertos*, twelve-year-old Gamaliel and his family gather to remember his grandparents. Lasky's text and Knight's color photographs explain and describe how Mexicans honor the dead by cleaning up their graves and preparing tables of remembrance, by processions of children dressed up as ghosts and ghouls, and by the sale of special candy, flowers, and candles. The story of Gamaliel's grandparents and his home-life are placed at the center of these celebrations. Connections are made between *los Días de Muertos* and All Saint's Day, All Soul's Day, and Hallows' Eve. Glossary included. *hc*
Author from the United States

46. Levy, Janice. **The Spirit of Tío Fernando /** *Es espíritu de tío Fernando*. Illustrated by Morella Fuenmayor. Chicago: Whitman, 1995. (Paperback: Whitman, 1995). Spanish translation by Teresa Mlawer. ISBN 0-8075-7585-2. 32p. (5-8). Picture book.

Young Fernando narrates this story of how the Day of the Dead is celebrated in his rural Mexican village. Throughout their preparations, he and his mother share memories of his Uncle Fernando, for whom he is named, who died only six months ago. They clean the house, set up an altar with Tío Fernando's picture and favorite foods, and make purchases in town for their nighttime visit to the cemetery. Illustrations by a Venezuelan artist capture details of Nando's home life and activity in the market, and text appears in both English and Spanish. *ss*
Author from the United States

47. Madrigal, Antonio Hernández. **Erandi's Braids.** Illustrated by Tomie dePaola. New York: Putnam, 1999. ISBN 0-3999-23212-5. 32p. (4-6). Picture book.

In the Mexican village of Patzcuaro, the beautiful hair of the Tarascan women is highly prized for wigs, eyelashes, and embroidery. So when Erandi's mother needs money for new fishing nets, she attempts to sell her hair, which turns out to be too short. Though fearful it may never grow back, Erandi impulsively decides to sell her own long hair, which brings enough to pay for a doll besides. DePaola's richly colored illustrations provide details of dress, pottery, architecture, and nature, giving cultural context to this tender story of family love. *sp*
Author from the United States

48. Martinez, Alejandro Cruz. **The Woman Who Outshone the Sun.** Illustrated by Fernando Olivera. Translated by Rosalma Zubizarreta, Harriet Rohmer, and David Schecter. San Francisco: Children's Book Press, 1991. ISBN 0-89239-101-4. 32p. (4-9). Picture book.

That fear breeds misunderstanding but acceptance generates forgiveness are two truths made clear in this legend about a strange, beautiful woman named Lucia who outshone the sun and charmed the river, the fish, and the otters. Her sudden appearance in the village, her quiet ways, and her magical bond with nature made some of the villagers uneasy. When their cruelty and meanness drive Lucia from the village, the river, fishes, and otters follow her. The elders' wise advice teaches the villagers about the process of understanding and apology as well as the importance of living in harmony so that balance can be restored. The bold colors of the symbolic paintings add a metaphorical touch. *bjk*
Author from the United States

49. Nye, Naomi Shihab, compiler. **This Tree Is Older Than You Are.** Illustrated by Mexican artists. New York: Simon & Schuster, 1998. ISBN 0-689-82087-9. 111p. (7-14). Poetry.

This collection of translated poetry represents the work of many Mexican poets. Including both Spanish and English text, Nye has gathered the work of numerous Mexican poets and artists to present a comprehensive picture of both contemporary culture and that of antiquity. This anthology of poems and some prose presents the ordinary in extraordinary ways using the talents of writers from all parts of Mexico. Both the text and full-color reproductions of various art by famous Mexican artists capture the spirit of the people and the land. *jbm*
Compiler from the United States

50. Paz, Octavio. **My Life with the Wave.** Translated and adapted by Catherine Cowan. Illustrated by Mark Buehner. New York: Lothrop, 1998. ISBN 0-688-12660-X. 32p. (4-8). Picture book.

A boy makes friends with an ocean wave and brings her home from the seashore with him. At first all is sunshine and light, but the wave grows restless and uncontrollable in the house and eventually must be returned to the ocean. Surreal oil and acrylic paintings capture the changing and changeless sea in one representative wave, lending form to a fantastic conceit. Look for hidden pictures on every page. *pm*

51. Sanroman, Susana. **Señora Regañona: A Mexican Bedtime Story.** Illustrated by Domi. Toronto: Groundwood, 1998. Originally published as *La señora regañona* by Fondo de Cultura Economica in 1997. ISBN 0-88899-320-X. 16p. (5-7). Picture book.

A first-person narrator tells this story from the perspective of a knowing child. Originally, the child was frightened of the night and kept a light on under the covers. One night, though, the child falls asleep and doesn't light the lamp. In a dream, the child glides out into the starry night, meets the terrifying Señora Regañona, and demands that she play. They do—and readers know the child will never be frightened by the night again. Vibrant, two-sided illustrations splashed in blues, reds, greens, and purples abstractly represent both the child and the night. *ebb*

52. Serrano, Francisco. **Our Lady of Guadalupe.** Pictures by Felipe Dávalos. Translated by Haydn Raulinson. Paper engineering by Eugenia Guzmán. Toronto: Groundwood, 1998. ISBN 0-88899-335-8. 14p. (5-12). Engineered book.

Our Lady of Guadalupe appears to Juan Diego, a young Mexican man, and tells him to go to the bishop and report that she wants her house built on the top of the hill of Tepeyac. At first the bishop does not believe Juan Diego, but when the Lady provides a miracle, he believes and builds a church. A beautifully crafted, sophisticated pop-up book that presents a complex mixture of Catholic and Aztec iconography. *djg*

53. Sola, Michele. **Angela Weaves a Dream: The Story of a Young Maya Artist.** Photographs by Jeffrey Jay Foxx. New York: Hyperion, 1997. ISBN 0-7868-2060-8. 48p. (7-12). Picture book.

Narrative, photographs and captions, myths and factual sidebars are woven together as we take part in Angela's year-long journey to become a skillful weaver so that she can enter the annual sampler contest. She learns the myths behind the Seven Sacred Designs as she works in the fields with

her grandfather. Her grandmother guides her in the basics of weaving and advises her to pay attention to her dreams, which will inspire her design. As the photography details Angela's daily life (chores, friends, weaving practice) we come to know her as a real person and share in her struggles, her warm family life, and in her delight at winning First Sampler Prize. Glossary, bibliography, map, and notes by author and photographer. *bjk*
Author from the United States

54. Tabor, Nancy Maria Grande. **A Taste of the Mexican Market.** Illustrated by the author. Watertown, MA: Charlesbridge, 1996. ISBN 0-88106-820-9. 32p. (4-9). Picture book.

A feast for the eyes with its colorful collage art, this bilingual text takes the reader on a shopping trip to a typical Mexican market. The bounty includes not only regional foods but also classification, shapes, and colors within a framework of math and botany. Includes ten "look and find" math questions at the end. *1996 Scientific American Young Readers Book Award. bjk*
Author from the United States

55. Treviño, Elizabeth Borton de. **El Güero: A True Adventure Story.** Illus. by Leslie W. Bowman. New York: Farrar, Straus & Giroux, 1989. ISBN 0-663-58559-7. 99p. (10-12). Novel.

In the late 1800s in Mexico and Baja California, Porfirio (El Güero), son of Judge Cayetano Treviño, tells about his father's banishment and his family's journey by land and boat to Ensenada, Baja California, where his father must set up court in a deserted region. Here, Captain Alanis, involved with unscrupulous adventurers and settlers, places the judge in jail. El Güero, with the help of the family's friend, Captain Forker, and an Indian guide manages to seek help from the Mexican officials in La Paz. Based on the boyhood of the author's father-in-law. Historical note, author's note, and map provided. *hc*
Author from the United States

56. Treviño, Elizabeth Borton de. **Leona: A Love Story.** New York: Farrar, Straus & Giroux, 1994. ISBN 0-374-34382-9. 151p. (10 up). Novel.

Set in Mexico, 1808, this novel is based on the story of the heroine of the Independence, Leona Vicario. Wealthy and well educated, Leona gradually becomes aware of the poverty and injustice around her. She falls in love with a young freedom fighter and runs away to join him. An author's note and glossary are appended. *djg*
Author from the United States

57. Urrutia, Maria Cristina, and Rebecca Orozco. **Cinco de Mayo: Yesterday and Today.** Illustrated with photographs and historic prints. Toronto: Groundwood, 1999. Originally published as *La Batalla del 5 de Mayo: ayer y hoy* by Ediciones Tecolote in 1996. ISBN 0-88899-355-2. 32p. (6-10). Informational book.

The historic battle fought on May 5, 1862, at Puebla, Mexico, in which the Mexicans defeated the French, is the subject of this small book. First-person accounts, illustrated with photographs of modern-day ceremonial re-enactments of the battle in the village of Tlaixpan, are interleaved with historic reports and illustrations of the actual battle. A note appended to the text places the battle in its historical context, and explains how a warlike occasion has been transformed into a time of myth and celebration. *lh*

58. Wolf, Bernard. **Beneath the Stone.** Photographs by the author. New York: Orchard, 1994. ISBN 0-531-06835-8. 32p. (7-9). Picture book.

With vibrant colorful photographs that share both the lifestyle and ancient culture of the Zapotecs, the story of Leo, six years old, and his family of weavers is told. Leo and his family live in Teotitlan, a Mexican village near Oaxaca City, famous for its intricate weavings, rich history, and colorful celebrations. As the family works and celebrates together, the story of this flourishing culture is shared through pictures and text about its language, customs, geographical features, and history. A map, pronunciation guide, and commentary about the Zapotec history enhance the reader's understanding. *jbm*

Author from the United States

Nicaragua

59. Rohmer, Harriet, and Octavio Chow. **The Invisible Hunters: A Legend from the Miskito Indians of Nicaragua/***Los cazadores invisibles: una leyenda de los indios miskitos de Nicaragua*. Spanish translation by Rosalma Zubizarreta and Alma Flor Ada. Illustrated by Joe Sam. San Francisco: Children's Book Press, 1987. ISBN 0-89239-031-X. 32p. (7-9). Picture book.

In this work the story appears on every page in both an English- and a Spanish-language version. Originating as a tribal folktale from Nicaragua, the legend of the invisible hunters emphasizes the problems that arise when outsiders bring new customs into a traditional culture. The hunters gain their powers of hunting invisibly by promising always to give away the meat from animals they kill to their tribe and to never hunt with guns. This fits in well with their culture. However, as they become famous hunters, traders from outside offer them gifts and money for meat, and then guns, so they can kill more animals. The hunters grow greedy and turn their backs on their hungry people. They end up becoming permanently invisible, and being banished from their village. *cc*

    Authors from the United States

Peru

60. Abelove, Joan. **Go and Come Back**. New York: DK, 1998. (Paperback: Puffin, 2000). ISBN 0-7894-2476-2. 177p. (12-14). Novel.

Two American anthropologists become the objects of cultural study themselves for Alicia, a Peruvian girl living in the Amazonian jungle. She and her no-nonsense kinfolk are polite and welcoming but not afraid to express their views on the white women's odd ways and beliefs. Brief missionary visits provided glimpses of the outside world, but the anthropologists' prolonged stay leads Alicia to see her world from another viewpoint. The story, based on actual people and events occurring in the 1970s, is laced with humor, frank talk about sexual relationships, and poignant moments of mutual understanding. *mm*

    Author from the United States

Puerto Rico

61. Belpré, Pura. **Firefly Summer**. Houston: Piñata, 1996. ISBN 1-555885-180-1. 207p. (8-12). Novel.

Belpré, well known as a librarian and storyteller in New York, grew up in Puerto Rico. This novel, written over forty years ago, was unpublished during her lifetime and discovered in her archives much later; its publication is part of an effort to recover the literary contributions of U.S. Hispanics. Set in Puerto Rico in the early part of the twentieth century, it recounts a summer in the life of Teresa, whose family lives on a large *finca*, or plantation, in the highlands of Puerto Rico. During the school year, she lives in San Juan with her aunt and uncle so she can go to school, so she appreciates even more her summer adventures. Readers will get a sense both of the privileged life she led and the customs and traditions particular to her culture. *ss*

    Author from the United States

Trinidad

62. Hodge, Merle. **For the Life of Laetitia**. New York: Farrar, Straus & Giroux, 1993. ISBN 0-374-32447-6. 214p. (10-14). Novel.

Laetitia lives with her mother's family in a village several hours away from the nearest secondary school. When she earns the chance to attend, she must live in the city with her father, whom she barely knows, and his family. In this portrait of life in rural Trinidad, Laetitia's family members, her school friends, and her teachers come alive, all desiring in some way to improve their lots in life. Like the other characters, Laetitia learns that hard work, sacrifice, and compromise are a necessary part of growing up. *ss*

63. Joseph, Lynn. **Jump Up Time: A Trinidad Carnival Story**. Illustrated by Linda Saport. New York: Clarion, 1998. ISBN 0-395-65012-7. 32p. (5-8). Picture book.

It's time for carnival and for six months the whole family has been working on Christine's costume. Lily wants to play *mas,* too; she doesn't want to wait until next year when she too will be old enough to wear a beautiful costume and jump up. But when her big sister is too nervous to jump up, it is her little sister who gives her the courage she needs. Island dialect is effectively used in this lively story illustrated in pastel drawings in glowing tropical colors. *djg*
Author from the United States

64. Rahaman, Vashanti. **A Little Salmon for Witness**. Illustrated by Sandra Speidel. New York: Lodestar, 1997. ISBN 0-525-67521-3. 32p. (4-9). Picture book.

On this Good Friday, which is also Grandmother's birthday, young Rajiv has a double dilemma—he has no money to buy a tin of salmon for the traditional extra touch (the witness) to the Good Friday dinner nor does he have a birthday gift to give to his beloved Aaji. Knowing how much the salmon would mean to her, he decides the salmon itself would be the perfect present. He goes from one neighbor to another to offer his services, finally undertaking a difficult gardening chore for the schoolmaster's wife who rewards him with real smoked salmon and more for his fine effort. The island dialogue in the text combines with rich pastel illustrations to radiate Caribbean ambience. *bjk*
Author from the United States

Venezuela

65. Horenstein, Henry. **Baseball in the Barrios.** Photographs by the author. San Diego: Gulliver, 1997. ISBN 0-15-200499-8. 32 p. (7-12). Picture book.

Thanks to Venezuela's year-round warmth, baseball has two seasons. A fifth-grade boy tells about the importance of baseball in Venezuelan culture, and about the many Venezuelan players who have come to the United States and played brilliant ball for the major leagues. Although primarily about baseball, the book also includes interesting information on life in a Caracas barrio, as well as a bit of the Spanish language. *cc*
Author from the United States

66. Schwartz, David M. **Yanomami: People of the Amazon.** Photographs by Victor Englebert. New York: Lothrop, 1995. ISBN 0-688-11157-2. 48p. (7-14). Informational book.

See Brazil for description.

Latin America – Mixed or Unspecified Settings

67. Agard, John, and Grace Nichols. **No Hickory No Dickory No Dock: Caribbean Nursery Rhymes.** Illustrated by Cynthia Jabar. Cambridge, MA: Candlewick, 1995. Originally published by Viking (U.K.) in 1991. ISBN 1-56402-156-4. 44p. (4-6). Poetry.

See Europe/United Kingdom for description.

68. Brusca, Maria Cristina, and Tona Wilson. **When Jaguars Ate the Moon and Other Stories about Animals and Plants of the Americas.** Illustrated by Maria Cristina Brusca. New York: Holt, 1995. ISBN 0-8050-2797-1. 42p. (5-10). Picture book.

This is an alphabetic arrangement of over thirty fantastic, fascinating, and funny stories that introduce young readers to plants and animals indigenous to the Americas. The rich and varied folklore of twenty-five native cultures is represented, from the extinct Selk'nam of Argentina to the Repulse Bay Eskimo of Alaska. Notes on the stories, a bibliography, and a map are appended. *djg*
Author from the United States

69. Delacre, Lulu. **Las Navidades, Popular Christmas Songs from Latin America.** Illustrated by the author. New York: Scholastic, 1990. ISBN 0-590-43548-5. 32p. (7-12). Picture book.

Sharing words to songs in both English and Spanish poetic form, Delacre revisits Christmas traditions of her childhood. Illustrations capture the mood of the book through facial expressions and detailed pictures that are captioned with interesting cultural facts pertaining to this celebration. Chronologically presented according to significant seasonal events, the book also provides music, recipes, and an invitation to readers to experience the many traditions described here through song. *jbm*

Author from the United States

70. Delacre, Lulu. **Salsa Stories**. New York: Scholastic, 2000. ISBN 0-590-63118-7. 144p. (9-14). Picture book.

This collection of stories begins with Carmen Teresa receiving a gift of an empty journal. She is deciding what to write in her journal when someone suggests collecting stories. The three generations of family members visiting her in the United States from different Latin American countries begin to tell stories from their life experiences. Within seven stories the reader learns much about customs and holidays from countries such as Peru, Mexico, Argentina, Cuba, and Puerto Rico. Since a particular food from each culture plays a significant role in each story, Carmen Teresa decides to record the many wonderful ethnic dishes that are part of her family's heritage. The recipes are provided as well as a glossary of Spanish terms used. The expressive linocut illustrations add character to the stories. *2000 Américas Commended List. jbm*

Author from the United States

71. DeSpain, Pleasant. **The Emerald Lizard: Fifteen Latin AmericanTales to Tell**. Translated by Mario Lamo-Jiménez. Illustrated by Don Bell. Little Rock: August House, 1999. ISBN 0-8748-3551-8. 192p. (7-12). Anthology.

Fifteen traditional tales, representing fifteen different cultures in Central and South America as well as the Caribbean, are retold for middle readers. While approachable for children, this rich and lyrical collection includes source notes as well as notes for storytellers. *djg*

Author from the United States

72. Garay, Luis. **Jade and Iron: Latin American Tales from Two Cultures**. Translated by Hugh Hazelton. Edited by Patricia Aldana. Illustrated by Luis Garay. Toronto: Groundwood, 1996. ISBN 0-88899-256-4. 64p. (7 up). Illustrated book.

See Canada for description.

73. Gershator, Phillis. **Sweet, Sweet Fig Banana**. Illustrations by Fritz

Millevoix. Chicago: Whitman, 1996. ISBN 0-8075-7693-X. 32p. (5-8). Picture book.

Soto plants a baby banana shoot in his yard. He waits patiently as the shoot grows in the warm sun. Soto goes to market and then the library while waiting for those fat, sweet, fig bananas to ripen. At last they ripen and Soto is happy to share with the market vendors and the librarian, too! Dialect, bright colors, and simple, primitive-style illustrations convey the Caribbean setting. *djg*

74. Hughes, Monica. **A Handful of Seeds**. Illustrated by Luis Garay. New York: Orchard, 1996. First published in Canada by Lester Publishing in 1993. ISBN 0-53109-498-7. 32p. (5-7). Picture book.

See Canada for description.

75. Isadora, Rachel. **Caribbean Dream**. New York: Putnam, 1998. ISBN 0-399-23230-3. 32p. (4-6). Picture book.

Isadora's poetical text builds on lines from "The Child's Return" by Phyllis Shand Alffrey quoted on the first page in which the remembrance of an island is a "childhood dream." On succeeding pages, short lyrical sentences—all using the word "meet"—link different aspects of setting and culture to evoke childhood experiences on a Caribbean island. For example, "Where waves meet sand we swim." Colorful full-page watercolor paintings complement each page of text depicting children smiling in friendship, swimming, running, singing, dancing, and listening to stories within the seascape and landscape settings of their island home. *hc*
Author from the United States

76. Jarmillo, Nelly Palacio. **Grandmother's Nursery Rhymes: Lullabies, Tongue Twisters and Riddles from South America/*Las Nanas de Abuelita***. Translated by Raquel Jaramillo. Illustrated by Elivera. New York: Holt, 1994. (Paperback: Turtleback, 1996). ISBN 0-8050-2555-3. 32p. (3-6). Picture book.

Traditional Latin American nursery rhymes are combined with riddles (*adivinanzas*) to invite participation and sharing. Explanatory information is provided for adults to reinforce the concepts that are presented. Whimsical watercolor illustrations are clearly placed on the pages to appeal to young children. *djg*
Author from the United States

77. Loya, Olga. *Momentos Magicos*/**Magic Moments: Tales from Latin**

America. Translated by Carmen Lizardo-Rivera. Little Rock: August House, 1998. ISBN 0-87483-497-X. 188p. (10 up). Anthology.

The stories in this collection are organized under four headings: scary stories, tricksters, strong women, and myths, with three or four stories in each section. The heaviest representation is from Mexico, though there are also stories from Colombia, Cuba, Nicaragua, and Puerto Rico. The author is a professional storyteller and the stories are meant to be shared aloud to acquaint listeners with various Latin American cultures. *djg*
Author from the United States

78. Orozco, Jose-Luis, translator. **Diez Deditos: Ten Little Fingers and Other Play Rhymes and Action Songs from Latin America**. Illustrated by Elisa Kleven. New York: Dutton, 1997. ISBN 0-525-45736-4. 56p. (2-8). Illustrated book.

A bilingual collection of thirty-four finger rhymes, play rhymes, and action songs and games with simple music for piano, voice, and guitar, background notes, and visual prompts. By the same author and illustrator team as the popular *De Colores and Other Latin American Folk songs for Children* (1994). The illustrations are engaging and provide opportunity to cue children to action movements. A back note explains that the Spanish alphabet has four letters more than the English alphabet and provides a glossary of the Spanish words contained in the book with their English translation and pronunciation guide. Also contains a subject index. A cassette or CD recording is available. *1998 Américas Award. djg*
Author from the United States

79. Reiser, Lynn. **Tortillas and Lullabies/Tortillas y Cancioncitas**. Translated by Rebecca Hart. Illustrated by "Corazones Valientes." New York: Greenwillow, 1998. ISBN 0-688-14628-7. 40p. (3-6). Picture book.

This bilingual picture book celebrates the cultural heritage and love of mothers and daughters by depicting in vibrant, full-color paintings how a great grandmother, a grandmother, a mother, and her young daughter make tortillas, gather flowers, wash a dress, and sing lullabies "in ways that are the same but different." The simple text, narrated by the young girl, is given in English at the top of each illustrated page and the corresponding text in Spanish is provided at the bottom. An author's note provides information about the artists and origin of the book. *hc*
Author from the United States

Related Information

Awards

Norma-Fundalectura Latin American Children's Literature Award

Established in 1996 to promote better books for children and young people in Latin America, this award is given to an unpublished work that has not already received another prize and is open to any author who is a citizen of a Latin American country; carries a cash prize of US $10,000 and ensures publication by Grupo Editorial Norma.

Pura Belpré Award

The Pura Belpré Award, established in 1996, is presented to a Latino/Latina writer and illustrator in the United States whose work best portrays, affirms, and celebrates the Latino cultural experience in an outstanding work of literature for children and youth.

Américas Award for Children's and Young Adult Literature

Sponsored by the National Consortium of Latin American Studies Programs, this award is given in recognition of U.S. works of fiction, poetry, folklore, or nonfiction published in the previous year in English or Spanish that authentically and engagingly portray Latin America, the Caribbean, or Latinos in the United States.

4
Canada and the Far North

80. Andrews, Jan. **Pa's Harvest**. Illustrated by Cybele Young. Toronto: Groundwood, 2000. ISBN 0-88899-405-2. 39p. (8-12). Autobiography.

This miniature book is the true story of Ephrem Carrier, who grew up on a farm during hard times. The father's potato crop is a bountiful harvest that provides tremendous hope for the family until they learn the market is saturated and the potatoes are worthless. His father's love and undying hope, however, are the greatest harvests of all. Simple illustrations depict farm life in sympathetic ways. *ebb*

81. Bannantyne-Cugnet, Jo. **A Prairie Alphabet**. Illustrated by Yvette Moore. Plattsburgh, NY: Tundra, 1993. ISBN 0-88776-292-1. 32p. (4-8). Picture book.

Alliterative sentences sum up the action in these twenty-six scratchboard and watercolor illustrations about life on the Canadian prairie. Beautiful scenery, good neighbors, fairs, and aspects of everyday life are stunningly portrayed. *djg*

82. Bannatyne-Cugnet, Jo. **From Far and Wide: A Canadian Citizenship Scrapbook**. Illustrated by Song Nan Zhang. Plattsburgh, NY: Tundra, 2000. ISBN 0-88776-443-6. 24p. (7-10). Picture book.

Xiao Ling Li narrates this story of how she became a Canadian citizen on National Flag Day, February 15, along with her mother and father and thirty-three other people from thirteen countries. Facts about citizenship and naturalization are skillfully woven into the narrative, and two pages at the end of the story list requirements and responsibilities of becoming a citizen. *ss*

83. Baskwill, Jane. **Somewhere**. Illustrated by Trish Hill. Glen Head, NY: Mondo, 1996. ISBN 1-57255-131-3. 24p. (4-8). Picture book.

Somewhere in the raindrop, a rainbow forms from light; a star lights up the night; and so begins a journey around the world from the forest to the desert, from the meadow to the arctic. Scratchboard and watercolor illustrations show us brilliantly the wonders of nature that occur all around the world, somewhere, on any given day. *djg*

84. Brewster, Hugh. **Anastasia's Album**. New York: Hyperion, 1996. First published by Madison Press in 1996. Photographs by Peter Christopher. ISBN 0-7868-0292-8. 64p. (10 up). Biography.

The story of the youngest daughter of Tsar Nicholas II is told with photographs and excerpts from letters and diary entries. This book offers a unique glimpse into the private world of the Romanovs. The story continues through the tsar's downfall and imprisonment in Siberia. An epilogue describes the death of the family as well as the mystery surrounding Anna Anderson. *djg*

85. Butler, Geoff. **The Hangashore**. Plattsburgh, NY: Tundra, 1998. ISBN 0-88776-336-7. 32p. (8-11). Picture book.

A hangashore is literally someone who is too lazy or unreliable to fish in the sea and describes a person without heart or courage—someone to be pitied. That's what young John calls the condescending new magistrate who comes to his small fishing village from England right after the end of World War II. John, the minister's son, is slow mentally but, as his father says, could teach the magistrate a thing or two. In a twist of fate, after the magistrate threatens to have him sent to an institution, John rescues the man from a boat that's being dragged by a whale, thereby changing both their lives. *ss*

86. Butler, Geoff. **The Killick: A Newfoundland Story**. Plattsburgh, NY: Tundra, 1995. (Paperback: Tundra, 1998). ISBN 0-88776-336-7. 32p. (10 up). Picture book.

A killick is a homemade anchor, made from sticks bound together to form a cage enclosing large rocks. This book paints a portrait of Newfoundland through three generations of one family. George and his mother live with his grandpa; his father has gone to mainland Canada to work since the closing of the fishery brought on by the disappearance of cod from the ocean. One day in early spring, George and his grandfather set out in the boat to visit the gravesite of his grandmother, buried on a nearby island, and are caught in a storm; for three days they drift with the ice. During their conversations, Grandpa makes George promise that "when his time comes," George will use the killick for his tombstone. *1996 Ruth Schwartz Children's Book Award. ss*

87. Carrier, Roch. **A Happy New Year's Day.** Illustrations by Gilles Pelletier. Plattsburgh, NY: Tundra, 1991. ISBN 0-88776-267-0. 24p. (7 up). Autobiography.

Carrier recalls what it was like growing up in a small village near the border between Quebec and Maine during the 1940s, especially on New Year's Day, when everyone gathered at his grandmother's house. And such a time it was, with his grandmother's cherry wine, well-wishers who traveled from house to house (imbibing at each), precious minutes of a long-distance phone call to a missed uncle, and dancing to violin and accordion music. Folk paintings capture details of the period and place, providing much to pore over again and again. *ss*

88. Clement, Gary. **The Great Poochini**. Toronto: Groundwood, 1999. ISBN 0-88899-331-5. 32p. (4-8). Picture book.

By day, Signor Poochini is an ordinary dog. By night he is the renowned opera singing canine lyric tenor. All is well until his unsuspecting owner leaves the house, locking the window and trapping him inside. Deep in despair, Poochini is resigned to missing his premier performance at the Muttropolitan Opera House. Enter the nefarious cat burglar, who once outsmarted by the clever, punning pooch, is able to attend the performance. *2000 Governor General's Award for Illustration. djg*

89. Clement, Gary. **Just Stay Put**. Toronto: Groundwood, 1995. ISBN 0-88899-239-4. 32p. (4-8). Picture book.

In this retelling of a familar tale, Mendel gets the urge to see Warsaw and sets out from his village of Chelm at dawn. Tired, he stops for a nap en route. To ensure going in the right direction when he wakes up, he takes off his boots and points them toward Warsaw, but while he is sleeping, a shepherd picks them up and carelessly sets them down again facing the other direction. Mendel returns to Chelm, thinking he is in a new place, and is baffled that it looks just like the village he left. Clement's clever illustrations comment on the story, showing Mendel as an off-kilter, good-spirited fellow with his head in the clouds, literally. The cover features him as oversized—a Gulliver in Lilliput—to set readers up for this tall tale. *ss*

90. Copeland, Eric. **Milton, My Father's Dog**. Illustrated by the author. Plattsburgh, NY: Tundra, 1994. ISBN 0-88776-339-1. 24p. (4-8). Picture book.

Fraser is thrilled when his parents promise him a puppy, but the English sheepdog they present him with is not the pet of his dreams. Milton is a drooling, flea-bitten, rampaging menace. Fraser's father adores him, spoiling him with ice cream and an elaborate doghouse. Fraser finds his father's antics ridiculous, but eventually becomes reconciled to the newest member of his family. The cheerful watercolor illustrations and smaller pencil drawings convey warmth and good humor. *mb*

91. de Thomasis, Antonio. **The Montreal of My Childhood.** Plattsburgh, NY: Tundra, 1994. Also published in a French-language edition, *Le Montréal de mon enfance*. ISBN 0-88776-343-X. 40p. (8 up). Picture book.

Illustrations capture details of life in the 1940s and 1950s in Montreal, when milk was still delivered by horse and wagon and street vendors made their way through the neighborhoods. Children spent much of their time outdoors, in the back alleys or lanes in front of the apartment buildings. They made scooters out of apple boxes and the wheels from roller skates; they made Jughead hats out of their father's castoff fedoras. The view is clearly nostalgic—of interest to older people no matter where they grew up and to young Quebecois who may be inclined to disbelieve their ancestor's tales of the olden days. Images on endpapers denote the popular culture of the times. *ss*

92. Doyle, Brian. **Uncle Ronald**. Toronto: Groundwood, 1996. ISBN 0-88899-266-1. 138p. (9-12). Novel.

Old Mickey is 112 years old and he can't remember what he had for lunch today, but he can remember, in vivid detail, what happened in November 1895. That was when he and his mother ran away from his abusive father to live with Uncle Ronald and the O'Malley girls, and when he at last he learns what it means to feel safe and live with a family who loves him. Tragedy blends seamlessly with humor in this portrait of the people of Gatineau Hills, Ottawa. *1997 Canadian Library Association Book of the Year. 1999 IBBY Honor List. djg*

93. Ellis, Deborah. **Looking for X**. Toronto: Groundwood, 2000. ISBN 0-88899-378-1. 132p. (9-12). Novel.

Living on public assistance in a poor section of Toronto with an ex-stripper mother and two autistic brothers sounds like a disastrous life for an eleven-year-old girl, but Khyber's life is surprisingly rich. She's well-read (she named herself after the Khyber Pass and would like to be an explorer), has a mother who pays attention to her, and loves her brothers. She may not have many school friends, but she has X, a homeless woman in whom she confides as they sit together in the park. Khyber's first-person narration of her life defies commonly held stereotypes in revealing a down-and-out family with self-respect and solid values. *2000 Governor General's Award. ss*

94. Ellis, Sarah. **The Young Writer's Companion**. Toronto: Groundwood, 1999. (Paperback: Groundwood, 2000). ISBN 0-88899-371-4. 128p. (8-12). Informational book.

Sarah Ellis encourages children to use journaling, making lists, doodling, and clipping interesting pictures and articles to get ideas for writing. Her format includes a variety of writing prompts followed by lined pages for writing. Sidebars with quotes from famous authors provide more insights into the reading/writing process. A bibliography to encourage further reading follows each set of writing prompts. For example, the section on keeping diaries includes a list of children's books written as journals. A unique gift for the young reader and writer. *chs*

95. Finley, Carol. **Art of the Far North: Inuit Sculpture, Drawing, and Printmaking**. Minneapolis: Lerner, 1998. ISBN 0-8225-2075-3. 56p. (11 up). Informational book.

This book features art from the Inuit of northern Canada, primarily artists living in the Northwest Territories and Nunavut, near the Arctic Circle. Whatever their form, these art pieces reflect in some way the ideas, history, and beliefs of those who created them. Specific pieces of art are shown and explained, often in the artists' own words, and a final section includes photographs of all of the artists whose work is discussed. *ss*
Author from United States

96. Friesen, Gayle. **Janey's Girl**. Toronto: Kids Can Press, 1998. ISBN 1-55074-461-5. 222p. (12 up). Novel.

Claire and her mother, Jane, finally come to terms during a one-month trip to Jane's hometown, but the process is intense and painful. Claire, who narrates in present tense with dry wit, donates bone marrow to Jamie, a six-year-old leukemia victim, against Jane's wishes. It infuriates Jane, who is controlling and overprotective, because Jamie is son to Claire's father, a man Claire had never met until the visit and Jane hadn't seen since leaving home a pregnant teenager. Claire's bravery forces Jane to face her tumultuous relationship with her controlling, overprotective father, who has recently died, and it provides the opportunity to reconcile with Claire's father. Most important, it paves the way for a more balanced mother/daughter relationship. Adult readers will be as happy for Jane as they are for Claire. *1999 CLA Young Adult Canadian Book Award. ebb*

97. Garay, Luis. **Jade and Iron: Latin American Tales from Two Cultures**. Translated by Hugh Hazelton. Edited by Patricia Aldana. Illustrated by

Luis Garay. Toronto: Groundwood, 1996. ISBN 0-88899-256-4. 64p. (7 up). Illustrated book.

Jade (for the stone that was precious to the original inhabitants of Latin America) *and Iron* (used for tools by the Europeans who conquered them) is a collection of tales from many different Latin American coun-tries. It is an introduction to a rich and complex culture; to the worlds that coexist and are still struggling to find a way to live together. Warriors and princesses, opossum, a giant worm, and a mysterious woman magician are among the characters represented in this collection. Garay's bold illustrations add power and strength to these tales. *djg*

98. Garay, Luis. **The Long Road**. Plattsburgh, NY: Tundra, 1997. ISBN 0-88776-408-8. 32p. (8-11). Picture book.

The long road for José begins in a Central American village attacked by soldiers while José and his mother are visiting Grandmother. Everyone they know has fled and they, too, begin the journey north to safety. After many bus rides, a nighttime trek past the border patrol, and an airplane ride, they end up in a North American city to begin their new life. Sticking close to José's point of view, Garay shows what it is like to come to a new country with literally nothing but a duffel bag of possessions and learn new ways while learning a new language. *ss*

99. Garrigue, Sheila. **The Eternal Spring of Mr. Ito**. New York: Bradbury Press, 1985. (Paperback: Aladdin Books, 1994). ISBN 0-02-737300-2. 163p. (10-12). Novel.

In 1941, Sara, an evacuee from England, lives with her uncle's family in Canada. She is cultivating her own bonsai tree under the direction of her uncle's gardener, Mr. Ito, when the Japanese attacks on Pearl Harbor and Hong Kong change the lives of her family and those of Mr. Ito and his family. Sara learns about the Japanese-Canadians' unfair deportation and visits the internment camp where Mr. Ito's family lives to return to them their special pine bonsai found in the cave where Mr. Ito had chosen to die. Sequel to *All the Children Were Sent Away*. *hc*
Author from United States.

100. Gay, Marie-Louise. **On My Island**. Toronto: Groundwood, 2000. Originally published in 1999 as *Sur mon île* by Éditions Milan, France. ISBN 0-88899-396-X. 38p. (3-7). Picture book.

Action-packed illustrations of flying fish, erupting volcanoes, circling dragons, and the like belie the text, in which a child bemoans, "On my island, nothing ever happens." The hand-lettered text is incorporated into the illustrations, executed in a combination of loose, scratchy pen-and-ink drawings with watercolor and collage touches, so that everything on the pages seems to be in constant motion. *ss*

101. Gay, Marie-Louise. **Stella: Star of the Sea**. Toronto: Groundwood, 1999. ISBN 0-88899-337-4. 32p. (4-8). Picture book.

Stella and little brother Sam are spending a day at the seashore. It is Sam's very first time and he has a million questions about everything he sees. Stella knows all the secrets and shares them with infinite patience, until a string of questions finally causes her to yell, "Are you ever coming in?" Whimsical watercolor illustrations bring this day at the beach to life. Sam and Stella continue their adventures while exploring the wonders of winter in *Stella, Queen of the Snow* (2000). *1999 IBBY Honor List; 2000 Ruth Schwartz Children's Book Award. djg*

102. Gillmore, Don.**The Fabulous Song**. Illustrated by Marie-Louise Gay. New York: Kane/Miller, 1998. Originally published by Stoddart, 1996. ISBN 0-916291-80-4. 32p. (4-8). Picture book.

Young Frederic (named after Frederic Chopin) Pipkin is born into a musical family. Unfortunately, he displays no talent when playing the piano, clarinet, oboe, or violin. His parents are ready to give up in their attempts to create a child prodigy when Frederic displays an unknown talent for conducting on his seventh birthday. Energetic cartoon illustrations complete this humorous story. *1996 Mr. Christie's Award. jr*

103. Gregory, Nan. **How Smudge Came**. Illustrated by Ron Lightburn. New York: Walker, 1995. Originally published by Red Deer College Press in 1995. ISBN 0-8027-7522-5. 30p. (6-8). Picture book.

This story is narrated in third person from the perspective of Cindy, a mentally disabled woman, with softly muted illustrations showcasing events as Cindy might understand them. The story begins when Cindy finds an abandoned puppy, hides him from her caregivers, and takes him to work at Hospice House. When the caregivers discover her secret, they take the puppy away and Cindy believes he is gone forever; the following day she arrives at work to find that the Hospice House residents and staff members have adopted him. This humane gesture, which is consistent with the overall tone of the book, provides a plausible—and perhaps the only viable—resolution to what would otherwise be a heartbreaking story. *1996 Sheila Egoff Prize. ebb*

104. Heneghan, James. **The Grave**. Toronto: Groundwood, 2000. ISBN 0-374-32765-3. 245p. (12 up). Novel.

This story is told by a first-person narrator named Tom Mullens, who begins by warning readers: his tale is too fantastic to believe. He's right! When the story begins, he is a thirteen-year-old loner who has been living in *fozzies* (foster homes) since he was abandoned as an infant in a Liverpool department store. When he learns a construction site has uncovered a massive grave, Tom is inexplicably drawn to it. It transports him through time to Ireland in 1847 when the potato famine is taking place, and he saves a loving family that turns out to be his own ancestors, two of whom are buried in the massive grave. Saying good-bye to the remaining family members is a painful but necessary conclusion to the book because it provides Tom with the opportunity to find his long-lost parents. *2000 Sheila Egoff Prize. ebb*

105. Heneghan, James. **Wish Me Luck**. New York: Farrar, Straus & Giroux, 1997. Simultaneously published in Canada by HarperCollins Canada, 1997. ISBN 0-374-38453-3. 195p. (10-12). Novel.

Twelve-year-old Jamie Monaghan lives with his family in Liverpool during World War II. As the bombings come closer, his parents decide to send him on a passenger liner, *City of Benares*, with other children who are traveling to safety in Canada. Several days into the voyage a German U-boat torpedoes the ship. Although Jamie's story is imagined, the historical details are based on an actual incident. *1998 Sheila Egoff Prize. pc*

106. Highet, Alistair. Based on a story by Fred Bernard. **The Yellow Train**. Illustrated by François Roca. Mankato, MN: Creative Editions, 2000. Originally published as *Le Train Jaune* by Editions du Seuil in 1998. ISBN 1-56846-128-3. 32p. (4-7). Picture book.

A grandfather relives his youth by taking his grandson on a dreamlike trip, conducting the yellow train he ran in his working days before cities dominated the landscape. Panoramic views of landscape and patterned, detailed city scenes characterize the large color illustrations that tell the story parallel to the text. *ak*

107. Holeman, Linda. **Mercy's Birds**. Plattsburgh, NY: Tundra, 1998. ISBN 0-88776-463-0 (paperback). 198p. (12-14). Novel.

Fifteen-year-old Mercy lives with her unemployed, clinically depressed mother and her fortune-telling, alcoholic aunt. Mercy's after-school job at a flower shop is the household's main source of grocery money; the rent is paid by the aunt's boyfriend, who has been sexually harassing Mercy. All of these problems are interwoven sensitively and believably and are brought to a conclusion that, while far from happily ever after, does hold out hope for the future. *pm*

108. Holubitsky, Katherine. **Alone at Ninety Foot**. Custer, WA: Orca, 1999. ISBN 1-55143-129-7. 168p. (12-16). Novel.

In diary style, Pamela Collins captures perfectly the pitch of junior high preoccupations and social exchanges, filtered through the mind of a teenager who is also trying to cope with her mother's suicide (which in turn was precipitated by the death of Pam's eight-month-old sibling due to SIDS). That the details of the plot work out to the reader's satisfaction— Pam accepts her father's girlfriend and also gets the cool guy at school— without the reader's ever feeling manipulated is testimony to the author's skill at creating a character we both like and trust. *2000 CLA Young Adult Canadian Book Award. ss*

109. Hughes, Monica. **A Handful of Seeds**. Illustrated by Luis Garay. New York: Orchard, 1996. First published in Canada by Lester Publishing in 1993. ISBN 0-53109-498-7. 32p. (5-7). Picture book.

Evicted from her country home after the death of her grandmother, an orphaned little girl moves to a barrio somewhere in Latin America, plants a garden using chili, corn, and bean seeds she has brought with her, and converts all the young urban gang members to farmers. Stylized scratchboard paintings temper the occasionally violent story, as when city police beat the children and trample their garden for no reason. *pm*

110. Jam, Teddy [Matt Cohen]. **The Fishing Summer**. Illustrated by Ange Zhang. Toronto: Groundwood, 1997. ISBN 0-88899-285-8. 32p. (7-10). Picture book.

The narrator of this story recounts childhood summers visiting his uncles, who lived in the house where they grew up and made their livelihood fishing in the Atlantic as had their father. The boy's hard work earns the respect of his uncles. Now the fishing factory is closed, and his uncles have moved away. Zhang's brilliantly colored illustrations capture the details of a way of life that has since vanished along with the fish. *djg,ss*

111. Jam, Teddy [Matt Cohen]. **The Stoneboat**. Illustrated by Ange Zhang. Toronto: Groundwood, 1999. ISBN 0-88899-368-4. 32p. (7-9). Picture book.

Mr. Richard is a giant of a man who owns the best land, works eighteen hours a day, and has more money than anyone else. Because of his French heritage, the townspeople have never accepted him as part of their community. When two brothers save him from drowning, they hope that he might forgive the large debt their father owes him. However, it takes a special neighborly gesture from the younger brother before Mr. Richard forgives the debt. This act eventually brings Mr. Richard and the boys' father together as friends, thus overcoming years of prejudice. The oil paintings in dark shades are especially effective in portraying the brute strength of this Bunyan-like character. *chs*

112. Jam, Teddy [Matt Cohen]. **ttuM**. Pictures by Harvey Chan. Toronto: Groundwood, 1999. ISBN 0-88899-373-0. 112p. (7-10). Novel.

Charlotte finds a stray dog (a mutt, her father says) who does things backward, and so she calls him ttuM. A new teacher, a month's stay at the cottage, and a running-away dog all combine in an entertaining mystery that provides enough clues to satisfy readers in the early grades, who may also be intrigued by the several instances of backward language. *ss*

113. Katz, Welwyn Wilton. **Beowulf**. Illustrated by Laszlo Gal. Toronto: Groundwood, 1999. ISBN 0-88899-365-X. 64p. (8 up). Illustrated book.

This retelling of the seminal Anglo-Saxon epic poem recasts the tale in prose form from the viewpoint of a young kinsman who accompanies his grandfather to Beowulf's castle, hearing tales of the hero's feats along the way and becoming part of the legend once there. The language is contemporary and lively while also exuding the flavor of the original, and this version will seduce young readers just as readily as previous tellings have captured their audiences. Gal's illustrations bring to life key scenes, and a genealogy chart included in the front will help keep straight the unfamiliar names. *ss*

114. Khan, Rukhsana. **Bedtime Ba-a-a-lk**. Illustrated by Kristi Frost. Toronto: Stoddart Kids, 1998. ISBN 0-7737-3068-0. 32p. (4-8). Picture book.

Night has fallen; time for gently aching limbs to rest. Time for sheep to take lullaby leaps. But the sheep, led by a feisty old ram, are uncooperative. They demand the little girl create a more appealing pasture in which to jump. Before it's over, there will be negotiation, compromise, and enough gentle laughter to send even the most reluctant little lamb over the fence to dreamland. *djg*

115. Khan, Rukhsana. **The Roses in My Carpet**. Illustrated by Ronald

Himler. New York: Holiday House, 1998. ISBN 0-8234-1399-3. 32p. (5-8). Picture book.

Jets screaming overhead, not enough to eat, the weight of responsibility for mother and sister—blessed darkness seems the only relief for a young boy in an Afghan refugee camp. His only recourse is to accept the support of a sponsor who will pay for his school and the opportunity to learn the skill of weaving. In so doing he is almost able to forget the danger as he becomes lost in weaving a pattern of roses. This story, based on the author's meeting with one such boy, is a poignant tribute to hope in the face of great difficulty. *djg*

116. King, Thomas. **A Coyote Columbus Story**. Illustrated by William Kent Monkman. Toronto: Groundwood, 1992. ISBN 0-88899-155-X. 32p. (7-9). Picture book.

With mocking humor, the author uses the traditional Native American character of Coyote to present a revisionist history of the coming of Europeans to America. What Coyote loves to do best is play ball, and everything ensues from that passion. Watercolor with gouache illustrations in predominantly fuchsia, chartreuse, orange, and bright blue contain numerous visual gags to complement the cleverly improbable text. *pm*

117. Kurelek, William. **Lumberjack**. Illustrated by the author. Boston: Houghton Mifflin, 1974. Originally published by Tundra in 1974. ISBN 0-395-19922-0. 48p. (10 up). Informational book.

In this plain but eloquent account Kurelek relates his experiences as a young lumberjack in Canadian logging camps. There is an elegiac quality here, as the author reflects on a way of life that vanished with the coming of the chain saw. Each section is illustrated by detailed oil paintings of experiences ranging from eating breakfast and doing laundry to cutting with a swede saw and dynamiting a logjam. *lh*

118. Lemieux, Michèle. **Stormy Night**. Translated by the author with assistance from David Shewan. Toronto: Kids Can Press, 1999. Originally published in Germany as *Gewitternacht* by Beltz & Gelberg in 1996. ISBN 1-55074-692-8. 240p. (10-12). Picture book.

After kissing her parents goodnight and putting herself to bed, a preteen girl stays awake with her dog, asking a series of open-ended questions ("Who am I?" "Is there life on other planets?") and sharing random thoughts ("Sometimes I feel completely lost." "I'd like to invent things that don't yet exist." "I'm scared of war."). Simple pen-and-ink drawings of the girl's bed (floating on the white page) or of her imaginings (some boxed, some full bleed) alternate with dark double-page images that record the stages of a thunderstorm enveloping her solitary house and, presumably, her psyche. *1997 Bologna Ragazzi Award winner; 2000 Elizabeth Mrazik-Cleaver Canadian Picture Book Award.* pm

119. Lewis, Paul. **Storm Boy**. Berkeley, CA: Tricycle Press, 1999 (first edition by Beyond Words in 1995). ISBN 1-883672-96-1. 32p. (4-7). Picture book.

During a terrible storm in the Pacific Northwest, a chief's son is lost at sea and is cared for in an unfamiliar village. This original, stunningly illustrated story draws on the mythology of the Haida, Tlingit, and other Native peoples who inhabit the Pacific Northwest; the rich symbolism of the art is explained in an afterword. A similar concept underlies the equally worthwhile *Frog Girl*, also by Lewis, who lives in Seattle. *ss*
    Author from United States

120. Littlechild, George. **This Land Is My Land**. Illustrated by the author. San Francisco: Children's Book Press, 1993. ISBN 0-89239-119-7. 32p. (7-9). Picture book.

This oversized book presents a collection of the author's mixed media paintings along with descriptions of his Plains Cree Indian background and the experiences of Native Americans in general. The author/artist states, "For me, working as an artist is my way of healing the pain of the past and helping the next generation of Indian people." *pm*

121. Lottridge, Celia Barker. **Wings to Fly**. Toronto: Groundwood, 1997. ISBN 0-88899-280-7. 210p. (9-12). Novel.

Set in the early 1900s on the Alberta prairie, this Canadian story will remind some of the Wilder books, focusing as it does on the everyday chores and acts of heroism that kept pioneer families alive. The anticipation of Christmas, a new family moving nearby, an outbreak of influenza that takes several lives—these and other adventures are told from twelve-year-old Josie's point of view. Josie is thinking ahead to what she might like to be when she grows up, and although the expectations for women of the time are made clear (they can be teachers or nurses, but just until they marry), readers know that she will find a way to follow her dream, whatever it turns out to be. *ss*

122. Lunn, Janet. **Charlotte**. Illustrated by Brian Deines. Plattsburgh, NY: Tundra, 1998. ISBN 0-88776-383-9. 32p. (10-12). Picture book.

At the end of the American War of Independence (or, depending on your perspective, the Revolutionary War), Loyalist families are exiled from New York. Ten-year-old Charlotte's father supported the revolution, but her uncle did not. When Charlotte visits her departing cousins to say good-bye, her father disowns her and she is forced to go to Nova Scotia with the exiles. Full-page oil paintings anchor the action in eighteenth-century America. An afterword contains a brief bio of the real Charlotte Haines, on whom the story is based. *pm*

123. Lunn, Janet. **The Hollow Tree**. New York: Viking, 2000. Originally published by Alfred A. Knopf Canada in 1997. ISBN 0-670-88949-0. 208p. (10-14). Novel.

The American Revolutionary War is part not only of U.S. history but also of Canadian history, as Lunn shows in this compelling story of fifteen-year-old Phoebe, whose cousin calls her Mouse because she is so timid. The war divides Phoebe's family—her father goes off to fight with the Patriots while her beloved cousin fights for the Tories. Neither man lives, but that is just the start of Phoebe's transformation as she carries out her cousin's mission to deliver a message and meets up again with relatives who are fleeing to Canada for refuge, all destined to become part of the Canadian mosaic. *1998 Canadian Governor General's Award. ss*

124. Manson, Ainslie. **A Dog Came, Too: A True Story.** Illustrated by Ann Blades. New York: McElderry, 1993. Originally published by Groundwood in 1992. ISBN 0-689-50567-1. 29p. (7-9). Picture book.

Based on the journal of explorer Alexander Mackenzie, this is the story of a working dog, called only Our Dog, who accompanied Mackenzie, two native guides, and seven voyageurs on an expedition across Canada to the Pacific Ocean (which was reached in July 1793). Blades's soft, realistic watercolor paintings maintain the focus on Our Dog, who served as a hunter, watchdog, and loyal friend—and was the "first dog to make the long journey to the Pacific Ocean." *ca*

125. Oppel, Kenneth. **Silverwing**. New York: Simon & Schuster, 1997. Originally published in Canada by HarperCollins in 1997. (Paperback: Aladdin, 1999). ISBN 0-689-81529-8. 218p. (9-12). Novel.

The name Silverwing describes a particular species of bats to which Shade belongs. Born in the colony's northern home, he is at once both the smallest (his nickname is Runt) and most curious of the newborns, and his curiosity causes him to challenge some of what he is taught. When the colony flies south to its winter hibernating spot, a storm comes up and Shade is separated from the rest of the bats. How he manages to rejoin them and what he learns along the way form the basis of this compelling fantasy, continued in *Sunwing*. *Silverwing: 1998 CLA Book of the Year Award; Sunwing: 2000 CLA Book of the Year Award. ss*

126. Service, Robert W. **The Shooting of Dan McGrew.** Illustrated by Ted Harrison. Boston: David R. Godine, 1988. First published by Kids Can Press in 1988. ISBN 0-87923-748-1. 30p. (8-12). Poetry.

A two-page introduction to this post–Gold Rush work of Robert Service begins the poem, which portrays the romance and hardships of that era. A classic read aloud since 1907, Ted Harrison's haunting portrayal of the dirty, half-crazed miner who wanders into the Malamute saloon one dark night with nothing but revenge on his mind as he sits down at the piano will not soon be forgotten. Harrison's bold colors and unique style were first seen in *The Cremation of Sam McGee* and later in *O, Canada. djg*

127. Simard, Rémy. **Mister Once-Upon-a-Time.** Illustrated by Pierre Pratt. Translated by David Homel. Toronto: Annick Press, 1998. Originally published as *Monsieur Iletaitunefois* in 1998. ISBN 1-55037-539-3. 25p. (4-8). Picture book.

Once upon a time everything changed in a village where the people had only one thing to do, that is, tell stories. That was the day Mister Once-Upon-a-Time showed up. Parents could no longer start their bedtime stories with "Once Upon a Time" for who would come knocking at their door? The police solve the problem by locking him in jail, but that is not the end of the story! *IBBY Honor List, 2000. djg*

128. Sterling, Shirley. **My Name Is Seepeetza.** Toronto: Groundwood, 1992. (Paperback: Groundwood, 1998). ISBN 0-88899-290-4. 126p. (10-12). Novel.

For the better part of the year, Seepeetza has to give up her Native American culture while she attends the Indian Residential School in Kalmak, British Columbia. She even has to forsake her given name and answer to "Martha Stone." Her sixth-grade teacher requires that she keep a journal. The entries, written between 1958 and 1959, reveal a marked contrast between the harsh, colorless days at school and the rich life of her visits with her extended, close-knit family at their home, Joyaska Ranch. *1993 Sheila Egoff Prize. mm*

129. Takashima, Shizuye. **A Child in Prison Camp**. Plattsburg, NY: Tundra, 1971. ISBN 0-88776-241-7. 100p. (9-12). Biography.

A Japanese Canadian girl recounts in words and paintings the three years she and her family spent in a Canadian internment camp during World War II. This story tells of the triumph of a courageous, loving family and their struggle to maintain decency in the midst of degrading circumstances. *1972 Amelia Frances Howard-Gibbon Illustrator's Award. djg*

130. Trottier, Maxine. **Dreamstones**. Illustrated by Stella East. Toronto: Stoddart Kids, 1999. ISBN 0-7737-3191-1. 24p. (7-9). Picture book.

A nineteenth-century naturalist stays too long in the Far North, and his ship becomes icebound. During the long Arctic winter, his young son wanders away from the ship but is saved by a mysterious man who—it is hinted— may be an Inukshuk, one of the strange, man-shaped stone figures that are "as old as time." Moody full-color paintings stretch across each spread, drawing the reader into the legend. *pm*

131. Valgardson, W. D. **The Divorced Kids Club and Other Stories**. Toronto: Groundwood, 2000. ISBN 0-88899-369-2. 184p. (8-12). Short stories.

Survival means many different things to the resourceful characters in these short stories. They draw on inner resources to survive and adapt, no matter how rocky their journeys may be. The reader meets seven unique protagonists, from a computer genius and a budding entrepreneur to a boy faced with a summer of hard labor after a shoplifting incident goes awry. *djg*

132. Valgardson, W. D. **Frances**. Toronto: Groundwood, 2000. ISBN 0-88899-386-2. 190p. (10-14). Novel.

Although not his own family's story, Valgardson draws on his Icelandic heritage in this contemporary story of Frances, her mother, and her grandmother, who live together in a beach town on Lake Winnepeg. An old trunk full of letters written in Icelandic leads Frances to look into her past, despite her grandmother's warning that some things are better left alone. Beyond the mystery of Frances's family secrets is the portrait of a resort town and a people who still carry many of the traditions and beliefs of their ancestors. *ss*

133. Valgardson, W. D. **Garbage Creek and Other Stories**. Illustrations by Michel Bisson. Toronto: Groundwood, 1997. ISBN 0-88899-339-0. 132p. (7-12). Short stories.

In eight wonderful short stories, characters Richard, Jim, Rainbow,

Sam, Tom, Johnny, and Erin all face situations every kid knows well, including putting on a brave front, adjusting to a new place, buying their hearts' desires, and trying to save the planet. *djg*

134. Valgardson, W. D. **Sarah and the People of Sand River**. Pictures by Ian Wallace. Toronto: Groundwood, 1996. ISBN 0-88899-255-6. 32p. (6-12). Novel.

Kindness rewarded is the theme of this illustrated work of historical fiction about a young girl in the late 1800s. Sarah, born and raised on the shores of Lake Winnipeg in a community of Icelandic settlers, is sent by her father to attend school in the city to learn English. She is mistreated and decides to return home but is overcome by a blizzard. Throughout the ordeal, she is aided by a raven and a Cree man and woman who assist her with gifts that help her survive. Only she can see them, and she becomes convinced that these mysterious helpers are the spirits of the People from Sand River, whom her mother assisted many years ago. *djg*

135. Van Camp, Richard. **A Man Called Raven**. Illustrated by George Littlechild. San Francisco: Children's Book Press, 1997. ISBN 0-89239-144-8. 32p. (4-9). Picture book.

Respect for every living thing is the theme of this story, which sweeps the reader into delightful tension as it weaves magic, realism, transformation, and mystery into the flow of mankind and nature. The author and illustrator draw on their different but compatible Native American backgrounds to craft a seamless blend of text and art to communicate a powerfully positive environmental message. *bjk*

136. Van Camp, Richard. **What's the Most Beautiful Thing You Know about Horses?** Illustrated by George Littlechild. San Francisco: Children's Book Press, 1998. ISBN 0-89239-154-5. 32p. (4-9). Picture book.

This whimsical interaction between author and reader begins like a diary entry and ends with a challenge (the title question). The author is a Dobrig Native American who knows a lot about dogs and nothing about horses, so he asks family and friends about horses and weaves their answers together in a fanciful way with the help of the wild and colorful paintings of the illustrator, a Plains Cree Native American who does know a lot about horses. *bjk*

137. van Kampen, Vlasta. **Beetle Bedlam**. Watertown, MA: Charlesbridge. 1997. Originally published by Key Porter in 1997. ISBN 0-88106-695-8.

30p. (7-9). Picture book.

When a bark beetle is put on trial, accused of killing trees, seven beetles from around the world are called as witnesses. Their evidence is worthless. In his own defense, the bark beetle declares, "I am not a tree murderer—I am a bark beetle!" and goes on to explain the necessity of laying its eggs under the bark of trees. The judge, a Goliath beetle, pardons the bark beetle after he promises to live only in sick or dead trees. This courtroom drama introduces various beetles, but their anthropomorphic characterization in the text and the watercolor illustrations that offer a clutter of oversized beetles (especially their menacing mouthparts) diminish the effectiveness of the book. A glossary offers information about the characteristics (including actual size) and behavior of the twelve beetles that appear in the illustrations. *ca*

138. Waboose, Jan Bourdeau. **Morning on the Lake**. Illustrated by Karen Reczuch. Toronto: Kids Can Press, 1998. ISBN 1-55074-373-2. 32p. (7-9). Picture book.

Three linked stories reflect the Ojibway respect for land and nature and the bonds between generations. A grandfather and grandchild encounter a family of loons on a mystical morning canoe ride on a northern lake. At noon they climb a high cliff for a bird's-eye view of the river and forest. An eagle surprises them and leaves behind the gift of one feather. At night they journey by moonlight into the forest, where they hear a bone-chilling howl and meet a pack of timber wolves. Full-page pencil and watercolor illustrations dramatically portray these encounters with wild creatures. Reproductions of Ojibway beadwork provide decoration. *chs*

139. Waboose, Jan Bourdeau. **SkySisters**. Illustrated by Brian Deines. Toronto: Kids Can Press, 2000. ISBN 1-55074-697-9. 32p. (5-8). Picture book.

Waboose, an Ojibway, draws on her own childhood experiences in northern Ontario to create this lyrical story of two Ojibway sisters journeying to Coyote Hill. Three animals—a white rabbit, deer, and coyote—welcome them as they climb up through the cold, dark, snowy night. The sisters create snow angels as they watch the sky and wait for the object of their journey. Finally, they see the SkySpirits, the Northern Lights, flicker and flow across the sky. Deines's full-page oil paintings beautifully portray two sisters bonding as they appreciate the wonders of nature. Includes translations and pronunciation for the Anishinawbe words. *chs*

140. Wallace, Ian. **Boy of the Deeps**. Illustrated by the author. New York: DK Ink, 1999. ISBN 0-7894-2569-6. 32p. (7-12). Picture book.

James's first day down in the Cape Breton coal mines, accompanied by his father, is filled with learning, hard work, the pride of a job well done, and the touching surprise his mother has packed in the twelve-year-old's lunch box. The day also brings a frightening accident as a ceiling of dust crumbles and falls on the father and son. Although set in Nova Scotia, the book is based on the author's grandfather's experiences as a miner in England. Each page of the text is faced by a full-color acrylic-on-canvas painting which conveys the intimate work setting and hardship of a miner's life. *1999 IBBY Honor List. sg*

141. Walters, Eric. **Caged Eagles.** Custer, WA: Orca, 2000. (Paperback: Orca, 2000). ISBN 1-55143-182-3. 256p. (11 up). Novel.

Three months after Pearl Harbor was bombed, Tadashi Fukushima and his family receive orders to leave home (a small fishing village on the Pacific coast) for an internment camp. Like their neighbors, most of whom are Japanese Canadians, they pack what they can in their fishing boats and travel in a caravan to Vancouver, where they are housed in horse stables in a racetrack before being sent elsewhere. Details of life in the camp and the decisions faced by those inside are told from this fourteen-year-old boy's point of view in a moving and sometimes suspenseful manner. *ss*

142. Watts, Irene N. **Good-bye Marianne: A Story of Growing Up in Nazi Germany**. Plattsburgh, NY: Tundra, 1998. ISBN 0-88776-445-2 (paperback). 105p. (9-12). Novel.

In November 1938, eleven-year-old Berliner Marianne Kohn heads for school worrying about her math test; she arrives to find the school doors closed to her because she is a Jew. With her father in hiding and her mother often gone, Marianne's lonely days at home are enlivened by the friendship of Ernest, who is visiting a neighbor. The two act out scenes from the novel *Emil and the Detectives*. Days pass with mounting signs of danger: troops in the streets, a search of her apartment by the Gestapo. Even Ernest wears the uniform of the boys' branch of the Hitler Youth and spouts hateful propaganda. When Marianne prepares to leave on the Kindertransporte, Ernest comes to say good-bye and to tell her that he is her friend and that "We [Germans] are not all the same." Based on the author's wartime experiences. *1998 Geoffrey Bilson Award for Historical Fiction for Young People*. See also the sequel: *Remember Me* (Tundra, 2000). *mn*

143. Weiler, Diana. **RanVan: The Defender**. Toronto: Groundwood, 1997. ISBN 0-88899-270-X. 172p. (10 up). Novel.

Rhan Van, fifteen, lives with his grandmother and spends his spare time and money playing a video game in the corner store opposite their apartment building (his video name, which can be only six characters, is RanVan). Then one late summer day a big silver car stops in front of the store and out falls a dark-haired teenage girl, who spurns his offer of help. Fall arrives, and the same girl turns up at Rhan's school. His obsession with her blinds him to the truth and feeds his desire to be in real life the knight he is in his video game. *ss*

144. Withrow, Sarah. **Bat Summer**. Toronto: Groundwood, 1999. ISBN 0-88899-352-8. 174p. (12 up). Novel.

Modern-day Toronto is the setting for this story told by Terence, a teenage boy whose best friend goes away to camp one summer. During the absence, Terence meets Lucy, a rather odd girl who plays chess, flies kites, and claims she is a bat. Terence knows his best friend would find Lucy strange, but this doesn't stop him from becoming her friend. Terence even begins believing he is part bat, too. When Lucy suddenly disappears, family and friends assume foul play, but Terence knows better. He finds her hiding place and eventually learns that Lucy is grieving the tragic death of her own best friend. In the process of helping Lucy heal, Terence grows as a person. *ebb*

145. Woods, Shirley. **Black Nell: The Adventures of a Coyote**. Illustrated by Celia Godkin. Toronto: Groundwood, 1998. ISBN 0-88899-316-8. 88p. (8-12). Novel.

A worthy addition to the notable Canadian tradition of the realistic animal story, this gripping novel tells the story of Nell, a black coyote, from her birth through young adulthood. At every stage of her life she is beset by danger, much of it caused by the loss of animal habitat to encroaching human settlement. She faces a forest fire, hunters, trappers, starvation, highways, and near death before she is rescued and set free again, this time near the more hospitable boundaries of Algonquin Park. *lh*

146. Wynne-Jones, Tim. **The Book of Changes**. New York: Orchard, 1995. Originally published in Canada by Groundwood in 1994. ISBN 0-531-09489-8. 143p. (8-12). Short stories.

Amelia and Tobias, first introduced in *Some of the Kinder Planets*, are now learning about China and the Chinese Book of Changes. The class is intrigued with this oracle of the future. The characters in this story as well as in the six other stories all learn that they can't rely on chance to make their futures. All make their way through these quirky and sometimes magical stories by the strength of their own characters. *djg*

147. Wynne-Jones, Tim. **The Maestro**. New York: Orchard, 1996. Originally published by Groundwood in 1995. ISBN 0-531-09544-4. 232p. (11 up). Novel.

Burl and his mother live in terror of his father, whose behavior is unpredictable. After one particularly bad incident, Burl runs away and stumbles on an isolated lake cabin, owned by an eccentric, famous Canadian pianist (modeled on Glenn Gould). Each time Burl thinks he's found safety, circumstances change, and he must again venture out into the wilderness. Wynne-Jones has written a literary coming-of-age story, filled with adventure and packed with meaning. *1995 Governor General's Award; 1998 IBBY Honor List. ss*

148. Wynne-Jones, Tim. **Stephen Fair**. New York: DK Ink, 1998. Simultaneously published in Canada by Groundwood. ISBN 0-7894-2495-9. 218p. (12 up). Novel.

Ex-hippie parents, now divorced; an older brother who left home at fifteen to escape the family tensions; a recurring nightmare seemingly inherited from his absent brother—these are some of the pieces of Stephen Fair's life that he can't make sense of. The imaginative storyline considers both the toll of family secrets and the ways in which our bodies remember what our minds may not and is told in an entertaining style full of smart dialogue and clever wordplay. *1998 CLA Book of the Year for Children. ss*

149. Yee, Paul. **The Boy in the Attic**. Illustrated by Gu Xiong. Toronto: Groundwood, 1998. ISBN 0-88899-330-7. 32p. (4-7). Picture book.

The move from rural China to big-city Canada is strange for seven-year-old Kai-Ming, and he spends the summer as an outsider in his new neighborhood, unable to understand the children or make sense of the street signs on the block. Helping him through this transition is the old-fashioned looking boy in the attic. Every day, Kai-Ming plays with him and the toys stowed away up there. By the time Kai-Ming's father finds a job and the family moves, Kai-Ming is ready to make friends with flesh-and-blood children. The presence of the spirit world is represented by the black butterfly that appears to Kai-Ming both in China near his grandmother's grave and in the attic when he meets the boy. *ss*

150. Yee, Paul. **Breakaway**. Toronto: Groundwood, 1997. ISBN 0-88899-289-0. 144p. (10-14). Novel.

Faced with poverty, back-breaking labor on the family farm, and racial prejudice, high school senior Kwok-ken Wong also struggles with difficult decisions concerning his family and his future. This powerfully crafted and gripping novel provides a vivid portrait of a Chinese Canadian family of the Pacific Northwest during the Great Depression. Equally important to the plot are Kwok's travails and triumphs on the soccer field, and his shifting alliances between the world of Chinatown and the all-white world of his high school, in neither of which he feels he belongs. *lh*

151. Yee, Paul. **Ghost Train.** Illustrated by Harvey Chan. Toronto: Groundwood, 1996. ISBN 0-88899-2572-2. 332p. (6-10). Picture book.

Arriving in Canada from China after her father has been killed in an accident while working on the railroad, young Choon-yi, a talented artist with only one arm, is summoned by her father's ghost to ride the trains and help the souls of many other dead Chinese workers return to their homelands. History meets ghost story in this moving tale, effectively illustrated by Chan's rich oil paintings. *1997 Governor General's Children's Literature Award; 1997 Ruth Schwartz Children's Literature Award. lh*

152. Yerxa, Leo. **A Fish Tale (Or, The Little One that Got Away).** Illustrated by Leo Yerxa. Toronto: Groundwood, 1995. ISBN 0-88899-247-5. 30p. (6-9). Picture book.

Far below the surface of the water, a young fish restlessly wonders about the world above. Are the stories true? Are there really humans and hooks and rods? Are there skies and rivers and other dimensions? As a dart-school failure, this little fish is easily lured upward by an experienced fish named Jack who tricks him into biting a hook. When the little fish is snared, Jack says he is on his way to heaven, but the little fish wants nothing of it, especially when he is looking into the eyes of a giant human. The fish's small-fry prayer—*please let me return to the deep*—is answered because he is too small to keep. As the little fish is tossed back into the water, though, he looks around and sees the world he never knew truly existed. Safely in the deep, he decides not to tell the others that the stories are true. *ebb*

153. Zagwÿn, Deborah Turney. **Apple Batter.** Berkeley, CA: Tricycle Press, 1999. ISBN 1-883672-92-9. 32p. (6-9). Picture book.

A loving relationship between a mother and son provides space for each other's passions—hers for gardening and his for baseball. Over the years, while the mother nurtures three apple trees (one for the past, one for the present, and one for the future), the son hones his baseball skills, each putting forth great effort despite sometimes discouraging results. In time, both succeed—the son hits a perfect ball that smashes into the mother's perfect apple, and mother makes apple crumble from the results. Enticing illustrations contain information about apple varieties, insects, and baseball stances. *ss*

154. Zagwÿn, Deborah Turney. **Hound without Howl**. Point Roberts, WA: Orca, 1994. ISBN 1-55143-019-3. 32p. (6-9). Picture book.

Opera-loving Howard longs for a companion to share his love of music, and Clayton the basset hound seems a perfect match. But despite Howard's creative attempts to coax a deep baying sound from Howard, the dog remains silent. Until, that is, he discovers the moon. Captivating illustrations framed in primary borders and sporting cleverly inserted humorous touches make this a picture book to return to again and again. *cl*

155. Zagwÿn, Deborah Turney. **Turtle Spring**. Berkeley, CA: Tricycle Press, 1998. ISBN 1-883672-53-8. 32p. (6-9). Picture book.

Clee's baby brother takes up most of her mother's time, and her father's job takes him away for the winter. Her comfort is the turtle Uncle Fishtank gives her, but it's a southern turtle not used to the northern climate, and when it's left out in the cold, Clee finds it in the compost pile, "stone cold." She mourns its loss while building a relationship with her baby brother, and when spring comes, they're both outside when the turtle emerges from the pile. An afterword explains the hibernation patterns of the Red-eared Slider turtle featured in the story. Another picture book about Clee and the natural setting where her family lives is *The Pumpkin Blanket* (Tricycle, 1995). *ss*

156. Zeman, Ludmilla. **The First Red Maple Leaf**. Tundra, 1997. ISBN 0-88776-419-3. (Paperback: Tundra, 1999). 24p. (5-8). Picture book.

In this original pourquoi tale, Zeman offers an explanation for Canada's changing seasons, symbolized by the maple leaf. Zeman arrived in Canada as a refugee, and she notes that "whatever the season, the red maple leaf shelters my new country. For me, it represents the sense of safety I felt when I first came here with my family." *ss*

157. Zhang, Song Nan. **The Children of China: An Artist's Journey**. Toronto: Tundra, 1998. (Paperback: Tundra, 1998). ISBN 0-88776-363-4. 32p. (10-12). Informational book.

Zhang pairs fifteen full-page paintings of people (especially children) with a first-person narrative exploring his impressions of the people as he journeyed throughout China sketching and photographing them. The result is a celebration of the diversity of minorities in China. An endpaper map pinpoints the regions where Zhang originally met the people portrayed in the paintings. *ca*

158. Zhang, Song Nan. **Cowboy on the Steppes.** Illustrated by the author. Plattsburgh, NY: Tundra, 1997. ISBN 0-88776-410-X. 32p. (8-12). Informational book.

During the Chinese Cultural Revolution, Yi Nan, along with millions of other young people, is forced to leave his home in Beijing to work in the countryside. A diary, beginning in August 1968, describes Yi Nan's life on the steppes of Inner Mongolia as he learns to be a cowboy, herding and tending cattle. Detailed colored paintings capture the beauty and ruggedness of the grasslands. *chs*

159. Zhang, Song Nan. **A Little Tiger in the Chinese Night: An Autobiography in Art.** Plattsburgh, NY: Tundra, 1993. ISBN 0-88776-320-0. 48p. (10-14). Autobiography.

Song Nan tells of the drastic changes in his life following World War II with the communist takeover of China in 1949. From the Cultural Revolution to the relaxing of policies following the death of Mao to the clamp down at Tiananmen Square the reader watches Song Nan grow as student, artist, husband, father, and finally as exile. Happy early memories of a tiger coming near his home and visits with his grandmother are followed by years of art school, work assignments in a coal mine, difficult years working on an aquatic farm, separation from his family, and ultimately a reunion in Canada. *djg*

160. Zhang, Song Nan, and Hao Yu Zhang. **A Time of Golden Dragons.** Illustrated by Song Nan Zhang. Plattsburgh, NY: Tundra. 2000. ISBN 0-88776-506-8. 21p. (10-12). Informational book.

When a dragon year in the twelve-year Chinese calendar coincides with a metal (gold) year of another cycle of about two years in length that moves through the elements of wood, fire, earth, metal, and water, a Golden Dragon Year occurs. The Zhangs created this book to mark the Year of the Golden Dragon (February 5, 2000–January 4, 2001). In a series of spreads, each with a richly colored, detailed illustration, the Zhangs explore dragon history, legends and lore about dragons, and the importance of the dragon as a symbol of the Chinese people. *ca*

Related Information

Organizations
The Canadian Children's Book Centre
www3.sympatico.ca/ccbc
c/o The Toronto Public Library, Northern District Branch, Lower Level, 40 Orchard View Blvd., Toronto, ON M4R 1B9; tel. 416-975-0010; fax 416-975-8970

Founded in 1976, this national, nonprofit organization promotes and encourages the reading, writing, and illustrating of Canadian children's books through such activities as Children's Book Week and the publications *Children's Book News* and *Our Choice*. The website has links to pages that provide names and addresses of Canadian publishers, bookstores, and related organizations as well as author web pages and an explanation of the Canadian children's book awards.

Awards
The Amelia Frances Howard-Gibbon Illustrator's Award
Given by the Canadian Association of Children's Librarians (CACL), this annual award is presented to the illustrator of an outstanding children's book (age 0-14) published during the previous calendar year in Canada; the illustrator must be a Canadian citizen or permanent resident of Canada.

Canadian Library Association Book of the Year for Children Award
Given by the Canadian Association of Children's Librarians (CACL), this annual award is presented to the author of an outstanding children's book published during the previous calendar year in Canada; the author must be a Canadian citizen or permanent resident of Canada.

Elizabeth Mrazik-Cleaver Canadian Picture Book Award
The award is administered by IBBY Canada and given to a Canadian illustrator of a picture book published in Canada in English or in French during the previous calendar year.

The Geoffrey Bilson Award for Historical Fiction for Young People
This annual prize is awarded to the author of an outstanding work of historical fiction for young people published during the previous year; the author must be Canadian.

Governor General's Literary Awards
Up to four annual awards (one each to an English-language writer, a French-language writer, an illustrator of an English-language book, and an

illustrator of a French-language book) are given by the Canada Council; all books for young people written or illustrated by a Canadian citizen in the previous year are eligible, whether published in Canada or abroad.

Information Book Award

Sponsored by the Children's Literature Roundtables of Canada, the Information Book Award is given to recognize an outstanding information book for children and young people five to fifteen years of age written in English by a Canadian citizen.

The Mr. Christie's Book Award

Six awards—three categories (seven and under; eight to eleven, and twelve and up) in English and French—are given, and the books are judged on the content of illustrations and text. Eligible books are published in the previous calendar year written and/or illustrated by a Canadian.

Ruth Schwartz Children's Book Award

Administered by the Ontario Arts Council Foundation, the Ontario Arts Council, and the Canadian Booksellers' Association, this prize recognizes authors and illustrators who demonstrate artistic excellence in Canadian children's literature. Winning books are selected by juries of children from a public school in Ontario.

Sheila A. Egoff Children's Book Prize

The Sheila A. Egoff Children's Book Prize is awarded annually as part of the British Columbia Book Prize program to what is judged to be the best children's book published in the previous year written by a writer who has been resident in British Columbia (or the Yukon) for three of the previous five years, published anywhere in the world.

Vicky Metcalf Award

This annual award carries a large cash prize and is presented by the Canadian Authors Association to a Canadian writer (citizen or landed immigrant) who has produced a body of work (more than three books) with appeal for children aged seven to seventeen.

A good source for lists of award winners, including most of those mentioned here, is **Globebooks.com**, the online book review magazine of the *Globe and Mail* at www.globebooks.com/search/awardsearch.html.

Websites
The Children's Literature Web Guide
www.ucalgary.ca/~dkbrown/index.html

Created and maintained by David K. Brown of the University of Calgary, this comprehensive site is international in scope and used by people all around the world.

Online Bookstores
Chapters Online
chapters.indigo.ca

With a separate category called Kids, this online venue of the Canadian bookstore chain makes it easy to browse in the children's section, where author profiles are posted periodically and featured books are described.

Journals
Canadian Children's Literature/Littérature canadienne pour la jeunesse
www.uoguelph.ca/englit/ccl

University of Guelph, Guelph, Ontario, Canada N1G 2W1 tel. 519-824-4120, x3189; fax 519-837-1315 E-mail: ccl@uoguelph.ca

This bilingual (English and French) journal of criticism and review covering Canadian books and other media for children and young adults was founded in 1975 and comes out quarterly. The website offers sample articles and pages, tables of contents of past issues, and information on how to subscribe.

The Looking Glass: New Perspective on Children's Books
www.the-looking-glass.net

Founded in 1997, this high-quality electronic journal about children's literature describes itself as combining an interest in the traditional with an eye to the modern. Although its contributors span the globe, they usually have a Canadian connection; the articles are international both in terms of topic and approach. Subscriptions are free but donations are welcome.

5
Asia

Afghanistan

161. Khan, Rukhsana. **The Roses in My Carpet**. Illustrated by Ronald Himler. New York: Holiday House, 1998. ISBN 0-8234-1399-3. 32p. (5-8). Picture book.
See Canada for description

162. McKay, Lawrence. **Caravan**. Illustrated by Darryl Ligasan. New York: Lee & Low, 1995. ISBN 1-880000-23-7. 32p. (7-12). Picture book.
This invitation to join ten-year-old Jura's rite of passage as he accompanies his father for his first caravan trip is made all the more intimate as the story is told in the first person, printed in stanzas and embellished with exquisite textured paintings. The reader shares Jura's pride in taking part in a sometimes dangerous journey while being responsible for three camels, his wonderment at city sights and sounds, and his thankfulness upon the safe return to his family camp (and mother and sisters) in the Hindu Kush Mountains. Author's note includes information about the caravaneers and their centuries-old route as well as vocabulary clarification. *bjk*
Author from the United States

Cambodia

163. Baillie, Allan. **Little Brother**. New York: Viking, 1985. Originally published by Penguin Books Australia in 1990. ISBN 0-670-84381-4. 144p. (8-12). Novel.
See Australia for description.

164. Coburn, Jewell Reinhart. **Angkat: The Cambodian Cinderella**. Illustrated by Eddie Flotte. Auburn, CA: Shen's Books, 1998. ISBN 1-885008-09-0. 32p. (5-10). Picture book.
Against the background of Cambodian landscapes and architecture, this variant of a Cinderella tale found in *Le Conte de Cendrillo Ches Les Cham* was first recorded by the French folklorist Adhemard Leclare in the

late 1800s. It is translated here with help from a Cambodian educator. The author and illustrator portray unique qualities of Cambodian art and life as Angkat endures great wrongs at the hands of her wicked stepmother and sister. Her kindness is rewarded by a delicate golden slipper, which brings her to the attention of the prince. *djg*
Author from the United States

165. Ho, Minfong. **The Clay Marble**. New York: Farrar, Straus & Giroux, 1991. (Paperback: Sunburst, 1993). ISBN 0-374-31340-7. 163p. (9-12). Novel.

As Vietnamese troops replace the Khmer Rouge, twelve-year-old Dara recounts her family's journey to the refugee camp, Nong Chan, on the Thai-Cambodian border where they camp. When fighting breaks out, Dara and her friend, Junta, are separated from their families, and Juntu makes Dara a "magic" clay marble to make her strong. The magic is within her, Dara discovers, as she copes with Junta's subsequent shooting by a guard at the base camp where their families have taken refuge and decides she can return home (alone, if need be) to rebuild their lives. A map and preface provide historical context. *NCSS-CBC Notable Children's Trade Book- Social Sciences; NCTE Children's Trade Book-Language Arts. hc*
Author from the United States

166. Ho, Minfong, and Saphan Ros. **The Two Brothers**. Illustrated by Jean and Mou-Sien Tseng. New York: Lothrop, 1995. ISBN 0-688-12550-6. 32p. (7-10). Picture book.

In a quiet Buddhist monastery in Cambodia, there once llived twin brothers named Kem and Sem. The two orphans studied hard and were eventually ordained as monks. After a time, they wished to see the world, and seeking blessings from the abbot they began their life outside the monastery. Kem immediately fulfills his destiny, but Sem, not following the wise advice of the abbot, suffers before he finally earns his reward. This story reflects the rich texture of Cambodian life, providing a brief glimpse of a Buddhist monastery, the royal court, village life, and a mythological monster. A detailed author's note sets this tale against the context of today's Cambodia. *djg*
Authors from the United States

167. Kuckreja, Madhovi. **Prince Norodom Sihanouk**. Broomall, PA: Chelsea House, 1990. ISBN 1-55546-851-9. 112p. (12 up). Biography.

Beginning with his abdication, the story of Prince Norodom Sihanouk is told against the setting of the turbulent politics of Cambodia. Retaining

his title of prince, Sihanouk abdicates his role as king to participate in party politics. Historical information about the land and people of Cambodia is given to understand the impact of his leadership. *djg*
   Author from the United States

168. Spagnoli, Cathy. **Judge Rabbit and the Tree Spirit: A Folktale from Cambodia**. Illustrated by Nancy Hom. San Francisco: Children's Book Press, 1991. ISBN 0-8239-071-9. 32p. (5-8) Picture book.

When a young man goes off to war, leaving his beautiful wife at home in sorrow, she is bewitched by the spirit of a banyan tree that turns itself into a creature identical to her husband. The real husband returns from war, the wife is confused by her two husbands, and it is up to Judge Rabbit to sort things out. *djg*
   Author from the United States

China

169. Bateson-Hill, Margaret. **Lao-Lao of Dragon Mountain**. Chinese text by Manyee Wan. Illustrated by Francesca Pelizzoli. Paper cuts by Sha-liu Qu. Originally published by De Agostini Editions (U.K.) in 1996; distributed by Stewart, Tabori & Chang. ISBN 1-899883-64-9. 32p. (4-8). Picture book.

See Europe/United Kingdom for description.

170. Jiang, Ji Li. **Red Scarf Girl: A Memoir of the Cultural Revolution**. New York: HarperCollins, 1997. ISBN 0-06-027585-5. 285p. (12-14). Biography.

Twelve-year-old Ji Li, an outstanding scholar and athlete, is proud to be a "Young Pioneer" and to take part in revolutionary activities but finds that she is excluded because of her family's class status. She witnesses the persecution of teachers and friends by neighborhood committees and the Red Guards until, finally, her family's apartment is ransacked and her father arrested. As her family's situation worsens and she is even asked to testify against her father, Ji Li realizes where her loyalties lie. In an epilogue, Ji Li writes of events after the Cultural Revolution. Glossary and foreword included. *ALA Best Books for Young Adults, 1998; Notable Children's Trade Book in the Field of Social Sciences, 1998. hc*
   Author from the United States

171. McCully, Emily Arnold. **Beautiful Warrior: The Legend of the Nun's Kung Fu**. New York: Levine/Scholastic, 1998. ISBN 0-590-37487-

7. 40p. (7-9). Picture book.

A daughter is born to the last Ming emperor of China. She is sent to tutors as if she were a son, excelling at martial arts. When the Ming Dynasty ends, she joins the monks at Shaolin Monastery to continue her studies in kung fu. She is given the name Wu Mei, meaning beautiful warrior. Wu Mei passes on her knowledge of martial arts to a young girl to save her from being forced into marriage by a gang leader. *pc*
Author from the United States

172. McMahon, Patricia. **Six Words, Many Turtles, and Three Days in Hong Kong**. Photographs by Susan G. Drinker. Boston: Houghton Mifflin, 1997. ISBN 0-395-68621-0. 45p. (7-12). Informational book.

More than a photographic essay, the narrative captures the spirit of a lively eight-year-old girl, Tsz Yan, who lives in a lively city about to experience change from British to Chinese ownership. The text is filled with typical, any child, age-appropriate thoughts as she negotiates her school day (backpack, daycare, friends, homework) and a family weekend. The photographs are candid, lending an intimate invitation to the reader to become part of Tsz Yan's life. Includes a pronunciation guide as well as an inset map of Hong Kong and a larger map showing Hong Kong in relation to China and Southeast Asia. *bjk*
Author from the United States

173. Mah, Adeline Yen. **Chinese Cinderella**. New York: Delacorte, 1999. (Paperback: Dell, 2001). ISBN 0-3853-2707-2. 224p. (11up). Biography.

This is an account of the author's childhood growing up in China, blamed by her siblings for "causing" their mother's death by giving birth to her, ignored by her father, and hated by her father's new wife. Her only moral support comes from her aunt and grandfather, who seem powerless to protect her. Despite being berated by her family members, sent off to a school and even to an orphanage, she persists in earning honors at school. Ultimately, she gets the chance to go to school in England and, like both the European Cinderella and her Chinese counterpart, Ye Xian, finds a new life. Supplementary information includes a guide to Chinese names and the symbols for numbers, along with a historical overview that helps explain the Yen family's position during the Cultural Revolution. *ss*
Author from the United States

174. Tsubakiyama, Margaret Holloway. **Mei-Mei Loves the Morning**. Illustrated by Cornelius Van Wright & Ying-Hwa Hu. Whitman, 1999.

ISBN 0-8075-5039-6. 32p. (4-8). Picture book.

Every morning, Mei-Mei and her grandpa go by bicycle to the park, carrying the family's pet songbird. They hang the bird's cage in the tree while they do tai-chi exercises with other people who have congregated there. Then they have their tea and return home. Scenes of everyday life in a big city in China offer fascinating details, such as the handkerchief covering a cyclist's nose and mouth to protect her from the pollution, a cyclist transporting a pig in a basket, and street vendors of all kinds. *ss*

Author from the United States

175. Yen, Clara. **Why Rat Comes First: A Story of the Chinese Zodiac.** Illustrated by Hideo C. Yoshida. San Francisco: Children's Book Press, 1991. ISBN 0-89239-072-7. 32p. (4-6). Picture book.

When the emperor of heaven, the Jade King, gives a feast for the animals of earth, only twelve show up, so he rewards their loyalty by naming the twelve years of the Chinese calendar cycle after them. Rat and Ox argue over who should be first, and the Jade King declares that a popularity contest will decide. This is not a traditional Chinese tale but a retelling of a story made up by the author's father. Stylized illustrations are ink and colored pencil. Includes summary of the Chinese zodiac for the years 1900-2019. *pm*

Author from the United States

176. Zhang, Song Nan. **The Children of China: An Artist's Journey.** Plattsburgh, NY: Tundra, 1998. (Paperback: Tundra, 1998). ISBN 0-88776-363-4. 32 p. (10-12). Informational book.

See Canada for description.

177. Zhang, Song Nan. **Cowboy on the Steppes.** Plattsburgh, NY: Tundra, 1997. ISBN 0-88776-410-X. 32p. (8-12). Informational book.

See Canada for description.

178. Zhang, Song Nan. **A Little Tiger in the Chinese Night: An Autobiography in Art.** Plattsburgh, NY: Tundra, 1993. ISBN 0-88776-320-0. 48p. (10-14). Autobiography.

See Canada for description.

179. Zhang, Song Nan, and Hao Yu Zhang . **A Time of Golden Dragons.** Illustrated by Song Nan Zhang. Plattsburgh, NY: Tundra, 2000. ISBN 0-88776-506-8. 21p. (10-12). Informational book.

See Canada for description.

Related Information

Awards
Chinese National Book Award
    This annual award, established in 1998, is for the most outstanding writing for children and young people in a book published in the preceding year.

India

180. Atkins, Jeannine. **Aani and the Tree Huggers.** Illustrated by Venantius J. Pinto. New York: Lee & Low, 1995. (Paperback: Lee & Low, 2000) ISBN 1-880000-24-5. 32p. (4-6). Picture book.
    When loggers come to cut down the forest around their village in India, young Aani and the other women hug the trees to protect them from the woodcutters. Stylized gouache paintings combine several styles from seventeenth-century northern Indian art to convey the energy and spiritual overtones of the 1970s Chipko Andolan (Hug the Tree Movement). Based on a true incident. *Smithsonian Notable Book for Children, 1995. pm*
    Author from the United States

181. Axworth, Anni. **Anni's India Diary.** Watertown, MA: Charlesbridge, 1992. ISBN 1-58089-050-4. 32p. (9-12). Picture book.
    Readers are introduced to India in a personal way through the diary entries of a fictional child traveling with her parents. Her impressions combine with illustrations of sights she sees along with way and facsimiles of tickets, postcards, and other items that give the feel of a scrapbook. The family's three-and-a half-month trip enables them to see much of India, and their route is sketched out in advance on a map on the title page. *ss*
    Author from the United States

182. Bash, Barbara. **In the Heart of the Village: The World of the Indian Banyan Tree.** Illustrated by the author. San Francisco: Sierra Club, 1996. ISBN 0-87156-575-7. 32p. (5-10). Picture book.
    This book, part of the Tree Tales series, describes the ecological, spiritual, and social importance of the Banyan tree to a small Indian village. This tree, with its aerial shoots that take root and form new trunks, becomes a forest unto itself. It is home to many creatures, and provides shade and sustenance to the villagers. Vibrant illustrations enhance the text, which is done in calligraphy by the author. *mb*
    Author from the United States

183. Bond, Ruskin. **Binya's Blue Umbrella**. Illustrated by Vera Rosenberry. Honesdale, PA: Boyds Mills, 1995. ISBN 1-56397-135-6. 69p. (8-12). Transitional book.

Ten-year-old Binya is fascinated by a blue umbrella owned by a sightseer who is equally fascinated by Binya's leopard-claw necklace. A trade is negotiated and from that point on, Binya and her umbrella are inseparable. She becomes the envy of the village; even the shopkeeper arranges for someone to steal the umbrella! He quickly finds out that "crime doesn't pay" when the failed deed is made public and his business suffers. In circular fashion, Binya compassionately gives the now well-worn umbrella to the shopkeeper and he gives her a bear-claw necklace. In spite of the emphasis on the color of the umbrella, the black pencil sketches perfectly capture the essence of this story set in rural India. *bjk*

184. Claire, Elizabeth, reteller. **The Little Brown Jay**. Illustrated by Miriam Katin. Glen Head, NY: Mondo, 1994. ISBN 1-879531-44-5. 24p. (5-8). Picture book.

This pourquoi tale explains where the blue jay got its sharp voice and beautiful color. A beautiful princess with an ugly voice loved a blind prince but could not get his attention. The jay gave her his voice to make her happy, and in exchange she wrapped him in her lovely blue scarf. When the prince heard the lovely singing voice of the princess, he fell in love with her. Following this folktale is a section that provides information about contemporary Indian society, illustrated with photographs. *ss*

Author from the United States

185. Gleeson, Brian. **The Tiger and the Brahmin**. Illustrated by Kurt Vargo. Rowayton, CT: Rabbit Ears Books, 1992. ISBN 0-88708-232-7; 0-88708-233-5 (cassette). 36p. (6-10). Picture book.

The Brahmin, a holy man known for bringing goodness and wisdom wherever he goes, discovers a tiger trapped in a cage. This is a conundrum, as he knows that the tiger will eat him if he is freed, but the tiger will surely die if left in the cage. Persuaded by the tiger's cunning argument, he frees the animal and is immediately pounced upon. The holy man is given one chance to save himself, but finally, it is the lowly jackal who comes to the Brahmin's aid and teaches him a lesson not found in his holy books. The excellent audio recording is read by Ben Kingsley with music by Ravi Shankar. This story is one of the We All Have Tales series and was recorded as a video series distributed by Uni; audio products are available on the Kid Rhino label of Rhino records; books and book/cassette packages are pub-

lished by Picture Book Studio and distributed by Simon and Schuster. *djg*
Author from the United States

186. Jaffrey, Madhur. **Robi Dobi: The Marvelous Adventures of an Indian Elephant.** Illustrated by Amanda Hall. New York: Dial, 1997. Originally published by Pavilion in 1996. ISBN 0-8037-2193-5. 76p. (7-10). Short stories. See Europe/United Kingdom for description.

187. Lewin, Ted. **Sacred River.** Illustrated by the author. New York: Clarion, 1995. ISBN 0-395-69846-4. 36p. (7-12). Picture book.

Simple, descriptive text, accompanied by detailed full-color illustrations, provide the reader with brief information about the Ganges River at Benares in India. Hindu pilgrims are shown in dazzling saris the color of jai flowers in long wooden boats, filling the dark stone steps called *ghats*. *djg*
Author from the United States

188. Rana, Indi. **The Roller Birds of Rampur.** New York: Holt, 1993. First published by Bodley Head in 1991. ISBN 0-8050-2670-3. 298p. (12 up). Novel.

Sheila Mehta is an IBBRCD, an Indian Born British Resident Confused Desi. Her family moved from India to England when she was seven, and her life is an intermingling of Indian and British ways. Unlike in India, where her future would be decided for her, she must chart her own path, and she hopes that a summer spent with relatives in India will help in her search for identity and a career. The book is filled with information about contemporary Indian politics, cultural practices, and religious belief as well as the sights and sounds of rural India and New Delhi. *ss*

189. Shepard, Aaron. **Savitri: A Tale of Ancient India.** Illustrated by Vera Rosenberry. Chicago: Albert Whitman, 1992. ISBN 0-8075-7251-9. 40p. (7-10). Picture book.

Set in the time of legend, the story of the princess Savitri is one of the best-known tales of the *Mahabharata* and tells the story of a young woman, as wise as she is kind, who wins the life of her husband back from Yama, the god of death. Sivitri chose her husband, Son of Truth, knowing that his fate is cast and that he will die in one year. When Yama arrives to take him, she bravely confronts him, winning her husband's soul back from Yama with her wit. Detailed watercolor illustrations convey the richness of ancient Indian culture. *djg*
Author from the United States

190. Staples, Suzanne Fisher. **Shiva's Fire.** New York: Farrar, Straus & Giroux, 2000. ISBN 0-374-36824-4. 275p. (12-14). Novel.

Born on the same day that a cyclone kills her father and devastates her South Indian village, Parvati is regarded with suspicion. Her unusual powers, her affinity with the Hindu god, Shiva, with her innate talent for dancing bring her to the attention of a famous guru who persuades Parvati to study to be a "devadasi" dedicated to a life of prayer and dance. After two years, Parvati returns to her village to perform at the Raja's palace. Here, she meets the Raja's son and learns that she can be "a magic of possibilities." Includes a glossary of Indian terms. *hc*

Author from the United States

191. Whelan, Gloria. **Homeless Bird.** New York: HarperCollins, 2000. ISBN 0-06-028454-4. 216p. (12 up). Novel.

Modern-day India is the setting for the story of Koly, a thirteen-year-old girl forced into an arranged marriage with a sickly boy who dies suddenly. Social customs require that Koly continue living with her in-laws, even though they disrespect her. When the father-in-law dies, Koly's mother-in-law abandons her in a large city, where she makes her way with her skillful and creative embroidery work. At the end of the story, Koly does fall in love, but she doesn't agree to marry the boy until she can do so on her own terms. The book includes a glossary of words in Hindi, Koly's native language. *ebb*

Author from the United States

Related Information

Online Bookstores
Balkatha
balkatha.com

This company offers a selection of worthwhile children's books from India in English, Gujarati, Hindi, Tamil, Malayalam, Marathi, and Kannada. Orders can be placed online or by phone or fax to a U.S. number.

Publications
Writer and Illustrator: Quarterly Journal of the Association of Writers and Illustrators for Children
Nehru House, 4 Bahadur Shah Zafar Marg, New Delhi 110002 India

Written in English and published by the Indian section of IBBY, this journal contains book-related news as well as reviews of children's books published in India in English and in regional languages. US $40/yr.

Indonesia (Bali)

192. Gelman, Rita Golden. **Rice Is Life**. Illustrated by Yangsook Choi. New York: Holt, 2000. ISBN 0-8050-5719-6. 32p. (7-9). Picture book.

Telling this story in two texts running parallel on each page, Gelman shares with readers her nine years of living with the Balinese and the significance of their rice fields, *sawah*. One text is poetry with well-chosen imagery that focuses on different animals that visit the *sawah* during each stage of growing the rice. The other text is well-researched information that narrates the story of planting from seedbeds to harvest. Bordered, colorful oil illustrations enclose the poetry while the prose text, with its own symbolic pictures, lies outside the border. *jbm*

Author from the United States

Japan

193. Brenner, Barbara, and Julie Takaya. **Chibi: A True Story from Japan**. Illustrated by June Otani. Clarion, 1996. ISBN 0-395-69623-2. 64p. (4-8). Informational.

Tokyo residents observe as a wild duck chooses Mitsui Office Park as a nesting site. The last duckling to hatch becomes the favorite of Mr. Sato, a news photographer; he names her Chibi, which means "tiny." Traffic is stopped when the duck family crosses a busy avenue to reach the great moat in the Emperor's garden, and the entire city worries when three ducklings, including tiny Chibi, go missing during a typhoon. Chibi survives (she reappears floating on a sheet of styrofoam). Includes a glossary and pronunciation guide of Japanese words in the text. Otani's watercolor and ink illustrations show the charming duck family and the crowds of duck watchers in present-day Tokyo. *ca*

Authors from the United States

194. Finley, Carol. **Art of Japan**. Minneapolis: Lerner, 1998. ISBN 0-8225-2077-X. 56p. (11 up). Informational book.

This book focuses on wood-block color prints, primarily *ukiyo-e*, which flourished during the Edo period (1750 to 1850) and had a great influence on later western artists such as Van Gogh and Whistler. The place of this artwork in Japanese society, the process used to create it, and characteristics of the art are explained in a clear text supported with illustrations, photographs, and maps. *ss*

Author from the United States

195. Gold, Alison Leslie. **A Special Fate: Chiune Sugihara: Hero of the Holocaust.** New York: Scholastic, 2000. ISBN 0-590-09525-4. 176p. (10-14). Biography.
See Europe/Lithuania for description.

196. Gollub, Matthew. **Cool Melons—Turn to Frogs! The Life and Poems of Issa.** Illustrated by Kazuko G. Stone. Calligraphy by Keiko Smith. New York: Lee & Low, 1998. ISBN 1-880000-71-7. 40p. (4-14). Picture book.
An homage to Issa, the eighteenth-century Japanese poet, is this blend of biographical narrative and haiku. Since Issa's life contained many elements of a tale (jealous stepmother, abandonment, extreme poverty, and loss), readers will come to understand the comfort and solace he took not only in observing nature but also in writing about it in haiku form. The illustrations are expressions of each haiku's mood and grace, with transcriptions in Japanese calligraphy in the outer margins of each page. One can only imagine Issa's very own brush strokes! Includes author's notes about the illustrator, the translations, and about the haiku form. *bjk*
Author from the United States

197. Higa, Tomiko. **The Girl with the White Flag: An Inspiring Story of Love and Courage in Wartime.** Translated by Dorothy Britton. New York: Kodansha America, 1991. Originally published as *Shirahata no shojo* by Kodansha International in 1991. ISBN 4-7700-1537-2. 127p. (12 up). Biography.
The author reveals the memories of her experiences during the final battles on Okinawa, Japan, which were revived when she viewed the famous photograph taken of her by American photographers. She relates the story of becoming separated from her family, ransacking the belongings of the dead for scraps of food, escaping death at the hands of a crazed Japanese soldier, and the kindness of an elderly couple. Her indomitable spirit in the struggle against hunger, suffering, and grief is a testament to a child's heroic refusal to succumb to the devastation of war. *djg*

198. Kroll, Virginia. **A Carp for Kimiko.** Illustrated by Ruth Roundtree. Watertown, MA: Charlesbridge, 1993. (Paperback: Charlesbridge, 1996). ISBN 0-88106-412-2. 32p. (4-6). Picture book.
Even though Japan's traditional Boy's Day is now Children's Day, Kimiko's parents fly the traditional carp kites only for her three brothers, not for their little girl. She reminds her mother that on the Doll Festival she let her little brother come to her "girls only" party. The next day, Kimiko is given her own carp—a small, beautiful, live fish swimming in a bowl of

water. Brightly colored illustrations feature traditional and contemporary designs and costumes of Japan. *pm*
Author from the United States

199. Kuklin, Susan. **Kodomo:Children of Japan**. New York: Putnam, 1995. ISBN 0-399-22613-3. 48p. (7-9). Informational book.

Kuklin's full-color photographs and introductions accompany the narratives and voices of seven Japanese schoolchildren from Hiroshima and Kyoto documenting their lives at home and at school. Special emphasis is given to the children's participation in traditional activities such as *kendo, judo,* and the study of calligraphy (*shudo*), *sado* (the tea ceremony), and Japanese dance. Other children are shown learning Japanese writing and math in school. Kuklin provides information on traditional and modern Japanese culture, including a section on Japanese writing. Japanese terms are interwoven throughout the text followed by symbols and/or characters. A glossary is included. *hc*
Author from the United States

200. Mori, Kyoko. **Shizuko's Daughter**. Holt, 1993. ISBN 0-8050-2557-X. 256p. (11 up). Novel.

Shizuko's daughter is Yuki, who is twelve when her mother commits suicide. After a year with her aunt, Yuki joins her father and his new wife, whose outright hostility she must endure silently. Even though her mother's relatives would gladly raise her, Japan's strong patrilinear society dictates that she stay with her father. Beauty abounds in this austere story in the form of both the writing and the objects described—Yuki's childhood clothes lovingly sewn by her mother, a pottery tea set they both watched being made, and Yuki's own sketches that will eventually aid in her liberation as she graduates from high school and is able to go away to art school. Mori's *One Bird* (Holt, 1995), also set in Japan, draws on some of the same elements but features a different character and situation. *ss*
Author from the United States

201. Navasky, Bruno. **Festival in My Heart: Poems by Japanese Children**. Selected and translated from the Japanese by Bruno Navasky. New York: Harry N. Abrams, 1993. ISBN 0-8109-3314-4. 120p. (10 up). Poetry.

This is a collection of poetry written by Japanese elementary school children. The poems were originally printed as a daily feature in the newspaper, *Yomiuri Shimbun*. The poems are accompanied by seventy-seven illustrations representing the wide scope of Japanese art, including

scroll paintings, wood-block prints, and ink paintings. *djg*
Author from the United States

202. Say, Allen. **The Ink-Keeper's Apprentice**. Boston: Houghton Mifflin, 1994. ISBN 039-5705-622. (Paperback: Puffin, 1996). 49p. (12-14). Novel.
Koichi Sei summons up courage to ask Noro Shinpei, the famous cartoonist, if he can be his disciple. For three years, he works with his master (Sensei) and the apprentice, Tokida, until his father, who is divorced from his mother, offers him the chance to emigrate to America. An artist's coming-of-age story in which the talented Koichi, who has lived on his own from the age of thirteen (although his grandmother and mother are nearby), is introduced to art and Tokyo's nightlife. In a foreword to the second edition, Say writes about the autobiographic nature of his work. *ALA Notable Book;. ALA Best Book for Young Adults. hc*
Author from the United States

203. Say, Allen. **Tea with Milk**. Boston: Houghton Mifflin, 1999. ISBN 0-395-90495-1. 32p. (4-8). Picture book.
May, who has grown up in San Francisco, is unhappy when her parents move back to Japan. She finds it difficult to adapt to Japanese culture, to wear a kimono, and to take lessons in calligraphy, flower arranging, and the tea ceremony while sitting for "long stretches" on the floor. When her parents hire a matchmaker, Masako (May) moves to Osaka, where she works in a department store. Here, she meets Joseph, who also speaks English and likes "tea with milk and sugar." Allen Say complements his text with graceful full-page watercolors portraying his mother as she struggles with traditional Japanese culture. *ALA Notable Children's Books, 2000. hc*
Author from the United States

204. Say, Allen. **Tree of Cranes**. Boston: Houghton Mifflin, 1991. ISBN 0-395-52024-X. 32p. (4-8). Picture book.
A small boy in Japan narrates how, on the day he is sent to bed because he has caught a chill playing in a neighbor's pond, his mother, despite her disapproval at his disobedience, has a surprise for him. Remembering her childhood in California, she digs up his special pine tree and decorates it with candles and paper cranes. Next day, he receives a samurai kite and builds a snowman with his papa. Say's luminous colorful watercolors evoke the serenity and beauty that is present in the young boy's home as his family celebrates his first Christmas. *hc*
Author from the United States

205. Takao, Yuko. **A Winter Concert**. Brookfield, CT: Millbrook, 1997. Originally published as *Fuyu no hi no konsato* by Cacoo-sha in 1995. ISBN 0-7613-0301-4. 32p. (4-8). Picture book.

One snowy afternoon a little mouse goes to a concert. The pianist begins to play and beautiful music fills the room. Black-and-white line drawings become filled with beautiful colors as the audience enjoys the beauty of the music. They leave the concert and take the colors with them to fill their homes and thoughts with the colorful, magical event. A perfect companion to Leo Lionni's *Frederick. djg*

206. Yagyu, Genichiro. **All about Scabs**. Translated by Amanda Mayer Stinchecum. Illustrated by the author. New York: Kane/Miller, 1998. Originally published as *Kasabuta-kun* by Fukuinkan Shoten in 1997. ISBN 0-916291-82-0. 28p. (4-8). Informational book.

Children's comments and questions about scabs are combined with simple informational text, such as how a scab is formed and why scabs are important. Comic-style illustrations add humor and child appeal. See also *Breasts* by the same author. *chs*

207. Yumoto, Kazumi. **The Spring Tone**. Translated by Cathy Hirano. New York: Farrar, Straus & Giroux, 1999. Originally published as *Haru No Orugan* by Tokuma in 1995. ISBN 0-374-37153-9. 166p. (10 up). Novel.

Tomomi is growing up and her life is full of unrest. She dreams of trans-forming into a monster, and the powerful monster will help her conquer the problems she has been powerless to control. The scent of spring constricts her chest and she struggles with worries about what will happen before the next spring arrives. This is a philosophical story about a senstive young woman struggling against her journey to adulthood. *djg*

208. Wells, Ruth. **A to Zen**. Illustrated by Yoshi. New York: Simon & Schuster, 1992. ISBN 0-88708-175-4. 22p. (7-12 up). Picture book.

By following the sounds available in Japanese of the Roman alphabet, Wells introduces readers to twenty-two topics providing insight into Japanese culture. The book opens "back to front" as a Japanese book does, the topics are written in both Roman alphabet and in Japanese, and the illustrations use the same techniques used to decorate kimono, painted dyes on silk cloth. The book provides a beautiful and accurate introduction to Japanese culture and life and will prompt many readers to want to learn more. *hr*

Author from the United States

Related Information

Awards
Nihon Ehon Award / Japan Picture Book Award
    This award for the most outstanding Japanese picture book published in the previous year was established to popularize picture-book art, to promote book reading, and to contribute to the development of picture-book publication.

Online Bookstore
Amazon.co. – Japan site
www.amazon.co.jp
    This site follows the amazon.com format but is only useful to those who can read Japanese and whose computers are set to decode Japanese.

Organizations
International Institute for Children's Literature, Osaka
www.iiclo.or.jp/english/english.htm
10-6 Banpaku-Koen, Senri Suita-Shi, 565-0826 Japan; tel. 81-6-6876-8800; e-mai: info@iiclo.or.jp
    This institute houses a research collection of children's books and offers reference services and seminars; it publishes an annual bulletin and a newsletter, which is available online, in English, at its website.

North Korea and South Korea

209. Holt, Daniel D., editor. **Tigers, Frogs and Rice Cakes: A Book of Korean Proverbs.** Illustrated by Lu Han Stickler. Auburn, CA: Shen's Books, 1998. ISBN 1-8850-0810-4. 32p. (5-8). Traditional.
    This collection of twenty Korean proverbs is arranged according to theme and includes cooperation, friendship, and eating. An author's note and explanations of each proverb are included. The watercolor illustrations provide a decorative setting for each proverb. *djg*
    Author from the United States

210. Park, Frances, and Ginger Park. **My Freedom Trip.** Illustrated by Debra Reid Jenkins. Honesdale, PA: Boyds Mills, 1998. ISBN 1-56397-468-1. 32p. (9-14). Picture book.
    Honoring the authors' mother's escape from North Korea, this story of her trip to freedom by little Soo underlines the adverse effects on relationships as friends and family members are separated, often without

further news and closure. The bittersweet ending is made all the more poignant by the oil paintings, which convey Soo's heartbreak at leaving her mother, her vulnerability yet trust in her gentle guide throughout the dark and dangerous journey, and the joy of her father as he met her on the other side of the river. Glossary of Korean words and characters. *bjk*

Authors from the United States

211. Park, Frances, and Ginger Park. **The Royal Bee.** Illustrated by Christopher Zhong-Yuan Zhang. Honesdale, PA: Boyds Mills, 2000. ISBN 1-56397-614-5. 32p. (7-9). Picture book.

Too poor to attend school, Song-ho is nevertheless drawn to it by the dream of learning to read and write, the dream of providing for his hardworking widowed mother. Listening through the school door each day, the boy learns enough to be chosen to represent the school at the Royal Bee. Song-ho wins the contest through his knowledge and particularly through his courage in speaking the truth about his humble origins. Bold oil paintings reinforce the nineteenth-century Korean setting and ways of life, emphasizing the contrast between the wealthy and the very poor. *sp*

Authors from the United States

212. Park, Linda Sue. **The Kite Fighters.** Decorations by Eung Won Park. New York: Clarion, 2000. ISBN 0-395-94041-9. 136p. (8-12). Novel.

Set in Korea in 1471, this is the story of two brothers, elder Kee-sup and younger Young-sup. Young-sup has a special talent in flying kites, but it is elder brother who must have the honor and fly the family kite in the New Year competition. Elder brother builds the kite that will be entered in the competition while younger brother tries to teach the elder what comes naturally to him. Easy to read conversational dialogue and an exciting kite competition make this historical fiction very approachable for contemporary readers. *djg*

Author from the United States

213. Park, Linda Sue. **Seesaw Girl.** Illustrated by Jean and Mou-Sien Tseng. New York: Clarion, 1999. ISBN 0-395-91514-7. 90p. (10-14). Novel.

Living in seventeenth-century Korea, twelve-year-old Jade Blossom leads a protected but restricted life due to her father's high position. Her bubbly, curious nature leads to an adventure that opens up a new world to her in terms of beauty, poverty, and awareness of social and gender differences. At a time when Korea is just beginning to question its isolationism, Jade Blossom has questions of her own and learns to channel

her lively spirit into problem solving, finding solutions to express her need to see over the Outer Wall of the family courtyard (hence the title of the book), to paint what she can't embroider, and to heed her mother's words, "Learn to make it enough." Includes author's notes on Korea's history of isolationism, the lives of aristocratic girls and women (1300-1880), and the Korean version of a seesaw. *bjk*
Author from the United States

214. Watkins, Yoko Kawashima. **So Far from the Bamboo Grove.** New York: Lothrop, 1986. (Paperback: Avon, 1994). ISBN 0-844-66810-9. 183p. (10-16). Novel.

In this riveting autobiographical account of eleven-year-old Yoko's escape from Korea to Japan with her sister and mother during World War II, the author writes clearly and movingly about their struggle for survival. Fleeing for their lives, they ran on foot at night, crowded onto railroad cars, always lacking food and water, always in fear. Through sheer determination and ingenuity, they eventually reached war-torn Japan where their mother died and they were reunited with their brother. *1987 ALA Notable Book; 1987 Parents' Choice Award; 1987 National Council of Teachers of English Teachers' Choice Award; 1986 School Library Journal Best Book of the Year; 1987 Judy Lopez Memorial Award for Work of Literary Excellence. fd*
Author from the United States

Laos

215. Cha, Dia. **Dia's Story Cloth.** Stitched by Chue and Nhia Thao Cha. Compendium by Joyce Herold. New York: Lee & Low, 1996. (Paperback: Lee & Low, 1998). ISBN 1-880000-34-2. 24p. (7-12). Picture book.

Photographs of a story cloth made for the author by her aunt and uncle tell the story of her Hmong family's search for freedom, which began long ago in China. Their journey continued to Laos, where her father joined the loyalist army and left to fight the communist regime. He never returned. At ten, the author and her family fled, escaping across the Mekong River and on to a refugee camp in Thailand. Four years letter, the small family came to America. This story cloth serves to preserve memories of their lives and culture and history. Extensive notes and a bibliography are appended. *djg*
Author from the United States

216. Xiong, Blia. **Nine-in-One, Grr! Grr!** Adapted by Cathy Spagnoli. Illustrated by Nancy Hom. San Francisco: Children's Book Press, 1989.

ISBN 0-89239-048-4. 32p. (4-6). Picture book.

In this Hmong folktale from Laos, a lonely tiger visits the god Shao in the sky to ask how many cubs she will have. She is promised nine a year for as long as she remembers Shao's words. But the clever Eu bird, fearing an overpopulation of tigers, tricks her into forgetting her mnemonic song. The full-page, bordered illustrations in silkscreen, watercolor, and colored pencil draw on Hmong embroidery motifs, as do the illuminated capitals on each page. *pm*

Author from the United States

Pakistan

217. Staples, Suzanne. **Haveli**. New York: Knopf, 1993. (Paperback: Random House, 1995). ISBN 0-679-84157-1. 264p. (12-14). Novel.

In a compelling sequel to *Shabanu*, Suzanne Staples has again evoked the life of arranged marriages in Pakistan. By creating a compelling adventure-and-love story Staples effortlessly draws her readers into the hopeless plight of a teenage woman, youngest wife to a wealthy landowner. Staples successfully maintains a balance between adept storytelling and realistic reporting. For mature readers, the book offers strong female characters and intricate details about the culture in Pakistan. *cc*

Author from the United States

218. Staples, Suzanne Fisher. **Shabanu: Daughter of the Wind**. New York: Knopf, 1989. ISBN 0-394-94815-2. 240p. (12-14). Novel.

Shabanu and her family prepare for the wedding of Shabanu's elder sister, Phulan, to her cousin, Hamir. Their plans are ruined when Nazir Mohammad, the landowner who envies Hamir's family's land, threatens to kidnap Phulan and Hamir is killed in a gunfight. Shabanu's life, too, is changed forever, as Phulan marries Murad, Hamir's younger brother, to whom Shabanu was promised. Shabanu, who has always enjoyed the freedom of the desert, must now accept her future as one of the wives of Rahim-sahib, Nazir's elder brother, in return for his protection of the family. Glossaries of names and terms. *1990 Newbery Honor Book; 1992 IBBY Honor List. hc*

Author from the United States

Philippines

219. Arcellana, Francisco. **The Mats**. Illustrated by Hermès Alègrè. New

York: Kane/Miller, 1999. Originally published by Tahanan in 1995. 20p. (8-10). Picture book.

Papa returns home from the southern provinces with sleeping mats made especially for each family member. The colorful illustrations show that the mats are objects of Philippine art, with no two alike. Each features a family member's name woven above a symbol representing a defining interest or personality trait. After everyone receives a mat, three still remain, and Papa explains they are memorials to three daughters who died as little girls. The father's homecoming ritual is rendered profound by a love deep enough to extend to all of his children, including those living only in the heart. *ebb*

Thailand

220. Ho, Minfong. **Hush! A Thai Lullaby**. Illustrated by Holly Meade. New York: Orchard Books, 1996. ISBN 0-531-09500-2. 29p. (1-6). Picture book.

Beautiful cut-paper collage illustrations and a lilting lullaby tell the story of a mother trying to put her baby to sleep, nervous that animal sounds will keep the child awake. Page by page, she asks all the area animals to "Hush." As she tries to quiet the surroundings, readers will delight in noticing the baby climb out of his bed. *1997 CCBC Choices; 1997 Caldecott Honor Book. hr*
Author from the United States

221. Ho, Minfong. **Rice without Rain**. New York: Lothrop, 1990. ISBN 0-688-06355-1. 236p. (12-14). Novel.

In northern Thailand in the 1970s, seventeen-year-old Jinda's father, influenced by Ned, a university student, refuses to pay the traditional rent of half the rice crop because of the poor harvest. Inthorn is imprisoned and Jinda, in love with Ned, goes to Bangkok to campaign for her father's freedom. When the military regime massacres students and her father dies in prison, Jinda returns to farm and family instead of joining Ned and the Thai Communists believing that "to live, and grow things" will achieve more than fighting for an "idea." A foreword provides the historical background to Ho's story. *ALA Best Book for Young Adults, 1991; Booklist Editor's Choice,1991. hc*
Author from the United States

222. MacDonald, Margaret Read. **The Girl Who Wore Too Much: A Folktale from Thailand**. Thai text by Supaporn Vathanaprida. Illustrated by Yvonne Lebrun Davis. Little Rock: August House, 1998. ISBN 0-87483-503-8. 32p. Picture book.

Aree's parents give her all she could want: beautiful silk dresses, golden earrings, silver bracelets, and ruby rings are showered on their vain, spoiled daughter. But when Aree cannot decide what to wear to a dance she tries to wear it all and finally learns a lesson. This modern adaptation of a story told in northeastern Thailand is brightly illustrated in contemporary Pu-Thai silk colors and Thai text. Source notes are appended. *djg*
Author from the United States

223. Shea, Pegi Deitz. **The Whispering Cloth: A Refugee's Story.** Illustrated by Anita Riggio. Stitched by You Yang. Honesdale, PA: Caroline House/Boyds Mills, 1995. 32p. ISBN 1-56397-134-8. Picture book.

Mai lives with her grandmother in Ban Vinai, a refugee camp near Chiang Khan, Thailand. She loves to listen to the older women as they stitch and talk. Mai diligently learns how to stitch the *pa'ndau* borders guided by her grandmother's careful instruction. Soon, she wishes to learn how to stitch her own embroidered story quilt. Grandmother tells her that she will not be ready for her own *pa'ndau* until she hears the whispers of her own story. The original *pa'ndau* stitched for this book tells Mai's own story while soft watercolor illustrations complete the story. *djg*
Author from the United States

Tibet

224. Halpern, Gina. **Where Is Tibet?** Ithaca, NY: Snow Lion, 1991, 1997. ISBN 0-937938-93-9. 48p. (4-8). Picture book.

Pema and Tahi, two Tibetan children, want to know how to find their homeland. Each sentence is written first in the Tibetan alphabet, then phonetically as the Tibetan is pronounced, and then in English. The book features a page presenting the English alphabet facing a page featuring the Tibetan alphabet. *djg*
Author from the United States

225. Sís, Peter. **Tibet through the Red Box.** Illustrated by the author. New York: Farrar, Straus & Giroux. 1999. ISBN 0-374-37552-6. 56p. (7-14). Picture book.

Given a red box that for many years hid his father's diary, the author weaves history, biography, and imagination as he tells of his father's wanderings in Tibet in 1950 while making a documentary on road construc-

tion. Through illustration format that delineates the various aspects of the story, luminous colors, and intricate detail full of mystical symbolism, Sis shares his father's account of wandering through Tibet during its invasion by China. His childhood memories of the fairytale-like stories his father told and the events detailed in the diary combine father and son's reflections in a book for all ages. *1999 Caldecott Honor Book. jbm*
Author from the United States

226. Whitesel, Cheryl Aylward. **Rebel: A Tibetan Odyssey**. New York: HarperCollins, 2000. ISBN 0-688-16735-7. 192p. (10-14). Novel.

Lost in a storm, a Tibetan boy, Thunder, is saved by a *fringie* (outsider), with whom contact is forbidden, and thus his family must send him away to the monastery where his uncle is a holy man. In this historical novel set in the early 1900s, Thunder struggles with his ⌣wn inquisitive nature, at odds with the ways of his people. Written from research, including first-hand accounts of early explorers in Tibet, this book is at once a captivating adventure story and a glimpse into a world apart. *ss*
Author from the United States

Vietnam

227. Breckler, Rosemary. **Sweet Dried Apples: A Vietnamese Wartime Childhood**. Illustrated by Deborah Kogan Ray. Boston: Houghton Mifflin, 1996. ISBN 0-395-73570-X. 32p. (7-9). Picture book.

The harsh realities of war are brought home to Lieu and younger brother Duc when Ba leaves to fight and their grandfather, Ong Noi, comes to live with them. They tease him, in spite of his stern ways, and help him gather herbs to make medicines. When their small village is bombed, grandfather uses all his medicines treating wounded soldiers and villagers, saving none of the bitter herbs, sweetened with the precious dried apples, for himself. This book was inspired by a true story. *djg*
Author from the United States

228. Huynh, Quang Nhuong. **The Land I Lost**. HarperCollins, 1982. (Paperback: HarperTrophy, 1986). ISBN 0-06-024592-1. 144p. (7-10). Autobiography.

The relationship between humans and animals pervades these stories of growing up in rural Vietnam: the strong and clever water buffalo that was both pet and work animal, the poisonous snake that was a self-appointed guardian of the author's home, the birds trained to sing certain songs.

Altogether, the stories form a picture of Vietnamese life and culture far removed from the images of war so often associated with this country. *ss*
Author from the United States

229. Keller, Holly. **Grandfather's Dream**. Illustrated by the author. New York: Greenwillow, 1994. ISBN 0-688-12340-6. 32p. (4-9). Picture book.
A bit of Vietnam War history, a dream shared by grandfather and grandson, and the need to balance wildlife conservation (specifically the Sarus crane) with maintaining enough rice paddies to ensure the village food supply—these are the components of a gentle story with a strong message. Though Grandfather's dream does come true, every reader will understand the challenge he gives at the end of the story in terms of global and personal responsibility and commitment to our planet and its inhabitants. Vietnamese culture comes alive through Keller's illustrations. A prologue details the plight of the Sarus crane in the Mekong Delta, and Keller devotes an endpaper to her participation in the 1992 Earthwatch project to save these cranes. *bjk*
Author from the United States

230. Pevsner, Stella, and Fay Tang. **Sing for Your Father, Su Phan**. New York: Clarion, 1997. (Paperback: Dell, 1999). ISBN 0-395-82267-X. 107p. (10-12). Novel.
Su Phan, who lives in a North Vietnamese village, always sings for her father when he returns from trading at sea. War comes to Vietnam and communist officials seize her father's ships. He builds a store but refuses to become a communist and is sent to prison. Su Phan's carefree life changes as the family tries to adjust to living without their father in a country at war. *pc*
Authors from the United States

Asia—Regional

231. Lee, Cynthia Chin. **A Is for Asia**. Illustrated by Yumi Heo. New York: Orchard, 1997. ISBN 0-531-33011-7. 32p. (4-12). Picture book.
This alphabet soup of a book honors and celebrates the diversity of the people, lands, and cultures of Asia. A true feast for the eyes are the illustrations that match key words linked to places ("B is for Batik, an Indonesian craft"). The topical theme layout develops visual literacy and map skills whether used as a read-aloud for young children or as an independent read for older ones. Includes a spread of alphabet samples of Asian languages. *bjk*
Author from the United States

6
North Africa and the Middle East

Egypt

232. Heide, Florence Parry, and Judith Heide Gilliland. **The Day of Ahmed's Secret**. Illustrated by Ted Lewin. New York: Lothrop, 1990. (Paperback: Mulberry, 1995). ISBN 0-688-08894-5. 32p. (4-9). Picture book.

Oh, to know the secret! We do know immediately that Ahmed is very proud of his very important job delivering butagaz (butane gas canisters) to his customers in the city of Cairo. At the end of this particular day, Ahmed will reveal the secret to his family. He thinks often about his happy surprise as he makes his rounds in the cacophony and kaleidoscope that is Cairo, which comes alive here through an excellent meld of first-person narration and realistic illustrations. The secret? Ahmed has learned to write his name, and at the end of the story there it is in flowing Arabic for all to see. The thrill of writing his own name and writing it over and over again will evoke powerful memories and responses in all readers and listeners of this book. *bjk*
    Authors from the United States

233. Oppenheim, Shulamith Levey. **The Hundredth Name**. Illustrated by Michael Hays. Honesdale, PA: Boyds Mills, 1995. (Paperback: Boyds Mills, 1997). ISBN 1-56397-183-6. 32p. (7-9). Picture book.

In ancient Egypt, a young boy, Salah, worries that his camel is sad. When his father tells him mortals only know 99 names for Allah, Salah fervently prays that the hundredth name will be revealed to his camel. The prayer is granted, explaining why camels hold their heads high and walk with pride, even today. Textured acrylic paintings on gessoed linen canvas add dignity to the gentle fable. *pm*
    Author from the United States

234. Rubalcaba, Jill. **The Wadjet Eye**. New York: Clarion, 2000. ISBN 0-395-68942-2. 133p. (11 up). Novel.

When his mother dies in 45 B.C., an Egyptian named Damon decides to tell his long-absent soldier father in person. En route to Caesar's army, he and his best friend are shipwrecked and then rescued by the crewmen of

Cleopatra. At her request, the boys travel to Rome to be spies and are rewarded with horses for the remaining journey. At a makeshift war hospital, Damon finds his father. Though heartbroken by his wife's death, he is overjoyed to see Damon, whose feelings are more complex. In the end, the reunited pair make plans for passage to Egypt. A glossary and author's note enhance the narrative with historical background. *ebb*
Author from the United States

Iraq

235. Alrawi, Karim. **The Girl Who Lost Her Smile**. Illustrated by Stefan Czernecki. Delray Beach, FL: Winslow, 2000. ISBN 1-890817-17-1. 32p. (3-7). Picture book.

Sunlight and moonlight are both dependent on Jehan's smile, and when she wakes up to find it gone, the whole town tries to help. Finally a Persian man shows her how to get it back by polishing a wall and uncovering its hidden beauty. This story, which comes from the Islamic tradition, is set in Baghdad, and Czernecki's stylized illustrations remove from the telling any notion of time, past or present, while capturing a strong sense of place. *ss*
Author from the United States

236. Heide, Florence Parry, and Judith Heide Gilliland. **The House of Wisdom**. Illustrated by Mary Grandpre. New York: DK, 1999. ISBN 0-7894-2562-9. 32p. (7-12). Picture book.

In richly combined pastel hues and descriptive prose, this book brings to life the great scholarly contributions of the Arabic civilization around 1000 A.D. Through the true story of Ishaq, son of Baghdad's greatest translator, the fervor for wisdom is sensed as he becomes old enough to travel in search of ancient manuscripts and becomes, himself, the greatest translator of Aristotle. An author's note explains chronologically the significance of the House of Wisdom in preserving the great intellectual contributions of the ancient world. *jbm*
Authors from the United States

Israel & Palestine

237. Ben-Ezer, Ehud. **Hosni the Dreamer: An Arabian Tale**. Illustrated by Uri Shulevitz. Farrar, Straus & Giroux, 1997. ISBN 0-374-33340-8. 32p. (4-9). Picture book.

Hosni, a poor shepherd living in an Arabian desert, dreams of going to the city. When the sheikh invites him to make a journey to the city, he uses his one gold dinar to purchase a piece of wisdom that will ultimately change his life forever. Ben-Ezer lives in Tel Aviv. *jr*

238. Carmi, Daniella. **Samir and Yonatan.** Translated by Yael Lotan. Scholastic, 2000. Originally published as *Samir ve-Yonatan 'al kokhav Ma'adim* in 1994. ISBN 0-439-13504-4. 186p. (10-12). Novel.

Samir, a Palestinian boy, is sent to an Israeli hospital to have a special knee surgery. Here he finds himself surrounded by a different language and culture and by the people on whom he blames the death of his younger brother. The hospital, though, represents comfort and safety, a contrast from Samir's home on the West Bank, a war zone where his brother was accidentally shot by an Israeli soldier. As Samir learns more about the lives and problems of the four Israeli children in his ward, he sees each as an individual and finds a true friend in Yonatan. Yonatan's magical computer journey to Mars cements their relationship. Includes glossary. *Honorable Mention, UNESCO Prize for Children's Literature in the Service of Tolerance; 2001 Batchelder Award. chs*

239. Dolphin, Laurie. **Neve Shalom/Wahat al-Salam: Oasis of Peace.** Photography by Ben Dolphin. New York: Scholastic, 1993. ISBN 0-590-45799-3. 48p. (7-14). Informational book.

Firm "belief in the peaceful coexistence between Arabs and Jews" is the basis for this photo essay about an Arab-Jewish community in Israel that accepts outsiders to its school, where Arab and Jewish children learn each other's language and culture. Schlomki and Mohammad are two ten-year-old boys who are supported by their parents as they form their friendship by learning to understand and accept each other and finding out they are not so different from each other after all. The cover illustration is an eloquent collaboration by the children of the school depicting their art of the Western Wall and the Dome of the Rock in the old city of Jerusalem. Notes on the concept of the village and school, the history of Israel, a glossary and comparison of Hebrew and Arabic are included. *bjk*

Author from the United States

240. Edwards, Michelle. **Chicken Man.** Illustrated by the author. New York: Lothrop, 1991. (Paperback: Mulberry Books, 1994). ISBN 0-688-09709-X. 31p. (4-9). Picture book.

The Chicken Man lives on a kibbutz in Israel. He loves to take care of the chickens, and he does such a good job that the chickens lay more eggs

than they ever have. However, his kibbutz rotates all work schedules and Chicken Man is repeatedly posted to other jobs. When the chickens rebel and refuse to lay any eggs the kibbutz work committee decides that Chicken Man should always work with the chickens for the good of the community. A light-hearted telling and wonderful illustrations make this an enjoyable examination of life on a kibbutz. *cc*
Author from the United States

241. Nye, Naomi Shibab. **Habibi**. New York: Simon & Schuster, 1997. (Paperback: Aladdin, 1999). ISBN 0-689-80149-1. 144p. (9-12). Novel.

Fourteen-year-old Liyana Abboud tells about her family's move from Missouri to Jerusalem, where her Palestinian father was born. Liyana writes about the difficulties in adjusting to a new life—an Armenian school, new languages, and learning to behave "appropriately"—as well as getting to know and love her grandmother, Sitti, and the Old City. The conflict between Palestinians and Israelis is interwoven with Liyana and her family's personal lives, especially when Liyana meets Omer, who is Jewish. Nye's rich and poetic text enables one to savor life in Jerusalem and the West Bank in all its complexity. *1998 Jane Addams Book Award; ALA Best Books for Young Adults 1998; ALA Notable Book, 1998; Middle East Book Award 2000.* *hc*
Author from the United States

242. Orlev, Uri. **Hairy Tuesday**. Illustrated by Jacky Gleich. Glen Head, NY: Mondo, 1999. English adaptation by Pamela Pollack. Published as *Der haarige Dienstag* by Beltz & Gelberg in 1998. ISBN 1-57255-651-X. 32p. (3-5). Picture book.

Every Tuesday evening, three-year-old Michael fights getting his hair washed. His sister has an idea—one Tuesday morning, she takes him to the barbershop to have his hair cut off, but that scares him even more, and he returns home determined not to cry anymore. But he does, even though him mother has promised him a surprise if he can make it through hair washing without tears. Though it takes several months, he eventually earns that surprise. Children are left to guess what it is from the book's final picture of a carrot lying next to a cloth-covered cage. Gleich's expressive paintings portray a contemporary family that could live in any country. *ss*

243. Schur, Maxine. **When I Left My Village**. Illustrated by Brian Pinkney. New York: Dial, 1996. ISBN 0-8057-1562-5. 64p. (7-12). Transitional book.

See Africa South of the Sahara/Ethiopia for description.
Author from the United States

244. Semel, Nava. **Flying Lessons.** Translated by Hillel Halkin. Simon & Schuster, 1995. Originally published as *Maurice Chaviv' el Melamed La'oof* by Am Oved in 1990. ISBN 0-689-80161-0. 120p. (10 up). Novel.

Set in 1955, just seven years after the creation of the nation-state Israel, this sparely written story is as much a portrait of an Israeli village as it is of the young girl, Hadara, who narrates. Hadara's father is a citrus grower, her mother is dead, and her next-door neighbor, a shoemaker originally from an island off the Tunisian coast, talks to her of flying through the air like a trapeze artist. Much of this book consists of Hadara's thoughts—her belief that she can learn to fly, and that flying will add a missing dimension to her life. What Hadara and the reader do not realize until the book's end is that the shoemaker, rather than having been in a circus, was in a concentration camp, where "flying" helped him survive. *ss*

245. Sha'ban, Mervet Akram, and Galit Fink (presented by Litsa Boudalika). **If You Could Be My Friend: Letters of Mervet Akram Sha'ban and Galit Fink.** Translated by Alison Landes. New York: Orchard Books, 1998. Originally published as *Si tu veux etre mon amie* by Gallimard in 1992. ISBN 0-531-30113-3. 118p. (12-14). Informational book.

In August 1988, two twelve-year-old girls started writing letters to each other that were delivered by their common acquaintance, Litsa Boudalika, a journalist covering the intifada, the "War of the Stones." Mervet, a Palestinian Muslim living in a refugee camp, and Galit, an Israeli Jew living ten miles away in Jerusalem, share their ideas, questions, and experiences. Their nineteen letters, spanning the course of three years, are each preceded by a brief news account. They allow us to see human faces behind the ongoing struggle for land, freedom, and security, and they help us understand how conflicting viewpoints can be justified. A detailed, unbiased, twenty-page historical overview, along with a map and glossary, provide key information about the two cultures. *rta*

246. Waldman, Neil. **Masada.** Illustrated by the author. New York: Morrow, 1998. ISBN 0-688-144-81-0. 64p. (10-14). Informational book.

Two thousand years of history are compressed into this book about Masada, the last Jewish stronghold in the Holy Land to fall to the Romans in 73 C.E. Ancient Jews and Romans come alive as the military strategy of both is described and as the will to conquer clashes with the will to survive. Later chapters fill us in on archaeological expeditions and finds from 1838 to the 1960s. The author's afterword gives credit to Josephus Flavius's *The Jewish War* (75 C.E.) for the basis of the book. Halftone paintings are subtle

but powerful, paying homage to the people who so courageously defended this fortress. Includes author's introduction, afterword, maps, timeline, glossary, bibliography, and art notes. *bjk*
    Author from the United States

247. Wolf, Bernard. **If I Forget Thee, O Jerusalem**. New York: Dutton, 1998. ISBN 0-525-45738-0. 64p. (8-12). Informational book.

This look at the city that is held sacred by three religions—Judaism, Christianity, Islam—begins with its history over a thousand years before the birth of Christ, when King David led a band of people to the site. We see the buildings as they are today and also models of them as they looked in Herod's time, while the text recounts the growth of the old city and the work of archaeologists in uncovering the past. Subsequent sections describe the religious practices of Jews, Muslims, and Christians in Jerusalem, and a final section offers a look at everyday life in modern Jerusalem, touching briefly on the conflict among groups of people who find it hard to coexist peacefully. *ss*
    Author from the United States

Lebanon

248. Heide, Florence Parry, and Judith Heide Gilliland. **Sami and the Time of the Troubles.** Illustrated by Ted Lewin. New York: Clarion, 1992. ISBN 0-395-55964-2. 32p. (9-14). Picture book.

Sami is a braver, more contemplative than usual ten-year-old who has known nothing other than civil war. He has wonderful role models in his life—a grandfather who teaches him the value of visualization and memory, a mother who understands that children can be comforted by the beauty of familiar objects, and an uncle who cares for Sami's family after Sami's father is killed in a bombing. Sami somehow knows that children are the hope for the future, with power enough to make a difference in stopping civil violence as they tried to do once before when marching with signs of hope and positive change. Lewin's realistic illustrations combine with the reality of first-person narrative to give a message of a peaceful future. *bjk*
    Author from the United States

Morocco

249. Lewin, Ted. **The Storytellers**. Illustrated by the author. New York: Lothrop, 1998. ISBN 0-688-15178-7. 36p. (4-8). Picture book.

Vivid watercolor paintings enhance a convincing description of the marketplace in Fez, Morocco, where young Abdul and his grandfather are walking to work. At the city's gate, the boy sends their white dove into the sky to bring back stories for his grandfather to tell the crowds that gather around them. Includes glossary of Arabic words. *pm*
Author from the United States

250. London, Jonathan. **Ali, Child of the Desert**. Illustrated by Ted Lewin. New York: Lothrop, 1997. ISBN 0-688-12560-3. 32p. (7-11). Picture book.

For the first time, Ali is accompanying his father on the yearly journey to the camel market in the Moroccan town of Rissani, three days through the desert. When they are caught in an unexpected sandstorm, Ali becomes separated, and he and the camel he has been riding kneel down to wait out the storm. When it is over, he is alone in the empty desert. How will he find his father? Heading west, he meets a Berber goatherd and his grandson and makes camp with them that night, but the next morning, they must move on. Ali's careful decisions along with the generosity of the Berber goatherd reunite him with his father. Lewin's paintings capture the ferocity of the blinding sandstorm and the colors of the desert at various times of day and night. *ss*
Author from the United States

North Africa—Regional

251. Kessler, Christina. **One Night: A Story from the Desert**. Illustrated by Ian Schoenherr. New York: Philomel, 1995. ISBN 0-399-22726-1. 32p. (4-9). Picture book.

Nomadic life with its freedom of space structured by morning and evening tea is the setting for young Muhamad's rite of passage to manhood. He must spend the night in the desert alone with his herd of goats when one of his goats delivers her kid. As Muhamad watches over his herd and comforts the she-goat he visualizes what his family is doing as he repeats bits of advice and information given to him concerning the stewardship of the land and the animals. He returns to his family the next morning in time for tea, secure in the knowledge that he has done well and is reaffirmed by his father's announcement that Muhamad now needs the blue turban of an adult male. Schoenherr's beautiful illustrations capture the dignity of the Tuareg people of the Sahara as well as the spaciousness of the desert. *bjk*
Author from the United States

7
Africa South of the Sahara

Cameroon

252. Bognomo, Joel Eboueme. **Madoulina: A Girl Who Wanted to Go to School**. Honesdale, PA: Boyds Mills, 1999. Originally published by Editions Akomba Mba, 1996. ISBN 1-56397-769-9. 32p. (4-8). Picture book.

Maduolina must give up her dream of becoming a doctor and leave school to help her mother sell fritters and produce so they can earn a living and keep younger brother Babo in school. When the teacher, Mr. Garba, becomes aware of her situation, he finds a way to help her earn the money needed for her family and return to school. *djg*

253. Njeng, Pierre Yves. **Vacation in the Village**. Honesdale, PA: Boyds Mills, 1999. Originally published by Editions Akomba Mba in 1996. ISBN 1-56397-768-0. 32p. (4-8). Picture book.

It is the last day of school, and Nwemb and Ngo are leaving to spend their vacation in a village outside the city with their grandparents and cousins. Having never been in the countryside, the children come to appreciate the simple village life, including family meals and Grandfather's stories about the customs of their ancestors. *djg*

Democratic Republic of Congo

254. Stanley, Sanna. **Monkey Sunday: A Story from a Congolese Village**. New York: Farrar, Straus & Giroux, 1998. ISBN 0-374-35018-3. 32p. (4-6). Picture book.

Author Sanna Stanley grew up in the Democratic Republic of Congo (formerly Zaire), where her parents were missionaries. In a note, she tells of her first Monkey Sunday. Her new Monkey Sunday takes place at the opening service of a Matondo, a Kikongo word that means "celebration of thanksgiving." Though her father thinks it will be impossible, young Luzolo pledges to sit still during the Matondo service. She nearly succeeds, even when the animals from the village wander

into the open shelter. But when a monkey drops a banana peel on her preacher father's head no one can sit still, not even Luzolo. *djg*
Author from the United States

255. Stanley, Sanna. **The Rains are Coming**. Illustrated by the author. New York: Greenwillow, 1993. ISBN 0-688-10948-9. 32p. (4-9). Picture book.
Aimee is the daughter of missionary parents who live in a village in the former Zaire. The illustrations and text together play out the tension of imminent rain (as in the beginning of the all important rainy season) versus the beginning of an outdoor birthday party. The authentic, softly tinted etchings remind us all that birthdays can be happily celebrated with friends no matter where we happen to be living. Includes author's notes. *bjk*
Author from the United States

Ethiopia

256. Kurtz, Jane. **Only a Pigeon**. Illustrated by E. B. Lewis. New York: Simon & Schuster, 1997. ISBN 0-689-80077-0. 32p. (7-9). Picture book.
Young Ondu-ahlem raises pigeons in his Addis Ababa neighborhood. Though some might say that his favorite bird, Chinkay, is only a pigeon, Ondu-ahlem thinks it is a very special bird. He protects this pigeon from predators and perils, with help from his younger brother Mamoosh. A glossary and author's note about raising pigeons in this culture are appended along with a photograph of the boy who inspired this story. *djg*
Author from the United States

257. Kurtz, Jane. **Pulling the Lion's Tail**. Illustrated by Floyd Cooper. New York: Simon & Shuster, 1995. ISBN 0-689-80324-9. 32p. (7-10). Picture book.
Set in a village in Ethiopia and emphasizing the cultural importance of respect for elders, this original story has at its heart a traditional folktale, "The Lion's Whiskers." To learn the secret of how to gain her new stepmother's affection, Almaz must bring her grandfather a hair from the tail of a lion. This lesson in developing patience and trust is of course the secret Grandfather has helped Almaz discover on her own. Cooper's muted impressionistic paintings give the story immediacy and a contemporary feeling. *sp*
Author from the United States

258. Kurtz, Jane. **The Storyteller's Beads**. San Diego: Harcourt Brace, 1998. ISBN 0-15-201074-2. 153p. (12-14). Novel.

Sahay, a member of the Kemant, who regard Ethiopian Jews (Falasha) as alien, gradually makes friends with Rahel, who is proud of her Beta-Israeli heritage, as they both flee from warring factions and famine in Ethiopia. When Sahay's uncle and Rahay's brother are captured and sent back, Sahay helps Rahel, who is blind, struggle on to the Red Cross camp in Sudan. Sahey listens to Rahel's stories, passed down to her by her beloved grandmother, and finally decides to accompany Rahel to Jerusalem so that she can survive for the sake of her family. A map, glossary, and historical note are provided. *hc*
Author from the United States

259. Schur, Maxine. **When I Left My Village**. Illustrated by Brian Pinkney. New York: Dial, 1996. ISBN 0-8057-1562-5. 64p. (7-12). Transitional book.

In a sequel to *Day of Delight: A Jewish Sabbath in Ethiopia* (Dial, 1994), Schur takes up the story of the Falasha, a vanishing tribe of black, Ethiopian Jews. She follows the experiences of one family forced by persecution and famine to flee the country. Narrated by one of the family's two sons, the book presents a child's-eye, personal view of the secret evacuation by Israeli agents of 10,000 Falasha from Sudanese refugee camps to new homes in Israel. *cc*
Author from the United States

Ghana

260. Chocolate, Debbi. **Kente Colors**. Illustrations by John Ward. New York: Walker, 1996. ISBN 0-8027-8388-0. 32p. (4-8). Picture book.

Kente colors bold and bright are brilliantly depicted in this concept picture book. Emerald, indigo, and ivory are some of the symbolic colors shown in the kente representing bountiful harvest, love, and joy. Patterns such as "Gold Dust," symbolizing wealth and royalty, are among the many shown in the rhyming narrative depicting scenes from Ghana. *djg*
Author from the United States

Kenya

261. Anderson, Laurie Halse. **Ndito Runs**. Illustrated by Anita van der Merwe. New York: Holt, 1996. 0-8050-3265-7. 29p. (4-6). Picture book.

As young Ndito leaves her village home and runs across the Kenyan countryside eager to get to school, she joyfully imagines becoming different animals. She floats by the tall grass like a gazelle, scampers over the savanna like a goat, hops under a baobab like a dik-dik, and gallops up the hillside like a wildebeest. Van der Merwe's acrylic paintings fill the pages with beautiful images of the Kenyan highlands. *ca*
Author from the United States

262. Burchell, Chris. **Hamadi and the Stolen Cattle**. Illustrated by Sean Creagh. Broomall, PA: Chelsea House, 1995. ISBN 0-7910-3160-8. First published by Heinemann International Literature and Textbooks in 1994. 60p. (JAWS-Level 3). Novel.

Hamadi is eleven years old and belongs to the Galla tribe of northern Kenya. He and his family are nomadic and have many cattle. Hamadi lives a quiet life until one day when his family is attacked by Shifta bandits and his cattle and camels are stolen. The Junior African Writers Series (JAWS) offers young readers original stories set in Africa. The stories are graded into five levels of language difficulty, with 1 being for beginning readers and 5 for young adults. *djg*

263. Kitsao, Jay. **McHeshi Goes on a Journey**. Nairobi, Kenya: Jacaranda Designs, 1995. Illustrated by Wanjiku Mathenge et al. ISBN 9-96688-425-4. 24p. (3-5). Picture book.

McHeshi and her Aunt Suda travel by bus, train, airplane, and boat from the girl's village near Nairobi to the Somali border. A simple maze and map accompany the text. Bright, colorful illustrations as well as English and Swahili text are imposed on batik designs. Other books in the series: *McHeshi Goes to School*; *McHeshi Goes to the Game Park*; *McHeshi Goes to the Market* (all 1995). *Jomo Kenyatta Award for Children's Literature; Best Children's Title at the Pan-African Book Fair. djg*

264. Quintana, Anton. **The Baboon King**. Translated by John Nieuwenhuizen. New York: Walker, 1999. Originally published as *De havianenkoning* by Em. Querido's Uitgeverij in 1982. First English-language edition published in Australia in 1996. ISBN 0-8027-8711-8. 183p. (12-14). Novel.

See Europe/The Netherlands for description.

265. Wilson-Max, Ken. **Furaha Means Happy, A Book of Swahili Words**. Illustrated by the author. New York: Hyperion, 2000. Published

simultaneously in the U.K. by David Bennett. ISBN 0-7868-0552-8. 26p. (4-9). Picture book.
See Europe/United Kingdom for description.

Liberia

266. Zemser, Amy Bronwen. **Beyond the Mango Tree**. New York: Greenwillow, 1998. (Paperback: HarperTrophy, 2000). ISBN 0-688-16005-0. 156p. (10-14). Novel.
The move from Boston to Liberia has resulted in an isolated life for Sarina, twelve. As the only child of absent parents (a chronically sick, possessive, but emotionally vacant mother and a father away at work much of the time), she longs for love and friendship. Meeting Boimi, a Liberian boy, fulfills her need for friendship, while visiting his warm, loving family reminds her of her own void. Sarina's emotional needs, coupled with her privileged existence, blind her to the economic poverty of the country, including Boimi's malnutrition. Sarina's point of view is maintained throughout this bittersweet novel in which she learns to see beyond the tree in her own yard. *ss*
Author from the United States

Nigeria

267. Olaleye, Isaac. **The Distant Talking Drum: Poems from Nigeria**. Paintings by Frane Lessac. Honesdale, PA: Wordsong/Boyds Mills, 1995. (Paperback: Boyds Mills, 2001). ISBN 1-56397-095-3. 32p. (8-12). Picture book.
Fifteen poems illustrated with full-page guache illustrations describe life and customs in a Nigerian village. Weavers, storytellers, and farmers, listen to the distant talking drums, deep in the rain forest. The sounds and smells of the market, children playing, and rain storms invite the reader to enjoy the beauty and simplicity of life captured by Olaleye. *djg*
Author from the United States

268. Onyefulu, Ifeoma. **A Is for Africa**. New York: Cobblehill, 1993. Originally published by Frances Lincoln in 1993. ISBN 0-525-65147-0. 32p. (5-8). Picture book.
The author, a member of the Igbo tribe in Nigeria, presents photographs that reflect the rich diversity of the African continent as a whole. Full-page color images begin the visual introduction to Africa, from

beads, canoe, and drum to xylophone, yams, and zigzag lanes and everything in between. *djg*

Sierra Leone

269. Kessler, Cristina. **No Condition Is Permanent**. New York: Philomel, 2000. ISBN 0-399-23486-1. 184p. (12 up). Novel.

Begrudgingly, fourteen-year-old Jodie accompanies her divorced anthropologist mother to Sierra Leone for a sabbatical year to be spent studying the life of women in a fishing village. Becoming friends with Khadi, a girl her own age, eases her transition into village life and motivates her to learn Krio, the intertribal language, but their relationship changes when Khadi begins her secret initiation into womanhood. When Jodie learns that this initiation includes female circumcision, her attempts at intervention cause them to be routed from the village. The story offers hope that this tradition will change, not because cultural outsiders condemn it, but because those inside the culture are coming to recognize that they can make different choices for their own daughters. *ss*
Author from the United States

270. Sandoval, Dolores. **Be Patient Abdul**. New York: McElderry, 1996. ISBN 0-689-50607-4. 32p. (5-8). Picture book.

Abdul, who lives in Sierra Leone, loves school, but it is expensive and he must earn the money to attend. Everyday he goes to the marketplace to sell oranges, but he does not earn enough money. Grandmother encourages him to be patient but it is not until the day of the Independence Day parade that he, with the help of his family, is able to accomplish his goal. *djg*
Author from the United States

South Africa

271. Angelou, Maya. **My Painted House, My Friendly Chicken, and Me.** Photographs by Margaret Courtney-Clarke. New York: Clarkson Potter. 1994. ISBN 0-517-59667-9. 40p. (4-9). Picture book.

Angelou focuses on the way the Ndebele women in South Africa incorporate art into their daily lives. The Ndebele paint the exteriors of all their house in bright, intricate designs. They also create elaborate beadwork for their clothes. An eight-year-old girl tells the story, intro-

ducing herself and her way of life through many color photographs. *cc*
Author from the United States

272. Coman, Carolyn. **Many Stones**. Asheville, NC: Front Street, 2000. 1-
886910-55-3. 158p. (12 up). Novel.

Post-apartheid South Africa is the emotional and geographical
backdrop for a story about reconciliation between a daughter and father,
estranged by divorce, and the reconciliation of both to the death of their
family member, twenty-one-year-old Laura, who was murdered in Cape
Town while working there as a volunteer. A year after Laura's death, Berry
and her father have traveled to South African from their respective homes
in the United States for a memorial service honoring their sister and
daughter. Coman lets Berry narrate this story, giving readers a chance to
see how her anger toward him for leaving the family manifests itself and
how forgiveness, crucial to the success of the new South Africa, can be
hers, too. In the course of the story, readers visit, along with Berry and her
father, sites of social and political import, including Soweto, Robben Island,
and Kruger Park. *ss*
Author from the United States

273. Daly, Niki. **The Boy on the Beach**. New York: McElderry, 1999.
ISBN 0-689-82175-1. 32p. (3-7). Picture book.

It's hot, hot, hot—a perfect day for a boy at the beach with his
mother and father. Between bright umbrellas and tropical towels, surfers
and sunbathers, they find their spot. But the boy is eager to experience
every beach activity, splashing, running, kangaroo jumping. Lost in the
sand dunes and found by a lifeguard, he eventually has a happy reunion
at the ice cream stand. A perfect end for a boy on this universal beach.
IBBY Honor List, 2000. djg

274. Daly, Niki. **Bravo, Zan Angelo!** New York: Farrar, Straus & Giroux,
1998. First published by Frances Lincoln (U.K.) in 1998. ISBN 0-374-
30953-1. 32p. (5-8). Picture book.

Daly's lively text and fluid art combine to bring alive Venice and the
street theater—*commedia dell'arte*—that flourished during the
Renaissance. Young Angelo's persistence in asking to join his
grandfather's troupe wins him a spot at the end of the performance as a
rooster. Not a big part, certainly, but one that he prepares for throughout
the day by putting together the right costume and observing the struts
and squawks of Bardolino, his aunt's rooster. Predictably, Angelo steals

the show. While young readers will identify with Angelo's success, readers of all ages will be drawn into the magic of the world Daly offers here. *ss*

275. Daly, Niki. **Jamela's Dress**. New York: Farrar, Straus & Giroux, 1999. First published by Frances Lincoln (U.K.) in 1999. ISBN 0-374-33667-9. 32p. (3-7). Picture book.

Jamela's mother has bought a length of fabric to make a dress to wear to Thelma's wedding, but before sewing she washes it and hangs it out to dry under the watchful eye of Jamela. But Jamela does more than just watch it—she wraps herself in it and parades through the neighborhood. Commotion ensues, the fabric is ruined, and Archie the photographer takes a picture. Fortunately, Archie's picture is used in the newspaper and he receives a handsome sum, enough to buy Jamela's mother a new piece of fabric. This is a universal story—what child hasn't ruined a parent's prize possession?—set in a specific place and offering a glimpse of life in a South African township. *1999 Vivian Wilkes Award; 1999 Parents' Choice Silver Honor Winner. ss*

276. Deetlefs, Rene. **The Song of Six Birds**. Illustrated by Lyn Gilbert. New York: Dutton, 1999. Originally published by Andersen Press in 1999. ISBN 0-525-46314-3. 32p. (4-6). Picture book.

A little girl find that she can't make beautiful music with the flute her mother gives her until she captures the sounds of six birds in it and acquires a bit of wisdom from the medicine man. The author and illustrator, both South African, convey the sounds and sights of communal village life with a well-paced text and vibrant single- and double-page illustrations. *sg*

277. McKee, Tim. **No More Strangers Now**. Photographs by Anne Blackshaw. Foreword by Archbishop Desmond Tutu. New York: DK Ink, 1998. ISBN 0-7894-2524-6. 108p. (12 up). Informational book.

Powerful personal narratives and photographs bring together twelve South African teenagers whose distinct voices illuminate their experiences under apartheid and the challenging years of freedom since. Teens reveal what it was like growing up in a country bitterly divided by racial separation. Included are stories of hope and a willingness to reach out, forgive, and heal, a testament to the power and resilience of the human spirit. *djg*
    Author from the United States

278. Moodie, Fiona. **Nabulela**. Illustrated by the author. New York:

Farrar, Straus & Giroux, 1997. Originally published by Andersen Press in 1996. ISBN 0-374-35486-3. 32p. (7-9). Picture book.

The name of this South African folktale comes from a lake-dwelling monster that eats people and terrorizes a village. Moodie retells the tale, concentrating on relationships between the village chief's daughter, Nandi, and the other girls her age. The chief spoils his daughter, arousing jealousy and hatred. The village girls trap Nandi where lions can attack her, but her dog leads the village men to the rescue. As punishment for the village girls, the chief orders them to trap Nabulela and bring its skin to him. The girls succeed, and the chief praises them and acknowledges his errors in spoiling Nandi. He agrees to treat all the girls equally. Moodie's colorful and imaginative illustrations enhance the story. *cc*

279. Sisulu, Elinor Batezat. **The Day Gogo Went to Vote.** Illustrated by Sharon Wilson. Boston: Little, Brown, 1996. (Paperback: Little, Brown, 1999). ISBN 0-316-70267-6. 32p. (7-9). Picture book.

Nelson Mandela called Sisulu's story of Gogo "inspiring and moving." And it is. The story centers on South Africa's first free election in 1994, and on great-grandmother Gogo, who is "older than the township." Through the eyes of six-year-old great-granddaughter Thembi, we follow the proud and homebound Gogo to the polls to cast her first ballot. Wilson's moody pastel illustrations richly complement a memorable text. *1999 Parents Choice Gold Award winner. rhm*

280. Stewart, Dianne. **Gift of the Sun: A Tale from South Africa.** Pictures by Jude Daly. New York: Farrar, Straus & Giroux, 1996. First published by Frances Lincoln in 1996 by arrangement with The Inkman, Cape Town, South Africa. ISBN 0-374-32425-5. 25p. (3-6). Picture book.

Thulani loves to bask all day in the sun and he soon gets tired of interrupting his rest to milk the cow. So early one morning he goes to market to trade the cow for an old billy goat. But his wife is angry and the goat eats all their seed corn, so off again to market to trade for a sheep. On and on the trades progress until he is able to trade for seed, but it is only sunflower seed, good for nothing but following the sun, just like Thulani. However, this time the trade proves useful and before long Thulani and his wife are reaping the rewards. Beautiful images of contemporary rural life in South Africa are portrayed by Jude Daly. *djg*

Related Information

Websites
Bookchat: Your Centre of Information on South African Children's Books
www.bookchat.co.za
This website offers lists of recommended books, a "book of the week," and news about South African writers and artists, with a link to the South African Children's Book Forum.

Bookstores
The Book Cottage
10 Harbour Road, Hermanus 7200 South Africa; tel. 0283-700834; fax 0283-70011

Sudan

281. Walgren, Judy. **The Lost Boys of Natinga**. Photographs by the author. Boston: Houghton Mifflin, 1998. ISBN 0-395-70558-4. 48p. (12-14). Informational book.

This photojournal alerts us to the plight of the orphan boys of the Natinga refugee camp and school in the Sudan. Most have lost everything and everyone in the civil war but find companionship, schooling, religion, and their basic needs met (if barely) at the camp. Responsibilities (preparing food, cleanliness, studying) are documented as well as needs (adequate medicine, food, schoolbooks, clothing). There is hope for preserving various tribal cultures and giving the boys a sense of belonging by organizing traditional games and opportunities to perform tribal songs and dances. A sober look at the effect of war on young lives. Includes a map and author's afterword. *bjk*
Author from the United States

Tanzania

282. Grimes, Nikki. **Is It Far to Zanzibar?** Illustrated by Betsy Lewin. New York: Lothrop, 2000. ISBN 0-688-13157-3. 32p. (4-12). Poetry.

People and places, sights and sounds of Tanzania are the focus of the thirteen poems in this book. The use of first person and sensory descriptions bring to life this African country as the poet experienced it. Watercolor illustrations add detail and delight to the sometimes whimsical nature of these poems. A map and glossary of African words provide

additional insight to this culture. *jbm*
Author from the United States

283. Mollel, Tololwa M. **Big Boy.** Illustrated by E. B. Lewis. New York: Clarion, 1995. (Paperback: Clarion, 1997) ISBN 0-389-567403-4. 28p. (4-6). Picture book.

Tired of being small, Oli sneaks away from home, is granted a wish by a magical bird, becomes a giant, and discovers that being big has drawbacks, too. Mythic elements in the story are smoothly integrated into a realistic framework by the author, an Arusha Maasai from Tanzania who adapted his motif from African folklore. Outstanding watercolor illustrations suit the beautifully written text. Includes glossary of Kiswahili terms used in the story. The author recently moved to the United States. *pm*

284. Stuve-Bodeen, Stephanie. **Elizabeti's Doll.** Illustrated by Christy Hale. New York: Lee & Low. 1998. ISBN 1-880000-70-9. 29p. (4-6). Picture book.

Elizabeti, a young Tanzanian girl, has a baby doll (actually a large rock) named Eva, which she lovingly nurtures while Mama cares for Elizabeti's new baby brother, Obedi. In the sequel, *Mama Elizabeti* (2000), Elizabeti has a new baby sister named Flora. Because of her practice with Eva, Elizabeti knows just what to do now that Mama is busy with the new baby and needs her to care for Obedi. Elizabeti soon learns, however, that minding a toddler is not as easy as taking care of a rock doll. Hale's appealing mixed-media illustrations capture the warm, loving relationship of the children, Mama, and Baba, their father, and daily life in their Tanzanian village. *1999 Ezra Jack Keats New Writer Award; ALA Notable Book; SLJ Best Books of 1998. ca*
Author from the United States

Zimbabwe

285. Farmer, Nancy. **Do You Know Me?** Illustrated by Shelley Jackson. New York: Orchard, 1993. (Paperback: Puffin, 1994). ISBN 0-531-08624-0. 105p. (7-9). Transitional book.

Uncle Zeka moves in with his nine-year-old niece, Tapiwa and her family in Harare after bandits burn his village in Mozambique. Tapiwa and her uncle enjoy unusual adventures together; their undertakings often getting them into trouble. Eventually Uncle Zeka's knowledge of bush

life-plants, animals, and ancestral medicine land him a job at a Medical Research Center where he is appreciated. *pc*
Author from the United States

286. Farmer, Nancy. **The Ear, the Eye and the Arm.** New York: Orchard, 1994. (Paperback: Puffin, 1995). ISBN 0-531-08679-8. 311p. (12-14). Novel.

General Matista's son, thirteen-year-old Tendai, and his siblings are kidnapped when they leave their protected home to explore Harare. Three mutant detectives, Ear, Eye, and Arm, follow the trail of the children as they escape from Dead Man's Vlei (where She Elephant puts them to work in a plastic mine) and from Resthaven, within whose walls the past is preserved. Eventually recaptured by She Elephant, the children are delivered to the deadly Masks but the detectives arrive in time to save Tendai from being sacrificed. Set in Zimbabwe in 2194, the story integrates Shona beliefs into a technologically advanced society. Glossary included. *1995 ALA Best Books for Young Adults; 1994 Golden Kite Fiction Honor Book. hc*
Author from the United States

287. Farmer, Nancy. **A Girl Named Disaster.** New York: Orchard, 1996. (Paperback: Puffin, 1998). ISBN 0-531-095-398. 309p. (12-14). Novel.

Nhamo, a young Shona woman, is told that she must marry an old man, brother of the man whom her father had murdered. With the aid of her grandmother, she escapes and sets out by boat to find her father's family in Mozambique. On her long journey, during which she communicates with her dead mother's spirit, she encounters near starvation and many dangers, finally reaching safety at Dr. Masuko's experimental station on the Zimbabwe/Mozambique border. Here, Nhamo receives the support that will enable her to become economically independent of her father's family. Glosssary and notes on Shona culture are included. *1997 Newbery Honor Book; 1997 ALA Best Books for Young Adults; 1996 National Book Award Finalist. hc*
Author from the United States

Africa—Regional

288. Ekwensi, Cyprian. **King Forever!** Illustrated by Shirley Bellwood. Broomall, PA: Chelsea House, 1994. First published by Heinemann International Literature and Textbooks, 1992. ISBN 0-7910-2921-2. 94p. (JAWS-Level 4). Novel.

Set in the kingdom of Bamanga, this is the story of King Sinanda, who wanted to rule forever. But he was an evil man and ruled his people in terror. He destroys his enemies in a violent coup, and becomes corrupted by his desire for power. Eventually, he too is overthrown in an action staged by his own Special Action Soldiers. The story concludes with the statement: King Sinada had forgotten one thing. "It is only death that rules for ever." The Junior African Writers Series (JAWS) offers young readers original stories set in Africa. The stories are graded into five levels of language difficulty, with 1 being for beginning readers and 5 for young adults. *djg*

289. Finley, Carol. **The Art of African Masks**. Minneapolis: Lerner, 1999. ISBN 0-8225-2078-8. 64p. (11 up). Informational book.

One of a series of four books of art around the world, this illustrated book focuses on the masks made by several different tribes in West and Central Africa. Masks have many functions in the private and public ceremonies of these cultures, both concealing identities and creating new ones from the spirit world. The descriptive text is augmented with photographs of masks being worn during ceremonies as well as those on display as art objects. *ss*
Author from the United States

290. Launko, Okinaba. **Ma'mi**. Illustrated by Chris Coady. Broomall, PA: Chelsea House, 1995. First published by Heinemann International Literature and Textbooks, 1994. ISBN 0-7910-3164-0. 89p. (JAWS-Level 5). Novel.

Ma'mi and her young son are desperately poor. She will do almost anything honorable to earn enough money to live and to help him complete his education. For ten years she keeps hidden the secret of his father's identity. But the boy's curiosity is strong and she has no choice but to reveal the terrible truth about why she left her husband. This a wrenching story about the extreme hardship of poverty and the power of money to corrupt. *djg*

291. Magombe, Paulinos Vincent. **Mr. Kalogo's Factory**. Illustrated by Mei-Yim Low. Broomall, PA: Chelsea House, 1995. First published by Heinemann International Literature and Textbooks, 1994. ISBN 0-7910-3021-0. 30p. (JAWS-Level 2). Transitional book.

Mafabi is a young boy and the son of a chief in the small village of Kyenyanja along the beautiful banks of the River Nile. He does not understand at first why his father is against the plan to build a new factory in his village. But the chief knows that a similar factory in a nearby town destroyed the river with pollution. *djg*

292. Medlicott, Mary, editor. **The River That Went to the Sky: Twelve Tales by African Storytellers.** Illustrated by Adelmola Akintola. New York: Kingfisher, 1995. (Paperback: issued as *Tales from Africa*, Kingfisher, 2000). ISBN 1-85697-608-4. 96p. (7-12). Short stories.
See Europe/United Kingdom for description.

293. Moss, Miriam. **This Is the Tree.** Illustrated by Adrienne Kennaway. New York: Kane/Miller. 2000. Originally published by Frances Lincoln in 2000. ISBN 0-916629-98-7. 27p. (4-9). Informational book.
See Europe/United Kingdom for description.

8
Australia and New Zealand

Australia

294. Baillie, Allan. **Little Brother**. New York: Viking, 1985. Originally published by Penguin Books Australia in 1990. ISBN 0-670-84381-4. 144p. (8-12). Novel.

Vithy and his brother are all that remains of the family after the Khmer Rouge invades their northern Cambodian village and forces everyone to go to a work camp farther south. The brothers escape but are separated in the process. Vithy must get to the Thai border on his own, straight through the jungles, bandits, and war zone. Vivid portraits of Phnom Penh and Angkor Wat, along with Vithy's reflections of life during peacetime, add cultural insight to this compelling story of a boy's ingenuity and persistence. *ss*

295. Baker, Jeannie. **The Hidden Forest**. Illustrated by the author. New York: Greenwillow, 2000. ISBN 0-688-15760-2. 32p. (6-10). Picture book.

Switching her environmental focus from Australia's arid inland (*The Story of Rosy Dock*, 1995), north coastal rain forest (*Where the Forest Meets the Sea*, 1987), and suburban fringe sprawl (*Window*, 1991), Baker explores the "mysterious, hidden world" of the undersea kelp forests of the southern temperate waters of Tasmania. She uses the simple plot of a young boy struggling to free his entangled fish trap, and his subsequent discovery of the beauty and diversity of this fragile marine environment, as a vehicle for highlighting her overt ecological message: the need to respect and protect the "wondrous living treasures" of our oceans. Her vivid, luminous collage constructions of pressed seaweed, sponges, sand, and translucent modeling clay dramatically bring to life the shimmering light, textures, and movement of an underwater wonderland. A concluding author's note provides information about kelp forests and their potential endangerment. *bt*

296. Baker, Jeannie. **The Story of Rosy Dock**. Illustrated by the author. New York: Greenwillow, 1995. Originally published by Random House Australia in 1995. ISBN 0-688-11493-8. 32p. (5-9). Picture book.

Baker continues her exploration of environmental concerns, moving from the encroachment of urban pollution (*Window*, 1991) to the insidious rural degradation that can result from the introduction of nonindigenous plant species. One old woman settler inadvertently wreaks havoc on an ancient corner of the central Australian desert by planting "rosy dock" seeds, brought from North Africa or Western Asia. The cycle of drought, floods, and dust storms scatters the seeds that over time produce, after the rare rainfalls, a "great red blanket" that pushes many native plants to extinction. Baker's ecological message about the dangers of unchecked exotic species is carried in an afterword and in her striking collage constructions, which are created in painstaking detail with natural materials from the landscape itself. *Honor, Australian Picture Book of the Year, 1996. bt*

297. Clarke, Judith. **The Lost Day.** New York: Holt, 1999. Originally published by Puffin in 1997. ISBN 0-8050-6152-5. 176p. (12-16). Novel.

Vinny and his mates enjoy the freedom of being nineteen years old and able to drink and dance until late at nightclubs in Melbourne, Australia. Yet on the Saturday night that Vinny disappears inexplicably from the crowded pavement outside their favorite club, a darker side emerges as his friends and family eventually realize that something is very wrong. Tension builds as the impact on each of those who care about Vinny is examined from their individual perspectives. When he reappears twelve hours later, having woken up groggy and bewildered on a train, Vinny pieces together a strange accounting for his "lost day," one that represents a realistic, cautionary message of the dangers of being drugged and molested through the spiking of drinks. Includes a glossary of Australian slang. *bt*

298. Clarke, Judith. **Night Train.** New York: Holt, 2000. Originally published by Penguin in 1998. ISBN 0-8050-6151-7. 200p. (12-16). Novel.

Unable to cope with the pressures of home and school, eighteen-year-old Luke spirals into a paralyzing depression. His growing desperation and retreat into his own inner world increasingly alienate him from the people who have tried unsuccessfully to support him. Overwhelmed by the fear that he is losing his mind, he goes out in search of the late night train that only he seems to be able to hear, and meets with a tragic death. The story begins with his funeral, and then shifts backwards and forwards through time and the perspectives of his family, teachers, and friends. This unrelentingly bleak portrait of adolescent depression sounds a grim warning of the dangers of ignoring or dismissing signs of distress from troubled teens. Includes a glossary of Australian slang. *Honor, Children's Book of the Year for Older Readers, 1999. bt*

299. Cresp, Gael. **The Tale of Gilbert Alexander Pig.** Illustrated by David Cox. New York: Barefoot, 2000. Originally published as *Biography of Gilbert Alexander Pig* by Benchmark in 1999. ISBN 1-84148-215-3. 32p. (7-9). Picture book.

In this variation on the traditional tale of "The Three Little Pigs," Gilbert Alexander Pig, a character based on Motown jazz trumpeter Gil Askey, sets out to seek his fortune. Along the way, the little black pig encounters a big white wolf determined to do him in, but music and interpersonal skills win the day, and the wolf and Gilbert play trumpets together happily ever after. *lh*

300. Crew, Gary. **Bright Star.** Illustrated by Anne Spudvilas. New York: Kane/Miller, 1997. Originally published by Lothian in 1996. ISBN 0-916291-75-8. 32 p. (6-10). Picture book.

Against the historical background of famous Australian astronomer John Tebbutt's (1834-1916) discovery of two of the greatest comets of the nineteenth century, Crew creates the inspirational story of a young girl who was able to break free of the confining domestic roles expected of women at this time. In a series of fictionalized meetings with the great "Star Man," Alicia's intellectual capabilities are confirmed and she is encouraged to "reach for the stars," to take control of her own destiny and follow her dreams of studying the mysteries of the universe. Spudvila's richly glowing oil paintings ably capture Alicia's change from frustration with her lot of needlework and milking cows while her brothers are free to come and go "like sparrows," to wonderment as her new mentor opens doors she had never dreamed possible. Includes an introductory note on Tebbutt. *bt*

301. Crew, Gary. **Memorial.** Illustrated by Shaun Tan. Port Melbourne, Victoria: Lothian, 1999 (distributed in the United States by Star Bright). ISBN 0-85091-983-5. 32p. (7-14). Picture book.

Four generations of one Australian family share personal memories of the old tree that stands at the town's crossroads, the site of public services memorializing the nation's involvement in many wars. Planted alongside a statue of "the unknown soldier" on the day that great-grandpa came home from the Great War, the tree is now under threat of being cut down by the town council. It is the young son who is prepared to take a stand on fighting for the preservation of this living memorial. "It's the fight in you they'll remember," Old Pa tells him. "That memory won't die." Tan's striking illustrations are photographed from layers of assembled collage constructions that include frayed canvas laced to old timber frames, faded photographs, and old stamps, merged into paintings that variously evoke haunting war time images through a muted palette, and occasional bright splashes of the more innocent between-war years. *Honor, Australian Picture Book of the Year, 2000. bt*

302. Egan, Ted. **The Drover's Boy**. Illustrated by Robert Ingpen. New York: Star Bright, 1998. Originally published by Lothian in 1997. ISBN 1-887734-52-X. 32 p. (10-15). Picture book.

Well-known Australian folk singer/songwriter Egan wrote the song that comprises the text of this book in 1981 as a tribute to the Aboriginal women who made a significant, previously unacknowledged contribution to the development of the pastoral industry. To get around the law forbidding their employment as cattle drovers (who moved herds across vast Outback distances), these skilled horsewomen were dressed as "boys," usually against their will. Egan's poignant story suggests that such forced unions with white bosses sometimes produced genuine loving relationships. The muted desert ochres of Hans Christian Andersen Medal winner Ingpen's evocative watercolor paintings, juxtaposed with collages of historical documents, create a profoundly moving visual experience. Includes the scored music of the song (which won the Heritage Award at the Australasian Country Music Awards in 1990) and an explanation of the historical background of this work of fiction, set in the 1920s. *bt*

303. Elgar, Susan. **The Brothers Gruesome**. Illustrated by Drahos Zak. Boston: Houghton Mifflin, 2000. Originally published by HarperCollins in 1999. ISBN 0-618-00515-3. 32p. (7-9). Picture book.

In double lines of iambic rhymes that move along in matter-of-fact tone, the acts of the three gruesome, incredibly ugly brothers become ever more dreadful as they devour everything in sight, from their mother on. "Off they stomped, singing 'We're kings of the area,' But they never counted on something bigger, hungrier, and hairier!" The full-page colored drawings are finely wrought, sculptured forms set against blank backgrounds to better emphasize the grotesque, misshapen features, huge teeth, spearlike tongues, and bulging bodies, shades of Hieronymus Bosch but subtly humorous. *km, sm*

304. Finley, Carol. **Aboriginal Art of Australia**. Minneapolis: Lerner, 1999. ISBN 0-8225-2076-1. 56p. (11 up). Informational book.

One of a series of four books of art around the world, this illustrated book focuses on the traditional artistic expressions of aboriginal culture,

which include rock painting and engraving, sand painting, and bark painting, as well as designs painted on the body and on objects used in everyday life. This kind of art functions as a carrier of cultural beliefs, and understanding the significance of particular designs increases appreciation for both Aboriginal art and culture. *ss*
Author from the United States

305. Fox, Mem. **A Bedtime Story**. Illustrated by Elivia Savadier. Glen Head, NY: Mondo, 1996. ISBN 1-57255-136-4. 24p. (1-3). Picture book.

Polly and "Bed Rabbit" want Mom and Dad to read a bedtime story, but they are engrossed in their own books. Only when Polly has satisfied her parents that she is truly ready for bed and "all snuggled in" do they leave their reading to read aloud to Polly until she falls asleep. Savadier's watercolors and pastel colored pencil drawings depict a loving family while the bright collages of books in Polly's room serve to emphasize the importance of reading and stories in a young child's life. *hc*

306. Fox, Mem. **The Straight Line Wonder**. Illustrated by Marc Rosenthal. Glen Head, NY: Mondo, 1997. Originally published by Horwitz in 1987. ISBN 1-57255-206-9. 16p. (4-6). Picture book.

In this allegorical dare-to-be-different tale, three straight lines are best friends. One of them one day decides to bend, boing, twist, and spring around, and—failing to heed their admonishments—is rejected by the other two. That only lasts until the maverick not-straight-anymore line becomes a famous movie star, and the two straight lines claim it again as good buddy, best friend. India ink straight lines sporting various watercolor hairdos and hats support the somewhat heavy-handed moralistic text. *rhm*

307. Germein, Katrina. **Big Rain Coming**. Illustrated by Bronwyn Bancroft. New York: Clarion, 1999. Originally published by Roland Harvey in 1999. ISBN 0-618-08344-8. 32p. (4-9). Picture book.

Everybody in this remote Aboriginal community in Australia's Northern Territory waits patiently all week for the long-promised rain. In the stifling heat, panting dogs dig themselves dusty holes to keep cool, fat frogs huddle around the rainwater tank, and kids drag their mattresses outside at night looking for a breeze. When the gathering storm clouds finally burst over the parched land, there is a joyful celebration in the drenching rain. Bancroft's vivid illustrations, painted in bright gouache and acrylic colors, convey the sense of eager anticipation and exuberant relief suggested by the spare text. Drawing on traditional motifs from her Aboriginal heritage,

Bancroft weaves through the pages a connecting thread of a brightly colored Rainbow Serpent, the Dreamtime creation spirit associated with water and life. *bt*

308. Graham, Bob. **Benny: An Adventure Story**. Illustrated by the author. Cambridge, MA: Candlewick, 1999. Originally published as *Buffy: An Adventure Story* by Walker (U.K.) in 1999. ISBN 0-7636-0813-0. 26p. (4-9). Picture book.

When Benny, the talented canine assistant of Brillo the Magician, outshines his jealous master, he is unceremoniously kicked out the stage door. Clutching his bag of tricks, Benny roams the countryside, seeking greater appreciation of his skills. After rejection as a dancing sheepdog, a plate-juggling kitchen dog, and a harmonica-playing guard dog, Benny comes to realize that "I am me. No more. No less." Busking on a city sidewalk, he wins the hearts of a musical Irish family, who adopt him. We last see Benny surrounded by the warm, exuberant family love found in most Graham books—and sharing the spotlight with young Mary in an after-dinner jig. *Australian Picture Book of the Year Shortlist, 2000. bt*

309. Graham, Bob. **Max**. Illustrated by the author. Cambridge, MA: Candlewick, 2000. Originally published by Walker (U.K.) in 2000. ISBN 0-7636-1138-7. 28p. (3-6). Picture book.

Max is an ordinary baby learning to do what other ordinary babies learn to do, such as walk, talk, and . . . fly? Well, maybe Max is not so ordinary after all. He's the son of superheroes Captain Lightning and Madame Thunderbolt. They fly, of course, in the course of performing heroic deeds. By the time Max goes to school, he still can't fly. He can't even hover. This is a problem until Max performs a sort of heroic deed of his own and, in doing so, learns a new skill. Graham's clever text and vivid ink and watercolor illustrations highlight this enjoyable book. *Nestlé Smarties Gold Medal, 2000; Honor, Australian Book of the Year for Early Childhood, 2001. rhm*

310. Graham, Bob. **Queenie, One of the Family**. Illustrated by the author. Cambridge, MA: Candlewick, 1997. Originally published as *Queenie the Bantam* by Walker (U.K.) in 1997. (Paperback: Candlewick, 2001). ISBN 0-7636-0359-7. 32p. (4-8).

When Caitlin's dad rescues a drowning hen from a lake, Queenie the bantam soon becomes one of this lovable family. When they take her back to her farm, she insists on returning daily to lay a fresh egg in the dog's bed basket, until Caitlin's baby brother is born. Graham's simple text and trademark witty pen and wash cartoon-style illustrations paint an intimate and authentic picture of a warm, loving family endearingly engaged in the small domestic dramas of a busy household. The circular story concludes with a delightfully satisfying twist. *Australian Picture Book of the Year Shortlist, 1998. bt*

311. Graham, Bob. **The Red Woolen Blanket.** Illustrated by the author. Boston: Little, Brown, 1988. Originally published as *The Red Woollen Blanket* by Walker (U.K.) in 1987. (Paperback: Candlewick, 1996). ISBN 0-316-32310-1. 26p. (4-8). Picture book.

Julia's attachment to her treasured red woolen blanket she received at birth will resonate with many young readers, as it did for Graham's daughter, for whom he first made up a story of "the adventures of an intrepid security blanket." Julia and blanket are inseparable, but as she grows bigger, the blanket gets smaller, with pieces lost to the vacuum cleaner and lawn mower. It is not until she starts school that she finally outgrows the need for her now postage-stamp-sized blanket. Sometime during the excitement of her first day, the "last threads of her blanket" disappear. Graham's delightful cartoonlike illustrations in his signature pen-and-wash style add a wealth of witty detail to this simply told yet endearing tale. *bt*

312. Graham, Bob. **Spirit of Hope.** Illustrated by the author. Glen Head, NY: Mondo, 1996. Originally published by Lothian in 1993. (Paperback: Mondo, 1996). ISBN 1-57255-202-6. 32p. (4-8). Picture book.

The Fairweathers, a large, happy, working-class family, are evicted from their humble house to make way for a new factory down by the dockyards where Mr. Fairweather works. Undaunted in their search for a new home, this loving family takes inspiration from their youngest child's toy houseboat and, with support from their factory friends, move their old house to an unexpected new site. Graham's endearing characters, depicted in his familiar pen-and-wash cartoon-style illustrations, glow warmly with exuberance and hope through the more gloomily juxtaposed industrial images of this setting. *bt*

313. Gray, Nigel. **Full House.** Illustrated by Bob Graham. Port Melbourne, Victoria: Lothian, 1998 (distributed in the United States by Star Bright). ISBN 0-85091-879-0. 20p. (2-4). Novelty book.

"My dog got fatter and fatter. I didn't know what was the matter. Then do you know what she did?" So begins a little girl's family saga. The dog goes into a cupboard and comes out thin, whereupon readers have a chance to lift the flap and discover why: two puppies. The same routine occurs with the little girl's cat—three kittens—and then the little girl's mother. By this time the child has caught on and so has the reader, but there's a final surprise in store. *ss*

314. Hill, Anthony. **The Burnt Stick**. Illustrated by Mark Sofilas. Boston: Houghton Mifflin, 1995. Originally published by Penguin Books Australia in 1994. ISBN 0-395-73974-8. 53p. (10-12). Transitional book.

In parts of Australia as late as 1960, it was the law to take children of mixed parentage from their Aborigine families to be raised at missions. In an attempt to prevent the white men from welfare from taking her four-year-old son, Liyan takes a burnt stick and rubs the soot over her son's skin to make him as dark as the other Aborigines. Twice she is successful. On a surprise third visit from welfare, her son John is taken away to be raised at the missionary home. *pc*

315. Hines, Sue. **Out of the Shadows**. New York: Morrow/Avon, 2000. Originally published by Random House Australia in 1998. ISBN 0-3808-1192-8. 160p. (14 up). Novel.

Two teenagers struggle to maintain their friendship while hiding secrets they fear will tear them apart. Rowanna Preston, whose mother was recently killed by a drunken driver, is living with Deb, her mother's lover. Jodie Waters is not only in the closet about her sexual identity but also hiding her attraction to Ro. By alternating the voices of Ro and Jodie, the author provides insight into each character, while examining complex issues of loss, bigotry, and self-discovery. *fd*

316. Ingpen, Robert. **The Dreamkeeper**. Illustrated by the author. New York: Star Bright, 1998. Originally published by Lothian in 1995. ISBN 1-88773-441-4. 40p. (6-10). Picture book.

Presented as a handwritten letter to his granddaughter, Alice Elizabeth, this magical tale tells how the Dreamkeeper collects the creatures, good and evil, that escape from our dreams in search of reality, and returns them to the peace and safety of the Dreamtree. Working in the world "just around the corner of your mind," the Dreamkeeper uses a variety of charms, tokens, and tricks to lure into his homemade traps a variety of mischief-seeking hairy trolls, rebellious angels, goblins, and witches. The strikingly detailed illustrations of this award-winning artist (1986 Hans Christian Andersen Award for Illustration) vividly bring to life this exploration of the magic of dreams and its intersection with reality, that elusive space between "what is really happening and what you imagine might happen." *bt*

317. Ingpen, Robert. **The Idle Bear.** Port Melbourne, Victoria: Lothian, 1986 (distributed in the United States by Star Bright). 32p. (2-4). Picture book.

Two bears, Ted and Teddy, have a discussion, which turns out to be rather void of content, since neither really knows what he is talking about. Ingpen has created bears so lifelike and appealing that one can almost imagine their conversation is real. *1986 Hans Christian Andersen Illustrator Medalist. ss*

318. Keneally, Thomas. **Ned Kelly & the City of the Bees.** Illustrated by Stephen Ryan. Boston: David R. Godine, 1981. First published by Jonathan Cape in 1978. ISBN 1-56792-022-5. 126p. (7-10). Novel.

When Ned Kelly gets an attack of appendicitis, he is rushed to the hospital. In bed, watching a bee on the ceiling, he suddenly starts to shrink until he is the size of the bee, Apis, who carries him off to its hive. There Ned spends a summer of adventure, learning firsthand about drones and queens, worker bees and wasps (the enemy), and occasionally eavesdropping on humans. Only in the fall, as the bees clear the hive of all nonessential members in preparation for winter, does Ned opt to return home, carried by Apis. Back in bed, he returns to his original size and the people who have been worried about him. "You were in a coma," his mother tells him, but he knows better. Keneally, author of *Schindler's List*, grew up in an Australian town like that described here. *ss*

319. Lester, Alison. **Celeste Sails to Spain.** Illustrated by the author. Boston: Houghton Mifflin, 1999. Originally published by Hodder in 1997. ISBN 0395973953. 32p. (4-8). Picture book.

In this fifth in her series, Lester again celebrates the individuality of ordinary young children getting about the business of growing up. We learn more about the unique personalities, interests, and accomplishments of the same seven spirited characters from earlier books. Initially they were engaged in the daily routines and small trials of preschoolers, eating, dressing, and playing, but now they are seven, and interested in outdoor adventures, sports, museums, and dreaming big dreams that take them to far-distant countries. Lester continues her successful formula of lining up six simply captioned panels of individual characters in ever-changing sequences across a spread, followed by a full page spotlighting the seventh child at a memorable moment. The lively line-and-watercolor illustrations provide a wealth of humorous detail, inviting readers into a visual game of comparison and prediction. Other titles in series: *Clive Eats Alligators* (1986), *Rosie Sips*

Spiders (1989), *Tessa Snaps Snakes* (1991), *When Frank Was Four* (1996), *Ernie Dances to the Didgeridoo* (2001). *bt*

320. Lester, Alison. **Imagine**. Illustrated by the author. Boston: Houghton Mifflin, 1990. Originally published by Allen & Unwin in 1989. (Paperback: Houghton Mifflin, 1993). ISBN 0-395-53753-3. 32p. (4-8). Picture book.
Two children's imaginative play is used as a springboard into an exploration of diverse wildlife environments, including a jungle, ocean, ice-cap, safari, farm, and Australian bushland. Lester prefaces each home-play scene with a rhymed text that begins with "Imagine . . ." and her opposing simple watercolor-and-line drawings humorously show creative props young readers could use to simulate such adventures, including dressing up the cat. Elaborately detailed spreads of the actual environment follow each imagined re-creation, overflowing with a bountiful range of indigenous animals, and inviting readers to search for matches with the names that are listed around each border. The child characters appear in these busy, colorful scenes, interacting in friendly ways with the wild animals. A final scene brings them back to the warm security of their own home. *bt*

321. Lester, Alison. **My Farm**. Illustrated by the author. Boston: Houghton Mifflin, 1994. Originally published by Allen & Unwin in 1992. ISBN 0-395-68193-6. (Paperback: Houghton Mifflin, 1999). 32p. (4-8). Picture book.
In this lively memoir, Lester re-creates the exuberance of her childhood spent on an Australian farm, where her parents raised livestock. Her delicately detailed pastel watercolor illustrations, sometimes clustered in miniature panels, and sometimes luxuriously spread over the entire page, together with her childlike narrative voice, portray a kaleidoscope of remembered events big and small. She evokes a sense of wonderment and delight as the four children find plenty of time for fun and imaginative play as they help out with the multitude of daily and seasonal chores: from milking the cow to hypnotizing the chickens, from mustering cattle to playing trick rodeo riders under the clothesline. Includes a brief explanation of Australian terms and seasons. *bt*

322. Lester, Alison. **The Quicksand Pony**. Boston: Houghton Mifflin, 1998. Originally published by Allen & Unwin in 1997. ISBN 0-395-93749-3. 162p. (10-14). Novel.
In her first novel, Lester has created an absorbing adventure inspired by two true stories: a female convict escapee who lived alone in rugged bushland; and a pony that became bogged in quicksand but floated free

with the rising tide. Set in Australian wild country near Lester's own farm, and told from alternating nonlinear perspectives, two parallel stories eventually converge to solve the years-old mystery of the disappearance of an emotionally disturbed seventeen-year-old girl and her baby. Faking their drowning, she takes refuge deep in the wilderness, and raises her son insulated from human contact. However, after her death, his growing need for human contact leads him to seek out ten-year-old Biddy, whose pony he rescues after it becomes stranded in quicksand during her family's spring cattle round up. *bt*

323. Marchetta, Melina. **Looking for Alibrandi**. New York: Orchard, 1999. Originally published by Penguin Australia in 1992. ISBN 0-531-30142-7. 250p. (12-14). Novel.

Bright, seventeen-year-old Josie, a high school senior in Sydney, is already contending with a loving, protective single mother and an old-fashioned Italian grandmother, when she meets the father she has never known. In the tumultuous year that follows, she learns many truths about family secrets, love, friends, and boyfriends, and most of all about herself. The Australian setting and conflicts between "Australians" and ethnic Italians are strongly portrayed, as is the culture of high school students. *2000 BILBY Award; 1993 Book of the Year for Older Readers. sg*

324. Marsden, John. **Checkers**. Boston: Houghton Mifflin, 1998. Originally published by Pan Macmillan Australia in 1996. (Paperback: Laurel Leaf, 2000). ISBN 0-395-85754-6. 122p. (12-16). Novel.

The perfect world of a teenage girl begins to spin out of control when she finds herself caught in the middle of an illegal "insider trading" deal in which her businessman father is involved. The media's relentless hounding eventually exposes the fraud, cruelly exploiting the girl's innocent love for her dog. The resulting political scandal tears apart her wealthy, privileged family, sending her into the juvenile ward of a psychiatric hospital, from where she narrates her story. Tension builds slowly through a complex interweaving of flashbacks and her ongoing struggle to come to terms with her role in the scandal. Only when she is finally able to open up to her therapy group do we learn the shocking truth of the real reason for her commitment. Includes a glossary of Australian slang. *bt*

325. Marsden, John. **The Dead of the Night**. Boston: Houghton Mifflin, 1997. Originally published by Pan Macmillan Australia in 1994. (Paperback: Laurel Leaf, 1999). ISBN 0-395-83734-0. 278p. (12-15). Novel.

This sequel to *Tomorrow, When the War Began* continues the riveting adventure story of a group of Australian teenagers who return from a camping trip to find their country overrun by foreign invaders and their world forever changed. The gritty, resourceful band is forced to fight desperately for their survival, turning to guerrilla and terrorist tactics. Breathtaking action and cliff-hanging suspense have enthralled addicted fans around the world, who have waited anxiously for each new installment of this outstandingly popular seven-part series. Titles include the following U.S. editions from Houghton Mifflin: *Tomorrow, When the War Began* (1995), *The Dead of the Night* (1997), *A Killing Frost* (1998), *Darkness Be My Friend* (1999), *Burning for Revenge* (2000), *The Night Is For Hunting* (2001), and the concluding *The Other Side of Dawn* (2002). *bt*

326. Marsden, John. **Norton's Hut**. Illustrated by Peter Gouldthorpe. New York: Star Bright, 1999. Originally published by Lothian in 1998. ISBN 1-887734-64-3. 32p. (9-14). Picture book.

A group of young hikers takes refuge from a blizzard in an abandoned hut deep in the Australian Alps. Their noisy confidence is subdued by the eerie presence of a mysterious stranger, who huddles silently over a fitful fire, and then vanishes during the night. Snowed in for three days, the teenagers wile away the hours before they can venture outside again to resume their journey. Gouldthorpe's vivid paintings inject a surreal quality into a tale that borders on the supernatural. The snow-swept outdoor panoramas, with inset frames that slice pieces out of the landscape, contrast starkly with the richly glowing yet ominously foreboding fire-lit scenes. We leave the teenagers huddled around a campfire, pondering over the chilling retelling by seasoned mountain men of the legend of a hut that burned down many years ago during a blizzard, incinerating the young man inside. *bt*

327. Marsden, John. **Prayer for the Twenty-First Century**. New York: Star Bright, 1998. Originally published by Lothian in 1997. ISBN 1 887734 42 2. 32p. (10-16). Picture book.

In his first picture book, one of Australia's leading authors for young adults speaks to readers of all ages with a heartfelt prayer that expresses universal hopes and fears: "May those who live in the shadows/Be seen by those who live in the sun." The spare, poetic text is strikingly and provocatively interpreted by designer Barbara Beckett, who draws on a wide variety of photographs and paintings by Australian and international artists, past and present, from Australian collections. Several are from an exhibition that showcases outstanding works from the visual arts program in New South Wales schools (e.g., the opening line, "May the road be free for the journey," faces a line drawing expressing the journey from Vietnam to Australia by the artist's family, who were boat people). *bt*

328. Mattingley, Christobel. **The Magic Saddle**. Illustrated by Patricia Mullins. New York: Simon & Schuster, 1996. Originally published by Hodder & Stoughton, Australia, in 1983. ISBN 0-689-80959-X. 32p. (4-8). Picture book.

In this gentle, heartwarming fantasy Jonni uses his imagination to extend the boundaries of his poor but loving family life. In exchange for the tiny rocking horse Christmas tree ornament that he gives to the Christ child in the town's Nativity scene, Jonni receives a gingerbread rocking horse with a magic saddle that is able to take him "over the mountains and far away" to the places of his dreams. The influence of Mattingley's childhood immersion in European fairy tales resonates in her story, which was inspired by a visit to the wintery Bavarian landscape of Germany. Mullin's striking illustrations, rendered in torn-tissue collage, lino block, crayon, and watercolor, capture the magical qualities and family warmth of this wordy tale. *bt*

329. Morimoto, Junko. **The Two Bullies**. Translated from the Japanese by Isao Morimoto. Illustrated by the author. Cambridge, MA: Candlewick, 1999. Originally published by Random House in 1997. ISBN 0-517-80061-6. 32p. (4-8). Picture book.

When ancient Japan's self-proclaimed strongest man traverses the vast ocean to challenge his Chinese counterpart, he loses his courage and flees back to Japan, but not before inadvertently intimidating his would-be opponent. Even though it turns out that both bullies are relieved to escape a showdown with such a seemingly invincible opponent, their reputations of great strength endure today in their respective cultures. The bold, calligraphy style watercolor brush strokes of this Japanese-Australian artist evoke the origins of this lighthearted story with folktale qualities. *Australian Picture Book of the Year, 1998. bt*

330. Moss, Sally. **Peter's Painting**. Illustrated by Meredith Thomas. Glen Head, NY: Mondo, 1995. ISBN 1-57255-013-9. 24p. (4-6). Picture book.

White-bordered spreads that show a small boy painting alternate with full-bleed spreads depicting what he has painted: a bird, a snake, a fish, a star, all of which come to life. When he paints a door, it opens and he steps into the painting. *pm*

331. Nix, Garth. **Sabriel.** New York: HarperCollins, 1995. ISBN 0-06-027322-4. 292p. (12-14). Novel.

When Sabriel's necromancer father, Abhorsen, disappears, Sabriel crosses into the Old Kingdom, taking with her his sword, his bells that have power in Death, and her knowledge of Charter Magic. Over the border, she encounters terrible creatures from the Dead. She also meets the cat, Mogget, a powerful "Free Magic" servant bound to Abhorsen's service, and the young man, Touchstone, a Charter mage and member of the old ruling royal family. Once Sabriel releases her father, temporarily, from Death, they all strive to overcome the evil Kerrigor, the most powerful of the "Greater Dead." Sabriel survives—the new Abhorsen. Sequel: *Lirael* (HarperCollins, 2001). *ALA Best Books for Young Adults, 1996; ALA Notable Children's Book, 1996; Best Fantasy Novel, Best Young Adult Novel, Aurealis Awards for Excellence in Australian Speculative Fiction, 1995. hc*

332. Oliver, Narelle. **The Best Beak in Boonaroo Bay.** Illustrated by the author. Golden, CO: Fulcrum, 1995. Originally published by Lothian in 1993. ISBN 1-55591-227-3. 32p. (4-9). Picture book.

In her third picture book exploring nature, Oliver tells a fanciful story of how the bickering water birds of Boonaroo Bay resolve their dispute over who has the best beak. A contest organized by the wise old pelican reveals that "we are all winners," that each beak is perfectly designed to catch its prey. Using her award-winning linocut technique, hand colored with watercolor, ink, and pastel, Oliver richly depicts the bird and plant life of a coastal mangrove swamp setting near her home in Queensland. *Australian Picture Book of the Year Shortlist, 1994. bt*

333. Oliver, Narelle. **The Hunt.** Illustrated by the author. New York: Star Bright, 1998 (paperback). Originally published by Lothian in 1995. ISBN 1-88773-443-0. 32p. (5-10). Picture book.

The simple story line of a Tawny Frogmouth owl searching the forest at twilight for food for her babies is an effective vehicle for teaching about the amazing powers of camouflage, as well as for showcasing Oliver's own amazing skill for rendering such animal trickery visible through her hand-colored linocuts. The spiders, frogs, moths, and stick insects found by the mother owl disappear into the colors, shapes, and textures of their environment, as does she herself when threatened by a larger predator in the food chain. A wealth of supplementary information is appended, including scientific names, scale drawings, and a bibliography. A key to the illustrated animals helps readers solve this "hide-and-seek" puzzle that entertains as it teaches. *1996 Australian Picture Book of the Year. bt*

334. Orr, Wendy. **Ark in the Park.** Illustrated by Kerry Millard. New York: Holt, 2000. Originally published by HarperCollins Australia in 1994. ISBN 0-8050-6221-1. 78p. (7-9). Transitional book.

Sophie, a lonely seven-year-old, lives in a high-rise apartment and longingly watches the activity at a marvelous pet shop, shaped like Noah's Ark, across the park from her building. When she finally visits on her birthday, she finds animal friends, wonderful substitute grandparents, and a sense of belonging. This charming story is illustrated with many lively black-and-white drawings that break up the text. *1995 Children's Book of the Year for Younger Readers. sg*

335. Orr, Wendy. **Peeling the Onion.** New York: Holiday House, 1997. Originally published by Allen & Unwin in 1996. (Paperback: Laurel Leaf, 1999). ISBN 0-8234-1289-X. 166p. (12-16). Novel.

Seventeen-year-old karate champion Anna's dreams are shattered when her neck is broken in an automobile accident. Fighting back from a near-death experience, she faces long-term, excruciating pain and debilitating injuries that leave deep physical and emotional scars. In a convincing present-tense, first-person narrative voice, Anna's long, painful road to recovery over nine months is documented, as she struggles desperately to find her real self through a haze of bitter anger, despair, and suicidal depression. "I am/peeling like an onion,/shedding papery protection,/and superficial skin." In an optimistic yet realistic ending, she is able to adjust to her changed relationships and future aspirations, with the support of her family and new boyfriend. Canadian-born Orr writes from the experience of a serious car accident that similarly changed the focus of her own life. *Australian Book of the Year for Older Readers Honor Book, 1997. bt*

336. Overend, Jenni. **Welcome with Love.** Illustrated by Julie Vivas. New York: Kane/Miller, 2000. Originally published as *Hello Baby* by ABC Books in 1999. ISBN 0-916291-96-0. 32p. (4-9). Picture book.

Jack, the youngest of three siblings, tells the story of his Mum's home birth in this loving and exceptionally candid book. The childlike text details the family's preparations, the birth, and the gentle family time after as the whole family goes to sleep around the fireplace. Vivas's strong but gentle warm-toned illustrations depict everybody's emotions surrounding this memorable event and include pictures of a panting, yelling Mum leaning on Dad and being supported by the family and then leaning over naked as the midwife catches the emerging baby. Because of its sensitive, intimate nature, this story will be best used by parents and children together. *Picture Book of the Year Shortlist,2000. sg*

337. Riddle, Tohby. **The Great Escape from the City Zoo.** Illustrated by the author. New York: Farrar, Straus & Giroux, 1999. Originally published by HarperCollins in 1997. ISBN 0-374-32776-9. 32p. (4-8). Picture book.

Under the soft sepia tones of a full moon, four animals break out of the City Zoo: an anteater, elephant, turtle, and flamingo. Disguised as people, they mingle in the city streets, and subsequently flee to the country to avoid detection by the relentlessly pursuing zookeepers. However, one by one, they give themselves away by reverting to their animal instincts, and they are taken back to the zoo—all but the flamingo, who disappears with only occasional reports of "unconfirmed sightings." The story is told as the truest account of a local legend passed down orally over generations, and cartoonist Riddle's soft whimsical drawings lighten the allegory of a prison breakout, scattering familiar cultural icons throughout, like King Kong, masterpieces of modern art, and even an allusion to the Beatles crossing Abbey Road. *bt*

338. Thompson, Colin. **Unknown.** Illustrated by Anna Pignataro. New York: Walker, 2000. Originally published by Hodder Headline Australia in 2000. ISBN 0-8027-8730-4. 31p. (4-9). Picture book.

Each new arrival at an animal shelter has on its cage a sign with a name, such as Stray, Owner Died, and Grown Too Large. A small, shy dog, Unknown, goes unnoticed by the people who come to the animal shelter seeking a dog to adopt until she becomes a hero during a fire that threatens the shelter. After she is featured in a front-page news article, hundreds of people want to adopt her. As Unknown leaves the shelter with her new family she makes a thought-provoking statement: "I got lucky. But it would be good if we could put all the humans in cages and walk along with our noses in the air and choose the ones WE wanted." *ca*

339. Walker, Kate. **Peter.** Boston: Houghton Mifflin, 1993. First published by Omnibus in 1991. (Paperback: Houghton, 2001). ISBN 0-395-64722-3. 170p. (13 up). Novel.

Peter, fifteen, is confused by his emotions. His friends are all talking about girls and are pushing him to make moves he's not ready for, while his older brother's friend, David, treats him like an equal and is easy to talk to. David is gay, so does that mean Peter is? Readers are privy to Peter's thoughts as he sorts through his feelings, and as often happens in real life, the novel's end brings no firm resolution. *1991 Australian Human Rights Award. ss*

340. Wild, Margaret. **Old Pig**. Illustrated by Ron Brooks. New York: Dial, 1996. Originally published by Allen & Unwin in 1995. ISBN 0-8037-1917-5. 30p. (4-8). Picture book.

Old Pig and her granddaughter have spent a loving life together, sharing household chores as well as the wonders of nature. When she senses her approaching death, Old Pig calmly puts her affairs in order and savors one last time the closeness with her beloved granddaughter as they take a final stroll together, feasting on the sights, smells, and sounds around them. The simple, lyrical text harmonizes perfectly with the warmly glowing autumnal tones and soft lines of the watercolor illustrations. This poignant tale presents death as a natural culmination of life, in the broader context of celebrating together the beauty of life that surrounds us. As such it offers opportunities to discuss the acceptance of the loss of a loved one and the need to make the most of the time we have with each other. *Australian Picture Book of the Year Shortlist, 1996. bt*

341. Wild, Margaret. **Rosie and Tortoise**. Illustrated by Ron Brooks. New York: DK, 1999. Originally published in Australia by Allen & Unwin in 1999. ISBN 0-7894-2630-7. 32p. (4-7). Picture book.

Rosie the hare can't wait for her baby brother to be born, but when he's born too small she becomes afraid to touch him. After Dad tells her a story about the tortoise who "slow and steady" found his way home, Rosie finally accepts that her little brother is growing slowly and steadily, too, and she dares to hold him at last. *lh*

342. Wild, Margaret. **Tom Goes to Kindergarten**. Illustrated by David Legge. Chicago: Albert Whitman, 2000. First published by ABC Books in 1999. ISBN 0-8075-8012-0. 32p. Picture book.

Everyday Tom Panda and his mother walk by the kindergarten and Tom sees the children building spaceships and playing astronauts and googly monsters. He looks forward to the day when he will be able to attend. At last the day arrives and the whole family walks Tom to school, but he does not want to stay. What are a good mother and father to do but stay and play. And what a good time they have! Humorous watercolor illustrations capture the kindergarten fun. *djg*

343. Winch, John. **The Old Woman Who Loved to Read**. New York: Holiday House, 1997. First published by Scholastic Australia in 1996. ISBN 0-8234-1281-4. 32p. (4-8). Picture book.

There was an old woman who loved to read, but alas it is too noisy in the city. She packs up her possessions and moves to the country where surely it will be quiet, but no! There are so many chores, inside and out. Unexpected animal visitors drop in and stay. Through fire and flood, she finds a quiet cozy winter afternoon to enjoy her books. Read together with Winch's *The Old Man Who Loved to Sing* (Scholastic, 1993) who fills his quiet country farm with song, to the delight of the animals who gather around to enjoy his music. *djg*

344. Winton, Tim. **The Deep**. Illustrated by Karen Louise. Berkeley, CA: Tricycle Press, 2000. Originally published by Sandcastle in 1978. ISBN 1-58246-024-8. 32p. (4-7). Picture book.

Alice's family lives on the seacoast, where the children spend their days playing in the sand and swimming. Although Alice loves the shallows, she is afraid of deep water. Only when lured out by dolphins does she realize that she is swimming in the deep. Realistic illustrations capture the blue of the water and the variety of fish in Western Australia. *ss*

Related Information

Annual Awards

Children's Book of the Year (categories include Early Childhood, Picture Books, Younger Readers, Older Readers, and Eve Pownall for Non-Fiction)

Nan Chauncy Award

A biennial award named after the noted Tasmanian author of children's books and created to honor people who have made an outstanding contribution to the field of Australian children's literature. The recipient must be an Australian citizen, no matter where residing, or a person who has been resident in Australia for at least five years.

Crichton Award

Recognizes new talent in the field of Australian children's book illustration. This award and the two listed above it are administered by the Children's Book Council of Australia.

Australian Children's Choice Awards
Organized by territory and administered by local bodies, these include BILBY (Queensland), COOL (Australian Capital Territory), CROW (South Australia), CYBER (Tasmania), KOALA (New South Wales), KROC (Northern Territory), YABBA (Victoria), WAYRBA (West Australia), and Dymocks (national).

Organizations
Children's Book Council of Australia
www.cbc.org.au
Contains information about Australian children's book awards, current shortlists and winners, and links to pages with information about Australian authors and illustrators.

Publish Australia
publishaustralia.com.au
Publish Australia is a national network of independent Australian publishers. This website offers a directory of members, online catalogs, relevant news items, and the opportunity to order books online.

Online Bookstores
Australian Online Bookshop
www.bookworm.com.au
A reliable, independent bookshop that handles international orders through the Internet.

Gleebooks Children's Bookshop
www.gleebooks.com.au
The virtual site of an independent bookstore in Sydney where you can browse, read the newsletter, and order online or by fax or email.

Websites
OzKidz Literature
www.ozkidz.gil.com.au/OzLit/ozlit.html
A comprehensive Aussie site for all information pertaining to children's and young adult books, with links to author sites, book reviews, academic articles, and lesson plans.

Ozlit
home.vicnet.net.au/~ozlit
An online database of children's literature of Australia and New Zealand.

Journals
Papers: Explorations into Children's Literature is Australia's only peer-reviewed journal focusing on children's texts from Australia and elsewhere. three issues/year. For information, write to Clare Bradford, Deakin University, 221 Burwood Highway, Burwood, Vic 3125, or e-mail clarex@deakin.edu.au; tel. 61-3-9244 6487; fax 61-3-9244 6755.

Magpies: Talking about Books for Children provides a current overview of children's literature in Australia through books reviews, award listings, author and illustrator profiles, and articles. six issues/year. Box 98, Grange, Queensland, Australia 4051; e-mail james@magpies.net.au; tel. 61-7-3356 4503; fax 61-7-3356 4649; www.magpies.net.au.

New Zealand

345. Boock, Paula. **Dare Truth or Promise.** Boston: Houghton Mifflin, 1999. Originally published by Longacre Press in 1997. ISBN 0-395-97117-9. 180p. (14 up). Novel.

In this beautifully written love story, two teenagers overcome homophobia, both external and internal, and after much pain and turmoil, embrace their lesbian identities. In one remarkable scene, a priest advises one of them to not be concerned with literal interpretations of the Bible, adding, "I think love comes from God. And so, to turn away from love, real love, it could be argued, is to turn away from God" (p. 158). The Boston: Houghton Mifflin edition includes a Kiwi glossary. *1998 New Zealand Post Children's Book of the Year; Esther Glen Award Shortlist, 1998. fd*

346. Cowley, Joy. **The Rusty, Trusty Tractor.** Illustrated by Olivier Dunrea. Honesdale, PA: Boyds Mills, 1999. ISBN 1-56397-565-3. 34p. (7-9). Picture book.

Mr. Hill, the implement dealer, laughs at Granpappy's old tractor and makes a bet with him that it won't last through the next planting and harvesting seasons. Grandson Micah watches his Granpappy plow up his field: "The tractor crawled along, *chugga, chugga, chugga,* like an old fishing boat, brown waves curling up behind the plow." When it's time to bale the hay, Micah worries that the tractor isn't big enough to pull the baler, but Granpappy talks to it like he would a favorite horse and the "rusty, trusty tractor shuddered across that field, dragging the big baling machine." Granpappy not only wins the bet, but also delivers Mr. Hill's comeuppance when he and his old tractor pull Mr. Hill's car out of the mud. The watercolor illustrations accurately capture farming and farm machinery. *chs*

347. Cowley, Joy. **Starbright and the Dream Eater.** New York: HarperCollins, 2000. First published by New York: Viking Penguin (N.Z.) in 1998. ISBN 0-06-028419-6. 199p. (12 up). Novel.

An outbreak of spindle sickness (named after the spell in "Sleeping Beauty") has mystified doctors and scientists alike. Some say it is a plan by aliens to take over the planet. It began in South America, has appeared in Africa and Australia, and now is in two neighboring small towns in Missouri. Each of the sites is connected: an Argentinian astronomer records an intergalactic warning sent in the language of an ancient indigenous group; an American journalist in South America on another assignment hears about it and investigates; the journalist has a twin, an obstetrics nurse, who delivers the child destined to thwart the plan. While the plot is hard to swallow, the character of the child, Starbright, and the circumstances of her birth are strong enough to pull the reader along. *ss*

348. Mahy, Margaret. **A Summery Saturday Morning.** Illustrated by Selina Young. New York: Viking, 1998. Originally published by Hamish Hamilton in 1998. ISBN 0-670-87943-6. 28p. (1-6). Picture book.

A rhyming text that begs to be read aloud describes all the unexpected adventures that ensue when the children take the dogs down the wiggly track on a summery Saturday morning. Lively watercolors follow as the children, dogs, cat, and geese interact along the beach. *1999 New Zealand Post Award Winner. sg*

349. Taylor, William. **The Blue Lawn.** Boston: Alyson, 1999. Originally published by HarperCollins New Zealand in 1994. ISBN 1-55583-493-0. 122p. (14 up). Novel.

In this fascinating book, the connection between two teenagers goes from curiosity to hostility to attraction to denial to acknowledgment. In spite of their confusion, David and Theo find the courage to talk to each other about their feelings. Subthemes revolve around Theo's grandmother, who is a Holocaust survivor. This is a poignant book with an interesting mixture of tenderness, vulnerability, and irreverence. *Lambda Literary Award Finalist. fd*

Related Information

Awards

Esther Glen Award, given to the New Zealand author of the book considered the most distinguished contribution to literature for children in the preceding year.

Russell Clark Award, given to a New Zealand illustrator responsible for the most distinguished illustrations for a children's or young adult's book. Non-fiction as well as fiction titles are eligible.

NZLIA Young People's Non-Fiction Award, given to the New Zealand author of the book that is considered to be the most distinguished contribution to nonfiction for young people.

The above three annual awards, as well as several others, are administered by the Library and Information Association of New Zealand Aotearoa.

The New Zealand Post Children's Book Awards, sponsored by the newspaper firm, recognize the best in New Zealand children's books in four categories: junior fiction, senior fiction, picture book, and nonfiction.

9
Europe

Austria

350. Janisch, Heinz, adapter. **Noah's Ark**. Translated by Rosemary Lanning. Illustrated by Lisbeth Zwerger. New York: North-South, 1997. First published as *Die Arche Noah* by Michael Neugebauer in 1997. ISBN 1-55858-784-5. 32p. (4-8). Picture book.

Janisch retains the feel of the biblical language for this retelling, which Zwerger sets in a landscape of her own imagination, populated by centaurs and unicorns as well as people and animals. Pairs of worms, ants, beetles, and other insects join the more media-friendly creatures in the procession on to the ark, some cast as scientific drawings in nineteenth-century treatises. *ss*

351. Krischanitz, Raoul. **Nobody Likes Me!** Translated by Rosemary Lanning. New York: North-South, 1999. Originally published as *Willst du mein Freund sein?* by Nord-Süd in 1999. ISBN 0-7358-1054-0. 26p. (3-7). Picture book.

As the day begins, Buddy, a bright chartreuse dog, comes over the hill into a new town. He wants to play, but each animal Buddy approaches, beginning with a fat brown mouse, is unfriendly. At the edge of the wood, Buddy begins to cry. A bright red fox helps him by suggesting he ask the others what is wrong. Buddy and the fox go to each animal; when Buddy explains that he only wants to be a friend, they follow Buddy and the fox. At last they come to the mouse, who has baked a cake and offers a piece to each of the animals. This simple cumulative story of friendship is illustrated with full-page painted illustrations, which use strong colors and bold simple shapes to guide the eye and help tell the story. *mn*

352. Orgel, Doris. **The Devil in Vienna**. New York: Dial, 1978. (Paperback: Puffin, 1988). ISBN 0-8037-1920-5. 246p. (10-14). Novel.

Ilse Dornenwald and her family live a comfortable, upper-class life in Vienna, where her father manages the family business and her mother is a book editor. Because the family is Jewish, they find their lives increasingly diminished and threatened after the Anschluss. The focus of the story is the friend-

ship between Ilse and Leiselotte Vessely, whose father becomes a member of the Nazi Party. Although their families forbid them to remain friends (for different reasons), they continue their friendship clandestinely, and it is this friendship that ultimately saves the Dornenwald family and provides their exit from Austria. While a work of fiction, the novel draws on the author's childhood experiences growing up in Vienna. *ss*
Author from the United States

353. Sansone, Adele. **The Little Green Goose.** Translated by J. Alison James. Illustrated by Alan Marks. New York: North-South, 1999. Originally published as *Das Grüne Küken* by Nord-Süd in 1999. ISBN 0-7358-1071-0. (4-6). Picture book.

Mr. Goose, who longs to be a parent, sets on a large egg that the farm dog finds while digging a hole. What hatches is a green dinosaur-like creature. Mr. Goose proudly introduces his "little green goose" to the barnyard animals. The chicks, however, tease the youngster, saying that he is not a goose and that Mr. Goose cannot be his real mother. "The little green goose" runs away to find his true mother. When his search fails, he returns to the farm where his "real mother"—or rather his Daddy—who loves him is. Marks's illustrations extend both the humor and the warm, cozy feeling of this story of an unusual adoption. *ca*

354. Weninger, Brigitte, adapter. **The Elf's Hat.** Translated by J. Alison James. Illustrated by John A. Rowe. New York: North-South, 2000. Originally published as *Die Zwergen Mütze* by Nord-Süd in 2000. ISBN 0-7358-1254-3. 29p. (4-6). Picture book.

In an adaptation of a Ukrainian tale, a variety of animals make their homes in a hat lost by an elf. The cumulative tale begins with a frog hopping into the hat, then a mouse, a hare, a hedgehog, and finally a bear. When a tiny flea crawls inside, the hat can expand no more. All the animals, except the flea, pop out and run away. When the elf returns to retrieve his hat, he is completely oblivious to the flea, who has made the hat his new home. The surrealistic paintings include many humorous details. *chs*

355. Weninger, Brigitte. **Special Delivery.** Translated by J. Alison James. Illustrated by Alexander Reichstein. New York: North-South, 2000. Originally published as *Was Kann Das Sein?* by Nord-Süd in 2000. ISBN 0-7358-1318-3. 27p. (3-5). Engineered book.

One morning the postman delivers a new vacuum cleaner to Mother, and not much later the same box again appears at the door. A guessing game ensues as Mother lifts the box and feels inside, wondering what it could be. Mother hears breathing inside and knows that the box contains "something special." The book ends with flaps like those on a cardboard box, which Mother opens to uncover a pop-up child. The book itself resembles a shipping carton covered with childlike drawings and stickers. *chs*

356. Weninger, Brigitte. **What Have You Done Davy?** Translated by Rosemary Lanning. Illustrated by Eve Tharlet. New York: North-South, 1996. Originally published as *Pauli! Du schlimmer Pauli!* by Nord-Süd in 1996. ISBN 1-55858-581-8. 32p. (4-6). Picture book.

Poor Davy! In his eagerness to play with his friends he inadvertently manages to crash, smash, and generally wreak havoc everywhere he goes. How he makes amends for his mischievous misdeeds results in a reassuring tale of family love and forgiveness. Expressive drawings capture every emotional nuance of Davy's up and down day. Other titles include *Where Have You Gone Davy? Will You Mind the Baby Davy? What's the Matter Davy?* and *Merry Christmas Davy!* *cl*

Other books illustrated by Lisbeth Zwerger, 1986 Hans Christian Andersen Medalist
357. Baum, L. Frank. **The Wizard of Oz**. Illustrated by Lisbeth Zwerger. New York: North-South, 1996. Originally published by Michael Neugebauer in 1996. ISBN 1-55858-638-5. 103p. (7-12). Novel.

The text is Baum's well-known story of young Dorothy's journey via tornado from Kansas to the fantasy world of Oz. Unlike any of the other versions, Zwerger's creates her own special world, one of a distant lightness and a more immediate intimacy. There is great emotional impact here: giant red poppies surround Dorothy; black, red-headed monkeys carry her off; a spooky wicked witch fills pages with evil. We get surrealism appropriate to the fantasy but very humanistic renderings of the heroes. *km, sm*
    Author from the United States

358. Carroll, Lewis. **Alice in Wonderland**. Illustrated by Lisbeth Zwerger. New York: North-South, 1999. Simultaneously published by Nord-Süd Verlag. ISBN 0-7358-1166-0. 103p. (7-12). Novel.

See Europe/United Kingdom for description.

Related Information

Awards

Österreichische Kinder- und Jugendbuchpreise/Austrian National Children's and Youth Book Awards
Sponsored by Federal Chancellery Department of the Arts, these awards are given in three categories: fiction, illustration, and translation.

Belgium

359. Ashbé, Jeanne. **What's Inside?** New York: Kane/Miller, 2000. Originally published as *Et dedans il y a . . .* by Pastel, L'École des Loisirs in 1997. ISBN 0-916291-97-9. 14p. (3-6). Picture book.

At first glance, this book for young children, translated from the French, appears to focus simply on the concept of "inside." Chapter 1 shows things we *can* open up (like a suitcase) and Chapter 2 things we *shouldn't* open up (like a teddy bear). In both cases, children will enjoy lifting the flaps to see "what's inside." In Chapter 3, however, the reader realizes that the focus of the book is actually pregnancy. What's inside Mommy's tummy when she's going to have a baby? This works well as an introduction to a concept that's difficult for small children to grasp, but it limits the appeal of the book to a rather specific audience. A nice feature of the book design is that the pages are laminated and quite sturdy, well-suited to a young child. *fk*

360. Coran, Pierre. **Family Tree.** Illustrated by Marie-José Sacré. Minneapolis: Carolrhoda, 1999. Originally published as *Meine Familie* by Bohem Press in 1997. ISBN 1-57505-219-9. 32p. (3-5). Picture book.

This book begins and ends with illustrations of the relatives in the narrator's family tree—great-grandmother, two sets of grandparents, and plenty of aunts and uncles, as well as two cousins. Only at the end do we find out that the narrator (a mere infant) came to this family in an airplane from a faraway country. "There, I no longer had a family. Here, everyone was expecting me." Colorful paintings show family members in their proper settings, from bandleader to sea lion tamer to mail carrier, and what a diverse and interesting family it is. *ss*

361. Guettier, Bénédicte. **The Father Who Had 10 Children.** New York: Dial, 1999. (Paperback: Puffin, 2001). Originally published by Casterman as *Le papa qui avait 10 enfants* in 1997. ISBN 0-8037-2446-2. 48p. (2-5). Picture book.

This oversized, cartoonlike book chronicles the daily routine of a single dad who cooks for, clothes, and drives to school his ten children (all the same size) before he himself goes to work, and then reverses the process in the evenings. He plans a getaway on a sailboat, leaving the kids with grandma, but finds he just can't do without them, so back he goes to bring them along on his adventure. *ss*

362. Vincent, Gabrielle. **A Day, a Dog.** Illustrated by the author. Asheville, NC: Front Street, 1999. Originally published as *un jour, un chien* by Éditions Duculot in 1982. ISBN 1-886910-51-0. 64p. (4-14). Picture book.

Without a written word Vincent conveys all the pathos and joy of a dog abandoned by his owners and searching for a haven. We hope he has found it at the end. The soft black strokes on the stark white paper create images that are simultaneously tentative, as if we are part of the creative process, and yet definitive enough to arouse our emotions. Vincent produces the vast emptiness of a lonely landscape and the claustrophobic alleyways of a city with equal conviction. *km, sm*

Czech Republic

363. Isaacs, Anne. **Torn Thread.** New York: Scholastic, 2000. ISBN 0-590-60363-9. 188p. (12 up). Novel.
See Poland for description.

364. Machalek, Jan. **Eva's Summer Vacation: A Story of the Czech Republic.** Norwalk, CT: Soundprints, 1999. ISBN 1-56899-802-3. 32p. (4-8). Picture book.

Set in contemporary times, this simple, first-person story describes a girl's trip from Prague, where she lives, to a relative's wedding in Moravia, a region in the southeastern part of the country. Illustrations are filled with realistic portraits of Prague's buildings and streets, images of the countryside, and details of rural life and traditional Moravian customs. Common Czech words, such as *pozdravuj* (hello), are introduced in the text and defined in a glossary. Also included is a map and a brief paragraph of facts about the country and the customs that figure in the story. *ss*
Author from the United States

365. Pacovská, Kveta. **Flying.** Translated by Andrew Clements. Illustrated by the author. New York: North-South Books, 1995. Originally published as *Türme* by Michael Neugebauer Verlag AG in 1995. ISBN 1-55858-

496-X. 42p. (6-8). Engineered book.

One tower whispers a secret to another that "flying is easy." When the moon overhears, she spreads the secret as she flies across the sky. Creatures in the story use all kinds of devices to take flight. The illustrations are a cubist collage style with intense colors, die-cuts, pop-ups, and a 3D foldout. Pacovská: *Hans Christian Andersen Medal for Illustration, 1992. chs*

366. Rubin, Susan Goldman. **Fireflies in the Dark: The Story of Friedl Dicker-Brandeis and the Children of Terezin.** New York: Holiday House, 2000. ISBN 0-8234-1461-2. (10-14). Picture book.

A teacher and artist always, Friedl Dicker-Brandeis took art supplies rather than personal items when she was sent to the Terezin concentration camp in the former Czechoslovakia. This book is a testimony of how one person made a difference in the lives of the children at the camp. Art helped the children focus on a happier past while giving them an outlet for dealing with the horrors of the present. Some of the results are reproduced and documented in picture-book format with a text that will appeal to older students studying the Holocaust. Extensive references: publications, videos, unpublished diaries, lectures, sound recordings, CD, websites. *bjk*
Author from the United States

367. Sís, Peter. **A Small Tall Tale from the Far Far North.** Illustrated by the author. New York: Knopf, 1993. (Paperback: Sunburst/FSG, 2001). ISBN 0-679-84345-0. 32p. (5-10). Picture book.

Jan Welzl was a Czech explorer in the late nineteenth century whose books recounting his journeys in the Arctic fueled the imagination of young Peter and his brother. Sís imagines Welzl's adventures traveling across Asia through Siberia to the Arctic and his activities once there. His inventive illustrations expand on the straightforward text, lending it the element of tall tale as promised in the title. *ss*
Author from the United States

368. Sís, Peter. **The Three Golden Keys.** Illustrated by the author. New York: Doubleday, 1994. ISBN 0-385-47292-7. 64p. (7-14). Picture book.

Returning to Prague, the city of his childhood, Sís reflects on the history and culture of this city he loves through a tale of fantasy. To open the door of his family home, he must find three keys. These keys each are found within Czech legends that he retells within the text. Significant to these stories are the pen-and-ink illustrations that contain mysterious ghostly figures. Using a subtle, single wash of color for each story, Sís recalls his

childhood with unique storytelling and enigmatic illustrations. *jbm*
Author from the United States

Related Information

Awards
Golden Strip Award/Zlatá stuha
Since 1992, this annual Award of the Albatros Publishing House (Výroc ní cena nakladatelství Albatros) has been the only national award devoted to new production of Czech publishing houses for children and youth.

Denmark

369. Andersen, Hans Christian. **The Emperor's New Clothes**. Translated and introduced by Naomi Lewis. Illustrated by Angela Barrett. Cambridge, MA: Candlewick, 1997. ISBN 0-7636-0119-5. 26p. (7-12). Picture book.

Andersen's tale of vanity and pride, popular since it was written in 1837, is magically translated by Naomi Lewis. Handsome watercolor illustrations bring to life the emperor's kingdom as well as his extravagant obsession with fashion. *IBBY Honor List, 2000. djg*

370. Andersen, Hans Christian. **The Swan's Stories**. Selected and translated by Brian Alderson. Illustrated by Chris Riddell. Cambridge, MA: Candlewick, 1997. Originally published by Walker Books (U.K.) in 1997. ISBN 1-56402-894-1. (7-10). Transitional book.

Alderson introduces this collection by comparing Hans Christian Andersen to one of his own characters, the ugly duckling evolving into a beautiful swan. Thus, the tales become the "Swan's Stories." The twelve well-translated tales range from familiar titles, such as "The Steadfast Tin Soldier" and "The Fir Tree," to rarely anthologized stories, such as "The Collar" and "The Darning Needle." Each of the tales is amply illustrated with humorous black-and-white drawings and full-page color plates. A modest glossary defines words and phrases that might stump contemporary children. *chs*

371. Levine, Ellen. **Darkness over Denmark: The Danish Resistance and the Rescue of the Jews**. New York: Holiday House, 2000. ISBN 0-8234-1447-7. 164p. (10-14). Informational book.

Levine provides a detailed and fascinating account of Germany's occupation of Denmark from April 9, 1940, to May 1945 that focuses on German policies toward the Danish Jews and the Danish rescue of the majority

of the 8,000-strong Jewish population from the Nazis. The drama of those years during which resistance grew to Germany's increasingly hard line is heightened by firsthand accounts obtained from interviews of selected Danes who experienced German attacks as well as of Danes who took part in rescues. Black-and-white photographs, an updated "Who's Who" of interviewees, a chronology, and bibliography are also provided. *hc*
Author from the United States

372. Lützen, Hanna. **Vlad the Undead**. Translated by the author. Toronto: Groundwood, 1998. Originally published as *Vlad* by Gyldendal in 1995. ISBN 0-88899-341-2. 190p. (12-16). Novel.

Lützen uses letters and diaries to convey this story, which is really three stories in one: the story of Vlad Dracula, the Romanian prince who lived in the Middle Ages; the story of Maresciu, a Romanian sea captain who takes a stranger aboard a ship bound for England and barely survives to dictate his horrifying story to the doctor attending his death; and the story of Lucia, a Danish medical student whose great-grandfather *was* that doctor and whose grandfather has given her the documents. Lucia, who becomes obsessed with the story, is soon part of it. This is a classy retelling of the Dracula legend, grounded in historical information about the medieval wars between the Ottoman Empire and its Christian neighbors. *ss*

Related Information

Organizations
Center for Børnelitteratur/Center for Children's Literature
www.cfb.dk

In English and Danish, the center's website includes a description of activities the center is engaged in, from maintaining a collection of children's books to disseminating the work of scholars. For those who read Danish, there are many useful links leading to bookstores and information sources.

Awards
Kulturministeriets børnebogspris/Ministry of Culture Children's Book Award

Awarded annually for Danish children's and young adult literature, either for an individual work or the entire work of an author; includes cash prize.

Kulturministeriets Illustratorpris/Ministry of Culture Illustration Prize
Awarded annually to a Danish illustrator, either for a particular work or for an illustrator's collected works; includes cash prize.

Other annual Danish children's book prizes include the Children's Librarian Culture Prize, the Danish Association of School Librarians Children's Book Prize, the Bookseller's Association Children's Book Prize, and the Danish School Library Association Children's Book Prize.

Finland

373. Jansson, Tove. **Moomin, Mymble, and Little My.** Illustrated by the author. Seattle: Blue Lantern, 1996. Originally published as *Hur gick det sen? Boken om Mymian, Mumintrollet och Lilla My* by Schildts Förlags in 1952. ISBN 1-893211-10-7. 28p. (2-6). Picture book.

The clever device of cutout pages, which pique the child's curiosity to turn the page, embellishes the adventure of Moomin and Mymble as they seek to find Mymble's sister, Little My. She is saved by Mymble, who cuts her out of the wicked vacuum cleaner. The text is printed in script, which adds to the fanciful nature of the tale. *rh*

Related Information

Online Bookstores
Bol.com
www.bol.fi
The Finnish version of Bol is organized a little differently from most of the other Bol.com country sites and is hard to negotiate for those without knowledge of Finnish.

France

374. Ardalan, Haydé. **Milton.** San Francisco: Chronicle, 2000. Originally published under the title *Moi, Milton* by La Joie de Lire in 1997. ISBN 0-8118-2762-3. 32p. (4-8). Picture book.

Milton is a cat, an exceptional cat, handsome, fearless, and curious, with retractable claws, good eyes, and expressive ears. He is an excellent hunter and tells the reader so. Life is good for a big cat, Milton. In spare text with stark, expressive, black-and-white illustrations, Ardalan conveys the essence of this proud cat's personality. Not just for cat lovers, this small picture book is a perfect companion to the 1998 Batchelder Honor book *Nero Corleone: A Cat's Story* by Elke Heidenrich (1997). *djg*

375. Axworthy, Anni. **Anni's Diary of France**. Watertown, MA: Charlesbridge, 1994. ISBN 1-879085-58-5. 32p. (10-14). Picture book.

Anni is about twelve years old as she accompanies her parents in this delightful, seven-week-long excursion. We visit Paris and then head through Normandy, Brittany, the Loire Valley, the Midi, and Provence. We discover that Carnac's standing stones are older than the pyramids, that Chenanceau was designed by women, and that pilgrims climbed the steps of Rocamadour on their hands and knees. Colorful drawings, interspersed with ticket stubs, cheese labels, stamps, and snapshots, surround the text on each page, giving the appearance of a scrapbook of joyful memories. Includes glossary of French words. *rta*

Author from the United States

376. Banks, Kate. **And If the Moon Could Talk**. Illustrated by Georg Hallensleben. New York: Farrar, Straus & Giroux, 1998. Originally published as *Si la lune pouvait parler* by Gallimard in 1998. ISBN 0-374-30299-5. 32p. (1-6). Picture book.

"Twilight blazes a trail across the bedroom wall" of a little boy as he prepares for bed. And if the moon could talk, it would tell of the stars flaring in a village, a papa reading to his child of sands blowing in the desert. The text and illustrations transport us from indoor to outdoor scenes as the books unfolds "like a banner across the sky." Rich, simple paintings that call to mind Clement Hurd's "Great Green Room" complement this eloquent text. *1998 Boston Globe-Horn Book Award for Best Picture Book of the Year. djg*

377. Banks, Kate. **Baboon**. Illustrated by Georg Hallensleben. Farrar, Straus & Giroux, 1997. Originally published by Gallimard in 1994. ISBN 0-374-30474-2. 28p. (1-3). Picture book.

Baby Baboon sees many things as his mother takes him on his first trip into the big world. They enter the great forest and Baboon concludes that the world is green. "Some of it," his mother wisely replies. With each new scene, Baboon learns more about the world. After traveling far and seeing many things, Baboon concludes that the world is big. "Yes," says his mother softly, "the world is big." Lush, large impressionistic paintings on thick glossy paper provide a context for the simple text and its lesson that the world is not as it first seems. *djg*

378. Banks, Kate. **The Night Worker.** Illustrated by Georg Hallensleben. New York: Farrar, Straus & Giroux, 2000. ISBN 0-374-35520-7. 36p. (4-6). Picture book.

Usually, Alex has to go to bed about the same time Pappa, a night-shift construction engineer, goes to work. But one night, Pappa hands his son a boy-size hard hat and takes Alex to work with him. Banks's sparse but compelling text and Hallensleben's shadowy nighttime illustrations convincingly portray the sights and sounds of a building project under way while the rest of the city sleeps. *2001 Charlotte Zolotow Award.* rhm

379. Bassède, Francine. **A Day with the Bellyflops.** New York: Orchard Books, 2000. Originally published by Siphano in 1998. ISBN: 0-531-30242-3. 26p. (3-6). Picture book.

Mrs. Bellyflop, an earnest, hardworking pig and single mother, has only two hours of work to do in her office. But Lily, Peter, and Wiggly can't seem to stay out of trouble long enough for her to finish in this humorous but all-too-realistic story. From the front endpapers of the busy family in sunshine to the story's end at night with a sleepy mother at her desk, the delightful watercolor scenes convey the mixed piggy emotions with affecting sympathy. *km, sm*

380. Bassède, Francine. **George's Store by the Shore.** Translated by Dominic Barth. New York: Orchard, 1998. Originally published as *Boutique de Georges a la plage* by Siphano in 1997. ISBN 0-531-33083-4. 24p. (4-6). Concept book.

Each day, George the duck and Mary the cat open their seaside store and count out their wares. Kids will enjoy counting the various items from page to page, then seeing (and counting) the whole display at the end of the book. Bassède's soft watercolor illustrations highlight her age-appropriate text. Sequel: *George Paints His House*, 1999. rhm

381. Bemelmans, Ludwig. **Madeline.** Illustrated by the author. New York: Viking, 1939. (Paperback: Puffin, 1998). 48p. (4-9). Picture book.

Our heroine, Madeline, is not only fearless but also believable (authentic illustrations see to that) and admirable—who among us would not also want to say "pooh-pooh" to the tiger in the zoo? Madeline's adventure has to do with an appendectomy and such is her popularity with the other little girls under Miss Clavel's care that they all want appendectomies, too! Bemelmans's rhyming text and illustrations in the original large-size format give a sense of spaciousness (and plenty

of room for mischief). Parisian scenes in the illustrations are identified at the end. *1940 Caldecott Honor Book.* Five other Madeline stories with the same opening lines that invite readers home to the "old house in Paris" are *Madeline's Rescue, Madeline's Christmas, Madeline and the Bad Hat, Madeline and the Gypsies,* and *Madeline in London. bjk*
Author from the United States

382. Butler, Nola, editor. **Travel Tales**. Various authors and illustrators. Translated by Toula Ballas. New York: Abrams, 1998. Originally published in France. ISBN 0-8109-389502. 80p. (mixed ages). Anthology.

Ten original tales, ranging from two to ten pages, form a showcase of contemporary French illustration and storytelling. Most of the stories are fantastic, with either animal or human characters, although in one story, the protagonist is a small blue carpet, Aziz, who goes to visit an older, more worldly relative. Most of the contributors will be new to American readers, although some may recognize Jacques Duquennoy from his Ghosts series. *ss*

383. Corentin, Philippe. **Papa!** Illustrated by the author. San Francisco: Chronicle, 1997. Originally published by L'École des Loisirs in 1995. ISBN 0-8118-1640-0. 32p. (4-6). Picture book.

This bedtime book about monsters has a decidedly different slant. Two children are in bed—a human child and a monster child, each tucked up in pajamas—and each, in turn, is horrified by the creature he finds in his bed. Pleas to their respective sets of parents bring them reassurance that "There's no such thing as monsters." Dubious, but worn out, the two finally snuggle down to share the bed and fall fast asleep. Cheerful cartoon illustrations make both humans and monsters approachable. Corentin: *1972 Children's Book Showcase Award. fk*

384. Davenier, Christine. **Leon and Albertine**. Translated by Dominic Barth. Illustrated by the author. New York: Orchard, 1997. First published as *Leon et Albertine* by Kaleidoscope in 1997. ISBN 0-531-30072-2. 36p. (4-6). Picture book.

Leon is a happy, normal pig—that is, until he falls I love with Albertine, who happens to be a chicken. With well-meant but poor advice from his friends, Leon embarks on a series of misadventures trying to make his true love notice him. Leon finally wins Albertine's heart by . . . well, by just being a pig. Exuberant watercolor illustrations complement Davenier's clever text. *rhm*

385. Dedieu, Thierry. **The Boy Who Ate Words**. Translated by Julie Harris and Lory Frankel. Illustrated by the author. New York: Abrams, 1997. Originally published by Editions du Seuil in 1996. ISBN 0-8109-1245-7. 38p. (8-12). Picture book.

This oversized picture book with full-page, cartoon illustrations depicts Gabby, a young boy who is enchanted by words. He enjoys asking questions, but when he has so many ideas that he has difficulty expressing them all, he invents his own language. Finally, he stops talking altogether and turns to body language and communication with animals and inanimate objects until his worried parents institutionalize him. There is hope, though, for Gabby when he becomes friends with a young girl who encourages him to again communicate in human words. *chs*

386. Dedieu, Thierry. **Hunting for Fur: The Adventures of Panda and Koala.** New York: Doubleday, 1998. Originally published as *Chasse a la Fourrure* by Editions du Seuil in 1998. ISBN 0-385-32636-X. 26p. (5-12). Picture book.

When Panda and Koala find Wolf, stripped of his fur and freezing in the snow, they take up their weapons and head for the city to put their plan into action. They trap the fur-wearing humans and forcefully take the furs, returning them to their rightful owners. After a very busy day, the two friends return to town, and passing a shop window filled with alligator purses, they plan a trip to Africa to help their cousins in need. *djg*

387. Dumas, Philippe. **A Farm.** Mankato, MN: Creative Editions, 1999. Originally published as *Une ferme* by L'École de Loisirs in 1997. ISBN 1-56846-169-0. (7-14). Picture book.

In a splendid, oversized format illustrated with lively, informative, and beautiful watercolor spreads, a large, nineteenth-century British farm is explored. Key messages of this peaceful, seemingly idyllic life—self-sufficiency and thrift—are established in the sage foreword and expertly woven into explanations of how this well-organized agricultural entity operated. Interesting details, such as the design of the garden gate lock and types of fowl raised, are presented in accurate drawings and captions. Broader social issues, such as the hard lives of the many servants upon whose labors the farm depended, are subtle and benign. Limited text. *cmt*

388. Francia, Silvia. **Roberta's Vacation.** New York: Kane/Miller, 1998. Originally published as *Les vacances de Roberta* by Editions du Seuil in 1996. ISBN 0916291839. 32p. (5-8). Picture book.

While visiting her grandparents, Roberta the dog is bored so she sets off alone for an adventure at the beach. She meets a bully dog, Jerome, who makes himself comfortable on her blanket and eats her snacks. Even before he's had time to digest, he dives into the water and sinks to the bottom. It's Roberta to the rescue, and her act of heroism turns them into best friends. *djg*

389. Gershator, Phillis. **When It Starts to Snow.** Illustrated by Martin Matje. New York: Henry Holt, 1998. ISBN 0-8050-5404-9. 32p. (2-5). Picture book.

What if it starts to snow? What do you do? Where do you go? Each time the author poses these questions, they are answered in rhymed text by various animals, "I creep into the house," says the mouse. Cold wins blow and the geese fly south, the beaver builds a lodge, fish lie low, farm animals hunker down, and bear finds it's time to sleep when the snow is deep. But the observant little boy can't sleep; he wants to play, and so he does in this lyric celebration of winter. The striking illustrations by a French illustrator well-known in his own country are what makes this worthy of inclusion here. *djg*

Author from the Virgin Islands

390. Gerstein, Mordicai. **Victor.** New York: Farrar, Straus & Giroux. 1998. ISBN 0-374-38142-9. 258p. (12-14). Novel.

Based on a true story occurring in France at the end of the eighteenth century, this novel recounts the life of a child abandoned in the woods at an extremely young age. When first discovered, Victor, as he came to be called, shows no signs of human upbringing and his skills resemble those of a wild animal. Authorities send him to a school for the deaf in Paris, where the teachers allow him to become a freak show, "The Savage of Aveyron." Victor becomes ill, and the doctor called to treat him, Jean-Marc-Gaspard Itard, takes an interest in the case. He pleads to become Victor's caretaker and begins a long process to educate Victor. Parallel stories present Itard's own development, and the life of a young girl, daughter to Itard's housekeeper. Using historical documents left by Victor's teacher, the author touches on educational philosophies, puberty, the French Revolution, and life in post-revolutionary Paris. *cc*

Author from the United States

391. Gerstein, Mordicai. **The Wild Boy.** New York: Farrar, Straus & Giroux, 1998. ISBN 0-374-38431-2. 39p. (4-8). Picture book.

Living alone in the forests, a wild boy is captured and taken to the nearest town. Unable to speak, he is taken to the Institute for Deaf-Mutes in

Paris where, diagnosed as a hopeless case, he is neglected until placed under the care of Dr. Itard. Victor's childhood is described as he learns to read, play, and adapt to civilized society. Lively illustrations with fluid lines depict Victor's changing emotions and his affinity with nature as he runs exuberantly with the wind or rolls in the snow. Based on the true story of Victor, the wild child of Aveyron. *ALA Notable Books, 1998; NYT Book Review Best Illustrated Book of the Year, 1998; SLJ Best Book of the Year, 1998.* hc

Author from the United States

392. Godard, Alex. **Idora**. Translated by Laura McKenna. New York: Kane/Miller, 1999. Originally published as *Idora* by Editions du Seuil in 1997. ISBN 0-916291-89-8. 32p. (4-6). Picture book.

When the Paris apartment house in which she lives is demolished, Idora, a lonely giraffe, turns her daydreams into reality. She buys a one-way ticket south and takes the express train to the sea, happily looking forward to a new life full of adventure. Full-page (and several double-page) illustrations feature Idora as a realistically drawn giraffe in human poses in beautifully depicted scenes of the city and country. *ca*

393. Godard, Alex. **Mama, Across the Sea.** Translated by George Wen. Illustrated by the author. New York: Holt, 2000. Originally published as *Maman-dlo* by Albin Michel in 1998. ISBN 0-8050-6161-4. 40p. (3-7). Picture book.

Set in Godard's childhood home of Guadeloupe, West Indies, this picture book is about Cecile, who lives with her grandparents while her Mama works in a city far away. Cecile yearns for Mama to return and collects shells and pink sand from Port Royal beach to send to her. One night, Cecile listens to a storyteller on the beach; the characters in his tale reflect her own feelings about waiting for her mother. The book ends with the beginning of Cecile's voyage to spend her school holiday with Mama. Illustrations portray the island, the sea, and Grandma's house in paintings full of light and shadow; the dominant blues, greens, and yellows are echoed in the vibrant plaid endpapers. *mn*

394. Lehmann, Christian. **Ultimate Game.** Translated by William Rodarmor. Boston: David R. Godine, 2000. Originally published as *No Pasaran, le Jeu* by L'École des Loisirs in 1996. ISBN 1-56792-107-8. 178p. (12-16). Novel.

The proprietor of a video store, a mysterious old man, gives three teenage boys a simple-looking computer game that catapults them into the virtual horrors of wars past and present, where each confronts his personal nightmare and resolution. The seventeen-year-old, who has a strong need for power and desire for violence, plays at being judge and jury, and finally victim. The strong narrative, fully drawn characters, and a vivid sense of place make for a riveting story. *2001Batchelder Honor Book. ak*

395. Luciani, Brigitte. **How Will We Get to the Beach?** Translated by Rosemary Lanning. Illustrated by Eve Tharlet. New York: North-South, 2000. Originally published as *Wer fährt mit ans Meer?* by Nord-Süd in 2000. ISBN 0-7358-1268-3. 34p. (3-6). Picture book.

On a summer's day, Roxanne decides to go to the beach and take along five things—a turtle, umbrella, book, ball, and baby. When her car won't start, Roxanne uses various modes of transportation, but none work out because in each case one of her five items won't fit. The repeated question "But something couldn't go with them. What was it?" creates a guessing game for readers. The illustrations add humor to this lighthearted story. The author was born in Germany and now lives in France, while the illustrator was born in France and spent her childhood in Germany. *chs*

396. Masurel, Claire, and Marie H. Henry. **Good Night!** San Francisco: Chronicle, 1994. Originally published as *Bonne Nuit!* by L'École des Loisirs in 1993. ISBN 0-8118-0644-8. 32p. (2-4). Picture book.

As part of her pre-bed ritual, a little girl rounds up her stuffed toys, talking to them in a voice that sounds positively parental: "Silly Max, it's not time to eat! It's time to go to bed." The repetitive text combined with detailed watercolor illustrations in soft hues make this a comforting and sleep-inducing reading experience. *ss*

397. Morgenstern, Susie. **Secret Letters from 0 to 10.** Translated by Gill Rosner. New York: Viking, 1998. Originally published as *Lettres d'amour de 0 a 10* by L'École des Loisirs in 1996. (Paperback: Puffin, 2000). ISBN 0-670-88007-8. 137p. (10-12). Novel.

Ernest Morlaisse has lived all of his ten years under the protection of his reclusive grandmother. The arrival of Victoria, a new classmate, means the opening of a whole new world beyond Ernest's bland and predictable life. With the help of Victoria and her large, boisterous family, Ernest learns the truth behind his father's disappearance the day after his birth. The story's international flavor is spiced with humor and elements of French city life. *mm*

398. Nikly, Michelle. **The Perfume of Memory.** Illustrated by Jean Claverie. New York: Arthur A. Levine/ Scholastic, 1999. Originally published as *Le Royaume des Parfums* by Albin Michel in 1997. ISBN 0-439-08206-4. 40p. (7-9). Picture book.

Equating scent with memory, Michelle Nikly weaves a tale with echoes of the Far East, while Jean Claverie's illustrations evoke an Arabian Nights atmosphere. A young girl, Yasmin, aspires to become Royal Perfume Maker, the most cherished position in her land. Unfortunately, girls are no longer allowed to make perfume, although at one time all children were trained in the art. Yasmin is able to overcome prejudice by thwarting a plot that removes the queen's memories. Armed with a tray of scents, Yasmin brings back the memories, and becomes Royal Perfume Maker. *cc*

399. Norac, Carl. **I Love You So Much.** Illustrated by Claude K. Dubois. New York: Doubleday, 1998. Originally published as *Les mots doux* by Pastel in 1996. ISBN 0-385-32512-6. 26p. (4-6). Picture book.

When Lola the hamster wakes up she has some special words on the tip of her tongue. But it takes her until the end of the day to finally tell her parents that she loves them. *pc*

400. Perrault, Charles. **Puss in Boots.** Translated by Anthea Bell. Illustrated by Giuliano Lunelli. New York: North-South, 1999. Originally published as *Der gestiefelte Kater* by Nord-Süd in 1999. ISBN 0-7358-1158-X. 26p. (4-8). Picture book.

In this spirited retelling of the traditional tale, the clever, resourceful cat manages to win a castle and a princess for his master, a poor miller's son. Lunelli's detailed, full-page illustrations and vignettes portray doll-like figures, a really wicked-looking magician, and a sleek, energetic puss, sometimes in near-surreal settings. The endpapers have his red boots standing out from an array of ordinary shoes. Illustrator is Italian. *km, sm*

401. Polacco, Patricia. **The Butterfly.** New York: Philomel, 2000. ISBN 0-399-23170-6. 48p. (8-10). Picture book.

It is France during the Second World War, and Monique wakes to find a girl with "sad eyes" sitting on her bed. Severine, Monique discovers, is hiding with her parents in the basement. One night, Severine is spotted by a neighbor, and Monique and her mother, Marcel, help Severine escape. The cruelty of the Nazis occupying the village is conveyed through Monique's perspective and Polacco's illustrations and is contrasted to the love in Monique's home, where a butterfly becomes a symbol of freedom. In an

author's note, Polacco tells about her great aunt Marcel Solliliage's involvement with the French Resistance. *hc*
Author from the United States

402. Rascal. **Socrates.** Illustrated by Gert Bogaerts. San Francisco: Chronicle, 1992. Originally published by L'École des Loisirs in 1992. (Paperback: Chronicle, 1992). ISBN 0-8118-1047-X. 26p. (4-7). Picture book.
An orphaned, homeless puppy roams the streets of a city searching for scraps of food. Full-page paintings depict this adorable, lonely dog whose luck seems to magically change when he dons a pair of glasses. Socrates finally finds a home when a street musician befriends him. *1992 American Bookseller "Pick of the Lists." chs*

403. Sanvoisin, Eric. **The Ink Drinker.** Illustrations by Martin Matje. Translated by Georges Moroz. New York: Delacorte, 1998. Originally published by Editions Nathan in 1996. ISBN 0-385-32591-6. 35p. (8-10). Transitional book.
From a hiding place in his father's bookstore, a little boy, who hates to read, observes the customers. He knows all the regulars and their habits, but then a new customer arrives. He is weird looking and instead of walking he floats like a ghost, but strangest of all is when he takes a straw from his pocket and drinks all the words out of the pages of a book. The boy follows the strange customer to the cemetery and discovers that he is a vampire! In a bizarre turn of events the little boy himself becomes an Ink Drinker, sucking up the flavor and excitement of the words, and for the first time in his life, discovers that he loves being the son of a bookstore owner. *djg*

404. Skurzynski, Gloria. **Spider's Voice.** New York: Atheneum, 1999. (Paperback: Aladdin, 2001). ISBN 0-689-82149-2. 200p. (12-14). Novel.
Aran, a mute peasant child, lives with his abusive father and brother in twelfth-century France. At twelve, he is sold to a man who specializes in creating freaks for the amusement of Paris nobles. It is Aran's inability to speak that saves him. He is just the servant the famous philosopher and teacher Peter Abelard needs because he cannot gossip about Abelard's forbidden relationship with the beautiful and brilliant Eloise. Aran (nicknamed "Spider") learns from the famous lovers about the power of words to both create and destroy, and what it means to have a voice. Includes a map and related website address. *mm*
Author from the United States

405. Ungerer, Tomi. **Tomi: A Childhood under the Nazis.** Illustrated by the author. Boulder: Roberts Reinhart, 1998. Originally published as *A la guerre comme à la guerre: dessins et souvenirs dènfance* by La Nuée Bleue in 1991. ISBN 1-57098-163-9. 176p. (12-14). Informational book.

Tomi Ungerer, a well-known Alsatian author and illustrator of children's books, provides an unusual, autobiographical account of World War II. Ungerer was seven in 1939 when the war broke out. His family never threw anything away, which is fortunate for it allowed him to thickly illustrate this book with examples of his childhood drawings, photographs of his family, propaganda materials from both Germany and the Allied troops, and the documents of daily life. The sheer variety of artifacts he displays tell a story on their own, with some of the illustrations presenting the horror of the German occupation his country experienced. His text emphasizes what everyday life was like for a child, highlighting problems in school and pranks he played, with the horror of the war mostly in the background. Ungerer: *1998 Hans Christian Andersen Medal for Illustration.* cc

Related Information

Awards
Le Baobab de l'Album
This annual award goes to a picture book.

Prix Totem
This award goes annually to books in five categories: picture book, fiction, nonfiction, translation, and comic strip.

Organizations and Websites
Le centre de promotion du livre de jeunesse/Center for the Promotion of Children's Books
www.ldj.tm.fr
The center's website contains news of French children's books, names and addresses of French publishers, current and past book awards, and a schedule of related book and art exhibits.

Site d'information sur la Littérature Jeunesse/Information on Literature for the Young
www.marmousse.net
Focused primarily on picture books, this site contains brief descriptions of new books, including a pick of the month.

Centre International d'Etudes en Littérature de Jeunesse

www.ricochet-jeunes.org
 The home page for this center provides an English-language option, and the site contains titles of numerous books and brief biographies of numerous authors and illustrators.

Online Bookstores
Alapage.com
www.alapage.com
 This online bookstore, similar in concept to amazon.com, offers French books, videos, and music.

Amazon.fr
www.amazon.fr
 The French site of amazon.com with everything you expect of the American site.

Bol.com
www. bol.fr
 The French version of Bol follows the familiar format of the online bookstore and is easy to negotiate, even for those who do not know French.

Germany

406. Bauer, Edith. **Walk the Dark Streets**. New York: Farrar, Straus & Giroux, 1998. ISBN 0-374-38229-8. 279p. (12-14). Novel.
 In 1933, Eva Bentheim sees Nazi flags flying in Thalstadt (a fictional town) in Germany. Highly descriptive, the novel documents how Eva's Jewish family and others suffer under the Nazi regime up to Eva's reluctant flight from her homeland in 1940—without her parents. Eva finds comfort through her romance with Arno as she experiences the escalation of violence, the closing of her sick father's bookstore (his arrest and rescue), the leaving of family members, and increasing isolation as she is barred from school and other public places. Also documented are outside events leading up to World War II. Sequel to *A Frost in the Night. hc*
 Author from the United States

407. Baumgart, Klaus. **Laura's Star**. Waukesha, WI: Little Tiger Press, 1997. Originally published in Germany in 1996 by Baumhaus Verlag. ISBN 1-888444-24-X. 28p. (4-8). Picture book.
 Laura is in bed one night wishing for a friend. Imagine her surprise

when she sees a steak of silver coming through the darkness toward her. Quickly running outside she finds a silver star. But the next day, the star is nowhere to be seen and she wonders if it was all dream. In this magical story richly illustrated in watercolor with a silver hologram star, a little girl learns that friendship sometimes means giving away the brightest treasures. *djg*

408. Buchholz, Quint. **The Collector of Moments.** Translated by Peter F. Neumeyer. Illustrated by the author. New York: Farrar, Straus & Giroux, 1999. Originally published as *Sammler der Augenblicke* by Carl Hanser Verlag in 1997. ISBN 0-374-31520-5. 42p. (7-14). Picture book.

In this dreamy, abstract story, a young boy who lives on an island treasures the time he spends with the family's boarder, Max, an enigmatic painter. Max doesn't allow the boy to see his works, which relate to fantastic stories he has told him, until he goes on a trip and leaves behind a private exhibit for the youngster. When Max finally moves away for good, he bequeaths the boy the priceless gifts of imagination and love for the power of art. Precise yet surreal pictures of the artist's stories, some softly colored and some black and white, are the star of this story. *2000 Mildred L. Batchelder Honor Award Winner. sg*

409. Craddock, Sonia. **Sleeping Boy.** Illustrated by Leonid Gore. New York: Atheneum, 1999. ISBN 0-689-81763-0. 32p. (7-9). Picture book.

A baby is born in Berlin, and the celebrating guests bestow wishes: a long life, good health. But the scorned Major Krieg arrives to case a curse: on his sixteenth birthday the boy will march off to war and not return. Using language and idioms of folklore, this story traces the arrival of poverty, war, the Berlin Wall. Peace does not occur until the Wall is finally destroyed, chip by chip, and the boy emerges from his metaphorical slumber. Elegant monochrome and subtly colored illustrations, presented in angular fragments, reveal details such as Nazi swastikas, grounding the tale in sober realism. *sp*

Author from the United States

410. Degens, T. **Freya on the Wall**. San Diego: Harcourt, 1997. ISBN 0-15-200210-3. 281p. (12 up). Novel.

Freya lives on the east side of the newly united Germany, and she shares an oral family history with her American cousin, Irene. Freya recounts her adventures with Winno, perceived betrayer and her one true love, as they live out a fairy tale told to them by Gran Dulla, Freya's grandmother. The Berlin Wall and the Chaos Theory play prominently as De-

gens uses a fractured timeline to show how chance and circumstance conspire to divide a family between East and West. The author, who grew up in Germany, immigrated to the United States in 1956 and now divides her time between Hamburg, Germany, and Portland, Oregon. *rlk*
Author from the United States

411. Enzenberger, Hans Magnus. **Lost in Time.** New York: Holt, 2000. Originally published as *Wo Warst Du, Robert?* by Carl Hanser Verlag in 1998. ISBN 0-8050-6571-7. 344p. (9-14). Novel.

Robert, a thirteen-year-old boy living in contemporary Germany, finds that when he rubs his eyes a certain way, odd things happen. One night while watching television, he is transported into the scene portrayed and finds himself in Siberia in 1956. The Communist officials are immediately suspicious of him, and he hides in a movie theater, where he enters the scene on screen and ends up in Australia in 1946. This happens seven times, with each occurrence landing Robert farther back in time. Finally, in Amsterdam in 1621, he is apprenticed to a painter and learns to paint his way back to his own time and place. *ss*

412. Enzensberger, Hans Magnus. **The Number Devil: A Mathematical Adventure.** Translated by Michael Henry Heim. Illustrated by Rotraut Susanne Berner. New York: Holt, 1998. Originally published as *Der Zahlenteufel; Ein Kopfkissenbuch fur alle, die Angst vur der Mathematik haben* by Carl Hanser Verlag in 1997. ISBN 0-8050-5770-6. 262p. (9-12). Novel.

Twelve-year-old Robert is plagued by bad dreams and a frustrating math teacher until one night when the number devil visits him. His dreams become contests in which Robert learns what math is really all about: zeros and ones, infinite series and irrational numbers, primes, patterns, and probability. The author writes with wit and insight. Readers will discover that they, too, can outsmart the number devil and learn a math trick or two. *djg*

413. Erlbruch, Wolf. **Mrs. Meyer the Bird.** Translated by Sabina Magyar and Susan Rich. New York: Orchard, 1997. Originally published as *Frau Meier, die Amsel* by Peter Hammer Verlag in 1995. ISBN 0-531-30017-X. 28p. (4-6). Picture book.

Mrs. Meyer, an obsessive worrier, adopts an abandoned baby blackbird. When she realizes that it is time for the bird to fly, she has a new worry: he won't. Mrs. Meyer must model the behavior. In teaching the bird to fly, Mrs. Meyer also learns to be free and daring. The text and mixed-media illustrations are embellished with amusing details of Mrs. Meyer's fretting and Mr. Meyer's "whatever you want, dear" attitude. *ca*

414. Gruber, Wilhelm. **The Upside-Down Reader**. Translated by J. Alison James. Illustrated by Marlies Rieper-Bastian. New York: North-South, 1998. Originally published as *Der Kopfstandleser* by Nord-Süd in 1998. (Paperback: North-South, 2000). ISBN 1-55858-974-0. 61p. (6-8). Transitional book.

In spite of older sister Tina's protests, preschooler Tim is allowed to sit across the table from her while she does homework. As Tina learns to read so does Tim, but he is doing it upside down. It is Grandma Lisa who helps Tim learn to read right side up and helps Tina realize that having two new readers in the family is okay. Cheery color illustrations add to the fun of this family story. *ca*

415. Hänel, Wolfram. **Rescue at Sea!** Translated by Rosemary Lanning. Illustrated by Ulrike Heyne. New York: North-South, 1999. Originally published as *Schiffshund in Not!* by Nord-Süd in 1999. ISBN 0-7358-1045-1. 60p. (6-9). Transitional book.

Watercolor illustrations fill the pages of this short sea adventure, told in six chapters. Nine-year-old Paul follows his father and the other village fishermen to the beach as they attempt to save a fishing boat caught at sea in a violent storm. Paul watches from the shoreline as all of the crew are saved in a daring rescue, but there is still someone aboard: the ship's dog. Paul climbs over rocks in the receding tide and coaxes the dog to jump from the ship and swim to him. For his bravery, Paul is allowed to keep "Johnny," the dog he has longed for. *mn*

416. Heidenreich, Elke. **Nero Corleone: A Cat's Story**. Translated by Doris Orgel. Illustrated by Quint Buchholz. New York: Viking, 1997. Originally published as *Nero Corleone: Eine Katzengeschichte* by Carl Hanser Verlag in 1995. ISBN 0-670-87395-0. 90p. (8-12). Transitional book.

Little Nero, an Italian-born black kitten, quickly learns to assert himself and influence others. So well does he assert himself that at six weeks of age he is known as Don Nero Corleone (Sir Nero, the lion-hearted). With his pudgy and loveable but simple sister, Rosa, in tow, Nero moves to Germany with a human couple he has adopted in his search for the good life. Nero's poignant return years later to his native Italy will pluck the heartstrings of pet lovers. This charming and delightful read is enhanced by surreal illustrations. Heidenreich knows cats. *rhm*

417. Heine, Helme. **The Boxer and the Princess**. Translated from the German. New York: McElderry, 1998. Originally published by Gertraud Middelhauve in 1997. ISBN 0-689-82195-6. 32p. (5-8). Picture book.

Max was different from the other rhinoceroses. He was gentle and sensitive. Max nods obediently when his father tells him, "life is hard . . . you will need a thick skin." In time Max adds the armor he needs to protect himself from life's troubles: boxing gloves to protect his hands, heavy boots for his feet, a suit of armor for his thin skin. At last he becomes so strong and tough that only cold and loneliness can penetrate his armor. It takes a very special princess to unlock the key to Max's heart. *djg*

418. Heine, Helme. **Friends.** New York: Atheneum, 1982. Originally published as *Freunde* by Gertraud Middellhauve in 1982. ISBN 0-689-50256-7. 32p. (3-6). Picture book.

Three improbable friends (a mouse, a pig, and a rooster) set off adventuring daily on their bicycle in this warm-fuzzy story. Though they always say, "Good friends always stick together," they find that concept difficult to execute when they decide to spend a night together in one or the other of their respective homes. Heine's bright, fresh watercolor illustrations perfectly complement his whimsical text. Sequel: *Friends Go Adventuring. rhm*

419. Holub, Josef. **The Robber and Me.** Translated by Elizabeth D. Crawford. New York: Holt, 1996. (Paperback: Dell, 1997). Originally published as *Bonifaz und der Räuber Knapp* by Beltz Verlag in 1996. ISBN 0-8050-5599-1. 213p. (9-12). Novel.

Eleven-year-old Boniface, sent by the Orphan's Court to live with his uncle, Emil Schroll, mayor of Graab in 1867, narrates how he is set down alone in the forest by a villainous driver and rescued by a man wearing a black hat. Boniface settles into his uncle's household and into school, making friends with Christian, whose father is known as "Robber Knapp." As officials attempt to arrest Knapp and persecute his family, Boniface finally tells what he knows—evidence that proves Knapp's innocence—and the identity of the real robber is unraveled. Includes translator's note providing a historical context and a glossary. *1998 Mildred L. Batchelder Award; ALA Notable Children's Book, 1998. hc*

420. Holzwarth, Werner. **I'm José and I'm Okay: Three Stories from Bolivia.** Translated by Laura McKenna. Illustrated by Yatiyawi Studios (Erlini Tola, Freddy Oporto, and Carlos Llanque). New York: Kane/Miller, 1999. Originally published as *Ich Heibe Jose und bin Zeimlich Okay!* by Peter Hammer Verlag, in 1996. ISBN 0-916291-90-1. 36p. (7-12). Picture book.

These short stories about a Bolivian orphan who faces obstacles in his uncle's auto repair shop and in a bicycle race are grittily realistic but hopeful. Expressive, action-filled illustrations add to the appeal to the reluctant reader. The book is the result of an international collaboration to encourage literacy through stories based on real people. *sg*

421. Jörg, Sabine. **Mina and the Bear.** Translated by Charise Neugebauer. Illustrated by Alexander Reichstein. New York: North-South, 1999. Originally published as *Mina und Bär* by Nord-Süd, 1999. ISBN 0-7358-1036-2. 48p. (5-8). Picture book.

A book-within-a-book relates the story of Mina, who desperately wants a stuffed toy bear. When she falls ill, her doctor gives her solace by telling her a story of his grandfather, who happened to be a bear. Mina is able to imagine that *her* family is part bear, too, and she no longer pines for the stuffed toy. *jr*

422. Kerner, Charlotte. **Blueprint.** Minneapolis: Lerner, 2000. Translated by Elizabeth D. Crawford. First published as *Blueprint/Blaupause* by Beltz & Gelberg in 1999. ISBN 0-8225-0080-9. 190p. (12 up). Novel.

Set approximately one generation into the future and inspired by the cloning of Dolly the sheep, this speculative novel explores the ramifications of cloning humans. Siri, cloned from her mother, Iris, a world-renown pianist and composer, tells her story as a flashback, from her perspective as a twenty-two-year-old soon after her mother has died of multiple sclerosis. While Siri took pleasure in their identicalness when she was a child, as she grew older she came to resent being brought into the world to fulfill her mother's musical ambitions. The author's afterword and acknowledgments will be of use to readers wishing to separate science from speculation. *2000 Deutscher Jugendliteraturpreis. ss*

423. Liersch, Anne. **A House Is Not a Home.** Illustrated by Christa Unzner. Translated by J. Alison James. New York: North-South, 1999. First published as *Ein Haus für alle* by Nord-Süd in 1999. ISBN 0-7358-1156-3. 28p. (5-8). Picture book.

Winter is coming and all the animals gather together to build a house, until Badger, a perfectionist, takes over and will not allow anyone to help. Eventually the happy friends become discouraged and band together to build their own house. Badger eventually becomes lonely in his perfect house, but he has a wonderful idea as the first snowflakes begin to fall. *djg*

424. Pressler, Mirjam. **Anne Frank: A Hidden Life.** Translated by Anthea Bell. New York: Dutton, 2000. Orginally published as *Ich Sehne Mich So: Die Lebengeschichte der Anne Frank* by Beltz Verlag in 1992. ISBN 0-

525-46330-5. 176p. (12-14). Informational book.

Anne Frank's life and death are situated in the wider historical context of events in Germany and the Netherlands that cause the Franks to emigrate to Amsterdam in 1933 and are the cause of their two years spent in hiding until captured in 1944. Pressler includes detailed information about the others hiding with the Franks and their "helpers" along with documenting what happened to the Franks after their capture. Including excerpts of Anne's diary previously omitted or edited, Pressler focuses on Anne's emotional, physical, and intellectual development and emphasizes Anne's literary ability. Included is the publishing history of Anne's diary. *hc*

425. Pressler, Mirjam. **Halinka**. Translated by Elizabeth D. Crawford. New York: Holt, 1998. ISBN 0-8050-5861-3. Originally published as *Wenn das Gluck kommt muss man ihm einen Stuhl hinstellen* by Beltz Verlag in 1994. 214p. (9-12). Novel.

Twelve-year-old Halinka lives in a home for emotionally disturbed girls in Germany just after World War II. She hides away all her thoughts until she discovers a secret room, where she keeps a diary of her most secret thoughts. Lonely and withdrawn, Halinka eventually opens up to Renata, another young girl. *2000 IBBY Honor Book for Translation*. *djg*

426. Rabinovici, Schoschana. **Thanks to My Mother**. Translated from the German by James Skofield (translated from Hebrew to German by Mirjam Pressler). New York: Dial, 1998. Originally published as *Danke meiner Mutter* by Alibaba Verlag in 1994. ISBN 0-8037-2235-4. 246p. (12-16). Autobiography.

When the Germans invade Vilnius in 1941, eight-year-old Susie Wecksler and her family are sent into the ghetto, where they endure increasing hardship and persecution. When the ghetto is liquidated in 1943, Susie's mother fights to save herself and Susie by hiding her in a backpack and making sure they are among the women sent to labor camps. Rabinovici (née Wecksler) recounts how her mother's courage and foresight help her to escape "selections" and survive starvation, illness, and journeys of death by boat and foot as they are sent from Kaiserwald to Stutthof to Tauentzien, where they are finally liberated. *1999 Batchelder Award. hc*

427. Ray, Karen. **To Cross a Line**. New York: Orchard, 1994. (Paperback: Puffin, 1995). ISBN 0-531-06831-5. 154p. (12-14). Novel.

Egon Katz is seventeen and working as a baker's apprentice in Barn-

trup in 1938 when he is involved in an accident with a Nazi businessman while delivering bread on his scooter. Arrest and a fine are followed by a summons to Gestapo headquarters. Egon, aided by his cousins and his brother Bruno, makes plans to escape Germany. His first two attempts fail; and he finally travels to Ellund on the Danish border, where a sympathetic innkeeper tells him where to cross. With the help of a compassionate Danish border guard Egon is free. Based on the author's father-in-law's escape from Nazi Germany. *hc*
Author from the United States

428. Ruepp, Krista. **Horses in the Fog**. Translated by J. Alison James. Illustrated by Ulrike Heyne. New York: North-South, 1997. Originally published as *Nebelpferde* by Nord-Süd in 1997. (Paperback: North-South, 1999). ISBN 1-55858-804-3. 61p. 7-9. Transitional book.

Charlie on Starbright and her new friend Mona on Merlin ride out through the shallow water to a sandbar off Outhorn Island. When a bank of fog suddenly rolls in, the girls and their horses are in danger. The stories about a sea ghost named Count Brineslime that Charlie has heard from Old Fig, the local storyteller, add to their fears. However, it is Old Fig's method of telling the direction of the tide that Charlie uses to get them safely back to shore. Realistic watercolor illustrations dramatically convey the setting and mood of this sequel to *Midnight Rider* (1995). *ca*

429. Schami, Rafik. **Albert & Lila**. Translated by Anthea Bell. Illustrated by Els Cools and Oliver Streich. New York: North-South. 1999. Originally published as *Albin und Lila* by Nord-Süd in 1999. ISBN 0-7358-1182-2. 24p. (4-6). Picture book.

Albert, a white-skinned pig, and Lila, an old hen who fears she'll end up in the cooking pot if the farmer finds out that she can no longer lay eggs, are barnyard outcasts who become best of friends. The joking and jeering of the pigs and hens at the expense of this odd pair turn to thanks, admiration, and apologies when Albert and Lila outwit a hungry fox by tricking him into believing that the hens have been moved to the pigsty. Albert and Lila sparkle with personality in Cools and Streich's comical paintings of barnyard scenes. *ca*

430. Scheffler, Ursel. **Be Brave, Little Lion!** Translated by J. Alison James. Illustrated by Ruth Scholte van Mast. New York: North-South, 2000. Originally published as *Pass auf, Lea Löwenkind!* by Nord-Süd in 2000. ISBN 0-7358-1264-0. 47p. (5-8). Transitional book.

Lea, an adventurous lion cub, explores the African grasslands until she meets a rhinoceros and runs away. Her father tells her, "A lion is never afraid." Her mother suggests caution, "Run away when someone is stronger than you." Later, after the rains come, Lea and her brothers splash in the water and roll in the "cool, gooey mud." Father lion decides to move the family to the mountains, away from hunters with guns. When a perplexed Lea asks if her father is afraid, her mother explains that her father is wise, "caution is not cowardly." Generous full-color watercolor illustrations are playful and beautifully depict the daily and seasonal changes on the African plains. *mn*

431. Scheffler, Ursel. **Grandpa's Amazing Computer**. Translated by Rosemary Lanning. Illustrated by Ruth Scholte van Mast. New York: North-South, 1997. Originally published as *Opa's Computer-Geheimnis* by Nord-Süd in 1997. (Paperback: North-South, 1999). ISBN 1-55858-795-0. 47p. (6-8). Transitional book.

On a weekend visit with his grandfather, Ollie, a computer-savvy nine-year-old, decides that his grandpa is out of step with the times and is in need of a computer. Ollie's constant chatter about computers leads Grandpa to show his grandson a very old computer. As he learns about the secrets of a sunflower-seed computer, which stores all the information needed to produce a whole plant, Ollie comes to agree that Grandpa does have an amazing computer. *ca*

432. Scheffler, Ursel. **The Spy in the Attic**. Translated by Marianne Martens. Illustrated by Christa Unzner. New York: North-South, 1997. Originally published as *Der Spion unterm Dach* by Nord-Süd in 1997. (Paperback: North-South, 1998). ISBN 1-55858-727-6. 63p. (7-9). Transitional book.

After seeing a late night delivery of some strange-looking boxes, Martin is convinced that Mr. Leon, the new tenant in the attic apartment, is a spy. He even appears to be in disguise (dark glasses, wig, and gloves). When Mr. Leon is ill and Martin is asked to walk his dog, the opportunity to do more sleuthing in the attic results in the proper identification of the mysterious man—and the making of a new friend. Watercolor illustrations with mysterious shadows in the background contribute to the suspenseful tone of this mystery. *ca*

433. Scheidl, Gerda Marie. **Tommy's New Sister**. Translated by J. Alison James. Illustrated by Christa Unzner. New York: North-South, 1999. Originally published as *Das neue Schwesterchen* by Nord-Süd in 1999. ISBN 0-7358-1056-7. (4-6). Picture book.

Unhappy about all the attention his new baby sister, Wendy, is getting, Tommy plots to get rid of her. There is nothing original about the ending: Tommy calms Wendy when no one else in the household heeds her crying and decides that he is proud to be a big brother. What's fun here are Tommy's imaginative plans for disposing of Wendy, such as sprinkling her with fairy dust (a mixture of flour, cocoa powder, and sugar) so that she can fly away like Wendy in *Peter Pan* and packing her in a box and mailing her to Granny. *ca*

434. Schneider, Antonie. **Good-Bye, Vivi!** Translated by J. Alison James. Illustrated by Maja Dusíková. New York: North-South, 1998. Originally published as *Leb wohl, Chaja!* by Nord-Süd in 1998. ISBN 1-55858-985-6. 26p. (4-7). Picture book.

When Granny comes to live with Molly and Will's family, she brings her old canary, Vivi, with her. The sickness and death of the canary leave the children sad and worried that Granny will die, too. Granny helps the children adjust to the loss of Vivi by sharing memories of the pet and, at the same time, prepares them for her own death. And when Granny does die the following spring, she has left for the children a memory book of pictures and stories, *Stories from My Vivi (Vivi means life!)* to help them remember her. Soft realistic watercolor illustrations contribute to the warm, gentle tone of this story of dealing with the death of a loved one. *ca*

435. Schneider, Antonie. **Luke the Lionhearted**. Translated by J. Alison James. Illustrated by Christina Kadmon. New York: North-South, 1998. Originally published as *Gustl Löwenmut* by Nord-Süd in 1998. ISBN 1-55858-976-7. 26p. (4-6). Picture book.

Luke's enjoyment of a visit to Aunt Molly's turns frightful when he sees a lion at the edge of the woods by her house. With reassurance from his aunt that lions don't come into houses, Luke falls asleep only to dream that the lion speaks to him. "Help me Luke the Lionhearted. I want to go home." The next morning Luke helps the zoo director locate and return the lion safely to the zoo. Bravery has replaced fear, and he has truly earned the name "Luke the Lionhearted." *ca*

436. Uebe, Ingrid. **Melinda and Nock and the Magic Spell**. Translated by J. Alison James. Illustrated by Alex de Wolf. New York: North-South, 1996. Originally published as *Melinda und der Zauber der Meerhexe* by

Nord-Süd in 1996. (Paperback: North-South, 1999). ISBN 1-55858-571-0. 62p. (6-8). Transitional book.

When Nock, a mischievous water sprite, teases the witch who lives in an undersea cave, she turns him into a sea horse. Melinda the mermaid bargains with the witch for her friend's release. She is to bring the witch the Seventh Wonder of the Sea, the most beautiful pearl in the world. Melinda and the sea horse search the Seven Seas for the jewel without luck, only to locate it right at the witch's door and to recover it in a clever way. The humorous ink and watercolor illustrations add to the fun of this fanciful undersea adventure. *ca*

437. Weigelt, Udo. **All-Weather Friends.** Translated by J. Alison James. Illustrated by Nicolas d'Aujourd'hui. New York: North-South. 1999. Originally published as *Alle Wetter* by Nord-Süd in 1999. ISBN 0-7358-1047-8. 26p. (4-6). Picture book.

All the animals expect Moss, a pond frog, to predict the weather because the humans in the house at the edge of the woods keep a weather frog in a jar for that purpose. Moss gives weather predicting a try, but he always gets it wrong. He seeks out the weather frog, rescues her from captivity by breaking the jar, and learns that frogs cannot really forecast the weather (people only think that they can according to European folklore). The two frogs hop off together and invite all the animals to stop worrying about the weather and to swim with them in the pond, a pleasant activity rain or shine. *ca*

438. Weigelt, Udo. **Hiding Horatio.** Translated by J. Alison James. Illustrated by Alexander Reichstein. New York: North-South, 1999. Originally published as *Rudolfo kommt* by Nord-Süd in 1999. ISBN 0-7358-1067-2. 26p. (3-7). Picture book.

The small woodland animals are afraid of the enormous lavender-gray stranger in the bowler hat and bow tie. He turns out to be Horatio the hippopotamus, who escaped from the circus and is trying to go home to Africa. It is decided that Africa is too far away and that Horatio should stay in the forest. Horatio avoids the men from the circus by disguising himself as a boulder, a bridge, four tree stumps, and, finally, an island. The illustrator's full-page paintings, using spatter-paint technique, add to the humor in this episode. The story ends with Horatio singing to all his new friends in the woods, as "the curtain of stars fell over the final song." *mn*

439. Wiesmüller, Dieter. **The Adventures of Marco and Polo.** Translated by Beate Peter. Illustrated by the author. New York: Walker, 2000. Originally published as *Pin Kaiser und Fip Husar* by Verlag Sauerländer in 1997. ISBN 0-8027-8729-0. 40p. (4-9). Picture book.

Marco Monkey comes to the South Polar Sea, where Polo Penguin becomes his guide. Then Marco takes Polo to his jungle home. But despite the wonders they see, the friends cannot find a place that suits them both, so they reluctantly return to where they belong. Despite the rather bland text, the double-page, colored scenes contribute factual information along with the visual attractiveness of both scenery and characters. The settings clearly show the blue chill that discomforts Marco and the yellow-green that overheats Polo. *km, sm*

Related Information

Library Collections

Internationale Jugendbibliothek / International Youth Library
www.ijb.de (in German only)
    This is a noncirculating collection of post-World War II children's books from all over the world. Schloss Blutenburg, D - 81247 Munich, Germany; e-mail: bib@ijb.de.

Institut für Jugendbuchforschung / Institute for Youth Book Research
www.uni-frankfurt.de/fb10/jubufo (in German only)
    Collected here are historical and contemporary children's books, primarily German-language. Johann Wolfgang Goethe-Universität, Grüneburgplatz 1, 60323 Frankfurt am Main tel. 49 69 798 32995; fax 49 69 798 32996; e-mail: jubufo@rz.uni-frankfurt.de.

Online Bookstores

Amazon.de
www.amazon.de

Adori
www.adorishop.de

Bol.com
www.bol.de

    All three of these sites are in German only but follow a familiar format and are therefore fairly easy to negotiate, especially if you know what title you would like to order.

Publications
Boersenblatt fuer den Deutschen Buchhandel
www.boersenblatt.net (in German)
Similar to *Publishers Weekly*, this journal carries information about the German-language book industry.

Awards
Deutscher Jugendliteraturpreis / The German Children's Literature Prize
Given to a book written by a German author or translated into the German language, this is the premier prize for children's literature in Germany and is presented annually at the Frankfurt Book Fair in October. Awards are made in four categories: picture book, children's book, young adult book, and nonfiction.

Greece

440. Aliki. **Marianthe's Story: Spoken Memories**. New York: Greenwillow, 1998. ISBN 0-688-15661-4. 30p. (7-10). Picture book.
This is Book Two of the back-to-back texts that comprise Marianthe's story, which begins in an American classroom where, not knowing English yet, she can only express herself through art. When Marianthe finally has the language skill to tell her life story, she describes the family's life (in Greece, although the country is actually not named), the war and famine that took her baby brother before she was born, and the hard conditions that finally caused her father to seek work elsewhere. Eventually the whole family is able to join Papa in that new land, which brings her story up to the present. Illustrations portray the details of Marianthe's family life and village. *ss*
Author from the United States

441. Bawden, Nina. **The Real Plato Jones**. New York: Clarion, 1993. Originally published by Hamish Hamilton (U.K.) in 1994. (Paperback: Puffin, 1996). ISBN 0-395-66972-3. 166p. (12-14). Novel.
See Europe/United Kingdom for description.

442. Bunting, Eve. **I Have an Olive Tree**. Illustrated by Karen Barbour. New York: HarperCollins, 1999. ISBN 0-06-027574-X. 32p. (5-8). Picture book.
This book begins in America when Sophia's grandfather gives her an olive tree for her birthday—an olive tree in Greece! His dying wish is to have her put her grandmother's beads on that tree, which is his way of

ensuring that her mother, born in Greece, will revisit her roots, and that Sophia will become acquainted with the country of her heritage. The bulk of the story describes this trip, with the climax occurring as Sophia sees the tree for the first time. Barbour's paintings contain the rich, saturated colors of the Mediterranean and incorporate designs and details suggestive of Greek folk art. *ss*

Author from the United States

443. Galloway, Priscilla. **Snake Dreamer**. New York: Delacorte, 1998. ISBN 0-385-32264-X. 231p. (12-16). Novel.

When nightmares of snakes leave young Dusa afraid to sleep, exhausted, and ill, her mother sends her to a clinic on an isolated Greek island run by two doctors, the Gorgon sisters, with an unusual specialty: they cure snake dreamers. But, from the moment Dusa arrives at the clinic, peculiar things begin to happen. In this unique adventure novel, the ancient Greek myth of Medusa and the Gorgons is weaved so cleverly into the realistic contemporary storyline that the reader is kept mesmerized until the very last page. This novel is evidence of the timeless nature and appeal of the myth in contemporary young adult literature. *des*

Author from the United States

444. Harrison, Barbara. **Theo**. New York: Clarion, 1999. ISBN 0-899-19959-3. 166p. (12-16). Novel.

When it is announced that all orphans are to be rounded up and sent to Germany by the Nazis, Theo and his older brother, Socrates, escape from Athens and travel to a small village in the countryside. Unfortunately an unpredictable turn of events leaves young Theo on his own without his brother to take care of him. His only true companion becomes his shadow puppet, Karagiozis, a beloved and heroic character in Greek puppet-shadow theater. With the splendid theatrical backdrop of World War II Greece, Theo's character develops from a young frightened boy into a young man who understands the meaning of heroism and can survive the harsh world around him. Includes a glossary of Greek words and phrases, a description of Greek shadow theater, as well as musical notation and lyrics of a Greek resistance song. *des*

Author from the United States

445. Marijanovic, Stanislav. **A Manual of House Monsters**. Glen Head, NY: Mondo, 1999. Text adaptation by Howard Goldsmith. Originally published as *A Family Guide to House Monsters* by Siphano in 1998. ISBN

1-57255-718-4. 26p. (7-9). Picture book.

These monsters, with the exception of Shadowy, the monster of the dark, are not particularly scary, but like Shadowy, they can cause trouble. Oopsalo, the monster of spills, makes you knock things over, while Chatterbug, who lives in the telephone, feeds off conversation (he especially likes long distance, the kind that costs lots of money). The fantastical creatures come straight from the artist's imagination and offer visual clues as to each monster's nature. Since the North American text was adapted from the British text, a comparison of the two versions would make an interesting study in language use. The author, born in Croatia, now lives in Greece. *ss*

446. Oppenheim, Shulamith Levey. **Yanni Rubbish**. Illustrated by Doug Chayka. Honesdale, PA: Boyds Mills, 1999. ISBN 1-56397-668-4. 32p. (5-8). Picture book.

Using the old cart and donkey, Yanni has taken over the family business of collecting garbage in his small Greek village while his dad is away in Germany working as a stonemason. He doesn't mind the job, but he does mind how his friends make fun of him. Rather than return their hurtful words, he finds a positive way to overcomes the situation. Inspired by an old photograph, he fixes up the cart and decorates the donkey with braided ribbon, creating a rubbish wagon that his friends will respect and want to ride on. Oil paintings with blurred lines create a contemplative mood while offering an intimate view of village life. *ss*

Author from the United States

447. Rosen, Billi. **Andi's War**. New York: Dutton, 1989. Originally published by Faber and Faber in 1988. (Paperback: Puffin, 1991). ISBN 0-525-44473-4. 136p. (12-14). Novel.

See Europe/United Kingdom for description.

448. Talley, Linda. **Plato's Journey**. Illustrated by Itoko Maeno. Kansas City: MarshMedia, 1998. ISBN 1-55942-100-2. 32p. (4-6). Picture book.

When Plato's friends flatter him and tell him that he may perhaps be "the fastest goat in the Peloponnese," he cannot but believe when he is told that he should travel to Olympia and compete in the great goat race. When reaching his destination he discovers that there is no such race and returns home having learned the importance of honesty and the consequences of lies. The amusing yet educational story is further complemented by vibrant watercolor illustrations of the Greek countryside and the an-

cient site of the Olympic games. Includes end pages giving information about Greece and the Olympic games as well as a page for parents and educators providing tips for activities and discussion. *des*
Author from the United States

449. Trivizas, Eugene. **The Three Little Wolves and the Big Bad Pig.** Illustrated by Helen Oxenbury. New York: McElderry, 1993. First published by Heinemann in 1998. ISBN 0-689-50569-8. 32p. (4-6). Picture book.

In this clever contemporary twist of the classic fairy tale, it is three little wolves who are frightened by a "Big Bad Pig." Trivizas's unparalleled imagination and wit is at its zenith and with Helen Oxenbury's distinctive and unique illustrations, the book offers a good hint at the richness and international appeal of contemporary Greek children's literature. *des*

Related Information

Awards
The Circle of Greek Children's Books (Greek Section of IBBY)

This group administers several annual awards, funded by cultural institutions or private donors. Awards are given for books published the previous year in the following categories: for younger children; for intermediate readers; for older children and young adults. A fourth award is given to a Greek children's book for its illustrations. The Penelope Delta Award is given for the body of work.

State Prize for Children's Literature

This annual prize, given to a book published in the previous year, is awarded in December and consists of a diploma and a sum of Drs. 5,000,000.

Diavazo Magazine Prize for Children's Literature

This is a new prize awarded for the first time for a book published in the previous year. It consists of a diploma and a sum of Drs. 500,000.

Websites
Greek Children's Literature Page
www.angelfire.com/pe/GrChildLit

This comprehensive site includes an historical overview of Greek children's literature from the past to the present, links to conferences, descriptions of the journals that focus on children's books, and news and information of all kinds relating to Greek authors and children's books.

Hungary

450. Siegal, Aranka. **Upon the Head of the Goat: A Childhood in Hungary 1939-1944**. New York: Farrar, Straus & Giroux, 1981. (Paperback: Puffin, 1994). ISBN 0-374-38059-7. 213p. (11 up). Autobiography.

Piri's family lives in Beregszász (then in Hungary, now part of Ukraine), the "big city" as compared to her grandmother's farm in nearby Ukraine. The war seems far away, and Piri's parents dismiss her grandmother's advice to send all the children to America. By the time they try to, it is too late to get papers and book passage. The family's life becomes more and more restricted, until finally they are forced to move into a ghetto. The book ends as they are being herded into a train car bound for Auschwitz. Siegal's story is continued in *Grace in the Wilderness: After the Liberation 1945-1948. 1982 Newbery Honor Book. ss*

Author from the United States

Related Information

Awards
Szep Magyar Konyv
Literally "The Fine Hungarian Book," this award is given out during Children's Book Week in Hungary.

Republic of Ireland

451. Bunting, Eve. **Market Day**. Pictures by Holly Berry. New York: HarperCollins, 1996. ISBN 0-06-025364-9. 32p. (5-8). Picture book.

The first Thursday of every month in this Irish village is market day and young Tess eagerly anticipates the sights and sounds: streets filled with horses, cows, and pigs, the honey man, and old Paddy Mahoney playing his pipes. And what to buy with the penny from father—a penny poke of gob stoppers from the sweetie stall? Eve Bunting reminisces about the sights and sounds of market day. *djg*

Author from the United States

452. Doyle, Roddy. **The Giggler Treatment**. Illustrated by Brian Ajhar. New York: Levine/New York: Scholastic, 2000. ISBN 0-439-16299-8. 112p. (7-10). Transitional book.

Most of the events in this story take place in the moments that elapse between the time Mister Mack's foot is twelve inches and the time that it is less than half an inch over the dog pooh in which he is about to step. Mister Mack, a biscuit taster, is due to get his treatment from the Gigglers, elflike creatures that make it their duty to give the giggler treatment to any adults who are mean to children. Broken down into chapters and chapters between chapters, the book also includes a glossary explaining such terms as biscuits and nappies for American children. *lh*

453. Fitzpatrick, Marie-Louise. **Lizzy and Skunk**. Illustrated by the author. New York: DK Ink, 2000. Originally published as *Izzy and Skunk* by David & Charles (U.K.) in 2000. ISBN-07894-6163-3. 26p. (3-6). Picture book.

Lizzy and her hand puppet Skunk do everything together, but the hand puppet paradoxically leads the way. That's because he is brave, and Lizzy isn't. On the left-hand side of each page, tiny illustrations depict Lizzy hesitating at one task or another; on the right-hand side, a corresponding full-page illustration depicts Skunk bravely taking on the task, with Lizzy seemingly in tow. Then the tables turn. A cat kidnaps Skunk and leaves him stranded in a tree. Lizzy rescues Skunk, and even young readers (who will recognize Lizzy has always had the potential to be brave), will sense she will be a brave girl thereafter. *Bisto Book of the Year, 2001. ebb*

454. Fitzpatrick, Marie-Louise. **The Long March**. Illustrated by the author. Hillsboro, OR: Beyond Words, 1998 (distributed by Tricycle). Originally published by Wolfhound in 1998. ISBN 1-885223-71-4. 32p. (10-14). Illustrated book.

This book chronicles an event in 1847 that is part of both Irish and Choctaw history: the donation of $170 collected from the meager assets of the Choctaw Indians to aid the Irish during the potato famine. The story is told from the perspective of Choona, a youth who doesn't understand why his people would want to help the Nahullo, or Europeans, who have taken their land. His grandmother explains that the Choctaw suffered greatly on the forced march from the southwestern United States to Indian Territory (present-day Oklahoma) and that helping the Irish endure similar hard times would be "like an arrow shot through time," a blessing for unborn Choctaw children. The illustrations, rendered in black-and-white pencil, accurately portray elements of Choctaw daily life. *RAI Special Merit Award, 1999. ss*

455. Heneghan, James. **The Grave**. Toronto: Groundwood, 2000. ISBN 0-374-32765-3. 245p. (12 up). Novel.

See Canada for description.

456. Lally, Soinbhe. **A Hive for the Honeybee.** Illustrated by Patience Brewster. New York: Scholastic, 1999. First published by Poolbeg (Ireland) in 1996. ISBN 0-590-51038-X. 226p. (12 up). Novel.

Thora is a diligent worker bee who tirelessly fans the wax combs of the hive with her wings and cleans up after the self-important drones. Soon, however, Thora wearies of her duties and begins to dream of idly resting in the sunshine on the petals of a rose. The pull of responsibility and the dreams of leisure are framed by the practicality of Belle, another worker bee, and the poet Alfred and the intellectual, but often ignored, Mo, two drones who aspire to mate with the virgin queen. This naturalistic story depicts the delicate balance of survival and examines the proscribed roles of society. *Bisto Book of the Year Shortlist, 1997. rlk*

457. MacGrory, Yvonne. **The Secret of the Ruby Ring.** Minneapolis: Milkweed, 1994. Originally published by The Children's Press (Ireland) in 1991. ISBN 0-91594-392-1. 189p. (9-12). Novel.

This time-travel novel offers everything one expects of the genre—a plausible vehicle for travel (the ruby ring), a main character who grows from the experience, and suspense as she tries to return to her own time. Lucy takes for granted her comfortable life until, wishing for a bigger house, she is transported back to 1885 as a maid in Langley Castle. Filled with details about the "upstairs-downstairs" life in a castle as well as the political situation brewing in Ireland, this book is truly a gem. *1991 Bisto Book of the Year. ss*

458. McBratney, Sam. **I'm Sorry.** Illustrated by Jennifer Eachus. New York: HarperCollins, 2000. ISBN 0-06-028686-5. 29p. (3-5). Picture book.

With the simple phrases and childlike observations of a toddler, this book begins by establishing for readers the friendship of a boy and girl who "love [each other] the best." As the softly muted and romanticized illustrations show, the pair does everything together until they quarrel one day, as children often do, for no apparent reason. After pretending not to care about the other one, the two finally apologize in the final pages of the story and are happy together once again. The author's choice not to reveal the children's names enhances the narrative and adds a universal quality. *ebb*

459. Taylor, Alice. **A Child's Treasury of Irish Rhymes.** Illustrated by Nicola Emoe. New York: Barefoot Books, 1999. First published by Barefoot (U.K.) in 1996. ISBN 1-902283-18-X. 48p. (0-6). Anthology.

Illustrations in secondary colors and a folk art style decorate twenty-six rhymes and poems from the Irish tradition. Compiler Alice Taylor states that "rhymes that we learn when we are young stick to our minds like cream to the inside of a jug." Her collection reflects her childhood in rural Ireland and presents a window into the past for contemporary children. *RAI Children's Book of the Year, 1996. chs*

460. Thompson, Kate. **Switchers**. New York: Hyperion, 1998. First published by Aran in 1994. ISBN 0-7868-0380-0. 220p. (9-12). Novel.

Tess is a switcher, someone who can change into the form of any animal she wishes. For years she has guarded this secret, until she meets Kevin and realizes that she is not alone. Together, with some guidance from Lizzie, the one adult who seems to understand their powers, they embark on a journey north to the arctic regions, fraught with danger and adventure. The two are able to defeat the enemy, but at a seemingly terrible cost. The adventure continues in the sequel, *Midnight's Choice* (1999), when Tess, in an attempt to save her friend, must choose between the forces of good embodied by Kevin in the form of a phoenix, risen from the ashes, and the powers of evil, embodied in Martin, who has chosen the form of a vampire. *djg*

461. Tompert, Ann. **Saint Patrick**. Illustrated by Michael Garland. Honesdale, PA: Boyds Mills, 1998. ISBN 1-56397-659-5. 32p. (7-10). Picture book.

This lush presentation pairs a straightforward text with inventive, collage-style illustrations to tell the story of the boy who was captured by pirates in fourth-century Britain and taken to Ireland to become slave to a chieftain. Not particularly religious before this point, he experiences a conversion. Eventually he escapes and returns home, but he cannot ignore the call to return to Ireland and "teach the Irish heathens." He prepares by studying in Gaul (present-day France) and then carries out his mission, baptizing and confirming people throughout Ireland. An author's note discusses the sources used. *ss*

Author from the United States

Related Information

Awards
Bisto Book of the Year Award
Sponsored by Children's Books Ireland and supported by RHM Foods, the Book of the Year and three Merit Awards recognize books by authors and/or illustrators born or residing in Ireland.

Europe 199

Eilís Dillon Memorial Award
This award to the author of an outstanding first children's book is awarded only at the discretion of the judges of the Bisto Award.

Reading Association of Ireland Award
Established in 1985, this program now presents two awards every other year: the RAI Children's Book Award and the RAI Special Merit Award. The RAI is affiliated with the International Reading Association.

Organizations
Children's Books Ireland (CBI)
This national children's book organization administers the Bisto awards, noted above, and runs seminars and conferences; it also publishes *Children's Books in Ireland*, which offers news and reviews of Irish children's books. For information about CBI or the journal it publishes, e-mail childrensbooksire@eircom.net.

Online Bookstores
Eason.ie
www.eason.ie
Several categories of children's books make it easy to browse this website, which features ratings and reader reviews.

Italy

462. Cockenpot, Marianne. **Eugenio**. Illustrated by Lorenzo Mattotti. Boston: Little, Brown, 1993. Originally published by Editions du Seuil in 1993. ISBN 0-316-14922-5. 28p. (4-6). Picture book.
Abandoned in infancy and raised by a circus magician, Eugenio becomes a popular clown. He feels something is missing from his life, so his circus friends offer advice that is varied, sometimes contradictory, and ultimately unhelpful. Then the fortune-teller tells him he needs someone to love; Eugenio immediately finds an abandoned infant on the steps of his circus trailer, and the story begins again. A dozen double-page chalky pastel drawings contain surreal touches (twin acrobats' tutus merge as a Moebius strip, rising campfire smoke forms a striking flower) contributing to a magical atmosphere. Preschoolers unable to follow the philosophical aspects of the text will nevertheless enjoy the colorful circus illustrations and pick up the basic message about love. *pm*

463. Daly, Niki. **Bravo, Zan Angelo!** Farrar, Straus & Giroux, 1998. First published by Frances Lincoln (U.K.) in 1998. ISBN 0-374-30953-1. 32p. (5-8). Picture book.

See Africa South of the Sahara/South Africa for description.

464. Fischetto, Laura. **Harlequin and the Green Dress.** Illustrated by Letizia Galli. New York: Delacorte, 1994. ISBN 0-385-31073-0. 32p. (7-9). Picture book.

Punch, Columbine, and other characters from Italy's *commedia dell'arte* (performance art popular from the sixteenth to the eighteenth century) tell this romantic farce that centers around a masked ball, mistaken identity, and a stolen green dress. Harlequin loves Columbine, Florindo loves Rosaura, and both cook up schemes to win their loved ones' hearts. But plans run awry and the clown Punch complicates the plot. Following the story is a two-page description of *commedia dell'arte* that explains its relevance to today's comedy. *cc*

465. Fleming, Candace. **Gabriella's Song.** Illustrated by Giselle Potter. New York: Atheneum, 1997. ISBN 0-689-80973-5. 32p. (3-8). Picture book.

To Gabriella, Venice is "the city of music." She hears melodies and rhythms around her as she walks home, including the songs of the street traders and the "jing-aling-ling of *lire.*" From these sounds she fashions a song that she passes on to others, including a composer who turns her song into a symphony. The fluid lines of Giselle Potter's cartoon-style illustrations (with musical notes dancing across the pages) evoke the lilting rhythm of Gabriella's song; while the ochre and blue-gray tones of the buildings, surrounded by expanses of sea and sky, evoke the beauty of Venice. An author's note tells about Venice's association with opera. *ALA Notable Children's Book, 1998. hc*
Author from the United States

466. Guarnieri, Paolo. **A Boy Named Giotto.** Translated by Jonathan Galassi. Illustrated by Bímba Landmann. New York: Farrar, Straus & Giroux, 1999. Originally published as *Un bambino di nome Giotto* by Edizione Arka in 1998. ISBN 0-374-30931-0. 26p. (7-12). Picture book.

The painting by a young shepherd boy inspired by the art of Cimabue impresses the artist enough to accept him as his student. Giotto goes on to outdo his master. The story, told simply but with feeling for the zeal and ambition of the youth, is illustrated in a style based on the paintings. The palette is rich with gold and umbers, while the varying sized, framed pictures of landscapes and interiors suggest the emerging

Renaissance perspective. *km, sm*

467. Parillo, Tony. **Michelangelo's Surprise**. Illustrated by the author. New York: Farrar, Straus & Giroux, 1998. ISBN 0-374-34961-4. 29p. (7-12). Picture book.

Based on an actual historical event, this book tells the story of Piero de Medici's plan for a festival following a heavy snowfall in Florence, Italy. Sandro, the youngest page in the palazzo, overhears the ruler summon Michelangelo, the sculptor. Sandro searches for his father to find out whether he knows why the sculptor has been summoned, only to find Michelangelo himself on his father's shoulders creating a sculpture, not out of stone, but out of snow! An afterword includes background information about Michelangelo. *hr*
Author from the United States

468. Scuderi, Lucia. **To Fly**. English-language text adaptation by Phillis Gershator and Robin Blum. New York: Kane/Miller, 1998. Originally published in 1997. ISBN 0-916291-79-0. 38p. (4-8). Picture book.

Peck, peck, pop—out hatch three baby birds. Walk, walk, walking until one disappears. In large fold-out pages the young reader finds one bird trying to fly, but too soon. Not to be discouraged, the bird tries and tries "To Fly!" and eventually does. Full pages fold up and out, truly extending the very simple text. *djg*

469. Testa, Fulvio. **A Long Trip to Z**. San Diego: Harcourt Brace, 1997. First published by Andersen Press in 1997. ISBN 0-15-201610-4. 28p. (4-7). Picture book.

A is for airplane, which flies out of the book and takes the reader on a fanciful ride, past the cage, through the crack in the door, to faraway islands, jungles, and even planets. Each letter is an imaginary journey, but the tired adventurer arrives yawning, back home just in time for bed. *djg*

470. Visconti, Guido. **The Genius of Leonardo**. Translated by Mark Roberts. Illustrated by Bimba Landmann. New York: Barefoot Books, 2000. Originally published As *Quel Genio de Leonardo* by Edizioni Arka in 2000. ISBN 1-84148-301-X. 40p. (9-13). Biography.

This sketch of Leonardo da Vinci's life and ideas is largely seen through the eyes of his lively and larcenous apprentice, Giacomo. Full-page, stylized color illustrations fill out some of the details of the paintings and setting. The endpapers are decorated with small drawings of Leonardo's studies. *ak*

Related Information

Online Bookstores
Bol.com
www.it.bol.com
The Italian version of Bol follows the familiar format of the online bookstore and is easy to negotiate, even for those who do not know the Italian language.

Lithuania

471. Gold, Alison Leslie. **A Special Fate: Chiune Sugihara: Hero of the Holocaust.** New York: Scholastic. 2000. ISBN 0-590-09525-4. 176p. (10-14). Biography.

Chiune Sugihara, Japanese vice consul in Lithuania in the 1940s, defied orders from his government and issued transit visas that permitted thousands of Jewish refugees to travel through the Soviet Union to Japan. Gold's inclusion of the stories of Masha Bernstein and Solly Ganor, two children who received visas from Sugihara, adds to this well-researched account (based in part on interviews with Sugihara's wife, Yukiko, and other witnesses) of Sugihara's incredible humanitarian deeds. In an epilogue, Gold covers Sugihara's life after the war and later honors in recognition of his rescue of 6,000 Jews during the Holocaust, including Israel's Righteous among the Nations Medal (1985) and the Nagasaki Peace Prize (1985). *ca*
Author from the United States

The Netherlands

472. Bos, Burny. **Meet the Molesons.** Translated by J. Alison James. Illustrated by Hans de Beer. New York: North-South, 1994. Originally published as *Familie Maulwurf Bitte recht freundlich!* by Nord-Süd in 1994. ISBN 1-55858-257-6. 46p. (7-9). Transitional book.

Eight generously illustrated chapters follow the adventures and misadventures of the Moleson family narrated in droll conversational style by young Dug (short for Dugless). Comic drawings capture the family's eccentric way of turning even the most ordinary activity into a not-to-be-forgotten experience. Other titles include *More from the Molesons* and *Leave*

It to the Molesons. cl

473. Bruna, Dick. **Miffy in the Hospital.** Translated by Patricia Crampton. New York: Kodansha America, 1999. Originally published as *Nijntje in het ziekenhuis* by Mercis Publishing in 1975. ISBN 1-56836-297-8. 26p. (4-7). Picture book.
Miffy the rabbit is not feeling very strong and her throat feels funny, too. When mother takes her to the doctor they must go right to the hospital. In simple text and illustration, Bruna is able to comfort and reassure the youngest child. One of a series of books recently rereleased about this charming rabbit, including *Miffy at the Museum, Miffy Is Crying, Miffy at the Zoo,* and *Miffy's Dream. djg*

474. de Vries, Anke. **Piggy's Birthday Dream.** Illustrated by Jung-Hee Spetter. Asheville, NC: Front Street/Lemniscaat, 1997. Originally published as *Lang zal ik leven!* by Lemniscaat in 1997. ISBN 1-886910-21-9. 26p. (4-6). Picture book.
Piggy, who is very shy, can't get up the nerve to invite anyone to her birthday party and so she celebrates alone. Then she goes to bed, falls asleep, and dreams how much fun the other animals have playing together. She is wishing that she had friends to play with when she is pleasantly awakened by the animals, who throw her a spectacular party. She is so pleased that she forgets to be shy. *pc*

475. Fisher, Leonard Everett. **Kinderdike.** Illustrated by the author. New York: Macmillan, 1994. ISBN 0-02-735365-6. 32p. (4-9). Picture book.
The tragic 1421 flood in Holland is told in rhyme accompanied by full-color paintings. The sparse text enriched by the lavish splashes of color tells the tale of a baby and kitten found alive on the dike after the floodwater recedes, a sign to the survivors to have the faith to rebuild, restore, and, in the process, to recover. *bjk*
Author from the United States

476. Hol, Coby. **The Birth of the Moon.** Translated by Sibylle Kazeroid. New York: North-South, 2000. Originally published as *La naissance de la lune* by Hatier Littérature Générale. ISBN 0-7358-1249-7. 24p. (4-6). Picture book.
When the animals ask the sun to shine at night so that they can see things, the sun explains that it must shine on the other side of the world, too, but offers them a "surprise": a tiny crescent moon. When they request

even more light, the sun has the moon grow larger night after night until it is a full moon. The animals soon take nighttime light for granted. The sun, sad and angered by their ungratefulness, takes the moon away. The animals apologize, and the sun agrees to provide a cycle of waxing and waning moon to remind them to appreciate its gift. The spare text for this original *pourquoi* tale is enriched by simple, well-composed illustrations done with torn and cut paper, spattered ink, and watercolors. *ca*

477. Holtwijk, Ineke. **Asphalt Angels**. Translated by Wanda Boeke. Asheville, NC: Front Street/Lemniscaat, 1999. Originally published as *Engelen van het Asfalt* by Lemniscaat in 1995. ISBN 1-886910-24-3. 184p. (14 up). Novel.

At thirteen, when Alex's foster mother dies and his abusive stepfather kicks him out of the house, his only recourse is to live on the streets of Rio de Janeiro. Faced with starvation and desperately needing a family, he joins the Asphalt Angels, a ragged group of children who live from hand to mouth by stealing. Alex's valiant hope for a better life, despite the horrible depravity he resists and the sorrow he endures, makes him a true hero. Graphic descriptions make this book suitable only for older, more mature, readers. Informative afterword and glossary of Portuguese terms. *Mildred L. Batchelder Honor Book, 2000. cmt*

478. Kraan, Hanna. **The Wicked Witch Is at It Again**. Translated by Wanda Boeke. Illustrated by Annemarie Haeringen. Asheville, NC: Front Street/Lemniscaat, 1997 (Paperback: Puffin, 1998). Originally published as *De bose heks is weer bezig!* by Lemniscaat in 1992. ISBN 0-14-130078-7. 128p. (7-9). Novel.

One of the author's very popular series about the misadventures of a group of animal friends who must share their forest with a witch, this book is every bit as good as its predecessors. In every chapter, the witch has cooked up some new mischief that the owl, the hedgehog, the hare, and other of their friends must try to counter. The reader gradually realizes that the witch is not really wicked, just mischievous and a bit lonely. The animals realize that their woods would be a lot less interesting without her wacky pranks. Other titles include *Tales of the Wicked Witch* and *Flowers for the Wicked Witch. fk*

479. Moeyaert, Bart. **Bare Hands**. Translated by David Colmer. Asheville, NC: Front Street, 1998. Originally published as *Blote handen* by E. M. Querido's Uitgeverij in 1995. ISBN 1-886910-32-4. 111p. (10-14). Novel.

The new year is supposed to be a time of new beginnings, but Ward is off to a bad start. On New Year's Eve, he accidentally kills a neighbor's duck and has to deal with the heartbreaking consequences. The fact that the neighbor, a coarse, lonely farmer, is courting his mother does not help matters. Their tense battle of wills is played out against a stark, cold, and windy landscape and comes to a climax under a night lit with a spectacular fireworks display. *1998 Deutscher Jungendliteraturpreis. mm*

480. Moeyaert, Bart. **Hornet's Nest.** Asheville, NC: Front Street, 2000. First published as *Wespennest* by E. M. Querido's Uitgeverij in 1995. ISBN 1-886910-48-0. 128p. (12 up). Novel.

The hornet's nest of the title refers to the small village where fourteen-year-old Susanna has grown up. From the outside it may appear calm, but under the surface it roils with resentments, grudges, and loyalties born of the past. A stranger who comes to town advises Susanna to either get out or stir up the nest; she chooses the latter by engineering a confrontation between a dog owner and those who have been complaining about the dogs. Told in chapters alternating between past and present, this moody story requires close reading and offers no pat ending. *ss*

481. Padt, Maartje, and Mylo Freeman. **Shanti.** New York: DK, 1998. English-language text by Lenny Hort. Originally published as *Shanti de Zebra* by Zirkoon uitgevers in 1998. ISBN 0-7894-2520-3. 32p. (5-8). Picture book.

Something is about to happen to Shanti, a young zebra on the African plains, but she does not know what it is. She falls behind her herd and encounters a lion, chameleon, monkeys, rhinoceros, viper, giraffe, turtle, crocodile, and elephants, all of whom tell her not to worry; she will not be alone for long. Then the wonderful thing she's been waiting for happens. She gives birth to a baby, and the herd returns to welcome her colt. Freeman's brilliantly colored batik paintings add to the mystery and intensity of this gentle tale. *lh*

482. Pallandt, Nicolas van. **Troll's Search for Summer.** Illustrated by the author. New York: Farrar, Straus & Giroux, 1994. Originally published by Lemniscaat in 1994. ISBN 0-374-36560-1. 24p. (5-7). Picture book.

When the wind blows Troll away from his cozy home, he is lost in the dark, spooky forest. Instead of searching for his small home, lost in winter, he decides to search for summer. In his search, he is joined by other creatures, who together circle back to Troll's home to await summer's warmth.

Detailed watercolor paintings depict mystical, nocturnal winter scenes. *chs*

483. Pelgrom, Els. **The Acorn Eaters.** Translated by Johanna H. Prins and Johanna W. Prins. New York: Farrar, Straus & Giroux. 1997. Originally published as *De eikelvreters* by E. M. Querido's Uitgeverij in 1989. ISBN 0-374-30029-1. 211p. (12-14). Novel.

A vivid depiction of rural Andalusia after the Spanish Civil War (1936-1939), where families live in limestone caves and eke out a living from the land. Young Santiago comes of age in this mountainous land of farms, olive groves, and gypsies. Through his innocent but intelligent eyes, he relates the everyday lives of his family and neighbors and the hardships they face. His ingenuity, determination, and love for his family see him through years of hunger, backbreaking labor, and oppression. Includes glossary of Spanish words and Spanish text of songs appearing in novel. *1990 Golden Pencil Award. mm*

484. Propp, Vera W. **When the Soldiers Were Gone.** New York: Putnam, 1999. (Paperback: Puffin, 2001). ISBN 0-399-23325-3. 102p. (8-12). Novel.

Henk loves living with Mama and Papa on the farm, so he's confused when a pale couple comes to visit and are introduced as his parents. Worse yet, Mama and Papa tell him he must go home with these people, who call him Benjamin. Set in the Netherlands directly after World War II, this is the story of a Jewish child hidden by a Christian family during the Nazi occupation. The details of how he was successfully protected unfold at about the same rate as he acclimates to his new life and identity, making this both an accessible and satisfying read. *ss*
Author from the United States

485. Quintana, Anton. **The Baboon King.** Translated by John Nieuwenhuizen. New York: Walker, 1999. Originally published as *De havianenkoning* by Em. Querido's Uitgeverij in 1982. First English-language edition published in Australia in 1996. ISBN 0-8027-8711-8. 183p. (12-14). Novel.

Morengáru, half Kikuyu and half Masai, has suffered the contempt of both tribes because he is different. Mistreated, ridiculed, and rejected since childhood, he is finally banished and retreats deep into the wilderness of Kenya. There, he is challenged by the leader of a troop of baboons, wins, and reluctantly becomes the new baboon king. Through his successful leadership of the troop, he gains a deeper understanding of tolerance and being different, realizes his own worth, and so decides to return to the human world. *2000 Mildred L. Batchelder Award. cmt*

486. Schubert, Dieter and Ingrid. **Abracadabra**. Translated by the publisher. Illustrated by Dieter Schubert. Asheville, NC: Front Street, 1997. Originally published in the Netherlands by Lemniscaat in 1996. ISBN 1-886910-17-0. 32p. (6-9). Picture book.

Macrobius the Magician casts spells on all the forest animals, giving the hare extraordinarily long ears and the fox the webbed feet of a goose. To get back at him the animals join forces to steal his wand, terrify him by impersonating a large beast, and threaten to turn him into a mushroom. The colorful illustrations contribute to the humor of this offbeat open-ended tale. *lh*

487. Schubert, Ingrid and Dieter. **Bear's Eggs**. Asheville, NC: Front Street, 1999. Originally published as *Dat komt er nou van . . .* by Lemniscaat in 1999. ISBN 1-886910-46-4. 28p. (3-7). Picture book.

Bear finds three eggs and builds a nest so they can hatch. Teaching goslings to swim and fly is a challenge for a land-bound creature like Bear, one that he meets with creativity. Watercolor illustrations capture Bear's many emotional responses, and observant children will notice recurring characters portrayed in the woodland setting. *ss*

488. Schubert, Ingrid and Dieter. **There's a Hole in My Bucket**. Translated by Heinrich Lieber. Illustrated by the authors. Asheville, NC: Front Street, 1998. Originally published as *En Gat in Mijn Emmer* by Lemniscaat in 1998. ISBN 1-886910-28-6. 24p. (2-6). Picture book.

Bear's flowers are wilting, and he can't water them because his bucket has a hole in it. His friend Hedgehog offers to help him fix it, but the two are unsuccessful in their efforts. However, a rainstorm solves the problem—temporarily. Endearing full-spread watercolor paintings that capture the humor of the retelling complement this winsome adaptation of a German folk song. *jr*

489. Spetter, Jung-Hee. **Lily and Trooper's Spring**. Asheville, NC: Front Street, 1999. Originally published as *Lentekriebels* by Lemniscaat in 1998. ISBN 1-886910-36-7. 26p. (4-6). Picture book.

Lily and her dog, Trooper, spend a perfect spring day listening to the birds, going on a picnic, running from the cow, climbing a tree, swinging, romping in the field with the sheep, and sliding into the mud with the pigs. Never daunted, Lily cleans herself up and sets off for more fun in the park. Brightly colored cartoon-style illustrations capture the springtime delight in this book, which completes the seasons series of *Lily and Trooper's Summer* (1998), *Lily and Trooper's Fall* (1998), and *Lily and Trooper's Winter* (1998). *djg*

490. Talbott, Hudson. **Forging Freedom: A True Story of Heroism during the Holocaust.** Illustrated by the author. New York: Putnam, 2000. ISBN 0-399-23434-9. 64p. (10-12). Informational book.

Talbott details the quiet heroism of Jaap Penraat, a Dutchman who helped 406 Jews escape Nazi-occupied Amsterdam during World War II. He follows both the growing popularity and dislike of Nazism through Penraat's boyhood into the war. Penraat as a young man uses the skills he learned at his father's printing shop to forge documents for his Jewish friends. As it becomes more obvious that the Nazis seek to eradicate the Jewish population, Penraat extends his plans to assist Jews to escape from Europe. Talbott's lavish and dramatic illustrations contribute highly to the work. *cc*

Author from the United States

Related Information

Awards

Jenny Smelik-IBBY Prize

This award is given annually to the author/illustrator/initiator of a work of children's fiction that contributes to better understanding of ethnic minorities.

Golden Brush Award

This is given for the year's most beautiful illustrations, with up to two Silver Brush Awards given to honorable mentions.

Golden Kiss Award

Established in 1997, this is the counterpart to the Golden Pencil for young adult novels; similarly, honor books are given the Silver Kiss Award.

Golden Pencil Award

This annual prize for the best children's book is considered the most important Dutch prize; honor books are called Silver Pencils and up to six are awarded annually.

The Netherlands shares a common language with Flanders, one of the federal states of Belgium, and a group of Flemish awards corresponds to the above. They are the **Book Lion** (with honor books called Book Cubs) given for text and the **Book Peacock** given for illustrations. Several other national prizes are awarded for children's books. The website of the Dutch publisher E. M. Querido's Uitgeverij offers a good explanation at www.querido.nl/summary.html.

Online Bookstores
Bol.com
www.nl.bol.com
   This site follows the familiar format of the online bookstore and is easy to negotiate, even for those who do not know Dutch.

Norway

491. Gaarder, Jostein. **Hello? Is Anybody There?** Translated by James Anderson. Illustrated by Sally Gardner. New York: Farrar, Straus & Giroux, 1998. First published as *Hallo? Er det noen her?* by Gyldendal Norsk in 1996. ISBN 0-374-32948-6. 144p. (8-12). Novel.
   Eight-year-old Joe is about to become a big brother, but when his mother leaves for the hospital, he suddenly has bigger problems than that. He finds a little boy from outer space hanging in a tree outside his window. Joe teaches Miko about the natural wonders and evolution of his world while learning how different it is in Miko's world in this fantasy work, reminiscent of *The Little Prince*, both in theme and in illustration. Joe learns that "traveling brings you farther out into the world. Dreaming draws you farther inside it. But maybe we can't travel in more than one direction at once." Whether a dream or real, Mika helps Joe adjust to the idea of a new baby in the house and instills a love of astronomy. *2000 IBBY Honor List. djg*

492. Kaldhol, Marit. **Goodbye Rune**. Illustrated by Wenche Oyen. Translated by Michael Crosby-Jones. English adaptation by Catherine Maggs. New York: Kane/Miller, 1987. Originally published as *Farvel, Rune* by Det Norske Samlaget in 1986. ISBN 0-916291-11-1. 26p. (6-10). Picture book.
   As long as Sara could remember, Rune had been her best friend. But when her friend dies, Sara struggles to understand. With the help of her parents she comes to terms with his death and her feelings of loss and sadness in this sensitively told story. Impressionistic watercolor illustrations provide a comforting touch. *djg*

493. Newth, Mette. **The Dark Light**. New York: Farrar, Straus & Giroux, 1998. Translated by Faith Ingwersen. First published by H. Aschehoug in

1995. ISBN 0-374-31701-1. 244p. (12-14). Novel.

In the early 1800s, thirteen-year-old Tora, stricken by leprosy after her mother's death from the same disease, is taken by her pastor to St. Jørgen's Hospital, Bergen. Here, in terrible conditions—hunger, overcrowding, deteriorating buildings—Tora learns to survive by helping others, especially the raging and despairing woman, Sunniva, who teaches Tora to read. As Tora, a model of courage, approaches her own death, she is reconciled with her father, who carries her to the mountain where her mother chose to die. A historical map of Bergen and a postscript with details about the diagnosis of leprosy by Norwegian doctors are provided. *ALA Best Books for Young Adults, 1999. hc*

494. Newth, Mette. **The Transformation**. Translated from the Norwegian by Faith Ingwersen. New York: Farrar, Straus & Giroux, 2000. Originally published as *Forandringen* by H. Aschehoug in 1997. ISBN 0-374-37752-9. 195p. (12-16). Novel.

Brendan, a young Irish monk, is sent to Greenland in the fifteenth century to convert the "heathens" to Christianity in accordance with a Bull issued by Pope Nicholas V. Through his relationship with the young woman, Navarana, who develops into a powerful shaman, Brendan undergoes a transformation. He journeys to the world's end to meet Raven, who has stolen the sun. Newth weaves together a story about the power of faith with elements of mysticism and myth set in a stark and beautiful land that also undergoes a transformation as the sun returns after three years of endless winter. *hc*

495. Sortland, Bjørn. **Anna's Art Adventure**. Translated by James Anderson. Illustrated by Lars Elling. Minneapolis: Carolrhoda, 1999. Originally published as *Raudt, blått og litt gult* by Det Norske Samlaget in 1993. ISBN 1-57505-376-4. (7-9). Picture book.

Anna, about seven, visits an art museum with her uncle and magically meets notable artists from the Old Masters to postmodernists, such as Rembrandt, Van Gogh, Chagall, Magritte, Mondrian, Munch, Dali, and Pollack. Outstanding works of the featured artists, rendered in styles remarkably faithful to the originals, serve to give young readers a short course on art history from the seventeenth century to present day. Young readers may appreciate the humor of Anna's desperate attempts to find a toilet, but the illustrations are the best part of the story. *cmt*

496. Sortland, Bjørn. **The Story of the Search for the Story**. Translated by James Anderson. Illustrated by Lars Elling. Minneapolis: Carolrhoda, 2000. Originally published as *Forteljinga om Jakta pa Forteljinga* by Det Norske Samlaget in 1995. ISBN 1-57505-375-6. 40p. (10-12). Picture book. When the loose letters fall out of Henry's book, leaving only blank pages, his Uncle Richard sends him to the library for a replacement. Along the way, Henry stumbles into a fantasy adventure where he meets famous writers from James Joyce to Salman Rushdie and creates his own story, which includes a discussion of censorship. Surrealistic paintings contribute to the sense of fantasy, and appended at the book's end are brief bios of the authors and characters Henry meets: James Joyce, Knut Hamsun, Virginia Woolf, Ernest Hemingway, Karen Blixen/Isaac Dinesen, Antoine de Saint-Exupery, Marcel Proust, Astrid Lindgren, Pippi Longstocking, William Shakespeare, Henrik Ibsen, Miguel Cervantes, Franz Kafka, and Salman Rushdie. *pm*

Related Information

Awards

Kulturdepartementets premiering / Norwegian Ministry of Culture Literary Prize
This annual prize is awarded in the categories of fiction, picture book, first book, nonfiction, translation, and illustration.

Publications

Tidsskriftet Alberto / Scandinavian journal of children's and young adult's literature
riff.hiof.no/~steinabl/asla3.html
The electronic version of this journal is named for Alberto, the character in Jostein Gaarder's *Sophie's World*; written in Norwegian, it has summaries in English and provides worthwhile links.

Organizations

Norskbarnebokinstitutt (NBI) / Norwegian Institute for Children's Books
www.barnebokinstituttet.no
Box 6719 St. Olavs plass, 0130 Oslo, Norway; tel. 47 22 11 12 80; fax 47 22 11 27 02; e-mail: biblioteket@barnebokinstituttet.no
NBI is a national center of expertise for literature for children and young people in Norway that serves the public as well as academic institutions in and outside of Norway; its website has an English-language option.

Poland

497. Isaacs, Anne. **Torn Thread**. New York: Scholastic Press, 2000. ISBN 0-590-60363-9. 188p. (12 up). Novel.

Eva Buchbinder was only twelve when she and her sister were sent from a loving home in Bedzin, Poland, to work in a Nazi slave-labor camp for girls and young women in Parchnitz, Czechoslovakia. From June 1943 until May 1943, Eva and Rachel lived and worked in such hazardous and filthy conditions that Rachel nearly died of typhus. Although they survived the Holocaust, an epilogue reveals to readers that the girls' father and extended family members were all sent to their deaths at Auschwitz in August 1943. An endnote provides historical facts regarding Eva, her family members, and the labor camp in Parchnitz. Depicted fictionally, this story is told in third person but from the perspective of Eva, a brave and strong girl. The author is Eva's daughter-in-law. *ebb*
Author from the United States

498. Lobel, Anita. **No Pretty Pictures: A Child of War**. New York: Greenwillow, 1998. ISBN 0-688-15935-4. 190p. (12-14). Autobiography.

Beginning with the marching of the Nazis into Kraków in 1939 when she was five years old, Lobel narrates how she and her brother hid in villages with their nanny, Niania, and later, in a convent. Eventually captured, they survive transports, marches, and concentration camps until taken to Sweden in 1945. Here, they are treated for tuberculosis and reunited with their parents before emigrating to the United States. Lobel tells how her time in Sweden awakened her love of books and art. An epilogue provides the full story of why she and her brother were saved when first arrested. *ALA Top 10 Best Books for Young Adults, 1999; ALA Notable Book, 1999. hc*
Author from the United States

499. Nieuwsma, Milton J. **Kinderlager: An Oral History of Young Holocaust Survivors**. New York: Holiday House, 1998. ISBN 0-8234-1358-6. 16p. (12 up). Informational book.

This book traces the lives of three Holocaust survivors who were children living in the Polish town of Tomaszo Mazowiecki when World War II shattered their innocence. The three survivors—Tova Friedman, Frieda Tenenbaum, and Rachel Hyams—tell their overlapping tragedies in first person, beginning with their prewar days, continuing with their imprisonment in the Kinderlager at Auschwitz-Birkenau, and ending at least momentarily with their liberation. Unlike many other Holocaust stories, however, these survivors' stories also chron-

icle the devastating long-term effects—including repressed memories, shared secrets, and failed relationships—the war had on them as a result of being children in concentration camps. Black-and-white family photographs enhance the stories; even those taken after the liberation help to illustrate the profound and immeasurable loss the survivors suffered. A glossary and epilogue render the stories even more accessible than they would be otherwise. *ebb*
Author from the United States

500. Radin, Ruth Yaffe. **Escape to the Forest.** Illustrated by Janet Hamlin. New York: HarperCollins, 2000. ISBN 0-06-028520-6. 90p. (9-12). Novel.

This fictional story, based on the life of an actual person, recounts the experiences of a Jewish family, inhabitants of a village in eastern Poland that is first invaded by the Russian army and then occupied by the Germans. Forced to move into a ghetto the family manages to survive and stay together; some members advocate escaping into the forest, where Tuvia Bielski and his band of resisters have formed camps, while others think they will be safer in the ghetto. Then they are ordered on a march to a line of waiting boxcars, and only three members of the family are able to melt into the sidelines and get away. They meet again at Tuvia's camp and become the only members of their family to survive the Holocaust. *ss*
Author from the United States

501. Silverman, Erica. **Raisel's Riddle.** Illustrated by Susan Gaber. New York: Farrar, Straus & Giroux, 1999. ISBN 0-374-36168-1. 32p. (7-12). Picture book.

In a Jewish version of the Cinderella tale set in Poland, a young girl's kindness to an old beggar enables her to attend a Purim costume ball, where she wins the heart of the rabbi's son with a profound riddle. *sg*
Author from the United States

Related Information

Awards
Book of the Year
Established in 1988 by the Polish Section of IBBY and financed by the Ministry of Culture and the Arts; awarded annually to living writers, artists, and publishers for outstanding accomplishments in the production of books for children.

Children's Best-Seller of the Year Award
Established in 1991 and given to the best Polish or foreign book pub-

lished in Poland. Two prizes are awarded, one selected by a jury of children (Little Dong) and the second by a jury of adults (Big Dong).

Kornel Makuszynski Literary Award
Established in 1994 by the Ksiaska dla Dziecka Foundation and the publisher of *Guliwer* magazine; awarded annually to a living Polish author for a book for younger children published in the preceding year.

Russia

502. Brewster, Hugh. **Anastasia's Album.** New York: Hyperion, 1996. First published by Madison Press in 1996. Photographs by Peter Christopher. ISBN 0-7868-0292-8. 64 pages. (10 up). Biography.
See Canada for description.

503. Gorbachev, Valeri. **Peter's Picture.** Illustrated by the author. New York: North-South, 2000. ISBN 1-55858-965-1. 32p. (1-6). Picture book.
Peter walks home from school proudly showing a picture of a flower he drew to all he meets, who in turn compliment the work by suggesting what to do with it. Smelling it, giving it to bees, and planting it are not acceptable to the young artist, so Peter is especially pleased when his mother and father immediately frame and hang his work. The pen-and-ink detail humorously personifies each animal character while soft watercolor shades add warmth to this family story. *jbm*
Author from the United States

504. Gukova, Julia. **All Mixed-Up: A Mixed-Up Matching Book.** New York: North-South, 2000. Originally published by Nord-Süd in 1999. ISBN 0-7358-1300-0. 32 p. (4-6). Picture book.
This clever toy book is essentially wordless. Phineas the photographer has photographed thirteen of his animal friends, but a mischievous witch has mixed his photos up. The gimmick is to flip the split pages to align the correct heads, bodies, and legs. Since Phineas has some unusual friends, it's harder—and more fun—than it sounds! A built-in answer key is itself a matching exercise since children can double-check their choices by matching the size and orientation of the answer key symbol. Intended for a younger audience, it will intrigue children as old as ten. *fk*

505. Marshak, Samuel. **The Absentminded Fellow.** Translated by Richard Pevear. Illustrated by Marc Rosenthal. New York: Farrar, Straus & Giroux, 1999. Adaptation of work originally published as *Vot Kakoi Rasseyannii* in the Soviet Union in 1928. ISBN 0-374-30013-5. 32p. (4-6). Picture book. From the moment he awakes, the amiable, confused fellow from Portobello Road is in such a hurry he rushes headlong from one humorous disaster to another to the dismay of all witnesses to his ineptitude. The illustrations in this rhyming tale are in vintage cartoon style, reminiscent of the classic Tintin comic books by Hergé, and they reinforce the feeling of wild motion and broad humor. *sg*

506. Prokofiev, Sergei. **Peter and the Wolf.** Adapted by Gerlinde Wiencirz. Translated by Anthea Bell. Illustrated by Julia Gukova. New York: North-South Books, 1999. Originally published as *Peter und der Wolf* by Nord-Süd in 1999. ISBN 0-7358-1188-1. 26p. (4-9). Picture book.

All the characters in the symphonic fairy tale are brought to life in their forest setting, along with Peter's house and the pond in the meadow, while Grandfather warns Peter of the dangerous wolf. When the hungry wolf turns up and gobbles the duck, Peter catches him with the help of the bird. Gukova's naturalistic, opaque and textured double-page paintings add details of place to the action. We see the transformation of the wolf from beast to victim to contented captive on the way to the zoo with the bumbling hunters. *km, sm*

507. Wassiljewa, Tatjana. **Hostage to War: A True Story.** Translated from the German translation of the original Russian by Anna Trenter. New York: Scholastic, 1997. German edition published by Beltz Verlag in 1994. ISBN 0-590-13446-9. 188p. (12-14). Novel.

Tatjana was thirteen when the Germans invaded Wyritza near Leningrad in 1941. In her diary, she records her journey to save the family from starvation, the death of her father, and how she was sent to Magdeburg as a captive laborer. In miserable conditions and always hungry, Tatjana slaves mainly in factories until 1944, when she escapes during bombing raids. It is 1946 before she is able to find her way back to Leningrad and her family. Back home, Tatjana has to fight for the right to continue her education but eventually graduates as a teacher. Historical note provided. *hc*

Related Information

Awards

Alexander Green Prize

Named for a romanticist, this prize, which includes a diploma and a monetary award, is usually given for literary works for children and young people that are imbued with romanticism and hope.

Slovak Republic

508. Winter, Kathryn. **Katarína**. New York: Farrar, Straus & Giroux, 1998. (Paperback: Scholastic, 1999). ISBN 0-374-33984-8. 257p. (12-14). Novel.

During World War II in Slovakia, Katarína, a young Jewish girl, lives with her loving Aunt Lena. As conditions worsen with the war, Katarína's aunt sends her to live with a family on a farm, telling them that Katarina is a Catholic orphan. It is discovered that Katarína is a Jew, and under pressure from people in the village, the family sends Katarína out on the road alone. Eventually Katarína finds a home in a Protestant orphanage, where she waits for the war to end. *pc*

Author from the United States

Spain

509. Alcantara, Ricardo. **Dog and Cat**. Translated by Elizabeth Uhlig. Illustrated by Gusti. Brookfield, CT: Millbrook, 1999. Originally published as *Chien et Chat* by Hachette in 1998. ISBN 0-7613-1420-2. 32p. (4-6). Picture book.

Child's-eye-view color drawings accompany this realistic story of a dog and cat during their first day in a new house. They act mean toward each other until becoming friends to face their common fear of the night. Young children will relate to this engaging tale, and older students may discover a lesson about ethnic prejudice. *rta*

510. Borton de Treviño, Elizabeth. **I, Juan de Pareja**. New York: Farrar, Straus & Giroux, 1965. ISBN 0-374-33531-1. 180p. (9-12). Novel.

The slave, Juan de Pareja, narrates the story of his life, as he is first sold, then abandoned by transporters, then finds his way into the household of seventeenth-century Spanish painter Velazquez. He learns to expertly mix paint and prepare canvases, and yearns to create his own works of art. This is the story, in Trevino's own words, of two men "who began in youth as master and slave, continued as companions in their maturity and ended as equals and friends." *1966 Newbery Medal. djg*

Author from the United States

511. Keselman, Gabriela. **The Gift**. Translated by Laura McKenna. Illustrated by Pep Montserrat. New York: Kane/Miller, 1999. Originally published as *El Regal* by La Galera in 1996. ISBN 0-916291-91-X. 52p. (3-7). Picture book.

Mr. and Mrs. Goodparents are sitting in their thinking chair, trying to decide on a special birthday gift for their son, Mikie. When they ask him what he wants, his clues only add to their confusion. Finally, they give him a big hug, which is what he wanted all along. Stylized art and fold-out pages that illustrate the parents' quirky ideas add to the fun. *Generalitat de Catalunya Illustrated Book for Children 1997; 1998 IBBY Honor List. jr*

512. Pelgrom, Els. **The Acorn Eaters.** Translated by Johanna H. Prins and Johanna W. Prins. New York: Farrar, Straus & Giroux. 1997. Originally published as *De eikelvreters* by E. M. Querido's Uitgeverij in 1989. ISBN 0-374-30029-1. 211p. (12-14). Novel.
See Europe/The Netherlands for description.

513. Vendrell, Carme Solé. **Jon's Moon.** New York: Kane/Miller, 1999. Originally published as *La Lluna D'en Joan* by Ediciones Hymsa in 1982. ISBN 0-916291-87-1. 32p. (7-9). Picture book.
During a terrible storm, a huge wave strikes Jon's father's tiny fishing boat and his spirit sinks to the bottom of the sea. When Jon's "silent, cold, and still" father returns home, John tucks him in bed, then seeks the help of the moon to recover his father's spirit from deep beneath the sea, where an octopus is holding it. Blinded by the moon's brilliance, the octopus drops the spirit. Upon returning home, Jon lovingly restores it to his father. The beautifully composed mixed-media illustrations feature a wide-eyed Peter and a quirky big-nosed full moon. *ca*

Related Information

Awards

Premio Lazarillo
Established in 1958, this is the oldest and most prestigious award for children's literature by Spanish or Spanish-speaking writers.

Comisión Católica Española de la Infancia Prize
Given to the publisher for a book written in Castilian by a Spanish or Spanish-speaking writer and published in the preceding year.

Catalonian International Award of Illustration
Awarded by the Generalitat de Catalunya, a region of Spain and home to the Catalan language.

Online Bookstores
Bol.com
www.es.bol.com

Spain's version of Bol follows the familiar format of the online bookstore and is easy to negotiate, even for those who do not know the Spanish language.

Sweden

514. Anderson, Lena. **Tea for Ten**. Translated by Elisabeth Kallick Dyssegaard. New York: R&S Books, 2000. Originally published as *Lilla Kotten får besök* by Eriksson & Lindgren in 1998. ISBN 91-29-64557-3. 26p. (2-5). Picture book.

Little Hedgehog is only one and feeling lonely, until, one by one, nine of her friends knock on her door and join her for tea and then they are ten. Simple rhyming text appears on each left-hand page. Numbers are written in large text; Arabic numerals do not appear in the book. Guests and their place settings can be counted in each new, detailed, full-page watercolor illustration. The book's characters, including Uncle Will, Frog, Elephant, and Duck, appear in the author/illustrator's earlier companion book, *Tick-Tock. mn*

515. Anderson, Lena. **Tick-Tock**. Illustrated by the author. New York: R&S Books, 1998. Originally published as *Tick-Tack* by Eriksson & Lindgren in 1996. ISBN 91-29-64074-1. 28p. (1-3). Picture book.

Four small friends spend the day with their grown-up friend Will. In a fresh approach to a book about telling time, the story begins at 1 P.M. and follows Hedgehog, Elephant, Duck, and Piglet each hour as they go to the park, have a picnic, and return home to get ready for bed. By 11 P.M., Will is absolutely exhausted. Will he ever get these four to bed? The book's humor, conveyed in engaging watercolor illustrations, will amuse adults as well as children. *fk*

516. Arrhenius, Peter. **The Penguin Quartet**. Illustrated by Ingela Peterson. Minneapolis: Carolrhoda, 1998. Originally published as *Pingvinvartetten* by Natur och Kultur in 1996. ISBN 1-575-05252-0. 28p. (5-8). Picture book.

One doesn't have to be a jazz aficionado to enjoy this book, although knowing that Herbie, Charlie, Miles, and Max might possibly refer to Hancock, Parker, Davis, and Roach is one of the many details that intensifies the reading experience for adults. On the face, it's a quirky story about four bored penguin dads on egg-sitting duty who take off for a concert tour in New York City with eggs in tow. The illustrations are full of jokes and allusions that will pass over the heads of most young readers and listeners. They, on the other hand, will be entertained by this story about four cool dads who love their eggs even more than their nightlife. *ss*

517. Björk, Christina. **Vendela in Venice.** Translated by Patricia Crampton. Illustrated by Inga-Karin Eriksson. New York: R&S Books, 1999. Originally published as *Vendela I Venedig* by Rabén & Sjögren in 1999. ISBN 91-29-64559-X. 93p. (7-12). Novel.

Vendela, a preteen girl from Stockholm with an interest in Venice, is taken there by her father in this exuberant first-person story. Part guidebook, part story, this engaging and well-designed book is lavishly illustrated with painting, photographs, and maps. It concludes with some traveler's tips, information about visiting museums and shops, suggested reading, and important dates in Venice's history. *2000 Batchelder Honor Book. sg*

518. Ingves, Gunilla. **To Pluto and Back: A Voyage in the Milky Way.** Translated by Steven T. Murray. New York: R&S Books, 1992. Originally published as *Resan I rymden* by Rabén & Sjögren in 1990. ISBN 91-29-62058-9. 61p. (5-9). Informational book.

Stina, Robin, and Tom have a big blue rocket built of boards high up in their big climbing tree. They have planned to take a trip into outer space, plotting a course to each of the planets, through the asteroid belts and on to the stars. They pack up their favorite things, clothes, and food and begin their space journey, zooming at the speed of light while sharing what they learn about the galaxy with the young readers. Books for learning more about the solar system and notes on planets, stars, and the moon are appended in this colorfully illustrated, imaginative journey through space. *djg*

519. Jeppson, Ann-Sofie. **Here Comes Pontus!** Translated by Frances Corry. Illustrated by Catarina Kruusval. New York: R&S Books, 2000. Originally published as *Här kommer Pontus!* by Rabén & Sjögren in 1998. ISBN 91-29-64561-1. 30p. (7-9). Picture book.

Pontus, a mischievous young New Forest pony, narrates his own story of being purchased for a "girl with a yellow mane" and going to live on a farm. In the month covered, Pontus adjusts to his new home, makes friends with a kitten in the stable, escapes unharmed from a barn fire, and is reunited with his brother when they are put out into neighboring paddocks for the summer. Illustrated boxed items add information on equipment, care, and training of ponies. Realistic watercolor-and-ink illustrations make this blending of story and information even more engaging. Index. *ca*

520. Klinting, Lars. **Bruno the Baker**. Translated by the publisher. Illustrated by the author. New York: Holt, 1997. Originally published as *Castor Bakar* by Alfabeta Bokförlag in 1996. ISBN 0-8050-5506-1. 32p. (5-9). Picture book.

Bruno the Beaver bakes a cake on his birthday. He and his friend Felix make sure they have a cookbook and all the ingredients before they start. Pleasant watercolor and colored pencil illustrations show each utensil and ingredient as the cake is mixed. While the cake bakes, the two friends tidy the kitchen, then set the table, just in time for friends to arrive. The pleasures of friendship and the simple joys of orderly work in a cozy old-fashioned kitchen are celebrated here. *lh*

521. Landström, Olaf and Lena. **Boo and Baa in Windy Weather**. Translated by Joan Sandin. New York: R&S Books, 1996. Originally published as *Bu och Bä I blåsväder* by Rabén & Sjögren in 1995. ISBN 91-29-63920-4. 26p. (2-4). Picture book.

This small-format book, one of four about a sheep couple, pairs an understated text with deceptively simple illustrations that work together to provide humor. When Boo and Baa take their sled to the store to buy groceries, for instance, they lose control going downhill and end up in a heap. The short text reads only "'That was quick!' says Baa. 'Quick as a bunny,' says Boo." Other titles in the series are *Boo and Baa on a Cleaning Spree*, *Boo and Baa in a Party Mood,* and *Boo and Baa at Sea. ss*

522. Lindgren, Astrid. **Do You Know Pippi Longstocking?** Translated by Elisabeth Kallick Dyssegaard. Illustrated by Ingrid Nyman. New York: R&S Books, 1999. Originally published as *Känner du Pippi Långstrump?* by Rabén & Sjögren in 1947. ISBN 91-29-64661-8. 28p. (4-8). Picture book.

When Pippi Longstocking moves into Villa Villekulla with her horse and monkey, Tommy and Annika have a new friend. Their adventures with Pippi are recounted in short episodes, including a pancake breakfast, a visit to the circus, and Pippi's birthday party. The bold primary colors and strong lines of the illustrations complement and extend this introduction to a unique, spunky girl who lives as she pleases and who can do anything from walking on the high wire to overpowering a circus strong man and the robbers who climb into her room. *hc*

523. Lindgren, Astrid. **Pippi's Extraordinary Ordinary Day.** Translated by Frances Lambora. Illustrated by Michael Chesworth. New York: Viking. 1999. ISBN 0-670-88073-6. 27 p. (4-6). Picture book.

When her friends Tommy and Annika have a Scrubbing Vacation (their school is being thoroughly cleaned), Pippi organizes a picnic outing that is packed with adventures, including Pippi's attempt to fly and an encounter with a bull. Chesworth's cartoonlike illustrations capture the craziness of Pippi's escapades perfectly. This book is from the Pippi Longstocking Storybook series, for which texts are excerpted from the original books. Also *Pippi Goes to School* (1998) and *Pippi Goes to the Circus* (1999). *ca*

524. Lindgren, Barbro. **Andrei's Search**. Translated by Elisabeth Kallick Dyssegaard. Illustrated by Eva Eriksson. New York: R&S Books, 2000. Originally published as *Andrejs Längtan* by Rabén & Sjögren in 1997. ISBN 91-29-64756-8. 26p. (2-7). Picture book.

Two small boys, Andrei and Little Vova, walk through St. Petersburg, depicted in Eriksson's watercolor illustrations accurately but with a dreamlike quality. The boys leave "a big house full of children (where) there were no mamas or papas" to look for Andrei's mother. During their search they meet a dog who looks a lot like Vova and a kind baker who gives them free pierogis; they wonder about a trolley that sends out sparks, an apple tree that flowers, and a tugboat that bobs. The boys find Mama in a house just like the one Andrei remembers in a joyful ending. Lindgren dedicates this unusual and compelling picture book to Korney Chukovsky, the Russian linguist and author of *From Two to Five*, who studied young children's use of language and story to make meaning. *msn*

525. Lindgren, Barbro. **Benny's Had Enough!** Translated by Elisabeth Kallick Dyssegaard. Illustrated by Olof Landström. New York: R&S Books, 1999. Originally published as *Nämen Benny* by Rabén & Sjögren in 1999. ISBN 91-29-64563-8. 26p. (4-6). Picture book.

Benny's had enough of his mother cleaning and straightening his stuff. He leaves home with his favorite toy, Little Piggy. After an unsuccessful hunt for a new home and a search for Little Piggy when it becomes lost, Benny decides home wasn't so bad. Landström's clever illustrations capture Benny's moods and also offer a fascinating glimpse of Benny's neighborhood. *pc*

526. Lindgren, Barbro. **Rosa Moves to Town**. Translated by Jennifer Hawkins. Illustrated by Eva Eriksson. Toronto: Groundwood, 1997. Originally published as *Rosa Flyttar Till Stan* by Eriksson & Lindgren in 1996. ISBN

0-88899-288-2. 26p. (4-6). Picture book.
Rosa, the ever curious terrier, finds much to explore in her new home in the city. However, her greatest adventure begins when she chews on her favorite toys and swallows her rubber banana and the trunk of her plastic elephant. When she cries from pain, her aunt rushes her to the pet hospital for emergency surgery. The illustrations humorously depict this playful, energetic dog. By the same duo: *Rosa Goes to Daycare* (2000). *chs*

527. Manning, Mick. **What a Viking!** Illustrated by Brita Granstrom. New York: Farrar, Straus & Giroux, 2000. Originally published as *Viklen Viking!* by Rabén & Sjögren, 2000. ISBN 91-29-64883-1. 32p. (4-9). Picture book.
First-person reminiscences by a retired Viking, now a farmer, provide a fascinating and surprisingly detailed look at Viking history, art, religion, and sports. Hand-lettered sidebars complement the typeset text. Realistic drawings of Viking artifacts are interspersed among whimsical cartoons of the narrator and his family. *pm*

528. Pohl, Peter, and Kinna Gieth. **I Miss You, I Miss You.** Translated by Roger Greenwald. New York: R&S Books, 1999. Originally published as *Jag saknar dig, jag saknar dig!* by Rabén & Sjögren in 1992. ISBN 91-29-63935-2. 249p. (12-14). Fiction.
Thirteen-year-old Tina and her identical twin sister, Cilla, are extremely close. When Cilla is struck and killed by a car, Tina struggles not just with her loss, but with the reactions of those around her. Her parents are barely coping with their grief. Their friends do not know how to behave around her and so avoid her, leaving Tina alone and desperate to fill the void in her life. Tina eventually finds new strength within herself and is finally able to put to rest her guilt and grief over Cilla's death. *djg*

529. Stark, Ulf. **Can You Whistle, Johanna? A Boy's Search for a Grandfather.** Translated by Ebba Segerberg. Oakland, CA: RDR Books, 1999. Originally published as *Kan du vissla, Johanna?* by Bonnier Carlsen in 1994. ISBN 1-57143-057-1. 48p. (7-9). Picture book.
Uffe and Berre, about eight, have a happy visit with Berre's grandfather, but then Uffe feels sad that he has never known a grandfather. The boys find an elderly gentleman in the park and decide to make him his grandfather. He lives in a retirement home and is confined to a wheelchair, but is still full of fun, stories, and spunk. Uffe and his pretend grandfather both benefit greatly from their relationship, and when the old man dies all too soon, he leaves Uffe with many happy memories. *Winner of the 1994*

German Youth Literature Prize. cmt

530. Wahl, Mats. **Grandfather's Laika.** Illustrated by Tord Nygren. Minneapolis: Carolrhoda, 1990. Originally published as *Farfars Lajka* by Carlsen if-Bökforlag in 1989. ISBN 0-87614-434-2. 32p. (4-8). Picture book.
    Laika, Grandfather's golden retriever, accompanies Grandfather each afternoon as he comes to pick up Matthew after kindergarten; Matthew, Grandfather, and Laika go for walks and enjoy each other's company while Matthew's parents are at work. Matthew narrates this story of how Laika gets sick and must be put to sleep. Loose pencil illustrations in muted colors underscore the relationship between the outdoor world and its inhabitants and capture the emotions of both grandson and grandfather. *ss*

Related Information

Awards
The August Prize
    This prize, named after August Strindberg, is the most prestigious Swedish literary prize for children's and young adult books.

Online Bookstores
Sweden Bookshop
www2.si.se/shop/swebook/swebook.html
    Instructions in English make it easy to search for titles from Swedish writers and artists either in Swedish editions or English-language translation.

Bol.com
www.bol.se
    The Swedish version of Bol is organized a little differently from the other Bol.com country sites, and knowledge of Swedish would be a prerequisite for negotiating this site.

Switzerland

531. Fazzi, Maura, and Peter Kühner. **The Circus of Mystery.** Translated by Rosemary Lanning. Illustrated by Maura Fazzi and Peter Kühner. New York: North-South, 1999. Originally published as *August und das rote Ding* by Nord-Süd in 1999. ISBN 0-7358-1168-7. 26p. (4-9). Picture book.
    A mysterious transformation occurs in Augustus's gray world, first depicted on the back jacket/cover and front endpapers, when he finds and

dons a red clown nose. The world and people around him then come alive with color, as from a junkyard he and his friends put together a "spectacular show." Double-page, crowded, realistic drawings with myriad intriguing details demanding close inspection illuminate the brief, matter-of-fact text. This fantastic world is filled with enough imaginative props to embellish any story. *km, sm*

532. Laukel, Hans Gerold. **The Desert Fox Family Book.** Translated by Rosemary Lanning. New York: North-South, 1996. Originally published as *Das Wüstenfuchs Kinder-Buch* by Michael Neugebauer/Nord-Süd in 1996. (Paperback: North-South, 1999). ISBN 1-55858-579-6. 64p. (7-9). Informational book.

In this photo essay from the animal family book series, Laukel's striking color photographs and clearly written text take readers to the North African Sahara to observe the desert fox, or fennec, an elusive small nocturnal mammal. Readers learn about the life cycle and behavior of the desert fox as Laukel records his observations of a mother fennec and her cubs. They also learn about the harshness of the fennec's habitat and the problems Laukel experienced in the field. *ca*

533. Obrist, Jürg. **Max and Molly and the Mystery of the Missing Honey.** Translated by Rosemary Lanning. New York: North-South, 2000. Originally published as *Max und Molli: Großvater und der Honigdieb* by Nord-Süd in 1989. ISBN 0-7358-1266-7. 48p. (4-7). Transitional book.

Max and Molly, twin bear cubs from other titles by Obrist, visit their grandpa every summer for a month of fun. Grandpa keeps bees and makes honey. When jars of honey start to disappear from the kitchen cupboard, Grandpa gets cranky and even blames the twins. The cubs solve the mystery: it was Grandpa walking in his sleep and eating the honey! This easy-to-read book is illustrated by the author with detail and humor. *msn*

534. Pfister, Marcus. **The Happy Hedgehog.** Translated by J. Alison James. New York: North-South. 2000. Originally published as *Der Glückliche Mischka* by Nord-Süd in 2000. ISBN 0-7358-1164-4. 24p. (4-6). Picture book.

Mikko, a little hedgehog, loves to spend time in his garden learning about the plants and animals found there. Grandfather Tarek scolds Mikko for wasting his time "squatting in the grass, sniffing the flowers" and tells him to go out and learn how others find fulfillment through striving toward important accomplishments. What Mikko learns is that the animals he meets (including a tortoise training to be the fastest tortoise in the world and a hare studying to be the most brilliant) are busy and ambitious but not enjoying life. Mikko does not want to be miserable in order to be happy in the future, and so he returns to his garden to do what he most enjoys. *ca*

Related Information

Awards
Die Blaue Brillenschlange / Blue Bookworm
Recognizes books published in German that have contributed in some way to a more prejudice-free image of people from other cultures (very often given to a translated book).

Prix Enfantaisie and Distinction Enfantaisie
Both of these awards honor French-language children's books in Switzerland; the first is chosen by children and the second is chosen by adults.

Online Bookstores
Bol.com
www.ch.bol.com
In German, this site is easy to negotiate, even for those who do not know the language.

United Kingdom
(includes England, Northern Ireland, Scotland, and Wales)

535. Agard, John. **The Calypso Alphabet.** New York: Holt, 1989. Originally published by Beanstalk Books in 1989. ISBN 0-8050-1177-3. 27p. (4-6). Picture book. **England.**
Twenty-six terms from the Caribbean Islands—from "A for Anancy" to "Z for zombie"—are given one-line definitions that have a rhythmic beat. For example, Anancy is defined as "Spiderman of tricky-tricky fame." The scratchboard artwork illustrates the terms in brightly colored Caribbean settings. A glossary elaborates on unfamiliar terms such as "kaiso," "lickerish," and "roti." *ca*

536. Agard, John, and Grace Nichols. **No Hickory No Dickory No Dock: Caribbean Nursery Rhymes.** Illustrated by Cynthia Jabar. Cambridge, MA: Candlewick, 1995. Originally published by Viking (U.K.) in 1991. ISBN 1-56402-156-4. 44p. (4-6). Poetry. **England.**
This is a collection of Caribbean nursery rhymes and chants, most

done in native dialect. Some share a distant kinship to Mother Goose, while others are directly related, such as "Humpty," the tale of what happened to Humpty Dumpty after all the king's horses and all the king's men couldn't put him together again. Richly colored scratchboard illustrations abound. *rhm*

537. Ahlberg, Allan. **The Bravest Ever Bear.** Illustrated by Paul Howard. Cambridge, MA: Candlewick, 1999. ISBN 0-7636-0783-5. 32p. (4-8). Picture book. **England.**

A young bear cub creates his own spin on a variety of fairy and nursery tales in a comic mix of overlapping stories. Older readers familiar with the tales will appreciate the parodies and silliness. *jr*

538. Alborough, Jez. **Duck in the Truck** New York: HarperCollins, 1999. Originally published by HarperCollins (U.K.) in 1999. ISBN 0-06-028685-7. 32p. (4-6). Picture book. **England.**

Alborough is a British author/illustrator with more than thirty children's books to his credit. *Duck in the Truck*, a rhyming tale reminiscent of "The House That Jack Built," is even more fun than some of his earlier titles. When Duck's truck gets stuck in the mud, his friends try to extricate him. A small sample: "This is the *slurp* and *squelch* and *suck!* as the Sheep steps slowly through the muck." Large, cheerful, cartoon-style illustrations make this a great book for a read-aloud in classrooms because everyone can see. But it's the good humor and, especially, the rich language and rollicking rhythm that will delight readers and listeners alike. *fk*

539. Almond, David. **Kit's Wilderness.** New York: Delacorte, 2000. Originally published by Hodder in 1999. ISBN 0-385-32665-3. 229p. (12-14). Novel. **England.**

Kit Watson, thirteen, and his family move to the coal mining village, Stoneygate, to care for his senile grandfather after his grandmother's death. Kit enjoys his grandfather's tales of his work in the coal mines; of "Little Silky," the comforting spirit child within the mines; and of the children who worked there a century ago. John Askew, another miner's son, runs a sinister game called "Death" and invites Kit to join the game in the "wilderness" of an old mine and Kit's imagination. Exploring his feelings and relationships, especially with his grandfather, Kit writes down the tales and forges new friendships with Allie, an aspiring actress, his parents, and the delinquent John Askew himself. *Carnegie Highly Commended Book, 1999. mr*

540. Almond, David. **Skellig**. New York: Delacorte, 1999. Originally published by Hodder in 1998. ISBN 0-385-32653-X. 182p. (10-14). Novel. **England.**

Michael is distressed when his family's plans for fixing up their new house are derailed after his mother gives birth prematurely. While his baby sister's life hangs in the balance, Michael discovers an odd, barely alive winged creature—something like a man, something like a bird, something like an angel—in his family's dilapidated garage. With the help of his new friend Mina, a homeschooled free spirit, he nurtures the creature, and in the process begins to address his own feelings of helplessness and despair. *1998 Whitbread Children's Book of the Year; 2000 Michael Printz Honor Book. mb*

541. Anholt, Catherine and Laurence. **Billy and the Big New School**. Chicago: Albert Whitman, 1999. Originally published by Orchard (U.K.) in 1997. ISBN 0-8075-0743-1. 32p. (5-8). Picture book. **England.**

Billy is starting at a new school. He is excited, but nervous, too. Billy wishes he could stay home with his mom, who comforts him and gives him a big hug. But it is not until Billy finds a young bird to nurture in his backyard that he learns that with comfort and support, he, like the young bird, can leave the nest to experience the wide world. Cartoon-style watercolor illustrations add warmth and charm to this story. *djg*

542. Anholt, Laurence. **Harry's Home**. Illustrated by Catherine Anholt. Farrar, Straus & Giroux, 2000. Originally published by Orchard (U.K.) in 1999. ISBN 0-374-32870-6. 32p. (4-6). Picture book. **England.**

Young Harry loves his urban life but is excited when Grandad comes to take him for a week to his farm far away. Harry and his grandad have a great time with the farm animals, especially a baby lamb, but he is as glad to return to his home in the city as his grandfather is to live in the country. Bright, happy illustrations depict both lifestyles as appealing choices. *sg*

543. Anholt, Laurence. **Sophie and the New Baby**. Illustrated by Catherine Anholt. Chicago: Albert Whitman, 2000. Originally published by Orchard (U.K.) in 1995. ISBN 0-8075-7550-X. 34p. (4-6). Picture book. **England.**

In the spring young Sophie learns that there will be a new baby by winter. She waits and waits and practices for the new baby by caring for her doll. Finally, the Winter Baby is born during the first snowfall. However, this baby brother is slow to get big enough to play with and Sophie feels lonely while waiting. Her parents are so busy with the baby that she finally asks: "When will he be going back again?" With parental understanding and time, Sophie grows to love her baby brother. The full-page impressionistic illustrations in watercolor and pencil detail the cycle of seasons as Sophie works through a familiar childhood crisis. *chs*

544. Atkins, Jeannine. **Mary Anning and the Sea Dragon**. Illustrated by Michael Dooling. New York: Farrar, Straus & Giroux, 1999. ISBN 0-374-34840-5. 28p. (5-12). Picture book. **England**.

Mary Anning, an eleven-year-old girl in England in the 1800s, hears her father's words ("Don't ever stop looking, Mary") as she digs at the beach looking for "curiosities" to sell in the family store. One day she discovers some teeth, the first part of what her brother calls a "sea dragon." She patiently and lovingly persists in digging out the fossil, the first of its kind found in England. The afterword describes how Mary continues with the work she loves, looking for fossils, for the rest of her life. *hr*

Author from the United States

545. Axtell, David. **We're Going on a Lion Hunt**. Illustrated by the author. New York: Henry Holt, 2000. Originally published by Macmillan (U.K.) in 1999. ISBN 0-8050-6159-2. 28p. (1-6). Picture book. **England**.

In this variation on a favorite storyteller's chant, two sisters are hunting for a lion on the African savanna. Vibrant, sunlit pictures, many with dominant green, yellow, brown, and blue tones, depict the little girls' exciting adventure against an expansive landscape filled with wildlife. This will be great fun to use with a group of children. *sg*

546. Balit, Christina. **Atlantis: The Legend of a Lost City**. Illustrated by the author. New York: Henry Holt, 2000. Originally published by Frances Lincoln in 1999. ISBN 0-8050-6334-X. 26p. (4-9). Picture book. **England**.

The eternally fascinating legend of Atlantis is clearly retold and adapted from Plato's *Timaeus* and *Civitas*. Stylized, detailed, double-page illustrations in rich Mediterranean colors are as powerful and intriguing as the tale. An endnote by historian Geoffrey Ashe presents different theories about the location and existence of Atlantis. *sg*

547. Banks, Lynne Reid. **Alice-by-Accident**. Illustrated by Caitlin Flanigan. New York: HarperCollins, 2000. ISBN 0380978652. 140p. (7-9). Novel. **England**.

Nine-year-old Alice, illegitimate daughter of a somewhat neurotic single mother, keeps two journals: one for a school assignment, complete with teacher comments and grades, and a private one for the things she cannot tell anyone. Her observations lead to her inevitable conclusion: "Babies aren't complicated, they're simple, it's just grown-ups that make things complicated for them." *pm*

548. Barber, Antonio. **The Mousehole Cat.** Illustrated by Nicola Bayley. New York: Macmillan, 1990 (Paperback: Aladdin, 1996). Originally published by Walker (U.K.) in 1990. ISBN 0-027-08331-4. 34p. (7-9). Picture book. **England.**

Mowzer, the cat, and his human, Tom, save the Cornish village of Mousehole from starvation when the great Storm-Cat prevents the fishermen from leaving the harbor in this traditional tale of courage and compassion and love. Mowzer tames the Storm-Cat with her singing and purring, which calms the Storm-Cat so that Tom can return their fully loaded fishing boat to the village for a pre-Christmas Eve feast with his neighbors and their cats, who guide them home with lanterns and candelight. Beautiful illustrations complement this story's message. Bayley: *1990 Commended for Kate Greenaway Award for Illustrations. mr*

549. Bateson-Hill, Margaret. **Lao-Lao of Dragon Mountain.** Chinese text by Manyee Wan. Illustrated by Francesca Pelizzoli. Papercuts by Sha-liu Qu. Originally published by De Agostini Editions (U.K.) in 1996; distributed by Stewart, Tabori & Chang. ISBN 1-899883-64-9. 32p. (4-8). Picture book. **England.**

Meshing elements of traditional Chinese folklore, the text and illustrations tell the story of Lao-Lao, a peasant woman, who is renown for her talent of paper cutting. When the emperor hears of her abilities, he takes her captive. The Ice Dragon rescues her, and flying to safety on his back, she covers the ground with beautiful cut papers. Templates and instructions to make a butterfly, flower, snowflake, and dragon paper cuts are included. An afterword discusses the development and use of Chinese writing. *djg*

550. Bawden, Nina. **Off the Road.** New York: Clarion, 1998. First published by Hamish Hamilton in 1998. (Paperback: Puffin, 2001). ISBN 0-395-91321-7. 192p. (10-14). Novel. **England.**

The year is 2040, and Tom and his parents are taking his grandfather to the Memory Theme Park. When Gandy goes "off the road" (escapes under the wall surrounding their community), Tom follows without thinking, assuming he will save his grandfather from the barbarians outside. What he finds out there makes him realize that the wall is not there to keep the barbarians out, as he has been told, but to keep residents of his community in. This provocative look at the future has a definite British setting and pairs well with Lowry's *The Giver*. *ss*

551. Bawden, Nina. **The Real Plato Jones.** New York: Clarion Books, 1993. Published by Hamish Hamilton (U.K.) in 1994. (Paperback: Puffin, 1996). ISBN 0-395-66972-3. 166p. (12-14). Novel. **England.**

Thirteen-year-old Plato Jones is forced to come to terms with his identity when he visits Greece to attend his Greek grandfather's funeral. There he finds out more about his family's history than he would have ever imagined. His Welsh grandfather was a World War II hero and his Greek one was considered a traitor. What had happened during the war and how would he discover the truth behind this mystery? Exquisitely written, with profound character analyses and realistic descriptions of the Greek setting, this novel is indispensable when examining the search for one's true identity and accepting one's national heritage. *1995 Shortlist, WH Smith Mind Boggling Books Award. des*

552. Binch, Caroline. **Since Dad Left.** Brookfield, CT: Millbrook, 1998. Originally published by Frances Lincoln in 1998. ISBN 0-7613-0290-5. 28p. (4-8). Picture book. **England.**

Six-year-old Sid doesn't understand why his parents don't live together anymore, but after a forced visit to his father, he gets over being mad. Beautiful, realistic illustrations depict Sid, his hippie parents, and a great many pets and domestic animals. *pm*

553. Blake, Quentin. **Clown.** New York: Henry Holt, 1995. Originally published by Jonathan Cape in 1995. ISBN 0-8050-4399-3. 32p. (3-5). Picture book. **England.**

A clown is thrown away along with a handful of other stuffed toys. He comes to life and manages to escape from the trash and has a series of adventures and misadventures until he is at last thrown into the window of an apartment building, where he becomes the perfect diversion for a crying baby and a harried babysitter. This is an eloquent, imaginative wordless picture book. *1996 Nestlé Smarties Bronze Medal; 1998 IBBY Honor Book;* Blake: *First UK Children's Laureate. djg*

554. Bloom, Valerie. **Fruits: A Caribbean Counting Poem.** Illustrated by David Axtell. New York: Holt, 1997. Originally published by Macmillan (U.K.) in 1997. ISBN 0-8050-5171-6. 24p. (4-9). Poetry. **England.**

Axtell's oil paintings, which feature two sisters, are as rich and colorful as the dialect of Bloom's poem, in which the narrator counts up to ten as she enjoys a feast of fruits native to the Caribbean (one pawpaw, two guava, and so on), and ends up with a stomachache from overeating. A glossary identifies the various fruits. *ca*

555. Branford, Henrietta. **Fire, Bed & Bone**. Cambridge, MA: Candlewick, 1998. Originally published by Walker (U.K.) in 1997. ISBN 0-7636-0338-4. 122p. (13 up). Novel. **England.**

When a kind peasant named Rufus is arrested for involvement in the 1381 Peasants' Revolt of Richard II's reign, life changes for his wife, their children, and his hunting dog. Told in first person by the dog, this story prompts sympathy for the human members of the family as they suffer separation, imprisonment, and ultimately Rufus's execution. Readers may sympathize even more for the wise hunting dog narrator. As a result of cruel treatment by temporary masters, she and her puppies escape the village and spend seasons in the wildwood, where they thrive. As the dog explains, however, she is not "truly wild," so when Rufus's family comes home to live at last in comfort and safety, she is happy to return to fire, bed, and bone. *1998 Guardian Children's Fiction Award; 1997 Nestlé Smarties Bronze Medal. ebb*

556. Brighton, Catherine. **The Fossil Girl: Mary Anning's Dinosaur Discovery**. Illustrated by the author. Brookfield, CT: Millbrook, 1999. Originally published by Frances Lincoln in 1999. ISBN 0-7613146-87. 28p. (4-8). Picture book. **England.**

A cartoon-panel format is used to tell the story of how twelve-year-old Mary Anning found an ichthyosaurus skeleton in Dorset, England, and chiseled away for months to unearth it. Brighton places commentary by the onlookers in bubbles (a range of attitudes from "She's brave" to "If God wanted you to find curiosities, Mary Anning, why did he bury them?") and also uses bubbles to convey Mary's own thoughts. Pairing this fictionalized biography with the one by Atkins, listed earlier in this section, would provide a useful look at the choices made by biographers as they reconstruct their subjects' lives. *pm*

557. Browne, Anthony. **Voices in the Park**. New York: DK Ink, 1998. Published simultaneously by Transworld Publisher. ISBN 0-7894-2522-X. 32p. (7-9). Picture book. **England.**

A bossy mother, her lonely son, a disheartened man, and a cheerful young girl give their own impressions of what they see in their own voice as they spend time at the park. As in all Browne's books, *Voices* is a visual delight and readers will interpret and reinterpret the events through the eyes of each character. *1998 Kurt Maschler Award;* Browne: *2000 Hans Christian Andersen Illustrator Medal Winner. djg*

558. Browne, Anthony. **Willy the Dreamer**. Cambridge, MA: Candlewick, 1998. Originally published by Walker (U.K.) in 1997. ISBN 0-7636-0378-3. 32p. (5-8). Picture book. **England.**

Willy the chimp dreams that he is a movie star or a singer or a sumo wrestler or a dancer. He dreams of being a hero and having adventures in the past and the future. Observant readers will find familiar elements from master artists on almost every page in this book, which is fifth in a series of books about Willy. Previous titles include: *Willy the Wimp* (1984), *Willy the Champ* (1985), *Willy and Hugh* (1991), and *Willy the Wizard* (1995). *djg*

559. Browne, Anthony. **Willy's Pictures**. Cambridge, MA: Candlewick, 2000. Published simultaneously by Walker (U.K.). ISBN 0-7636-0962-5. 32p. (5-8). Picture book. **England**.

Browne's trademark chimp becomes an artist in this book, beginning with the turnabout on the cover in which he paints a self-portrait that looks very much like Browne himself. Each of Willy's pictures, under which Willy adds a short commentary, is a variation on a classic painting. The originals, along with identification and description, are reproduced in a fold-out section at the book's end, making this book both an exercise in observation (look for the paintbrushes in each of Willy's paintings) and an introduction to art history. *ss*

560. Burgess, Melvin. **Copper Treasure.** Illustrated by Richard Williams. New York: Holt, 2000. Originally published by A & C Black in 1998. ISBN 0-8050-6381-1. 104p. (10-12). Novel. **England**.

In this exciting adventure story set in Victorian London, three lads who earn their bread by retrieving salvage from the muddy banks of the Thames River devise a desperate plan to salvage a valuable roll of sheet copper they see fall into the river. Humor and tragedy blend in a book that gives a wonderful picture of the difficult boyhood of impoverished children of the time. Includes a glossary and a chart of monetary units in Victorian England. *sg*

561. Burgess, Melvin. **Kite**. New York: Farrar, Straus & Giroux, 2000. Originally published by Andersen Press in 1997. ISBN 0-374-34228-8. 182p. (12-14). Novel. **England.**

Taylor Mase's dad is the gamekeeper on an estate in England in 1964 where pheasant are raised for sport hunting. Any wild creature that might prey on the game birds is considered "vermin" and it is Mr. Mase's job to exterminate it. Taylor collects bird's eggs with his best friend, Alan; and this is how the boys secretly hatch, raise, and release Teresa, a red kite. When the landowner spots Teresa and wounds her, he orders his gamekeeper to kill the bird, although only twenty-four red kites exist in England. How Teresa survives, with Taylor's courageous help, is the dramatic heart of the story. This novel has an unsentimental, sometimes graphic style, and includes excellent explanations "for American readers" in the author's note and afterword. *mn*

562. Burgess, Melvin. **Smack.** New York: Holt, 1998. (Paperback: Avon, 1999). First published as *Junk* by Andersen Press in 1996. ISBN 0-8050-5801-X. 327p. (12 up). Novel. **England.**

Fourteen-year-old Tar runs away from an abusive situation in his home and thinks he has found the perfect life in a squat, living with other runaways and dropouts from society. He convinces his girlfriend, Gemma, to run away and join him in his new home and live together with his new friends. When Gemma and her friends invite him to take his first hit of smack, he thinks things will only get better, but things quickly change for the worse. They must steal to get money to get more drugs, Gemma becomes distant and withdrawn, and things begin to fall apart. This is a penetrating and disturbing story about the ecstasies and horrors of heroin use. *1996 Carnegie Medal Winner; 1997 Guardian Prize; Publishers Weekly Best Book of the Year for 1998. djg*

563. Carroll, Lewis. **Alice's Adventures in Wonderland.** Illustrated by Helen Oxenbury. Originally published by Walker (U.K.) in 1999. ISBN 0-7636-0804-1. 206p. (8-12). Novel. **England.**

Oxenbury's artwork in this liberally illustrated and beautiful edition of Carroll's unabridged classic ranges from full-color watercolors on single pages and spreads to the many sketches that are integrated with the text. Oxenbury brings a freshness and charm to the text through her depiction of a modern-day Alice, with long blond hair, blue sleeveless tunic, and white sneakers, and through the liveliness and humor of her drawings, which evoke the droll and fantastic nature of Alice's "curious dream." A photograph of Carroll and an "author's note" (Christmas, 1896) are included in the prefatory material. *2000 Kate Greenaway Medal; 1999 Kurt Maschler Award. hc*

564. Carroll, Lewis. **Alice in Wonderland.** Illustrated by Lisbeth Zwerger. New York: North-South, 1999. Simultaneously published by Nord-Süd Verlag. ISBN 0-7358-1166-0. 103p. (7-12). Novel. **England.**
The text is Carroll's original tale of the strange adventures of a young girl who falls down a rabbit hole into another world. The bits of colored drawings that are integrated here and there plus occasional full-page scenes offer Zwerger's unique visual interpretation of the classic characters. She creates a nostalgic, dreamy, almost delicate world with consistent underpinnings of sly humor. A long-haired Alice in red stockings, white dress, and dark vest is attractively innocent; there is no hint of malice or danger here. *km, sm*

565. Cecil, Laura. **Noah and the Space Ark.** Illustrated by Emma Chichester Clark. Minneapolis: Carolrhoda, 1998. Originally published by Hamish Hamilton in 1997. ISBN 1-57505-255-5. 30p. (5-8). Picture book. **England.**
In this futuristic retelling of the Bible story, Noah and his family care for the small animals that live in the last green space left on a crowded and very polluted Earth. When a drought threatens even this safe haven, Noah builds a spaceship that will take his family and the animals to a new planet. After traveling forty days and nights, they find a new home on an unspoiled planet full of animals, trees, and plenty of fresh air. The detailed watercolor illustrations add bits of humor to this cautionary story. *chs*

566. Child, Lauren. **Clarice Bean, That's Me.** Cambridge, MA: Candlewick, 1999. Originally published by Orchard (U.K.) in 1999. ISBN 0-7636-0961-7. 28p. (7-9). Picture book. **England.**
Clarice describes her prickly relationships with family members in this archly funny modern tale. Many different typefaces and bold, multimedia illustrations enhance the chaotic feel of her family, which is actually pretty happy, despite mischievous Clarice's frequent bouts of pouting. *sg*

567. Cole, Babette. **Hair in Funny Places: A Book about Puberty.** Illustrated by the author. New York: Hyperion, 2000. Originally published by Random House (U.K.) in 1999. ISBN 0-7868-0590-0. 32p. (7-12). Informational book. **England.**
A teddy bear reveals to a young girl the mysteries of growing up. Accompanied by drawings full of humor, teddy explains that bodily changes

result from the machinations of Mr. and Mrs. Hormone. This frank depiction of the changes of puberty contains drawings of unclad teenagers, male and female. *cc*

568. Collicutt, Paul. **This Train.** Illustrated by the author. New York: Farrar, Straus & Giroux, 1999. ISBN 0-374-37493-7. 28p. (4-6). Picture book. **England.**

Most children are fascinated by trains. Collicutt's book depicts different kinds of trains in numerous locales. One might run on steam while another runs on electricity, but all the trains do their work in all kinds of weather. Vibrant paintings support a simple text that includes a number of contrasts: long/short, bridge/tunnel, uphill/downhill, and so on. Endpapers identify actual trains used in the illustrations. By the same author: *This Plane* and *This Boat*. *1999 Parents' Choice Gold Award winner*. *rhm*

569. Cooke, Trish. **The Grandad Tree.** Illustrated by Sharon Wilson. Cambridge, MA: Candlewick, 2000. ISBN 0-7636-0815-7. 24p. (5-8). Picture book. **England.**

Vin and Leigh's grandad planted an apple tree that "grew and grew." Impressionistic illustrations depict Grandad first as a small boy on a tropical island, next as a grown man surrounded by extended family, and finally with Vin and Leigh playing under the apple tree as seasons pass. These images, however, are all memories, because their grandad has recently died. Although textual clues, such as word choice and verb tense, have hinted at this, it is explicitly revealed to readers halfway through the book, and then they, too, can participate as Vin and Leigh learn to mourn in healthy ways. *ebb*

570. Cooper, Helen. **Pumpkin Soup.** Illustrated by the author. New York: Farrar, Straus & Giroux, 1999. Originally published by Doubleday/Transworld in 1998. ISBN 0-385-40794-7. 32p. (1-6). Picture book. **England.**

Enchanting illustrations and highly imaginative graphic design star in this tale of three friends. Bright, detailed, and humorous artwork will delight young children. The actual story concerns a cat, a squirrel, and a duck who live together. They cook pumpkin soup every evening, with the cat chopping the pumpkin, the squirrel stirring the soup, and the duck adding the salt. All proceeds smoothly until the duck decides he wants to stir, and the other two animals won't let him. When the duck runs away, the cat and squirrel realize how much they value his company. Duck does return, cat and squirrel let him stir, and all seems happy, though the ending acknowledges that friends living together will run up against disagreements. *1999 Kate Greenaway Medal. cc*

571. Cooper, Susan. **The Boggart.** New York: McElderry, 1993. ISBN 0-689-50576-0. (Paperback: Aladdin, 1995). 196p. (9-12). Novel. **Scotland.**
Visiting Scotland to view a castle they have inherited, a family accidentally transports the Boggart (an invisible magical creature) back to Canada. Ten-year-old Jessup and his sister Emily combine computer technology with Old Magic to return the Boggart to Scotland. Sequel: *The Boggart and the Monster* (1999). *pm*
    Author from the United States

572. Cross, Gillian. **Tightrope.** New York: Holiday House, 1999. Originally published by Oxford University Press in 1999. ISBN 0-8234-1512-0. 216p. (12-14). Novel. **England.**
Ashley is regarded as a responsible girl caring for her diasabled mother, but Ashley, an accomplished gymnast, is also "Cindy," who leaves her signature on the walls of high places. After she sprays her name on the wall of a local business owned by "Fat Annie," threatening anonymous letters arrive and a stalker lurks outside her home. Ashley turns to Eddie Beale, the local gang leader, for help but discovers that Eddie has used her mother and herself as pawns and has framed an innocent man. A plural narrative reveals what others in Ashley's family and neighborhood know and see. *hc*

573. Crossley-Holland, Kevin. **The World of King Arthur and His Court: People, Places, Legend, and Lore.** Illustrated by Peter Malone. New York: Dutton, 1999. Originally published by Orion in 1998. ISBN 0-525-46167-1. 125p. (12-14). Informational book. **England.**
Arthurian legends, the documented history of King Arthur, and the mysteries surrounding his legend and those of the other knights of the Round Table, as well as intriguing excerpts from medieval texts and general information about life and geography of the times, are collected in this generous compendium. Beautifully illustrated with glowing paintings reminiscent of medieval manuscripts, this elegantly produced book will please all lovers of King Arthur and the Middle Ages. *sg*

574. Doherty, Berlie. **The Snake-Stone.** New York: Orchard, 1996. Originally published by Hamish Hamilton in 1995. (Paperback: Puffin, 1998). ISBN 0-531-095-126. 166p. (10-12). Novel. **England.**
Fifteen-year-old James, training to be a champion diver, loses his con-

centration as he thinks about being adopted. Who was his mother and had she wanted him when he was born? The only clues to his past are a torn envelope with remnants of an address and the words, "Look after Sammy," along with a beautiful ammonite. James's quest takes him to Derbyshire, where he climbs over Horsenose Tor to the valley below. Here, he meets the woman who had given birth to him as a young girl and whose words of pain and loss are interspersed with James's story. *hc*

575. Doherty, Berlie. **Street Child.** New York: Orchard, 1994. Originally published by Hamish Hamilton in 1993. ISBN 0-531-06864-1. 154p. (10-12). Novel. **England.**

After his mother dies, Jim escapes from his miserable life in the workhouse. He finds temporary shelter with his mother's friend, Rosie, until Rosie's grandfather discovers him and sends him to work for the cruel barge worker, Nick Grimes. Forced to shovel coal until he drops, ill-treated and starving, Jim finally escapes and makes his way back to London, where he sleeps on the roofs with other destitute boys until rescued by Dr. Barnardo. Based on the real story of Jim Jarvis who was rescued from destitution in the 1860s by Dr. Barnardo, founder of Barnardo's Homes for Children. *hc*

576. Doherty, Berlie. **Willa and Old Miss Annie.** Illustrated by Kim Lewis. Cambridge, MA: Candlewick, 1994. ISBN 1-56402-331-1. 92p. (7-10). Transitional book. **England.**

Willa has moved to another country with her parents, leaving her best friend behind. Convinced she will never have another friend, she is afraid when she meets Old Miss Annie, whose hair looks like wool. But she is curious about the ghost who cries in Miss Annie's backyard. Doherty tells three stories about a lonely goat, a forgotten pony, and an orphaned fox and into each are woven the stories of little Willa, Old Miss Annie, and shy Ruth. *1994 Carnegie Highly Commended List. djg*

577. Doyle, Malachy. **Jody's Beans.** Illustrated by Judith Allibone. Cambridge, MA: Candlewick, 1999. ISBN 0-7636-0687-1. 25p. (4-7). Picture book. **Wales.**

Over the course of a year, Jody's kindhearted and steadfast grandfather teaches her how to plant, nurture, harvest, and cook beans, and then the pair begins the entire process again. By following the grandfather's instructions, readers of all ages may be inspired to plant and care for their own bean towers. A subject index reinforces the planting process, and so do the whimsical illustrations that simultaneously reveal two additional cycles: the changing of season and the pregnancy of Jody's mother. *ebb*

578. Dunbar, James. **When I Was Young**. Illustrated by Martin Remphry. Minneapolis: Carolrhoda, 1999. Originally published by Franklin Watts (U.K.) in 1998. ISBN 1-57505-359-4. 32p. (7-9). Picture book. **England.**

Seven-year-old Josh learns the importance of passing down family memories when he asks his grandmother what it was like when she was young. She tells him of her life in the 1950s and about the stories her grandfather told about England in the 1890s. The family stories continue all the way back through the generations to the 1600s. The final pages of the book include a family portrait gallery and a section of "useful information" for each of the generations. The details included in the lighthearted watercolor illustrations will help readers better understand the 300 years of English history. *chs*

579. Ellwand, David. **Alfred's Party**. Illustrated with photographs by the author. New York: Dutton, 2000. Originally published by Templar in 2000. ISBN 0-525-46385-2. 32p. (7-10). Picture puzzle book. **England.**

Alfred, the author's pointer dog, stars in this "I Spy" type book, and his charming posed photographs alternate with hand-colored photographs of cluttered pages in which the reader hunts for hidden objects. An earlier book along similar lines, *Alfred's Camera,* was first published in England in 1998 by Ragged Bears, and also in the United States by Dutton in that same year. *lh*

580. Fanelli, Sara. **Dear Diary**. Illustrated by the author. Cambridge, MA: Candlewick, 2000. Simultaneously published by Walker (U.K.). ISBN 0-7636-0965-X. 36p. (4-9). Picture book. **England.**

From endpages full of scribbles and faces to a variety of collage illustrations supporting the narrative, Lucy's diary highlights a typical child's day at school and then at home. While her narrative takes only a few pages, other points of view are also part of her diary. A chair at school, a spider and firefly who were at the school party, a fork rescued by the dog, and the dog each gives its perspective on Lucy's day as she continues writing in her diary. The detailed collage, a variety of print forms, and the atypical book format, to include classical quotes about journaling, make this book unique. *Honorable Mention, 2001 Bologna Ragazzi Award. jbm*

581. Fanelli, Sara. **My Map Book**. Illustrated by Sara Fanelli. New York: HarperCollins, 1995. Originally published by ABC, All Books for Children, in 1995. ISBN 0-06-026455-1. 25p. (1-3). Picture book. **England.**

How do you explain what a map is to a child? One way is by sharing a child's simple illustrations that clearly demonstrate some possibilities for mapping. The child narrator of this book shows us twelve maps she has designed and labeled. Some maps are predictable: a map of her bedroom and a map of her neighborhood. Other maps are creative and funny: a map of her day, a map of her dog, and a map of her heart. All the maps are double-paged color drawings and feature a variety of map perspectives. The book contains two poster-sized maps. *pas*

582. Fanelli, Sara. **Wolf**. Illustrated by Sara Fanelli. New York: Dial, 1997. Originally published by Reed in 1997. ISBN 0-8037-2093-9. 33p. (1-3). Picture book. **England.**

On a sunny day, a wolf walks into the city to find some new friends. Despite his acts of friendship, most of the people he meets believe wolves are fierce and scary, and they chase him away. When he finally finds a listener for his tales of misadventures, his tormentors realize they have been mean to judge him without getting to know him. Fanelli's eclectic use of newspaper, ticket stubs, ledger entries, crayons, painted paper cutouts, photographs, primitive drawings, and playful type settings present a visually appealing experience. Children will want to examine each page and the meaning of friendship. *pas*

583. Farjeon, Eleanor. **Elsie Piddock Skips in Her Sleep**. Illustrated by Charlotte Voake. Cambridge, MA: Candlewick, 1997. ISBN 0-7636-0133-0. 61p. (4-8). Transitional book. **England.**

Elsie Piddock was "a born skipper." At seven years old, summoned by Andy Spandy, Skipping Master of the fairies, to skip with the fairies on Mount Caburn, she masters all the fairy skips. For a prize, she is given a rope with handles of candy so she may "suck sweet all" her life. When an unscrupulous lord threatens to build on Mount Caburn, Elsie, 109 years old, returns with her skipping rope to skip as she has never skipped before. First published in 1937, Farjeon's classic story, complemented by Voake's delicate illustrations, retains its charm in this edition. *hc*

584. Fine, Anne. **The Tulip Touch**. New York: Little, Brown, 1997. ISBN 0-316-28325-8. Originally published Hamish Hamilton in 1996. 149p. (12 up). Novel. **England.**

When her parents take over the management of a hotel, Natalie befriends her new neighbor Tulip. She quickly comes under the spell of this strange girl and wants to be a loyal friend, but as Tulip's actions become increasingly unpredictable and reckless, Natalie becomes frightened. She must do something to break free from Tulip, but does she have the strength?

1996 Carnegie Highly Commended List; 1996 Whitbread Children's Book of the Year. djg

585. French, Vivian. **Growing Frogs.** Illustrated by Alison Bartlett. Cambridge, MA: Candlewick, 2000. Simultaneously published by Walker (U.K.). ISBN 0-7636-0317-1. 28p. (4-6). Informational book. **England.**

This charming book about the life cycle of frogs is set within the framework of the story of a little girl and her mother who collect frog spawn, care for it, and watch it grow. Careful observation is stressed and tips for replicating the experience are included. The bright, cheerful, acrylic paintings make the project even more inviting. *sg*

586. Garner, Alan. **The Well of the Wind.** Illustrated by Hervé Blondon. New York: DK, 1998. ISBN 0-7894-2519-X. 45p. (4-9). Picture book. **England.**

Using spare, poetic language Alan Garner presents a stripped-down fairy tale. A poor man takes in a brother and sister set adrift on the sea in a crystal box. The man dies, a witch appears and sets the brother on three quests. He fails the final test and his sister must rescue him. With courage, intelligence, and perseverance she succeeds. The combination of sparse prose and a seemingly formulaic story leads readers to create their own texts. Deceptively simple illustrations complement the deceptively simple telling of the fantasy. This would be an excellent book to spark discussions. *cc*

587. Geras, Adèle. **The Fabulous Fantoras: Book Two: Family Photographs.** Illustrated by Eric Brace. New York: Avon, 1999. (Paperback: Avon, 2000). 152p. (10-12). Novel. **England.**

In this sequel to *The Fabulous Fantoras: Book 1: Family Files* (1998), Ozymandias, the family cat, narrates more wacky adventures of the very unusual Fantora family as he tells the stories behind the framed photographs on the Family Wall, including vegetarian vampire Auntie Varvara's wedding. *ca*

588. Gerrard, Roy. **The Roman Twins.** Illustrated by the author. New York: Farrar, Straus & Giroux. 1998. Originally published by Hamish Hamilton in 1998. ISBN 0-374-36339-0. 32p. (4-9). Picture book. **England.**

Brother and sister twins serve as slaves to Slobus Pompius and his wife in ancient Rome. With the help of a horse and two friends the twins win a chariot race, save Rome from barbarians (led by Wulfus the Unwashed One), and finally gain their freedom. Gerrard's extremely detailed illustrations, his rhyming verse, and his signature short, chubby people combine to make this a satisfying tale where friendship and courage win over greed and sloth. *cc*

589. Gibbie, Mike. **Small Brown Dog's Bad Remembering Day.** Illustrated by Barbara Nascimbeni. New York: Dutton, 2000. First published by Macmillan (London) in 1999. ISBN 0-525-46397-6. 28p. (3-7). **England.**

Small brown dog wakes up one morning and can't remember anything, including his name. He asks everyone he meets, and each person remembers one more detail of his life. He discovers, among other things, that he has a small pink nose, likes splashing in puddles, chases squirrels, has a bad case of fleas, all told in cumulative style. In the illustrations, a mouse follows the small brown dog from place to place and is not acknowledged until the last page, when the dog finally discovers his name and the mouse says, "But I could have told you that!" *ss*

590. Gilchrist, Cherry. **A Calendar of Festivals.** Illustrated by Helen Cann. New York: Barefoot, 1998. Originally published by Barefoot Books Ltd. in 1998. ISBN 1-901223-68-X. 80p. (7-9). Informational book. **England.**

Origins of eight religious and secular holidays from around the world are clearly explained in full-page tellings and followed by a legend or folktale associated with the holiday. Appealingly designed, the book includes many full-color illustrations and attractive borders with appropriate motifs. Holidays include: Purim, Holi, Vesak, Tanabata, Halloween, Christmas, Kwanzaa, and Russian New Year. The last page is a list of sources. *sg*

591. Godden, Rumer. **Premlata and the Festival of Lights.** Illustrated by Ian Andrew. New York: Greenwillow, 1997. Originally published by Macmillan (U.K.) in 1996. (Paperback: HarperCollins, 1999). ISBN 0-688-15136-1. 58p. (7-9). Transitional book. **England.**

Premlata, a determined seven-year-old, sets out to salvage her family's Festival of Lights celebration. Her mother had to sell their *deepas*, the traditional oil lamps that are lit on the night of the festival to guide the goddess Kali as she goes about trying to rid the world of evil and bad luck. Prem could use some good luck: Her Dadi has died and her mother struggles to support their family of four. Prem's good-hearted but impetuous attempts to save the day nearly fail, but their kind landlord and a special friend come to the rescue. *mm*

592. Goodall, Jane. **Dr. White.** Illustrated by Julie Litty. New York: North-South, 1999. ISBN 0-7358-1063-X. 32p. (4-9). Picture book. **England.**

Delicate pastel illustrations showcase the power of animals to help heal the body and spirit. "Dr. White," a small friendly dog, makes the rounds daily at a children's hospital, providing companionship, hope, and love to his young patients. Banished from the wards by a health inspector, Dr. White's persistence and role in healing the inspector's little girl win him a permanent place as a valued member of the hospital staff. *cl*

593. Griff [Andrew Griffen]. **Shark-Mad Stanley.** Illustrated by the author. New York: Hyperion, 2000. Originally published by Ticktock in 1999. ISBN 0-7868-0594-3. 32p. (4-6). Picture book. **England.**

Stanley explores the possibilities of owning a shark through comparisons with his pet goldfish. Although he begins optimistically, the more he learns about sharks the less sure he is that they would make good pets. Amusing illustrations keep the tone of the book light. Part of an educational series (*Tiger-Time for Stanley* has also been published), a free CD accompanies the book but adds little to the content. *cc*

594. Haughton, Emma. **Rainy Day.** Illustrated by Angelo Rinaldi. Minneapolis: Carolrhoda, 2000. Originally published by Transworld in 2000. ISBN 1-57505-452-3. 28p. (5-8). Picture book. **England.**

Nick visits his father shortly after his parents' separation. When rain ruins their plan to attend the fair, they instead take a long walk through the city and a park to the sea. The rainy setting, shown in full-page impressionistic paintings, matches the sadness of both father and son as they consider how much they miss each other. At the end of their walk, when Dad tells Nick, "Things will get better . . . I promise," the sun breaks symbolically through the grayness. *chs*

595. Heap, Sue. **Cowboy Baby.** Illustrated by Sue Heap. Cambridge, MA: Candlewick, 1998. Simultaneously published by Walker. ISBN 0-7636-0437-2. 32p. (2-5). Picture book. **England.**

Sheriff Pa wants Cowboy Baby to come to bed, but Cowboy Baby insists he can't until he finds his toys, Texas Ted, Denver Dog, and Hank the Horse. Sheriff Pa sends Cowboy Baby off to find his toys, and the search ends in a game of bedtime hide and seek. Sheriff Pa lassos a twinkling star to deputize his little boy, who is now ready to come inside to sleep. *Cowboy Kid*, a sequel written by Max Eilenberg with Heap's illustrations, also focuses on bedtime. *1998 Nestlé Smarties Book Prize. jr*

596. Henderson, Kathy. **The Baby Dances.** Illustrated by Tony Kerins.

Cambridge, MA: Candlewick, 1999. ISBN 0-7636-0374-0. 24p. (1-3). Picture book. **England.**
A brief lyrical text and full-page chalk pastel illustrations in soft colors record the growth of a baby during her first year—from her birth, through the stages of rolling over, sitting up, crawling, and standing, to her first independent steps with which she staggers and prances and dances into her brother's arms. Small pencil sketches beneath the text show the brother and parents together with the baby. *ca*

597. Henderson, Kathy. **The Storm.** Cambridge, MA: Candlewick, 1999. ISBN 0-7636-0904-8. 28p. (7-9). Picture book. **England.**
A little boy, Jim, lives by the sea in an unnamed land, and one late winter morning proclaims to the wind and the sea, "All this is mine!" The wind and the sea, however, don't agree, and a ferocious gale unleashes wind, rain, hail, and waves, threatening the seashore home of Jim and his mother. After safely riding out the storm in Grandma's inland, upland home, Jim tells the wind and the sea, "All this is yours." Storm-moody mixed-media illustrations add character to this story. *pm, rhm*

598. Hendry, Diana. **Back Soon.** Illustrated by Carol Thompson. Mahwah, NJ: BridgeWater, 1995. Originally published by Julia MacRae in 1993. (Paperback: BridgeWater, 1995). ISBN 0-8167-3487-9. 32p. (4-6). Picture book. **England.**
Kitten Herbert's mother always seems to be leaving him at home in the care of relatives and going off with a breezy "Back soon!" But it never is soon enough for Herbert, and when he uses this "back soon" routine, Mother doesn't seem to notice his absence. One morning, however, Herbert has so much fun in the garden that he forgets his promise to be back soon. His reunion with Mother, who has missed him, is joyous as they agree that it is nice to have time to yourself—as long as you remember to come back soon. Thompson's watercolors feature a charming, playful Herbert and a mother who is a real feline fashion plate. *ca*

599. Hiçyilmaz, Gaye. **Smiling for Strangers.** New York: Farrar, Straus & Giroux, 2000. Originally published, in somewhat different form, by Orion in 1998. ISBN 0-374-37081-8. 152p. (12-14). Novel. **England.**
Fourteen-year-old Nina and her grandfather fled Sarajevo and are hiding in their mountain cottage when soldiers find them. Nina's wounded grandfather urges her to get a safe ride out of the valley on a rescue convoy by "smiling at strangers." Nina's journey, first to Italy and then to England,

and her own pilgrimage on foot to the south of England, is told with harsh honesty. Throughout this harrowing story about a young refugee of the war in Yugoslavia, horrible incidents battle with flashbacks of happy times before the war. Readers will be rewarded by startling and, ultimately, happy surprises in the book's closing chapters. *msn*

600. Hoffman, Mary. **Starring Grace**. Illustrated by Caroline Binch. New York: Fogelman, 2000. ISBN 0-8037-2559-0. 95p. (7-9). Novel. **England**.

Grace of the picture books *Amazing Grace* and *Boundless Grace* now stars in her own chapter book. It is the beginning of summer vacation, and Grace and her four friends plan to make the most of it. Their play transforms Grace's backyard into a circus, a shuttle launch pad, and a hospital. However, the best adventure of all is when they audition for the musical *Annie*. They all get minor parts as orphans, but Grace's dreams come true when she unexpectedly fills in for an actor with laryngitis. One black-and-white drawing by Caroline Binch appears in each chapter. *chs*

601. Hoffman, Mary. **Three Wise Women**. Illustrated by Lynne Russell. New York: Dial, 1999. ISBN 0-803-72466-7. 25p. (4-9). Picture book. **England**.

A tribute to women and their gifts is the focus of this fictional account of the history of Christianity. Both parallel and in contrast to the story of the three wise men bearing expensive gifts to honor the birth of Jesus, this story celebrates the humble gifts of bread, story, and a kiss—all used later in the life of Christ. The illustrations in oil pastels create a mood of drama and realism as they richly tell the story of women from three different cultures who followed the same star. *jbm*

602. Hollyer, Beatrice. **Wake Up, World! A Day in the Life of Children around the World**. New York: Holt, 1999. Originally published by Frances Lincoln in 1999. ISBN 0-8050-6293-9. 44p. (7-9). Picture book. **England**.

This photo essay describes a day in the life of eight children from around the world, specifically from the United Kingdom, Russia, the United States, Vietnam, Brazil, Ghana, India, and Australia. Each set of activities includes colored photos, captions, and quotations to give readers a personal introduction to the lives of the children. Readers will notice similarities as well as cultural differences. For example, Linh from Vietnam sleeps under a mosquito net; Anusibuno from Ghana rubs shea butter on his skin to protect him from the wind and sun; and Cidinha from Brazil helps her mother break babassu nuts, which they sell to the villagers for making soap. An outline map of the world and short descriptions of each country add to the geographic and cultural content. *chs*

603. Hooper, Meredith. **River Story**. Illustrated by Bee Willey. Cambridge, MA: Candlewick, 2000. Originally published by Walker (U.K.) in 2000. ISBN 0-7636-0792-4. 30p. (5-8). Picture book. **England.**

A river begins high in the mountains, flows over a waterfall and down into the meadows as it widens and moves toward a city. Finally, "fresh water meets salt water" as the river reaches the sea. The rhythm of the poetic text matches the flow of the river. Full-page watercolor illustrations in lustrous blues, greens, and yellows depict the movement of the water as it races down the mountain and winds toward the sea. A map on the last spread summarizes the river's journey and includes captions that reinforce the vocabulary words learned in context. *chs*

604. Horowitz, Anthony. **The Devil and His Boy**. New York: Philomel, 2000. Originally published by Walker (U.K.) in 1998. ISBN 0-399-23432-2. 182p. (10-12). Novel. **England.**

Thirteen-year-old Tom Falconer experiences Elizabethan England, first as an unpaid servant at a country inn, then as a runaway in London. In an elaborate plot Tom finds himself the pawn of traitors, the target of a murderer, and a member of a theater company (the title refers to the name of a play). Before the end his acquaintances number Moll Cutpurse, William Shakespeare, and Queen Elizabeth. Historical detail adds depth to this adventure story. *cc*

605. Houghton, Eric. **The Crooked Apple Tree**. Illustrated by Caroline Gold. New York: Barefoot, 1999. ISBN 1-902283-597. 20p. (6-10). **England**.

After moving into a new house, Ben and Kate are disappointed to see nothing but a crooked apple tree in the backyard. "What good is a tree?" they complain. As seasons pass, however, the changing tree inspires the children to play pretending games that transform them into fanciful characters from other worlds and realities. The colorful, double-page illustrations depict the children transformed and transported in their imaginative play. After a year passes, the family celebrates the one-year anniversary of their moving day, and the father, who has been taking pictures of the apple tree games throughout the story, presents the children with a scrapbook entitled, "What Good Is a Tree?" *ebb*

606. Hughes, Shirley. **Abel's Moon**. New York: DK Ink, 1999. Simultaneously published in England by Random House (U.K.). ISBN 0-7894-4601-4. 32p. (4-6). Picture book. **England.**

When Abel Grable, whose work involves extensive world travel, returns home he tells his family stories of his adventures, and before he leaves again, he writes them down. After reading the stories over and over, the older boys, Adam and Noah, decide to have their own adventures—including building a moon machine from their father's writing table—so that they will have tales to tell him on his return. Hughes's watercolor illustrations communicate the warmth of a loving family and the fun of the imaginative play of the children. *ca*

607. Hughes, Shirley. **Alfie's ABC**. New York: Lothrop, 1998. Originally published by Red Fox/ Random House (U.K.) in 1997. ISBN 0-688-16126-X. 30p. (1-3). Picture book. **England.**

For each letter of the alphabet there is a one-sentence story and a warm and cozy illustration featuring Alfie and his little sister, Annie Rose, playfully involved in day-to-day activities with each other and with family and friends. For example, "S is for seaside, swimming, and sand castles." In *Alfie's 123* (2000) one little boy—Alfie, of course—is joined by sister, Annie Rose, and friends and family members in activities that illustrate the numbers from one to ten. *ca*

608. Hutchins, Pat. **Ten Red Apples**. Illustrated by the author. New York: Greenwillow, 2000. ISBN 0-688-16797-7. 32p. (4-6). Picture book. **England.**

In this rhyming counting book, filled with animal sounds and illustrated in bold folklike art in cheerful primary colors, ten red apples on the tree are eaten one by one by a succession of farm animals. The flat doll-like farmer attempts in vain to chase them away, shouting, "Save some for me!" The horse, cow, donkey, goat, pig, sheep, goose, duck, and hen make off with the apples, until there is only one left for the farmer and his wife. Then, they all spy another apple-laden tree. "Yippee, fiddle-dee-fee!" *lh*

609. Inkpen, Mick. **In Wibbly's Garden**. New York: Viking, 2000. Originally published by Hodder & Stoughton in 2000. ISBN 0-670-89121-5. 16p. (2-4). Engineered book. **England**.

In this lift-the-flap book, Wibbly Pig searches for his lost stuffed animal, Piggly. He finds a snail, a ladybug, a caterpillar, an unidentifiable insect, and a bean, all of which he puts under a flowerpot. Next thing you know, a beanstalk is growing, and as Wibbly climbs up, he meets a giant who is looking for his magic hen. Wibbly remembers passing a hen on his climb up, and so will children. They can raise a flap of leaves to find the hen, then raise another flap (the hen's wing) to find Piggly. Under everything is the golden egg. Unlike in the folktale, this giant is gentle, and he and Wibbly part as friends. *ss*

610. Jaffrey, Madhur. **Robi Dobi: The Marvelous Adventures of an Indian Elephant.** Illustrated by Amanda Hall. New York: Dial, 1997. Originally published by Pavilion in 1996. ISBN 0-8037-2193-5. 76p. (7-10). Short stories. **England.**

When Robi Dobi hears a cry for help from little Kabbi Wahabbi the mouse, he brings him into his ear for protection, and so begins this collection of eight stories of daring rescues from exotic creatures inspired by stories told to the author by her father. The author draws on some of the great myths of Indian folklore while adding a modern spirit to these adventures. Stylized black-and-white alternate with vibrant watercolor illustrations to capture the Indian culture. *djg*

611. James, Simon. **Days Like This: A Collection of Small Poems.** Selected and illustrated by Simon James. Cambridge, MA: Candlewick, 2000. Originally published by Walker (U.K.) in 1999. ISBN 0-7636-0812-2. 45p. (4-9). Poetry. **England.**

Traditional poems along with those written by James and others including Ogden Nash, Charlotte Zolotow, and Eve Merriam, appear in this collection enlivened with James's full page pen-and-ink and watercolor illustrations. The feelings and adventures of young children are captured in poems such as "Sleeping Outdoors," "First Day at School," "The Guppy," and "Bouncing." An index of titles appears at the end. *msn*

612. Jarvis, Robin. **The Dark Portal.** New York: SeaStar, 2000. Originally published by Macdonald Young in 1989. ISBN 1-58717-021-3. 243p. (8-12). Novel. **England.**

Book 1 of the Deptford Mice Trilogy introduces the mice, who live peacefully in a quiet house in the Skirtings. Then Albert is drawn through the grill into the dark and sinister world of the sewers, the domain of the rats. Attempts at rescue fail, but his daughter and a few brave mice refuse to give in to the evil forces that seem to be growing stronger. A gripping story of good and evil, set in a gritty underground world, this is a tale of riveting adventure and heroism. Readers will look forward to further adventures in *The Crystal Prison* and *The Final Reckoning*. *djg*

613. Jay, Alison. **Picture This.** New York: Dutton, 2000. Originally published by Templar in 1999. ISBN 0-525-46380-1. 32p. (3-8). Picture book. **England**. This word book invites children to peruse its large fresh-colored paintings with cracked glaze surfaces that give them an antique appearance. One enters Jay's imaginative world by following the scenes depicted on the antique clock on the first page through various seasons. For example, the distant hill in the illustration featuring a dog jumping over a meadow in spring is foregrounded in the following spread. The playful use of nursery rhymes and the ingenuity with which Jay transposes the same images into other contexts on different pages construct a stunning visual experience while the single word per page is clearly printed for young readers. *hc*

614. King-Smith, Dick. **The Spotty Pig**. Pictures by Mary Wormell. New York: Farrar, Straus & Giroux, 1997. (Paperback: Sunburst, 1999.) Originally published by Victor Gollancz in 1997. ISBN 0-374-371547. 32p. (4-6). Picture book. **England**.

Peter, the spotted pig, does not like his spots. He attempts to fade his spots in the summer sun, cover them with dirt while rolling in the autumn leaves, freeze them away in the winter snow, and wash them away in the spring rain. Each time, his friend Joe the cat assures him that his spots have grown, just as he has. But all ends well when he meets Penny, another spotted pig. Bright, strong linocuts illustrate the simple text. *djg*

615. Kitamura, Satoshi. **Me and My Cat?** New York: Farrar, Straus & Giroux, 2000. Originally published by Andersen Press in 1999. ISBN 0-374-34906-1. 32p. (4-9). Picture book. **England**.

A crazy day ensues after a witch enters Nicholas's room at night and switches his body with his cat's. Nicholas and Leonardo, the cat, describe their unsettling day, illustrated with exaggerated, humorous pictures that extend the fun of the story. The witch returns and admits she has had the wrong address, leading to an additional twist to the story's last page. *1999 Nestlé Smarties Silver Medal. sg*

616. Kitamura, Satoshi. **Sheep in Wolves' Clothing**. Illustrated by the author. New York: Farrar, Straus & Giroux, 1996. Originally published by Andersen Press in 1995. ISBN 0-374-36780-9. 32p. (6-8). Picture book. **England**.

When they go for a swim, three sheep are tricked into leaving their beautiful woolly coats in the care of some conniving wolves. The chilly sheep search for their coats, and with the help of cousin Elliott Baa, private detective, and a gang of cats playing rugby with a ball of yarn, they track down their coats and overpower the wolves. But it is too late. The wolves have knit the wool into sweaters, which the sheep wear back to the meadow, making them sheep in wolves' clothing. *lh*

617. Laird, Elizabeth. **A Book of Promises**. Illustrated by Michael Frith. New York: DK Ink, 2000. Originally published by Dorling Kindersley in 1999. ISBN 0-7894-2547-5. 30p. (all ages). Picture book. **England.**

This oversized book is a series of fifteen two-sided illustrations that foreground family members of all ages but in different combinations and in varied settings. Most important, each of these large illustrations features a single promise. Adult readers will recognize these promises as, collectively, profound vows of love and assurance that children ages 5 through 105 should make and keep for those they love. *ebb*

618. Lewington, Anna. **Antonio's Rain Forest**. Photographs by Edward Parker. Minneapolis: Carolrhoda, 1993. Originally published by Wayland in 1992. ISBN 0-87614-749-X. 48p. (7-9). Informational book. **England.**

Outstanding color photographs accompany a first-person essay about a young boy and his family in the Brazilian rain forest. The father is a *seringueiro,* or rubber tapper, harvesting and processing sap from wild rubber trees. One of the main emphases is how the family got out from under the control of the "rubber barons." Seven full-page sidebars provide history and overview of the rubber industry. Includes maps, glossary, index, bibliography, addresses of conservation organizations in the United States, and a list of things young readers can do to support preservation of the rain forest. *pm*

619. Lewis, Kim. **Little Calf.** Illustrated by the author. Cambridge, MA: Candlewick, 2000. ISBN 0-7636-0899-8. 20p. (1-3). Picture book. **England.**

A preschool girl is filled with wonder on the day a calf is born on her family's farm. A short text and soft, realistic, colored pencil illustrations make this a good story to share with early listeners. Full-color endpapers picturing an overview of the farm suggest a British setting. *sg*

620. Lewis, Naomi, compiler. **Rocking Horse Land and Other Classic Tales of Dolls and Toys**. Illustrated by Angela Barrett. Cambridge, MA: Candlewick, 2000. Originally published as *The Silent Playmate: A Collection of Doll Stories* by Victor Gollancz in 1979. ISBN 0-7636-0897-1. 127p. (7-9). Short stories. **England.**

This anthology includes six classic stories about treasured dolls or toys: Mrs. Fairstar's "The Memories of a London Doll," Hans Christian Andersen's "The Steadfast Tin Soldier," Ruth Ainsworth's "Rag Bag," Naomi Lewis's retelling of "Vasilissa, Baba Yaga, and the Little Doll," Laurence Housman's "Rocking Horse Land," and E. Nesbit's "The Town in the Library." Each selection is introduced with Lewis's notes on the author and the origin of the story and an intricate cut-paper black silhouette. In addition, Barrett has created softly colored pencil and watercolor illustrations, some full-page and others small, which are scattered through the texts. *ca*

621. Lia, Simone. **Red's Great Chase**. New York: Dutton, 2000. Originally published by Methuen in 1999. ISBN 0-525-46213-9. 24p. (4-8). Picture book. **England.**

"You never know when a scary monster might jump out," Red thinks, and that is just what happens. The big blue monster chases Red out of the basement, out of the house, into town, through the jungle, and across the blue mountains in this fast-paced, action-packed tale. Children can follow the chase through the maze depicted on the endpapers and will enjoy the bold, brightly colored illustrations. *djg*

622. McAllister, Angela. **The Clever Cowboy.** Illustrated by Katherine Lodge. New York: DK Ink, 1998. Published simultaneously by Dorling Kindersley (U.K.). ISBN 0-7894-3491-1. 24p. (3-6). Picture book. **England.**

Clever Cowboy enters a pancake-tossing contest in Yippieville, and tosses his pancake so high it covers up the sun. Yippieville is pitched into darkness, and Clever Cowboy is in danger of losing because his pancake doesn't come down. He wins anyway when an outlaw, Six-Shooter Sam (actually his long-lost sister Kate in disguise), retrieves the pancake by lassoing it after being catapulted to the moon by Clever Cowboy's "giant elasticated-one-seater-frying-pan" catapult. The placement of the text for this original tall tale from the Old West is as frenetic as the wacky, colorful, detailed illustrations. *ca*

623. McAllister, Margaret. **Hold My Hand and Run**. New York: Dutton, 2000. Originally published by Oxford University Press in 1999. ISBN 0-525-46391-7. 150p. (9-12). Novel. **England.**

In July 1628, thirteen-year-old Kezia Clare vows to run away with her six-year-old half-sister Beth. After the death of her beloved stepmother, Kezia helped to care for Beth and to run her father's house. But when Aunt Latimer arrived, Canon Clare became distant from his daughters and allowed his tyrannical sister full authority in household matters. Kezia chafes under her aunt's iron rule and fears that the younger, more delicate Beth will not survive the cruelty and beatings. What follows is an exciting, often harrowing, survival story, with well-drawn characters, fascinating settings, and a satisfying surprise ending. *mn*

624. McCaughrean, Geraldine. **Beauty and the Beast.** Illustrated by Gary Blythe. Minneapolis: Carolrhoda, 2000. Originally published by Transworld in 1999. ISBN 1-57505-491-4. 28p. (7-9). Picture book. **England.**

The classic tale of Beauty and the Beast is retold in rich, evocative language. Each spread has a full-page, full-color illustration plus a black-and-white vignette on the facing text page. The mixed-media art combines realistic figures with a fantasy background for a surreal effect. *pm*

625. McCaughrean, Geraldine. **The Pirate's Son.** New York: Scholastic,1998. Originally published as *Plundering Paradise* by Oxford University in 1996. (Paperback: Point, 1999). ISBN 0-590-23044-4. 294p. (10-14). Novel. **England.**

One day in 1717, fourteen-year-old Nathan and his sister, Maud, are living a dull life with their parson father. The next, their father is dead and they are on a pirate ship bound for Madagascar. Their destiny becomes entwined with that of Tamo White, a pirate's son. Tamo is torn between following his father's ways and his Malagasy mother's desire for a better future for Tamo in England. While Maud comes to thrive on the island and Tamo resigns himself to his fate, the virtuous Nathan is left to deal with the cruel irony of wealth gained unintentionally through piracy. *1996 Nestlé Smarties Book Prize Bronze Award. mm*

626. McCaughrean, Geraldine. **The Stones Are Hatching.** New York: HarperCollins, 2000. Originally published by Oxford University Press in 1999. ISBN 0-06-028765-9. 240p. (10-14). Novel. **England.**

The Stoor Worm—the World Eater—is waking after being asleep for hundreds of years, and its Hatchlings are bringing terror to Britain. An ordinary boy, Phelim Green, is chosen to make the journey to the Stoor Worm's lair to kill it and its Hatchlings. The reluctant hero has only three companions, Maiden (Alexia, a wise young witch); Fool (Sweeney, an old soldier); and Horse (Obby Oss), as he sets out to save the world. McCaughrean draws on Celtic legends in this adventure-filled, well-crafted fantasy. *ca*

627. McClure, Gillian. **Selkie.** New York: Farrar, Straus & Giroux. 1999. Originally published by Doubleday/Transworld in 1999. ISBN 0-374-

36709-4. 30p. (4-6). Picture book. **England.**

Although warned to stay away from Seal Island, Peter is drawn by the "cries of the seals on the wind." At low tide Peter follows an oysterman's path across the sands to reach the island. There he rescues a selkie who has been caught in the oysterman's net. In gratitude, she teaches Peter the "secret language of the sea." They have been seen, however, and the oysterman recaptures the selkie and takes her sealskin. Peter then finds the sealskin in the man's cottage and returns the selkie to Seal Island. The knowledge of the sea that the selkie has taught him, in turn, allows Peter to return safely home in spite of the dangerous rising tide. The softly colored scenes of the sea and island, many bordered with symbols of the sea, are the most magical part of this original selkie tale. *ca*

628. McDonnell, Flora. **I Love Animals.** Cambridge, MA: Candlewick, 1994. Originally published by Walker in 1994. ISBN 1-56402-387-7. 32p. (1-3). Picture book. **Northern Ireland.**

The author/illustrator paints a lovely farmyard scene inspired by her home in Northern Ireland, which depicts a little girl telling about all the animals she loves. Her dog, Jock, the ducks waddling to the water, the goat racing across the field, the donkey braying, the cow swishing her tail are but a few of the animals portrayed in bright acrylic and gouache paintings in this large-formatted book for young children. *1995 Mother Goose Award. djg*

629. McDonnell, Flora. **I Love Boats.** Cambridge, MA: Candlewick, 1995. Originally published by Walker in 1995. ISBN 1-56402-539-X. 32p. (1-3). Picture book. **Northern Ireland.**

A little girl describes all the kinds of boats she loves, including a houseboat, a dredger, a lobster boat, a ferry, a cargo boat, a tug and more. You see the boats at work in the large acrylic and gouache illustrations, but surprise!—they are all floating in her bath at the end. *djg*

630. McNaughton, Colin. **Wish You Were Here (and I Wasn't): A Book of Poems and Pictures for Globe Trotters.** Illustrated by the author. Cambridge, MA: Candlewick, 2000. Originally published by Walker (U.K.) in 1999. ISBN 0-7637-0271-X. 61p. (7-12). Poetry. **England.**

Children will enjoy this funny collection of poems loosely based on the themes of travel and vacations, and it would be a wonderful read-aloud choice. Colorful ink-and-watercolor illustrations in cartoon style extend the fun. *sg*

631. Medlicott, Mary, editor. **The River That Went to the Sky: Twelve Tales by African Storytellers.** Illustrated by Adelmola Akintola. New York: Kingfisher, 1995. (Paperback: issued as *Tales from Africa*, Kingfisher, 2000). ISBN 1-85697-608-4. 96p. (7-12). Short stories. **England.**

Gathered here are twelve stories from Malawi, Angola, Morocco, Ghana, Nigeria, South Africa, Kenya, West Africa, Botswana, Egypt, Sierra Leone, and Zimbabwe, which combine nine stories based on folktales and three original stories to introduce the reader to the diverse landscape of African cultures. Many of the contributors are working storytellers and musicians, helping to keep Africa's oral traditions alive. The stories are illustrated with striking, rich-colored illustrations by a Nigerian artist. Map and source notes are included. *djg*

632. Micklethwait, Lucy. **A Child's Book of Art: Discover Great Paintings.** New York: DK Ink, 1999. Originally published as *Discover Great Paintings: A Child's Book of Art* by Dorling Kindersley (U.K.) in 1993. ISBN 0-7894-4283-3. 31p. (4-9). Informational book. **England.**

The author introduces the child to a variety of paintings by famous artists using familiar themes such as family, home, pets, and gardens. In a note to parents, Micklethwait encourages adults to help children look for details and talk about colors or how the pictures make them feel. Plenty of opportunity for discussion with this book and others in the series including: *A Child's Book of Play in Art* (1996), *Spot a Dog: A Child's Book of Art* (1995) and *Spot a Cat: A Child's Book of Art* (1995). *djg*

633. Micklethwait, Lucy. **I Spy a Freight Train: Transportation in Art.** New York: Greenwillow, 1996. Originally published as *I Spy: Transport in Art* by Collins in 1996. ISBN 0-688-14700-3. unpaginated. (4-9). Picture book. **England.**

Children can study each of eleven paintings by a variety of artists spanning the globe and the centuries to spy out a car, a ship, a bicycle, a freight train, and other forms of transportation. Other books in this series are *I Spy a Lion: Animals in Art* (1994), *I Spy Two Eyes: Numbers in Art* (1993), and *I Spy: An Alphabet in Art* (1992). In each book, the galleries, museums, and copyright holders of the pictures in the book are acknowledged. *djg*

634. Mockford, Caroline. **What's This?** New York: Barefoot, 2000. ISBN 1-84148-018-5. 32p. (3-5). Picture book. **England.**

Bird finds a seed lying on the ground and wonders, "What's this?" A little girl comes along and together they plant the seed, keep it watered, and care for it until it eventually grows into a sunflower. In the fall, they share the seeds with the little girl's classmates and the following summer, all have beautiful sunflowers. Simple text and bold primitive-style illustrations are supplemented with additional information on roots, shoots, flowers, and seeds. *djg*

635. Moore, Inga. **A Big Day for Little Jack.** Cambridge, MA: Candlewick, 1994. Originally published by Walker (U.K.) in 1994. ISBN 1-56402-418-0. 28p. (3-5). Picture book. **England.**

Little Jack, an anthropomorphic rabbit, is invited to his first party. Apprehensive about the new experience, he takes a stuffed toy with him, then meets a new friend and has a wonderful time. Soft colored-pencil illustrations enhance the gentle quality of the reassuring message. *pm*

636. Moss, Miriam. **This Is the Tree.** Illustrated by Adrienne Kennaway. New York: Kane/Miller, 2000. Originally published by Frances Lincoln in 2000. ISBN 0-916629-98-7. 27p. (4-9). Informational book. **England.**

A lyrical text (each sentence of which begins with "This is the tree") and watercolor illustrations featuring the baobab and the creatures who live in or depend on the tree against a backdrop of the savanna in all kinds of weather and at all times of the day give readers a look at the fascinating baobab and the abundance of wildlife that surrounds it. Interesting facts about the baobab are presented in a spread at the end. *ca*

637. Mulherin, Jennifer, and Abigail Frost. **The Best-Loved Plays of Shakespeare.** New York: Star Bright, 2000. Originally published by Cherrytree Press in 1993. ISBN 1-887734-62-7. 158p. (11 up). Informational. **England.**

This book beautifully showcases ten Shakespearean plays: *A Midsummer Night's Dream, The Merchant of Venice, As You Like It, Twelfth Night, Romeo and Juliet, Julius Caesar, Macbeth, Hamlet, King Lear,* and *Othello.* For each play, readers will find accessible plot summaries, useful character descriptions, and romantic color illustrations. The book begins with information about Shakespeare's life and times, and it ends with a one-page fact sheet featuring a list of each of Shakespeare's plays and a time line spanning Shakespeare's life from 1564 to 1616. The time line identifies both historical events and Shakespeare's milestones, including the dates he wrote all of his plays. *ebb*

638. Newsome, Jill. **Shadow.** Illustrated by Claudio Muñoz. New York:

DK Ink, 1999. Simultaneously published by Dorling Kindersley (U.K.). ISBN 0-7894-2631-5. 32p. (5-7). Picture book. **England.**
Dramatic watercolor and India ink illustrations accompany this emotional tale of a little girl's difficulty in adjusting to her family's move to a new neighborhood. Rosy walks through frightening woods, and faces looming strangers and night fears, until her discovery of an injured rabbit in the snowy woods gives her a new interest in life, and eventually leads her to friendship. Illustrator Muñoz now lives in London, although he spent his childhood in Chile. *lh*

639. Nicholson, William. **The Wind Singer.** New York: Hyperion, 2000. First published by Egmont in 2000. ISBN 0-7868-0569-2. 358p. (9-12). Novel. **England.**
Aramanth is a perfectly structured city with its inhabitants neatly ordered in a caste system, which is reconfigured each year by the results of the high examination. Children are properly trained at home and at school. Everyone is seemingly happy, except for the Hath family. Hanno struggles with the exams, Ira recognizes the undercurrents of unhappiness in the society, and the exuberant twins Kestrel and Bowman are not intimidated by the cruel schoolmaster Maslo Inch. A harsh punishment triggers Kestrel to break all the rules and begin a quest which takes her far beyond the walls of Aramanth, meeting allies and enemies, to face the sinister Morah and find the Wind Singer, which will break the spell which has controlled the city for generations. Children will enjoy this fast-paced adventure, filled with suspense and humor, and look forward to the next two books in the Wind on Fire Trilogy. *2000 Nestlé Smarties Gold Medal. djg*

640. Oram, Hiawyn. **Kiss It Better.** Illustrated by Frédéric Joos. New York: Dutton, 1999. Originally published by Andersen Press in 1999. ISBN 0-525-46386-0. 25p. (3-5). Picture book. **England.**
When Little Bear hits her head, bumps her paw, and loses her best friend, kisses and Band-Aids from Big Bear soothe her feelings. In a role reversal, when Little Bear finds Big Bear crying over a letter, she plies the adult bear with kisses, hugs, and lots of Band-Aids. The rounded soft shapes in the cartoon-style illustrations add to the story's message of care and love. Since the gender of Big Bear is not stated, the book is perfect for sharing by fathers or mothers. *chs*

641. Oram, Hiawyn. **Princess Chamomile's Garden.** Illustrated by Susan Varley. New York: Dutton, 2000. Originally published by Andersen Press in 2000. ISBN 0-525-46387-9. 27p. (5-8). Picture book. **England.**

Princess Chamomile helps the royal gardener until she becomes overwhelmed by the hard work needed to maintain the large palace gardens. The princess plans a space more her size and spends months working with the gardeners to create her perfect garden. The watercolor illustrations depict appealing mouse characters with warmth and humor. The book closes with a three-page foldout of the princess's garden. *chs*

642. Oram, Hiawyn. **The Wrong Overcoat.** Illustrations by Mark Birchall. Minneapolis: Carolrhoda, 2000. Originally published by Andersen Press in 1999. ISBN 1-57505-453-1. 24p. (4-8). Picture book. **England.**

Chimp has a new overcoat. Even though his family and friends think it suits him perfectly, Chimp thinks it's too long, he doesn't like the color, and the sleeves are too tight. He sets out to solve the problem and readers will be surprised at his ingenuity. Watercolor illustrations perfectly convey Chimp's frustration and then his delight. *djg*

643. Paul, Korky, and Valerie Thomas. **Winnie Flies Again.** Illustrated by Korky Paul. New York: Kane/Miller, 2000. Originally published by Oxford University Press in 1999. ISBN 0-916291-94-4. 28p. (4-6). Picture book. **England.**

Poor Winnie the witch has always enjoyed travel by broomstick, but now she has so many accidents she tries other modes of transportation with similar results. The problem is solved when she gets a pair of eyeglasses. Detailed, zany illustrations take full advantage of the oversized pages. This is one of a series of books about Winnie. *sg*

644. Penney, Ian. **Ian Penney's ABC.** New York: Abrams, 1998. Originally published by National Trust in 1998. ISBN 0-8109-4350-6. 28p. (3-6). Picture book. **England.**

For each letter of the alphabet, a rich and colorful scene is filled with figures and objects that begin with the letter for that page. Upper and lower cases are given for each letter, followed by a word identifying a prominent object in the accompanying illustration. In a formal design, each letter of the alphabet (upper and lower case) is found on the red, yellow, and green borders framing each picture. For added fun, an acorn is hidden in the illustrations, many of which feature country homes and parks preserved by the National Trust in England, Ireland, and Wales. *hc*

645. Pirotta, Saviour. **Turtle Bay.** Illustrated by Nilesh Mistry. New York:

Farrar, Straus & Giroux, 1997. First published by Frances Lincoln in 1997. ISBN 0-374-37888-6. 22p. (4-6). Picture book. **England.**
Young Taro loves to spend time with his wise friend, Jiro-San. Together they walk along the shore, swim, and dive for sponges. Other children laugh when they see the old man sweeping the beach, but Taro soon learns that he is preparing for the coming of the sea turtles. *djg*

646. Pow, Tom. **Who Is the World For?** Illustrated by Robert Ingpen. Cambridge, MA: Candlewick, 2000. Originally published as *Ar gyfer pwy mae'r byd?* by Cymdeithas Lyfrau Ceredigion in 2000. ISBN 0-7636-1280-4. 32p. (4-8). Picture book. **Scotland.**
Animal offspring ask their parents "Who is the world for?" Each of the parents answers "The world is for you" by focusing on the beauty of their habitat. The mother bear notes deep caves, spring rivers, and forests, while a father Arctic hare finds beauty in the northern world of ice and snow. When a young boy asks his father the same question, he replies that the world is for everyone, animals and human alike. Ingpen's large-scale watercolor and pencil illustrations capture the beauty of each habitat and reinforce the environmental message of the lyrical text. *chs*

647. Price, Susan. **The Sterkarm Handshake.** New York: HarperCollins, 2000. Originally published by Scholastic (U.K.) in 1998. ISBN 0-06-028959-7. 440p. (12 up). Novel. **England.**
The Sterkarms, sixteenth-century inhabitants of the land along the Scotland-England border, are invaded by foreigners from the twenty-first century, who arrive via a time tube created by a British corporation in search of new frontiers. Each group has something to gain: the corporation intends to profit from resources still existing in the sixteenth century but depleted in their own, while the Sterkarms, notorious plunderers, see a chance for new booty. A cultural anthropologist sent from the twenty-first century becomes involved with the favored son of the Sterkarm chief, facilitating and complicating the inevitable battle that ensues. *1999 Guardian Children's Fiction Award. ss*

648. Pullman, Philip. **The Amber Spyglass.** New York: Knopf, 2000. ISBN 0-679-87926-9. 518p. (12-14). Novel. **England.**
In Book 3 of His Dark Materials, Pullman continues the story of Will and Lyra as they join forces with Lord Asriel, Iorek Byrnison, Serifina Pekkala, and the ghosts of the dead against the grim plans of the Consistorial Court of Discipline and the Authority's regent, Metatron. The children

grow in wisdom as they journey into the land of the dead, meet with Dr. Malone in the land of the "mulefa," and learn about the true meaning of Dust. They finally realize, as do Lord Asriel and Mrs. Coulter, what they must sacrifice to preserve Dust and build for the future. *ALA Notable Children's Book, 2001.* Books 1 and 2: *The Golden Compass* (1997) and *The Subtle Knife* (1998). *The Golden Compass,* published in England as *The Northern Lights,* won both the 1996 Carnegie and Guardian awards. *hc*

649. Rennison, Louise. **Angus, Thongs and Full-Frontal Snogging: Confessions of Georgia Nicholson.** New York: HarperCollins, 2000. Originally published by Piccadilly Press in 1999. (Paperback, HarperCollins, 2001). ISBN 0-06-028814-0. 247p. (12-14). Novel. **England.**

Fourteen-year-old Georgia's diary details her obsessions with her body, boys, and snogging (kissing), as well as family problems, in this very funny novel that owes much to Helen Fielding's *Bridget Jones's Diary* (1998) for the older set. Although very British in tone, Georgia's problems and concerns will have appeal to American teens. There is a sequel, *On the Bright Side, I'm Now the Girlfriend of a Sex God,* published in 2001. Includes "Georgia's Glossary" of English and slang terms used. *sg*

650. Repchuck, Caroline. **The Forgotten Garden.** Illustrated by Ian Andrew. From an original idea by Mike Jolley. Brookfield, CT: Millbrook Press, 1997. Originally published by Templar. ISBN 0-7613-0141-0. 32p. (8-12). Picture book. **England.**

A man enters an overgrown garden. Memories dance around him and inspire him to take out the old garden sheers and begin to entice mysterious shapes from tangled bushes. The perceptive reader first discovers a set of initials carved in a tree and later reads a monument dedicated to the parents of Ben Green. The last illustration shows a fathers handing a young boy garden sheers and the reader suddenly understands. Soft illustrations set the tone for this lovely nostalgic tale. *djg*

651. Rosen, Billi. **Andi's War.** New York: Dutton, 1989. Originally published by Faber and Faber in 1988. (Paperback: Puffin, 1991). ISBN 0-525-44473-4. 136p. (12-14). Novel. **England.**

Andi's War tells the story of a young Greek girl coming of age in Greece during the Civil War, which broke out between the Communist partisans and the loyalists. The author does justice to the complexity of the Greek Civil War, capturing the reality and harshness of life during that time with clarity, sensitivity, and as much objectivity as possible. With her partisan parents fighting in the mountains and with only the guidance of her grand-mother, Andi comes to terms with death, loss, and fear and develops into a strong, dynamic leader. It is a novel telling not only of the physical war surrounding the heroine and highlighting its futility, but also of the emotional war being waged within the consciousness of an adolescent girl. *Andi's War* is the first part of Rosen's trilogy based on Andi's life. *1987 Faber/ Guardian/Jackanory Children's Competition for unpublished authors for children; 1993 Prix Enfance du Monde Natha Caputo (UNICEF). des*

652. Ross, Tony. **I Want to Be.** Illustrated by the author. New York: Kane/Miller, 1993. Originally published by Andersen Press in 1993. ISBN 0-916291-46-4. 28p. (4-6). Picture book. **England.**

In this sequel to *I Want My Potty*, the unnamed little princess asks her mother, father, and various courtiers how to grow up but is dissatisfied with their answers. Finally the maid asks what the princess herself wants to be and receives a childlike answer. Whimsical ink-and-watercolor illustrations enhance the slight text, adding charm and age-appropriate humor. Also by Ross: *Wash Your Hands! pm*

653. Rowe, John. **Can You Spot the Spotted Dog?** Illustrated by the author. New York: Delacorte, 1996. Originally published by Hutchinson in 1996. ISBN 0-385-32207-0. 24p. (3-6). Picture book. **England.**

A charmingly illustrated hidden picture book with a twist: it's cumulative. On the first spread, there is just one creature—the spotted dog—to find, but by the end of the book, there are twelve. For added fun, the final spread features a mirror, so that the last "creature" to be found is the reader! The cumulative text also makes the book a good one for emerging readers. *mb*

654. Rowe, John A. **Monkey Trouble.** Illustrated by the author. New York: North-South Books, 1999. Originally published as *Affenzoff* by Nord-Süd in 1999. ISBN 0-7358-1033-8. 30p. (5-8). Picture book. **England.**

Little Monkey, who never listens, defies orders and climbs the tallest tree he can find. A cyclone blows him out of the tree and into a great circular adventure. He becomes the victim of mistaken identity as he searches for his way home. The refrain "Oh, if only he had listened" at the end of each episode reminds readers of Little Monkey's initial act of defiance. Even the framed surrealistic paintings cannot contain Little Monkey, as bits of the pictures break out of the frames and spill over to the text page. *chs*

655. Rowling, J. K. **Harry Potter and the Sorcerer's Stone**. New York: Scholastic, 1998. Originally published as *Harry Potter and the Philosopher's Stone* by Bloomsbury in 1997. (Paperback: Scholastic, 1998). ISBN 0-590-35340-3. 309p. (8 up). Novel. **Scotland**.

This first in a projected series of seven novels introduces Harry Potter, whose eleventh birthday is the occasion for an acceptance letter from Hogwarts School of Witchcraft and Wizardry. Harry, whose aunt and uncle begrudgingly took him in after his parents' deaths, is unaware of his wizardly ancestry or his fame in the wizard world as one who has survived an encounter with the evil Voldemort. Thus begins Harry's seven years as a Hogwarts student, where he learns to play Quidditch and pursues studies in such subjects as charms, potions, and the history of magic while fending off attacks from those who wish him harm. Other books in the series to date: *Harry Potter and the Chamber of Secrets, Harry Potter and the Prisoner of Azkaban,* and *Harry Potter and the Goblet of Fire.* Awards garnered by books in this series: *1999 Whitbread Children's Book of the Year Award*; *1999, 1998, and 1997 Nestlé Smarties Gold Medals. ss*

656. Sharratt, Nick. **Split Ends**. New York: Phyllis Fogelman, 2000. First published by Egmont in 2000. ISBN 0-8037-2521-3. 24p. (3-7). Engineered book. **England**.

Twelve stiff pages, each split in thirds, provide a mix-and-match of hairstyles, earrings, and facial features. Make a man with green ponytails and a beard or a woman with a blue flattop and purple lipstick. Sturdy spiral binding will hold up to hours of manipulation. *ss*

657. Simmons, Steven J. **Percy to the Rescue.** Illustrated by Kim Howard. Watertown, MA: Charlesbridge, 1998. 0-88106-390-8. 29p. (4-6). Picture book.

A pigeon named Percy enjoys visiting famous places in London. On one of his daily visits to Kensington Gardens, where an elderly woman, Matilda, feeds him crumbs, Percy sees two boys become stranded on an island in the middle of Hyde Park's Serpentine Lake as their boat floats away. Percy flies to the island, and the boys write a note seeking help for Percy to deliver. Only Matilda pays attention to Percy. She gets the bobbies, and Percy guides the rescue team to the boys. The endpapers feature a map of Percy's London. What is fun here is the bird's-eye tour of London. *ca*
Author from the United States

658. Souhami, Jessica. **No Dinner! The Story of the Old Woman and the Pumpkin**. New York: Marshall Cavendish, 1999. First published by Frances

Lincoln in 1999. ISBN 0-7614-5059-9. 28p. (4-8). Picture book. **England.**
There was once a frail old woman who wanted to visit her granddaughter on the other side of the forest, but how to avoid those fierce hungry animals? The crafty woman convinces wolf, bear, and tiger to wait until the return trip when she is nice and fat. No dinner! It is the clever granddaughter who thinks of a way to get her grandmother safely home. This adaptation of a traditional Asian tale is illustrated with brilliant watercolors. *djg*

659. Stevenson, Robert Louis. **My Shadow.** Illustrated by Penny Dale. Cambridge, MA: Candlewick, 1999. ISBN 0-7636-0923-4. 24p. (2-6). Poetry. **England.**
Stevenson's classic poem (from *A Child's Garden of Verses*, 1885) has been cheerfully re-illustrated in spritely, appealing watercolors. The child narrator observes and plays with his shadow in a variety of situations, including an ethnically mixed preschool group. *pm*

660. Stojic, Manya. **Rain.** Illustrated by the author. New York: Crown, 2000. Originally published by David Bennet in 2000. ISBN 0-517-80085-3. 32p. (4-6). Picture book. **England.**
Brief, simple, repetitive phrases printed in bold, black, sans serif typeface proclaim the importance of rain to the animals of the African plains. The word of the coming rain spreads from animal to animal, and each takes its own pleasure in the aftermath, until the sun dries the soil and the wait for rain begins again. The double pages are flooded with intense, contrasting colors. The animals are rendered in unblended brush strokes that stimulate emotion and empathy. *km, sm*

661. Sturtevant, Katherine. **At the Sign of the Star.** New York: Farrar, Straus & Giroux 2000. ISBN 0-374-30449-1. 140p. (9-12). Novel. **England.**
When her father remarries, twelve-year-old Meg Moore stands to lose her inheritance—her father's thriving bookselling business and his life among the great literary men of 1677 London. She fears the comet she saw in the night sky over London may foretell a dreary marriage for her and a life away from the world of books. This wonderfully written, quiet novel takes the reader through the streets of London and into the playhouses, as we watch this intelligent, independent girl discover that she indeed has a hand in her own fate. *ds*
Author from the United States

662. Sutcliff, Rosemary. **Sword Song.** New York: Farrar, Straus & Giroux,

1997. First published by The Bodley Head in 1997. ISBN 0-374-37363-9. 272p. (10-12). Novel. **England.**

Sixteen-year-old Bjarni Sigurdson, exiled from his settlement for five years for drowning a monk who kicked his dog, sets sail with Heriolf, the merchant, to Dublin. For five years, Bjarni, accompanied by his new black hound, hires his sword out to island chiefs, Onund Treefoot and Thorstein the Red, respectively. After the death of Thorstein, Bjarni returns home with the young woman, Angelhard, who has been driven from her Welsh home by an unscrupulous relative. In her last book, Sutcliff describes the daily life, culture, and feuds of the Viking settlers on the islands off the west coast of Scotland. *hc*

663. Waddell, Martin. **The Big Big Sea.** Illustrated by Jennifer Eachus. Cambridge, MA: Candlewick, 1994. Originally published by Walker (U.K.) in 1994. ISBN 1-56402-066-5. 24p. (5-6). Picture book. **Northern Ireland.**

A simply written text invites readers to participate as a daughter and her mother frolic on the beach of the Northern Sea. It is late at night, and the silvery illustrations show every earthly object bathed in soft shadows or moon glow as the happy pair doff their shoes, splash the waves, and study their footprints. *ebb*

664. Waddell, Martin. **Rosie's Babies.** Illustrated by Penny Dale. Cambridge, MA: Candlewick, 1999. Originally published by Walker (U.K.) in 1992. ISBN 0-7636-0718-5. 22p. (3-7). Picture book. **Northern Ireland.**

Inspired by real-life events, this story re-creates a conversation between a mother and her young daughter. The mother, who is bathing, nursing, and bedding a new baby, plays along when Rosie importantly announces she has her own two babies: a teddy bear and a stuffed rabbit. By asking questions, the mother learns what Rosie's babies eat, how they behave, and what they play. Each full-page illustration, depicting Rosie's babies participating in fanciful pursuits, is complemented by a smaller illustration of Rosie talking with her mother as she works with the baby. This side-by-side effect grounds the story in reality, while confirming that the mother, though busy, still has time for Rosie. *ebb*

665. Waddell, Martin. **Who Do You Love?** Illustrated by Camilla Ashforth. Cambridge, MA: Candlewick, 1999. ISBN 0-7636-0586-7. 25p. (3-7). Picture book. **Northern Ireland.**

It's bedtime for a kitten named Holly, but not until she and the mama cat have played their nightly go-to-bed game. "Who do you love?" the mama asks again and again as the day winds down to a comfortable close, and Holly responds each time by naming family or friends and then invoking cherished memories of them. These memories, which are depicted in soft, watercolor illustrations filling entire pages, invite readers to participate in not only the bedtime game but also Holly's childhood relationships. Sweetest of all the relationships, though, is the one she shares with the mama cat, whose name (much to the mama's feigned chagrin) is "saved for last" in the bedtime ritual. *ebb*

666. Waite, Judy. **The Stray Kitten.** Illustrated by Gavin Rowe. New York: Crocodile, 2000. Simultaneously published by Little Tiger (U.K.). ISBN 1-56656-356-9. 28p. (4-6). Picture book. **England.**

A hungry "scrap of a kitten," born in the mean streets of Any City, learns to fend for himself. He learns to be careful, to be quick, to be patient, and to fight. Later, when he's a starving cat and the world seems desolate, he learns not to care. Ultimately, the cat is rescued from the jaws of a bulldozer by a caring boy, and at last he learns to love. A sparse but eloquent text complements Rowe's vibrant paintings. *rhm*

667. Wallace, Karen. **Scarlette Beane.** Illustrated by Jon Berkeley. New York: Dial, 2000. Originally published by Oxford University Press in 1999. ISBN 0-8037-2475-6. 28p. (4-6). Picture book. **England.**

When Scarlette is five years old, her family of avid gardeners gives her a vegetable garden of her own. When she goes to bed after planning her seeds, her fingers glow like green lights and in the morning gigantic vegetables appear in her garden. Everyone in the village comes to help harvest and Mrs. Beane makes a wonderful soup in a concrete mixer. That night Scarlette plants some more magic seeds and a castle made of vegetables appears. Glowing, thickly painted pictures make the whole process of growing things seem magical and alluring. *sg*

668. Watts, Bernadette. **Harvey Hare, Postman Extraordinaire.** Illustrated by the author. New York: North-South, 1997. Originally published as *Hase Hannes der Postbote* by Nord-Süd (Switzerland) in 1997. (Paperback: North-South, 1999). ISBN 1-55858-687-3. 32p. (4-6). Picture book. **England.**

Harvey Hare faithfully carries the mail to the woodland animals through summer heat, autumn storms, and winter chill. When spring arrives, the animals present Harvey with a thank-you gift: a beautiful umbrella to protect him from all kinds of weather. Sweet, old-fashioned illustrations are perfect for this gentle tale that reinforces familiar lessons about hard work and gratitude. Sequels include *Happy Birthday, Harvey Hare!* and *Harvey Hare's Christmas. mb*

669. White, Kathryn. **When They Fight**. Illustrated by Cliff Wright. Delray Beach, FL: Winslow Press, 2000. Originally published as *Good Day, Bad Day* by Oxford University Press in 2000. ISBN 1-890817-46-5. 28p. (4-8). Picture book. **England.**

When mother and father badger fight, the world shakes, the house quakes, and little badger feels cold and lonely, frightened and sad. But when they are friends, little badger floats on clouds, the world smiles, and he feels safe and warm. Then he knows that he loves his mom and dad and that they love him. An introduction by a psychologist explains that children find it difficult to express their feelings in a stressful family situation. This book helps a child explore this family interaction in a simple way. *djg*

670. Whybrow, Ian. **Little Wolf's Book of Badness**. Illustrated by Tony Ross. Minneapolis: Carolrhoda, 2000. Originally published by HarperCollins (U.K.) in 1995. ISBN 1-57505-410-8. 130p. (7-10). Transitional book. **England.**

Little Wolf has been sent by his parents to attend Cunning College for Brute Beasts operated by his uncle, Big Bad, in the Frettnin Forest. The story is told through his letters home to Mom and Dad, written as he walks the miles to Big Bad, begging to come home every step of the way. The letters continue as Little Wolf struggles to learn the Nine Rules of Badness, and Uncle Big Bad steals his ideas for trapping the little girl in red and her grandma. Encounters with a pack of cub scouts camping nearby lead to a hilarious ending, although a sad one for Uncle Big Bad. Sequels are *Little Wolf's Diary of Daring Deeds* and *Little Wolf's Haunted Hall for Small Horrors. lh*

671. Whybrow, Ian. **Quacky Quack-Quack**. Illustrated by Russell Ayto. Cambridge, MA: Candlewick, 1998. Originally published by Walker (U.K.) in 1991. ISBN 0-7636-0510-7. 30p. (3-7). Picture book. **England.**

Mommy gave baby some bread to feed the ducks, but baby starts to eat it instead. The ducks swarm around baby and begin to make a lot of duck noises. What a commotion! But big brother knows what to do. Watercolor line drawings and funny detail add to a book that will be sure to make children laugh. *Mother Goose Award. djg*

672. Whybrow, Ian. **Sammy and the Dinosaurs.** Illustrated by Adrian Reynolds. New York: Orchard, 1999. Originally published by David & Charles in 1999. ISBN 0-531-30207-5. 26p. (4-8). Picture book. **England.**
One day, while Sammy is helping Gran clean the attic, he finds a box of dinosaurs. He takes the box downstairs, cleans them, and fixes the broken ones and hurries off to the library to find out their names. From that day on they are inseparable, until he leaves them on the train. *djg*

673. Williams, Marcia. **Bravo, Mr. William Shakespeare!** Cambridge, MA: Candlewick, 2000. Published simultaneously by Walker (U.K.). ISBN 0-7636-1209-X. 36p. (10-12). Picture book. **England.**
Here, in truncated comic book format, are seven of Shakespeare's plays: *As You Like It, Antony and Cleopatra, Richard III, Twelfth Night, King Lear, The Merchant of Venice,* and *Much Ado about Nothing.* A rowdy bunch of Globe theatergoers inhabit the borders of each page, offering commentary on the action. The plot of each play is described in text boxes beneath each frame of the bountiful illustrations. The dialogue of the characters, printed in small italics, is pure Bill Shakespeare. So if young readers can get past the mega-busy artwork, the border kibitzing, and the tiny type, they can come away with a smattering of Elizabethan English and an acquaintance with the Bard at his best. *rhm*

674. Willis, Jeanne. **The Boy Who Lost His Belly Button.** Illustrated by Tony Ross. New York: DK, 2000. Originally published by Andersen Press in 1999. ISBN 0-7894-6164-1. 26p. (3-6). Picture book. **England.**
Once upon a time, a little boy wakes up and finds that his belly button is missing, so he leaves the city and canoes into the jungle to search for it. Whimsical, two-sided illustrations depicting the boy during his search complement the story line, which is comprised primarily of dialogue between the boy and various jungle animals. All of these animals have only their own belly buttons, except for one: the crocodile. He reasonably explains that he took the boy's belly button to wash the lint out. The story culminates with the boy slowly wading into a swamp where he grabs his belly button and replaces it on his stomach. *ebb*

675. Willis, Jeanne. **Susan Laughs.** Illustrated by Tony Ross. New York: Holt, 2000. Originally published by Andersen Press in 1999. ISBN 0-8050-6501-6. 28p. (3-7). Picture book. **England.**
Susan laughs; Susan sings; Susan flies; Susan swings. Susan is pictured with family members, schoolmates, and friends having fun doing the

same things as children the world over. Susan through and through—just like me, just like you—is shown in the last picture seated in her wheelchair. Whimsical watercolor illustrations subtly convey the message without sentimentality. *djg*

676. Wilson-Max, Ken. **Furaha Means Happy: A Book of Swahili Words**. Illustrated by the author. New York: Hyperion, 2000. Published simultaneously in the U.K. by David Bennett. ISBN 0-7868-0552-8. 26p. (4-9). Picture book. **England**.

Wambui and her family, who live in Kenya, go to the lake to picnic. As the rather simple story is told, certain words are identified with their pictures in both English and Swahili, thus making this book interesting for a wider range of readers other than emergent ones. Figures in bold colors outlined in black emphasize the concept nature of this book, and a map at the beginning and pronunciation guide at the end help readers to interact more with the setting. Born in Zimbabwe, the author now lives in London and has also written and illustrated *Halala Means Welcome: A Book of Zulu Words*. *jbm*

677. Wormell, Christopher. **Blue Rabbit and Friends**. New York: Phyllis Fogelman, 2000. Originally published by Jonathan Cape in 1999. ISBN 0-8037-2499-3. 32p. (1-5). Picture book. **England.**

Unhappy with his cave in the forest, Blue Rabbit sets out to find another home. He meets Bear, dissatisfied with his wet pool, Goose, who does not like "Rover's" kennel, and Dog, who is cramped in his hole under a cover sprinkled with daisies. The friends change homes, except for Blue Rabbit, who decides to "keep looking" and see the world. Framed in black against a white background, the linoleum block prints are characterized by heavy black lines, bold colors, and shading, giving objects—blocks, a round dish, a kennel—and animals figures a solid, three-dimensional quality. *hc*

678. Wormell, Mary. **Why Not?** New York: Farrar, Straus & Giroux, 2000. ISBN 0-374-38422-3. 32p. (2-5). Picture book. **Scotland**.

Barnaby, a calico kitten, is bold and independent as he follows his mom home for supper. "Don't chase the chickens, Barnaby!" Mom warns. "Why not?" he asks. "Because I'll chase *you*," warns the rooster. Barnaby has similar encounters with a crow, a ram, and a horse as he leaps and climbs over the farm until he finds himself stuck in a hay bale. He doesn't want any help from the other animals. Why not? Because he can get out by himself and walk home with his mom in time for supper! Action in Wormell's lively illustrations, in color with bold black outlining resembling linoleum prints, moves from left to right. The typeface is large and similarly bold. *mn*

Related Information

Awards

Carnegie Medal
The Carnegie Medal is Britain's oldest and most prestigious children's book award. It was first won by Arthur Ransome in 1936 and is awarded annually by the Library Association for "outstanding writing in a children's book."

Kate Greenaway Medal
Instituted in 1955 and awarded annually by the Library Association for "outstanding illustration in a children's book." It was first won by Edward Ardizzone in 1956. Past and current winners for both the Carnegie and Greenaway medals are listed at the Library Association website.

Guardian Children's Fiction Award
The *Guardian* newspaper sponsors and administers this award, given annually to an outstanding work of fiction (not picture books) for children written by a British or Commonwealth author, first published in the United Kingdom during the previous calendar year. The winner is chosen by a panel of authors and the review editor for the *Guardian's* children's books section.

Nestlé Smarties Book Prize
The Nestlé Smarties Book Prize was established in 1985 by Booktrust, with medals awarded to books in three age categories (under 5, 6-8, and 9-11) written in English by a U. K. citizen, or an author residing in the United Kingdom in the year ending October 31. A panel of adult judges chooses a shortlist and schoolchildren enter a competition to determine which classes will vote on the winners.

Kurt Maschler Award
The award, administered by the Booktrust, is made to the author and illustrator of a children's book that combines excellence in both text and illustration. Entries for the award must have been published during the preceding year.

Whitbread Children's Book of the Year Award
This annual award, sponsored by a British corporation, is given to books by authors who have been residents in the United Kingdom or Eire

for three years for books published in the preceding year ending October 31. Since 1999, the winner of the Whitbread Children's Book of the Year Award is also considered for the overall Whitbread Book of the Year Award, which carries a large cash prize.

Many other awards, in addition to those listed here, are described at the website of the Booktrust (see *Organizations* below).

Online Publications
ACHUKA
www.achuka.co.uk
ACHUKA describes itself quite rightly as the "Chock-Full, Eyes-Peeled, Independent Children's Books Site." Book news and reviews, author and illustrator interviews are all here, with reports from correspondents in the United States, Australia/New Zealand, Canada, and Europe, back issues on file, and a search engine to access it all.

The Bookseller
www.thebookseller.com
This is the British equivalent of *Publishers Weekly*, providing news about books and publishing business to publishers, booksellers, and others in the industry. Especially useful are the links to the websites of British publishers.

Online Bookstores
WH Smith
www.whsmith.co.uk
All online bookstores are not alike. This one has a children's section, with features such as Star Author section, Fun Stuff (competitions, crossword), a children's best-seller list, and well-written reviews by young people.

Amazon.uk
www.amazon.co.uk
Like its American counterpart, this site posts customer reviews and also classifies children's books into age categories that can be browsed.

Organizations
The Library Association
www.la-hq.org.uk/index.html
This professional group for librarians and information managers is the British counterpart to the American Library Association.

Booktrust

www.booktrusted.com/index.html

The mission of this independent educational organization is to work for and with all those concerned with children and what they read. Each year Young Booktrust produces resources for National Children's Book Week. Its well-organized website offers book news, links to prize lists (including many awards not listed above), publishers' addresses, bookstores, and anything else you could possibly want.

Other
Children's Laureate

www.childrenslaureate.org

Sponsored by the British bookstore Waterstone's and supported by British publishers, this honorary two-year position was created in 1998 to acknowledge the importance of exceptional children's authors in creating the readers of tomorrow. Thus far, two appointments have been made: Quentin Blake (1999-2001) and Anne Fine (2001-2003). The website gives more information about the activities of the post as well as biographies of each of the laureates.

Yugoslavia

679. Filipovic, Zlata. **Zlata's Diary: A Child's Life in Sarajevo**. Introduction by Janine Di Giovanni. Translated by Christina Pribichevich-Zoric. New York: Viking, 1994. Originally published in Croat by UNICEF in 1993. 200p. (10-14). Autobiography.

Zlata begins this diary just before her eleventh birthday in 1991. She writes of birthday parties and rock groups, supermodels and ski champions. But within months the tone of the entries changes, and where once there was peace, now there is war. We read about a world, circumscribed by violence, in which Zlata and her family are confined to their apartment. Because it is too dangerous to attend school, the diary becomes Zlata's only solace. *djg*

680. Hiçyilmaz, Gaye. **Smiling for Strangers**. New York: Farrar, Straus & Giroux, 2000. Originally published, in somewhat different form, by Orion in 1998. ISBN 0-374-37081-8. 152p. (12-14). Novel.

See Europe/United Kingdom for description.

681. I Dream of Peace: Images of War by Children of Former Yugoslavia. Preface by Maurice Sendak. Introduction by James P. Grant, executive director, UNICEF. New York: HarperCollins, 1994. ISBN 0-06-251128-9. 80p. (8-12). Informational.

Aleksandar of Sarajevo, severely burned in an explosion says, "When I close my eyes, I dream of peace." This collection of children's words and artistic expressions is a testament both to the horrors that children like Aleksandar endure and to the hope that burns within them. Full-color reproductions of children's art portray the cruel realities of war as experienced by children whose homes and schools have been bombed and who have witnessed the brutality of war firsthand. Their poetry cries out to those who hear words such as ten-year-old Sandra's: "Don't ever hurt the children. They're not guilty of anything." Maurice Sendak observes that "these fierce images do not speak of blame, only of sick despair that blossoms into radiant hope." *djg*

682. Lorbiecki, Marybeth. **My Palace of Leaves in Sarajevo.** Illustrated by Herbert Tauss. New York: Dial, 1997. ISBN 0-8037-2033-5. 56p. (10-12) Novel.

A series of letters presents the four-year pen-pal relationship between a young girl in what is now Bosnia-Herzegovina and her cousin in Minnesota. The correspondence begins in 1991, just before the Yugoslav People's Army invaded Croatia. Nadja describes her family's increasingly difficult life in a war zone, while Alex tries to send support in words and in packages of supplies. Eight illustrations in charcoal, oil paints, and oil crayons on canvas portray the Bosnian family. Includes map of the former Yugoslavia and addresses for sending donations to aid Bosnians. *pm*

Author from the United States

683. Marx, Trish. **One Boy from Kosovo.** Photographs by Cindy Karp. New York: HarperCollins, 2000. ISBN 0-688-17732-8. 32p. (9-13). Informational book.

An introductory chapter sets the historical and political stage for this sobering journey of a twelve-year-old boy and his family, Albanians from Kosovo forced to live in a refugee camp in Macedonia. As Edi and his family deal with the basics (food, shelter, clothing) of the camp routine, we know from the text and photos that family love endures and life goes on with time for play, volunteer work, journal writing, etc. The epilogue reports a happy ending as the family is repatriated after the war is over. *bjk*

684. Mead, Alice. **Adem's Cross**. New York: Farrar, Straus & Giroux, 1996. ISBN 0-374-30057-7. 132p. (10 up). Novel.

Adem, a fourteen-year-old ethnic Albanian, bears the physical and emotional scars of the war with the Serbian-dominated Kosovo. The first day of school brings the now familiar tear gas attacks and ritualistic beatings of Albanian teachers, and Adem's older sister, Fatmira, soon announces in confidence that she will carry out a nonviolent act of defiance against Serb aggression. It becomes apparent to Adem that his future and survival are at the whims and mercy of his oppressors, and he is forced into making a fateful decision. Mead portrays the life-and-death struggle of a minority culture during the Yugoslav war of the 1990s. *rlk*

10
Global

Multinational Books

685. Adler, Naomi. **Play Me a Story: Nine Tales about Musical Instruments.** Illustrated by Greta Cencetti. Brookfield, CT: Millbrook, 1998. First published in by Barefoot Books in 1997. ISBN 0-7613-0401-0. 80p. (mixed ages). Anthology.

This book is a collection of tales originating in nine countries around the world that feature musical instruments native to that country. Some tales are as well-known as the "Pied Piper of Hamelin," from Germany, and others, not so well-known, like "Didgeridoo Magic" from Australia's Aboriginal people. Credits for the stories are appended. *djg*

686. Beeler, Selby B. **Throw Your Tooth on the Roof: Tooth Traditions from around the World.** Illustrated by G. Brian Karas. Boston: Houghton Mifflin, 1998. ISBN 0-395-89108-6. 32p. (4-9). Picture book.

This book will connect with children all over the world as it explores the universal and riveting ritual of what to do with lost baby teeth. Beginning with our own Tooth Fairy, the author quickly introduces a parade of other helpers (mice, rats, birds, squirrels, the moon) as well as places other than our own under the pillow (in a slipper, up on the roof, in a pot, in a field, in the river, in a glass of water, in a hole in the ground). The comical illustrations offer visual clues to each country, and the book ends with two spreads of informative illustrations, tooth facts, and vocabulary. The book begs to be used in a variety of ways: to develop, compare, and contrast charts, graphs, map skills, a writing model. *bjk*
Author from the United States

687. Hamanaka, Sheila, compiler. **On the Wings of Peace: In Memory of Hiroshima and Nagasaki.** New York: Clarion, 1995. ISBN 0-395-72619-0. 144p. (8-12). Anthology.

This book is dedicated to the memory of the people who died at Hiroshima and Nagasaki. Sixty writers and illustrators speak out for peace in this collection of stories, poems, and art. Literature has been translated

from Spanish, Japanese, Danish, Persian, and Portuguese. Each piece is exquisitely illustrated by renowned children's book illustrators. From a moving story of nuclear destruction by Yoko Kawashima Watkins to a story by Milton Meltzer on the Quakers, from a story of the struggles in the West Bank by Omar Castañeda to letter from Baghdad by Barbara Bedway, these stories take us on a journey—on the wings of peace. Extensive bibliographies are appended along with biographical notes on all contributors. *1997 UNESCO Honor Book. djg*
Compiler from the United States

688. Harshman, Marc. **All the Way to Morning**. Illustrated by Felipe Davalos. New York: Marshall Cavendish, 1999. ISBN 0-7614-5042-4. 32p. (3-8). Picture book.

A father and son go camping, and as the boy crawls into his sleeping bag, Dad says: "As the earth turns day into night, kids just like you get ready to sleep and listen, too." Children from twelve countries are portrayed in full-color spreads listening to the night sounds in and around their homes. *djg*
Author from the United States

689. Hollyer, Beatrice. **Wake Up, World! A Day in the Life of Children around the World**. New York: Holt, 1999. Originally published by Frances Lincoln in 1999. ISBN 0-8050-6293-9. 44p. (7-9). Picture book. **England**.

See Europe/United Kingdom for description.

690. Jaffe, Nina. **Patakin: World Tales of Drums and Drummers**. With drawings by Ellen Eagle. New York: Holt, 1994. ISBN 0-8050-3005-0. 145p. (8-12). Short stories.

This collection of stories will introduce readers to drums and drummers from many cultures, including Haiti, Ghana, Fiji, Korea, India, Ireland, and Venezuela. The story follows introductory information about each culture and the use of the drum within that culture. Source notes are included for each story along with a bibliography as well as a discography. *djg*
Author from the United States

691. Jaffe, Nina, and Steve Zeitlin. **The Cow of No Color: Riddle Stories and Justice Tales from Around the World**. Pictures by Whitney Sherman. New York: Holt, 1998. ISBN 0-8050-3736-5. 162p. (8-12). Short stories.

Each of the stories in this collection from around the world turns on the question of justice. After the authors describe each problem, they

give the reader a chance to solve it before revealing the answer as it appears in the original tale. *djg*
Author from the United States

692. Lankford, Mary D. **Hopscotch around the World**. Illustrated by Karen Milone. New York: Morrow, 1992. ISBN 0-688-08420-6. 48p. (7-12). Informational book.

Nineteen hopscotch games from all over the world are gathered together in a collection that sparks interest in the variations of patterns, objects, and shapes while bringing children of diverse cultures together. Each version is clearly explained with differences linked to each country's geography, culture, or climate. Appealing illustrations are representative of each country. Includes a world map, author's note, and bibliography. *bjk*
Author from the United States

693. Mahy, Margaret, editor. **Don't Read This! And Other Tales of the Unnatural**. Illustrations by The Tjong Khing. Asheville, NC: Front Street/ Lemniscaat, 1998. Previously published as *Fingers on the Back of the Neck and Other Ghost Stories* and *Lees dit niet en andere griezelver-halen* by Lemniscaat in 1997. ISBN 1-886910-22-7. 213p. (10-14). Short stories.

This book was conceived, created, and published in cooperation with the International Board of Books for Young People. Eleven stories of murder, aliens, ghosts, and forsaken places by world-renown children's authors Margaret Mahy (New Zealand), Charles Mungoshi (Zimbabwe), Susan Cooper (United Kingdom), Roberto Piumini (Italy), Klaus Kordon (Germany), Eiko Kadono (Japan), Paul Biegel (Netherlands), Kit Pearson (Canada), Bjarne Reuter (Denmark), Uri Orlev (Israel), and Jordi Sierra I Fabra (Spain) are included in this anthology, which is guaranteed to raise the hair on the back of the neck. *djg*

694. Mazer, Anne, editor. **A Walk in My World: International Short Stories about Youth**. New York: Persea Books, 1998. ISBN 0-89255-237-9. 223p. (12 up). Short stories.

Anne Mazer tells us that these sixteen classic stories were chosen to take readers into the heart of another culture. Written by some of the world's best writers, these stories transport the reader all over the globe to show both the ordinary and the extraordinary. The reader will discover what it's like to live in another culture and meet kindred spirits on their own journeys to adulthood. Biographical notes on all the authors are appended. *djg*
Editor from the United States

695. Pohrt, Tom. **Having a Wonderful Time.** New York: Farrar, Straus & Giroux, 1999. ISBN 0-374-32898-6. 32p. (6-9). Picture book.

Eva and her sophisticated cat, Sam, are tired of winter. They check their passports and book passage on the zeppelin *La Grande Banane* and begin a fantastic trip around the world with destinations in several ports of call. They dine in the Crocodile Café and meet a lizard hotel proprietor. Soft watercolor illustrations complement the story. *djg*
Author from the United States

696. Preiss, Byron, editor. **The Best Children's Books in the World: A Treasury of Illustrated Stories.** New York: Abrams, 1996. ISBN 0-8109-1246-5. 320p. (all ages). Anthology.

This important collection is truly many books in one and offers a unique opportunity to see the work of writers and illustrators in the forms published in their own countries and languages. The oversized format encompasses reproduction of the original page spreads with English translations alongside. An introduction by Jeffrey Garrett emphasizes the value of this collection, and introductions to each book offer information about the author, illustrator, and book. The fifteen books reproduced here represent Belgium, Brazil, China, England, Germany and Russia, Ghana and Austria, Iran, Israel, New Zealand, Norway, Russia, Slovakia and Germany, Spain, Sri Lanka, and Switzerland. In some cases, this rich source is our only access to the work of some of the world's greatest contemporary award-winning artists and writers. *ss*
Editor from the United States

697. Siegel, Alice, and Margo McLoone. **The Blackbirch Kid's Almanac of Geography.** Woodbridge, CT: Blackbirch, 2000. ISBN 1-56711-300-1. 336p. (10-14). Informational book.

Most almanacs are equally useful for looking up facts and for browsing; this one definitely excels in the browsing category. Even though it is tightly packed with information, the design remains clean and appealing. Covering such areas as animals, world currencies, physical geography, foods, religions, fine arts, and world cities, it contains photos, diagrams, and maps that are eye-catching and of interest rather than simply decorative. Includes an index. *ss*
Author from the United States

698. Simmons, Lesley Ann. **Meet Kofi, Maria & Sunita: Family Life in Ghana, Peru & India.** Peterborough, NH: Cobblestone, 1996. ISBN

0-942389-12-3. 80p. (8-12). Illustrated book.

In three separate stories, the everyday life of a child is presented. Each child lives in a country helped by the World Bank, which lends money to developing countries to make improvements that will bring the people better living conditions. For instance, Kofi's life—and that of his whole family—changed for the better when a well was built in their village; Kofi could go to school because he no longer had to help his mother fetch water from the stream far from home. All three narratives are accompanied by American schoolchildren's illustrations, and a section in the back poses questions that will involve the reader. *ss*

Author from the United States

699. Solheim, James. **It's Disgusting and We Ate It!** New York: Simon & Schuster, 1998. ISBN 0-689-80675-2. 48p. (7-10). Informational book.

Subtitled "True Food Facts from around the World and throughout History," this collection features poems, facts, statistics, and stories about unusual foods and eating habits accompanied by humorous illustrations. *djg*

Author from the United States

700. Sturges, Philemon. **Sacred Places.** Illustrated by Giles Laroche. New York: Putnam, 2000. ISBN 0-399-23317-2. 38p. (4-14). Picture book.

This stunning multireligion book brings Buddhists, Christians, Hindus, Jews, and Muslims together in the spirit of sacred architecture. Age levels are brought together as well—each paper relief illustration of a sacred place is accompanied by a large type comment for younger readers and a more detailed description/explanation for older readers. This is a wonderful reference for any social studies curriculum—simple, positive, and inclusive, honoring differences while describing places that can and should be shared by us all. Includes notes to the reader on each religion as well as a site map. *bjk*

Author from the United States

701. Yorinks, Arthur. **The Alphabet Atlas.** Illustrated by Adrienne Yorinks. Letter art by Jeanyee Wong. Delray Beach, FL: Winslow Press, 1999. ISBN 1-890817-14-7. 60p. (4-14). Picture book.

This alphabet book introduces young explorers to twenty-six areas of the world from Australia to Zimbabwe, Egypt to Oman. Stunning quilts use fabrics, cloths, and textiles native to each region to illustrate one or two simple facts about each place. *djg*

Author from the United States

Geography Series

These series have been selected as among the most outstanding of the many country and geography series currently in print. Some of these series originate in the United States; those that have originated elsewhere have been heavily edited for American readers.

Count Your Way Through . . . Minneapolis: Carolrhoda. 24p. (6-9). Volumes currently available: Brazil, Canada, China, France, Germany, Greece, India, Ireland, Israel, Italy, Japan, Korea, Mexico, Russia, and the Arab World.

Author Jim Haskins works with all different illustrators to create this picture book series. In each book, numbers one through ten are used to discuss a particular element of a country's geography, culture, and history. For instance, in *Count Your Way through Italy*, number one (*uno*) stands for Mount Etna; number two (*due*) is for the mythological brothers Remus and Romulus; nine (*nove*) is for nine products for which Italy is known. Of course, with this restricted format the books provide only a taste of information, but it is enough to attract children's interest and give them some good background. One to three paragraphs are written for each number, printed in large type. Illustrations are in paint or colored pencil, done in a style to match the culture being studied. A pronunciation guide to the numbers is included at the back. *sdl*

Country Insights. Austin, TX: Raintree Steck-Vaughn. 48p. (9-12). Volumes currently available: Brazil, China, Cuba, Czech Republic, Denmark, France, India, Jamaica, Japan, Kenya, Mexico, and Pakistan.

Everyday life of contemporary people is reflected by comparing various topics in a city and in a town. For instance, in *Japan*, the city Okazaki is compared to the village Narai in chapters headed "Landscape and Climate," "Home Life," "Japan at Work," "Going to School," "Japan at Play," and "The Future." The pages are large and so is the type, with the margins often shaped around photographs, drawings, diagrams, and maps for a fresh appearance. Paragraphs have two to six sentences, and some pages may have as many as four paragraphs. Back of the book material includes a glossary, a page of further information (with books, videos, and addresses), and an index. *sdl*

Cultures of the World. New York: Marshall Cavendish. 128 p. (10-14) Volumes currently available: Afghanistan, Algeria, Angola, Argentina,

Armenia, Australia, Austria, Bahamas, Bahrain, Bangladesh, Barbados, Belarus, Belgium, Belize, Bhutan, Bolivia, Brazil, Britain, Bulgaria, Burma, Cambodia, Cameroon, Canada, Chile, China, Colombia, Costa Rica, Croatia, Cuba, Cyprus, Czech Republic, Democratic Republic of the Congo, Denmark, Dominican Republic, Ecuador, Egypt, El Salvador, Eritrea, Estonia, Ethiopia, Fiji, Finland, France, Georgia, Germany, Ghana, Greece, Grenada, Guyana, Haiti, Honduras, Hong Kong, Hungary, Iceland, India, Indonesia, Iran, Iraq, Ireland, Israel, Italy, Ivory Coast, Jamaica, Japan, Jordan, Kazakhstan, Kenya, Korea, Kuwait, Laos, Latvia, Lebanon, Liberia, Libya, Lithuania, Luxembourg, Madagascar, Malaysia, Maldives, Malta, Mexico, Moldova, Mongolia, Morocco, Nepal, Netherlands, New Zealand, Nicaragua, Niger, Nigeria, Norway, Pakistan, Panama, Papua New Guinea, Paraguay, Peru, Philippines, Poland, Portugal, Puerto Rico, Romania, Russia, Saudi Arabia, Scotland, Senegal, Singapore, Somalia, South Africa, Spain, Sri Lanka, Sudan, Sweden, Switzerland, Syria, Tahiti, Taiwan, Tanzania, Thailand, Tibet, Trinidad and Tobago, Tunisia, Turkey, Ukraine, Uruguay, Venezuela, Vietnam, Wales, Yemen, Zambia, and Zimbabwe.

This very extensive series began publishing in 1994, with new titles continuing to be released in 2001. The volumes are completely consistent, each with twelve chapters following an introduction: "Geography," "History," "Government," "Economy," "Italians" (or "New Zealanders," or "Moldovans," depending), "Lifestyle," "Religion," "Language," "Arts," "Leisure," "Festivals," and "Food." Type size is fairly small, but the copious color photographs help alleviate the density of text on a page. The writing style of the books on less prominent countries (Tahiti, for example) can be bland, while volumes on countries where the author has more personal familiarity are generally livelier. Back of the book material is brief, with a single page of "Quick Notes" (national flower, average rainfall), a glossary, a short list for further reading, and an index. *sdl*

Enchantment of the World Second Series. Chicago: Children's Press. 144p. (10-14).

Volumes currently available: Albania, Argentina, Australia, Austria, the Bahamas, Belgium, Bolivia, Brazil, Canada, Chile, Colombia, Costa Rica, Cuba, the Dominican Republic, Ecuador, Egypt, England, Finland, France, Ghana, Haiti, Iraq, Israel, Italy, Japan, Kuwait, Libya, Madagascar, Mexico, Morocco, Netherlands, Niger, Norway, Oman, People's Republic of China, Peru, Philippines, Poland, Romania, Serbia, South Africa, Sweden, Switzerland, and Thailand.

Like *Cultures of the World* from Marshall Cavendish, this is designed to answer all of the questions young report writers generally need to cover. It discusses geography, history, industry, and culture. Chapter headings in *Italy*, for example, are "Not a Museum," "Mountains and Coasts," "Empires and Republics," "A New Time," "A New Nation," "Constitution and Capital," "Industry and Division," "Trying to Make Italians," "The Intertwined Church," "Statues, Songs, and Soccer," and "The Best of Life." There are plentiful color photographs, art reproductions, and maps, all laid out in an attractive design. From a reading perspective, everything here is on a middle-grade level, with medium type size, sentence length, and vocabulary. Some volumes are more sparkling than others in tone, but all are readable. A time line at the back compares world history side by side with Italian history. A good deal of additional information is found under "Fast Facts," and the lists of places "To Find Out More" includes nonfiction, biography, fiction, videos, organization addresses, and websites. There is also an index. *sdl*

Exploring Cultures of the World. New York: Benchmark Books. 64p. (8-12). Volumes currently available: Australia, Brazil, Canada, Chile, China, Colombia, Egypt, Germany, Hungary, India, Iran, Italy, Japan, Kenya, Korea, Mexico, Nigeria, Peru, Poland, Russia, South Africa, Spain, Turkey, Ukraine, and Vietnam.

A short story or anecdote from a country's history opens each book, setting a tone and providing context for what follows. These tall books have large type, short sentences, and a somewhat conversational style, making them unusually accessible. They do offer ample information, with fairly long paragraphs, several to a page. Each spread includes at least one large color photograph, and boxes give additional information on special subjects such as common phrases in the country's language, or rules for a game children play. The books all have a map at the beginning and are divided into five chapters: "Geography and History," "The People," "Family Life," "Festivals, and Food," "School and Recreation," and "The Arts." Back of the book matter features "Country Facts" (geography, flag, holidays, etc.), a two-page glossary, a list for further reading, and an index. *sdl*

Families around the World. (A Family from...) Austin, TX: Raintree Steck-Vaughn. 32p. (8-12). Volumes currently available: Bosnia, Brazil, China, Ethiopia, Germany, Guatemala, Iraq, Japan, South Africa, and Vietnam.

In this creatively designed series, the first page shows a family with all of their material possessions displayed in a photograph taken outside their home. The next spread introduces each family member by name and age, and there is a close-up of some of the family members with a quotation from one of them. On each set of pages, a portion of the original photograph is boxed and highlighted to show the person or thing being addressed; additional color photographs are enormous and dominate the text. The type size is very large, and sentences are short, with easy vocabulary. Each book follows the family through their day, showing what they eat, how they spend their time, and what happens on special occasions. The last spread gives each family the opportunity to tell what their hopes are for the future. Information in boxes helps explain anything confusing in the text or gives background on the country as a whole. The final three pages include a pronunciation guide, glossary, list of books to read, and an index. *sdl*

Globe-trotters Club. Minneapolis: Carolrhoda. 48p. (8-11).

Volumes currently available: Argentina, Australia, Brazil, Canada, China, Costa Rica, Egypt, France, India, Indonesia, Israel, Jamaica, Japan, Kenya, Madagascar, Mexico, Nigeria, Norway, Philippines, Poland, Puerto Rico, Russia, Saudi Arabia, South Africa, Venezuela, and Vietnam.

The text of these books makes frequent use of the second-person to achieve the flavor of a travelogue, as readers are taken on a tour of the physical, cultural, historical, social, artistic, and economic elements of a country. Each spread covers a single topic as indicated by a heading in the style of a chapter title. *Kenya*, for instance, includes such topics as "Country and City Life," "Mosque, Church, or Altar," and "Story Time." The main text on each spread consists of four to five paragraphs, with additional information provided in picture captions and boxed features. Each book includes a glossary, pronunciation guide, list of related books, and index. *ss*

Modern Nations of the World. Farmington Hills, MI: Lucent. Pages vary. (11-15).

Volumes currently available: Austria, Brazil, Canada, China, Cuba, Egypt, England, Ethiopia, Germany, Greece, Haiti, India, Ireland, Italy, Japan, Jordan, Kenya, Mexico, Norway, Poland, Russia, Saudi Arabia, Scotland, Somalia, South Africa, South Korea, Spain, Sweden, Switzerland, Taiwan, the United States, and Vietnam.

While this series lacks the enticing color photographs of most others, it features lively, intelligent writing. The type size is small, sentences are long, and paragraphs average four to seven sentences, so this series is for children working at a high reading level. Its strength is in its coverage of history, politics, and society, as each writer is careful to present the facts in context. The number and organization of chapters vary. The volume on Canada, for example, has a lengthy introduction followed by five chapters headed: "Taming the Land," "Toward a Modern Nation," "A Nation of Diversity," "The Culture of Canada," and "Contemporary Canada." Back matter is ample, with a "Facts About" section with lists of the populations of various cities and other demographics, a well-fleshed chronology, an extensive list both of works consulted and suggestions for reading, and an index. *sdl*

A Ticket to . . . Minneapolis: Carolrhoda. 48p. (7-9).

Volumes currently available: Argentina, Australia, Brazil, Canada, China, Costa Rica, Egypt, France, India, Indonesia, Israel, Jamaica, Japan, Kenya, Madagascar, Mexico, Nigeria, Norway, Philippines, Poland, Puerto Rico, Russia, Saudi Arabia, South Africa, Venezuela, and Vietnam.

In a format similar to that of the Globe-trotters Club listed above, the books in this series introduce basic facts about a country and its culture to a younger set of readers. The main text on each spread is delivered in a paragraph of six to eight short sentences set in large type and is usually accompanied by a boxed feature that contains a suggested activity, a quiz, or additional information that extends the text. Back matter includes a glossary, a pronunciation guide, and suggestions for further reading, along with an index. *ss*

World's Children. (Children of ...) Minneapolis: Carolrhoda. 48p. (8-11).

Volumes currently available: Belize, Bolivia, China, Cuba, Dominica, the Ecuadorean Highlands, Egypt, Guatemala, Hawaii, India, Israel, Mauritania, Micronesia, Morocco, Nepal, Northern Ireland, Philippines, the Sierra Madre, Slovakia, the Tlingit, Vietnam, and Yucatan. Also available: *Grandchildren of the Incas, Grandchildren of the Lakota, Grandchildren of the Vikings.*

Outstanding color photographs are the focus in this series, which shows the children of a country going about their normal daily lives. The photographers have clearly spent the time necessary to make children comfortable, so the pictures are generally natural, close up, and capture real moments in a very appealing way. The text usually singles out a few children to discuss from different areas of the country, using them to talk about school, play, work, family, and community relationships. Each spread has two to four paragraphs, with additional information given in photograph captions. The series includes a number of rarely covered cultures. A pronunciation guide and an index are included. *sdl*

The World in Conflict. Minneapolis: Lerner Books. Pages vary. (12-16). Volumes currently available: Bosnia, Cyprus, East Timor, Haiti, Kurdistan, Northern Ireland, Quebec, Rwanda, South Africa, Sri Lanka, Sudan, and Tibet. This series strives to give students a balanced and fair account of some of the world's recent conflicts. They are frequently between ethnic groups that have been locked in dispute for centuries, but these authors do an excellent job of sorting through conflicting claims and providing background information. Text is in small type and dense, with small color photographs and maps. The books begin with a vocabulary list, introducing terms such as *coup d'etat* and *assimilate*, which is an intelligent choice that gives students the best chance for understanding. The foreword is the same in each book, offering possible reasons why this period has seen so many conflicts. The books then fall into similar, though not identical chapters. *Kurdistan*, for example, has these chapter headings: "Introduction" (geography, population, culture, etc.), "The Recent Conflict and Its Effects," "The Conflict's Roots," "Entrenched Positions," "The Present Conflict," and "What's Being Done to Solve the Problem?" An epilogue in each book gives the most up-to-date information available, and always suggests where students can go to get updates, including newspapers and Internet sources. Additional back of the book material includes a chronology, bibliography, and index, and a brief explanation of the author's credentials. *sdl*

Part 3

Resources

11
Children's Book Awards

United States
Mildred Batchelder Award

This award, sponsored by the ALA's Association for Library Service to Children, is given to the American publisher of a children's book considered to be the most outstanding of those books originally published in a country other than the United States in a language other than English, and subsequently translated and published in the United States during the previous year. Before 1979, there was a lapse of two years between the original publication date and the award date; to convert to the new system, two awards were announced in 1979: one for 1978 and one for 1979. Beginning in 1994, honor recipients were also selected.

1968 Knopf. *The Little Man* by Erich Kästner, translated from German by James Kirkup. Illustrated by Rick Schreiter.

1969 Scribner. *Don't Take Teddy* by Babbis Friis-Baastad, translated from Norwegian by Lise Sömme McKinnon.

1970 Holt. *Wildcat Under Glass* by Alki Zei, translated from Greek by Edward Fenton.

1971 Pantheon. *In the Land of UR: The Discovery of Ancient Mesopotamia* by Hans Baumann, translated from German by Stella Humphries. Illustrated by Hans Peter Renner.

1972 Holt. *Friedrich* by Hans Peter Richter, translated from German by Edite Kroll.

1973 Morrow. *Pulga* by Siny Rose Van Iterson, translated from Dutch by Alexander and Alison Gode.

1974 Dutton. *Petro's War* by Alki Zei, translated from Greek by Edward Fenton.

1975 Crown. *An Old Tale Carved Out of Stone* by Aleksandr M. Linevski, translated from Russian by Maria Polushkin.

1976 Walck. *The Cat and Mouse Who Shared a House* by Ruth Hürlimann, translated from German by Anthea Bell.

1977 Atheneum. *The Leopard* by
Cecil Bödker, translated
from Danish by Gunnar
Poulsen.

1978 No award.

1979 Two awards given:
Watts. *Konrad* by Christine
Nöstlinger, translated from
German (Austrian) by
Anthea Bell. Illustrated by
Carol Nicklaus.
Harcourt. *Rabbit Island* by
Jörg Steiner, translated from
German by Ann Conrad
Lammers. Illustrated by Jörg
Müller.

1980 Dutton. *The Sound of
Dragon's Feet* by Alki Zei,
translated from Greek by
Edward Fenton.

1981 Morrow. *The Winter When
Time Was Frozen* by Els
Pelgrom, translated from
Dutch by Raphael and
Maryka Rudnik.

1982 Bradbury. *The Battle Horse*
by Harry Kullman, translated
from Swedish by George
Blecher and Lone Thygesen-
Blecher.

1983 Lothrop. *Hiroshima No
Pika* by Toshi Maruki,
translated from Japanese
through Kurita-Bando
Literary Agency.

1984 Viking. *Ronia, the Robber's
Daughter* by Astrid
Lindgren, translated from
Swedish by Patricia
Crampton.

1985 Houghton. *The Island on
Bird Street* by Uri Orlev,
translated from Hebrew by
Hillel Halkin.

1986 Creative Education. *Rose
Blanche* by Christophe
Gallaz and Roberto
Innocenti, translated from
French by Martha Coventry
and Richard Graglia.
Illustrated by Roberto
Innocenti.

1987 Lothrop. *No Hero for the
Kaiser* by Rudolf Frank,
translated from German by
Patricia Crampton. Illustrated
by Klaus Steffans.

1988 McElderry. *If You Didn't
Have Me* by Ulf Nilsson,
translated from Swedish by
Lone Thygesen-Blecher and
George Blecher. Illustrated by
Eva Eriksson.

1989 Lothrop. *Crutches* by Peter
Härtling, translated from
German by Elizabeth D.
Crawford.

1990 Dutton. *Buster's World* by
Bjarne Reuter, translated
from Danish by Anthea
Bell.

1991 Dutton. *A Hand Full of
Stars* by Rafik Schami,
translated from German by
Rika Lesser.
Honor book:
Houghton. *Two Short and One
Long* by Nina Ring
Aamundsen, translated from
Norwegian by the author.

1992 Houghton. *The Man from the Other Side* by Uri Orlev, translated from Hebrew by Hillel Halkin.

1993 No award.

1994 Farrar. *The Apprentice* by Pilar Molina Llorente, translated from Spanish by Robin Longshaw. Illustrated by Juan Ramón Alonso.

Honor books:

Viking. *Anne Frank: Beyond the Diary* by Ruud van der Rol and Rian Verhoeven, translated from Dutch by Tony Langham and Plym Peters.

Farrar. *The Princess in the Garden* by Annemie and Margriet Heymans, translated from Dutch by Johanna H. Prins and Johanna W. Prins.

1995 Dutton. *The Boys from St. Petrie* by Bjarne Reuter, translated from Danish by Anthea Bell.

Honor book:

Lothrop. *Sister Shako and Kolo the Goat* by Vedat Dalokay, translated from Turkish by Güner Ener.

1996 Houghton. *The Lady with the Hat* by Uri Orlev, translated from Hebrew by Hillel Halkin.

Honor books:

Holt. *Damned Strong Love: The True Story of Willi G. and Stephan K.* by Lutz Van Dijk, translated from German by Elizabeth D. Crawford.

Walker. *Star of Fear, Star of Hope* by Jo Hoestlandt, translated from French by Mark Polizzotti.

1997 Farrar. *The Friends* by Kazumi Yumoto, translated from Japanese by Cathy Hirano.

1998 Holt. *The Robber and Me* by Josef Holub, translated from German by Elizabeth D. Crawford.

Honor books:

Scholastic. *Hostage to War: A True Story* by Tatjana Wassiljewa, translated from German by Anna Trenter.

Viking. *Nero Corleone: A Cat's Story* by Elke Heidenrich, translated from German by Doris Orgel.

1999 Dial. *Thanks to My Mother* by Schoschana Rabinovici, translated from German by James Skofield.

2000 Walker. *The Baboon King* by Anton Quintana, translated from Dutch by John Niewenhuizen.

Honor books:

Farrar. *Collector of Moments* by Quint Buchholz, translated from German by Peter F. Neumeyer.

R&S Books. *Vendela in Venice* by Christina Björk, translated from Swedish by Patricia Crampton. Illustrated

by Inga-Karin Eriksson, Front Street. *Asphalt Angels* by Ineke Holtwijk, translated from Dutch by Wanda Boeke.
2001 Author A. Levine/Scholastic. *Samir and Yonatan* by Daniella Carmi, translated from Hebrew by Yael Lotan.
Honor book:
David R. Godine. *Ultimate Game* by Christian Lehmann, translated from French by William Rodarmor.

International Hans Christian Andersen Award

This international award, sponsored by the International Board on Books for Young People, is given every two years to a living author and, since 1966, to a living illustrator whose complete works have made important international contributions to children's literature.

1956 Eleanor Farjeon (UK)
1958 Astrid Lindgren (Sweden)
1960 Erich Kästner (Germany)
1962 Meindert DeJong (USA)
1964 René Guillot (France)
1966 Author: Tove Jansson (Finland)
Illustrator: Alois Carigiet (Switzerland)
1968 Authors: James Krüss (Germany) and José Maria Sanchez-Silva (Spain)
Illustrator: Jirí Trnka (Czechoslovakia)
1970 Author: Gianni Rodari (Italy)
Illustrator: Maurice Sendak (USA)
1972 Author: Scott O'Dell (USA)
Illustrator: Ib Spang Olsen (Denmark)
1974 Author: Maria Gripe (Sweden)

Illustrator: Farshid Mesghali (Iran)
1976 Author: Cecil Bödker (Denmark)
Illustrator: Tatjana Mawrina (USSR)
1978 Author: Paula Fox (USA)
Illustrator: Svend Otto S. (Denmark)
1980 Author: Bohumil Riha (Czechoslovakia)
Illustrator: Suekichi Akaba (Japan)
1982 Author: Lygia Bojunga Nunes (Brazil)
Illustrator: Zbigniew Rychlicki (Poland)
1984 Author: Christine Nöstlinger (Austria)
Illustrator: Mitsumasa Anno (Japan)

1986 Author: Patricia Wrightson
(Australia)
Illustrator: Robert Ingpen
(Australia)
1988 Author: Annie M. G. Schmidt
(Netherlands)
Illustrator: Dušan Kalláy
(Czechoslovakia)
1990 Author: Tormod Haugen
(Norway)
Illustrator: Lisbeth Zwerger
(Austria)
1992 Author: Virginia Hamilton
(USA)
Illustrator: Kveta Pacovská
(Czechoslovakia)

1994 Author: Michio Mado
(Japan)
Illustrator: Jörg Müller
(Switzerland)
1996 Author: Uri Orlev (Israel)
Illustrator: Klaus Ensikat
(Germany)
1998 Author: Katherine Paterson
(USA)
Illustrator: Tomi Ungerer
(France)
2000 Author: Ana Maria
Machado (Brazil)
Illustrator: Anthony Browne
(UK)

Janusz Korczak Literary Award

Funded by the Ministry of Culture and the Arts at the initiative of the Polish section of IBBY, this award was established in 1979 in memory of the famous Polish writer and teacher who died in a Nazi concentration camp along with the orphaned children to whom he had dedicated his life. The prize is awarded biennially to living authors whose books for or about children contribute to international understanding among young people from all over the world. The awards are presented in two categories: books for children and books about children. After 1987, the award was temporarily suspended; it resumed in 1990, at which time additional books were named as distinctions.

1979 Astrid Lindgren (Sweden)
Sergiej Michalkow (USSR)
Bohumil Riha (Czecho-
slovakia)
1981 Michael Ende (Germany)
Jan Navratil (Czechoslovakia)
Katherine Paterson (USA)

1983 Ewa Nowacka (Poland)
Dieo Dickman (Czecho-
slovakia)
Mirjam Pressler (Germany)
1985 Luczezar Stanczew
(Bulgaria)
Maria Winn (USA)

1987 Maria Borowa (Poland)
  Albert Lichanow (USSR)
1990 Uri Orlev (Israel)
  Halina Filipczuk (Poland)
Distinctions:
  Marion Dane Bauer (USA)
  Revan Inanishvili (USSR)
1992 Joanna Rudnianska (Poland)
  Robert Coles (USA)
Distinction:
  "Guliwer," a periodical about
  children's books (Poland)
1994 Ofra Belbert-Avni (Israel)
  Mats Wahl (Sweden)
Distinction:
  Joanna Papuzinska (Poland)
1996 Jostein Gaarder (Norway)
  Viliem Klimacek and Desider
  Toth (Slovak Republic)

  Gertruda Skotnicka (Poland)
Distinction:
  Trude de John (Netherlands)
1998 Reinhardt Jung (Austria)
  Oleg F. Kurguzov (Russia)
Special Awards:
  Lars H. Gustofsson
  (Sweden)
  Annouchka Gravel
  Caluchko (Canada)
Distinctions:
  Murti Bunanta (Indonesia)
  Rukhsana Khan (Canada)
2000 Annika Thor (Sweden)
Distinctions:
  Andri Snaer Magnason
  (Iceland)
  Bina Stampe Zmavc
  (Slovenia)

UNESCO Prize for Children's Literature in the Service of Tolerance

The United Nations Educational, Scientific, and Cultural Organization established this prize to carry the message of the United Nations Year for Tolerance beyond 1995. The prize is awarded every two years in recognition of works for the young that best embody the concepts and ideals of tolerance and peace and promote mutual understanding based on respect for other peoples and cultures. There are two categories: books for children under thirteen and those for thirteen-to-eighteen-year-olds. The author of the prize-winning book in each category receives a cash award of US $8,000, donated by the Fundación Santa María /Ediciones S.M. of Spain.

1997
Under 13: *Something Else* by
  Kathryn Cave (UK)
Honorable mentions:
  To Bounce or Not to Bounce
  by Naif Abdulrahman Al-

Mutawa (Kuwait); *Le petit
garcon bleu* (Little Blue Boy)
by Fatou Keïta (Côte d'Ivoire);
*The Primer of Children's
Rights* by Ljubivoje Rsumovic
(Yugoslavia)

13-18: *Neun Leben* (Nine Lives)
by Chen Danyan (China)
Honorable mentions:
Samir und Jonathan by
Daniella Carmi (Israel); *Once
There Was a Hunter* by Eleni
Sarantiti (Greece); *On the
Wings of Peace*, compiled by
Sheila Hamanaka (USA)
1999
Under 13: *Sosu's Call* by Meshack
Asare (Ghana)
Honorable mentions:
Hoe gaat het? Goed (How
Are You? Fine) by Anke
Kranendonk (Netherlands);
Lines and Circles by Fatma
Al-Maadoul (Egypt); *Mon
ami Jim* (My Friend Jim) by
Kitty Crowther (Belgium)
13-18: *A Different Kind of Hero*
by Ann R. Blakeslee (USA)
Honorable mentions:
Contact by C. B. Peper
(South Africa); *A Swallow
in Winter* by Billi
Economou-Rosen (Greece)
2001
Under 13: *La guerre* (The War)
by Anaïs Vaugelade (France)

Honorable mentions:
My Brother is Different and
My Friend, a two-book series
by Najla Nusayr Bashour
(Lebanon); *La cosa più
importante* (The Most
Important Thing) by
Antonella Abbatiello (Italy);
The A.O.K. Project by
Vivienne Joseph (New
Zealand)
13-18: *Istgahe Mir* (The Mir
Space Station) by Violet
Razeqpanah (Iran)
Honorable mentions:
Angela by James Moloney
(Australia); *La noche en que
Vlado se fue* (The Night
Vlado Left) by Manuel
Quinto (Spain); *Café au lait
et pain aux raisins* (Coffee
with Milk and Raisin Rolls),
the French version of a book
originally written by German
author Carolin Philipps,
translated from the German
by Jeanne Étoré (France)

Other prominent international awards include the Tehran International Biennale of Illustrations, the Biennale of Illustrations Brataslava, and the Bologna Book Fair Ragazzi awards.

12
Organizations

The following organizations have been more fully described in Part 1 and are listed here for easy reference. While numerous organizations work on behalf of international literacy and children's literature, these are the most closely associated with USBBY in North America.

United States Board on Books for Young People (USBBY)
USBBY Secretariat
PO Box 8139
Newark, DE 19714-8139
e-mail: acutts@reading.org
website: www.usbby.org

USBBY Patrons

American Library Association
50 E. Huron, Chicago, IL 60611
tel. 800-545-2433
fax 312-440-9374
e-mail: ala@ala.org
website: www.ala.org

Children's Book Council
2 W. 37th Street, 2nd fl.
New York, NY 10018-7480
tel. 212-966-1990
fax 212-966-2073
e-mail: info@cbcbooks.org
website: www.cbcbooks.org

International Reading Association
800 Barksdale Rd., Box 8139

Newark, DE 19714-8139
tel. 302-731-1600
fax 302-731-1057
website: www.reading.org

National Council of Teachers of English
1111 W. Kenyon Rd.
Urbana, IL 61801-1096
tel: 800-369-6283
fax 217-328-9625
e-mail: public_info@ncte.org
wesite: www.ncte.org

International

International Board on Books for Young People (IBBY)
IBBY Secretariat
Nonnenweg 12, Fostfach
CH - 4003 Basel, Switzerland
e-mail: ibby@eye.ch
website: www..ibby.org

IBBY Documentation Centre of Books for Disabled Young People
Box 1140, N – 0317 Oslo, Norway
fax 47 22 85 80 02

International Youth Library
Schloss Blutenburg
D - 81247 Munich, Germany
e-mail: bib@ijb.de
website: www.ijb.de

**International Research Society
for Children's Literature**
fax 61 2 9514 5556
website: www.education.uts.edu.au/
centres/crea/irscl

**The International Federation
of Library Associations and
Institutions**
Box 95312, 2509 CH The Hague,
Netherlands
fax 31 70 3834827
e-mail: IFLA@ifla.org
website: www.ifla.org

13
Publishers

The North American publishers listed here have an international focus or consistently include international titles on their publishing lists. A more comprehensive list of names and addresses of children's book publishers can be obtained from the Children's Book Council (see Chapter 12 for contact information). The addresses below are current at the time of publication but subject to change. For updated information, consult the current edition of *Books in Print* or *Literary Marketplace*, available in most libraries, or visit the Children's Book Council website.

Abrams Books for Young Readers
100 Fifth Avenue
New York, NY 10011
tel. 212-645-8437
fax 212-645-8437
website: www.abramsbooks.com
　　As a publisher of art books, this company publishes an outstanding selection of international children's picture books.

Barefoot Books
3 Bow Street, 3rd Floor
Cambridge, MA 02138
tel. 617-576-0660
fax 617-576-0049
website: www.barefoot-books.com
　　This is the U.S. counterpart of a British company, recently established to bring its books to the American market and to work with American writers and artists.

Candlewick Press
2067 Massachusetts Avenue
Cambridge, MA 02140
tel. 617-661-3330
website: www.candlewick.com
　　The U.S. branch of London-based Walker Publishers provides a vehicle for bringing the works of some of the best British authors and illustrators to this country.

Charlesbridge Publishing
85 Main Street
Watertown, MA 02472
tel. 617-926-0329
website: www.charlesbridge.com
e-mail: books@charlesbridge.com
　　Among this publisher's eclectic offerings are children's books with a social justice theme.

Clarion Books
215 Park Avenue S.
New York, NY 10003
tel. 212-420-5800
　　The late Dorothy Briley, a tireless promoter of internationalism,

brought many authors and illustrators of note to this list.

The Creative Company
123 S. Broad Street, Box 227
Mankato, MN 56002
tel. 507-388-6273
fax 507-388-2746

This division of Creative Education regularly publishes a number of high quality international picture books, primarily from France and Germany.

DK Publishing, Inc.
95 Madison Avenue
New York, NY 10016
tel. 212-213-4800
fax 212-698-4828
website: www.dkonline.com

DK, the U.S. sister company of Dorling Kindersley, England, specializes in beautifully photographed informational books in a variety of formats for all ages, many originating in England. DK also produces companion CD-ROMs and videos.

Farrar, Straus & Giroux
19 Union Square West
New York, NY 10003
tel. 212-741-6900
fax 212-633-2427
website: www.fsbassociates.com/fsg

As a result of a translation and distribution agreement with the largest Swedish publisher of children's books, Rabén and Sjögren, this company publishes a number of translated Swedish picture books every year. In addition, the company publishes translated fiction for young adults.

Front Street Books
20 Battery Park Avenue
Asheville, NC 28801
tel. 828 236-3097
fax 828 236-3098
website: www.frontstreetbooks.com

A small press that publishes a number of books in translation, including books from the Dutch publisher Lemniscaat.

David R. Godine, Publisher
9 Hamilton Place
Boston, MA 02108-4715
tel. 617-451-9600
fax 617-350-0250
website: www.godine.com

Godine's reputation for fine bookmaking extends to the choices he makes when publishing international books.

Groundwood Books
720 Bathurst St., Suite 500
Torongo, Ontario M5S 2R4 Canada
tel. 416-537-2501
fax 416-537-4647
website: www.groundwoodbooks.com

A Canadian company, Groundwood also has a Latino imprint, Libros Tigrillo, dedicated to books from Spanish-speaking people living in this hemisphere.

Handprint Books
413 Sixth Avenue
Brooklyn, NY 11215-3310
tel. 718-768-3696
fax 718-369-0844
e-mail: publisher@
handprintbooks.com
website: www.handprintbooks.com
      This newly established publishing firm also distributes Ragged Bear Books, a British publisher of books for the very young.

Kane/Miller Book Publishers
Box 8515, La Jolla, CA 92038
tel. 800-968-1930
website: www.kanemiller.com
      This small press specializes in children's picture books from around the world, both in translation and from English-language countries.

Lerner Publications Company/ Carolrhoda Books
241 First Avenue N.
Minneapolis, MN 55401-1607
tel. 800-328-4929
fax 800-332-1132
website: www.lernerbooks.com
      These two sister companies publish international fiction and high-quality nonfiction for children in series.

Margaret K. McElderry Books/ Simon & Schuster
1230 Avenue of the Americas
New York, NY 10020
website: www.simonsays.com
      Margaret K. McElderry, child-

ren's book publisher and editor, is recognized for her leadership in bringing international children's books to the United States.

The Millbrook Press
2 Old New Milford Road
Brookfield, CT 06804
tel. 203-740-2220
website: www.millbrookpress.com
e-mail: millbrook@booksys.com
      Known primarily for its nonfiction series, this publisher also takes on international picture books that might be too culturally specific for larger publishers.

Mondo Publishing
980 Avenue of Americas
New York, NY 10018
tel. 212-268-3560; 888-88-MONDO
fax 212-268-3561
website: www.mondopub.com
      Mondo's eclectic list contains selections from Australia, Canada, and New Zealand as well as an excellent series of folktales from around the world.

North-South Books
11 East 26th Street, 17th Fl.
New York, NY 10010
tel. 212-706-4545
fax 212-706-4546
website: www.northsouth.com
      North-South Books is the English-language imprint of Nord-Süd Verlag, the Swiss children's book publisher. The company emphasizes high-quality multinational copub-

lications featuring lesser-known authors and illustrators, and regularly reissues older international titles. North-South also publishes the English-language editions of Michael Neugebauer Books, another Swiss publisher.

Soundprint Books
353 Main Avenue
Norwalk, CT 06851
tel. 800-228-7839 or 203-846-2274
fax 203-846-1776
Although the company publishes book-and-cassette packages and also specializes in stuffed toys, books are available separately.

Star Bright Books
3325 West 38th St., Ste 511
New York, NY 10018
tel. 800-788-4439
fax 212-564-3984
e-mail: starbrightbk@earthlink.net
This small press publishes a few original titles and also distri-

butes all Lothian books from Australia that have not been reprinted in U.S. editions.

Tundra Books
Box 1030, Plattsburgh, NY 12901
tel. 416-598-4786; fax 416-598-4002
website: www.tundrabooks.com
A Canadian-owned and managed company with a New York State address, Tundra specializes in French-English bilingual, Canadian, and Native American books for children and exceptional picture-book art.

Walker and Company
435 Hudson Street
New York, NY 10014
tel. 212-727-8300
This independent American publisher has no affiliation with the British publisher of the same name, and given their short annual lists, the proportion of international books is significant.

14
Sources for Foreign-Language and Bilingual Books

The following distributors and publishers are sources for books in other languages, most often imported from other countries but in some cases written and published in the United States to serve a distinct language community. These sources can be useful in finding books that have not been published in the United States as well as in locating the original-language edition of a book published in translation or other books by the same author or illustrator. This list was compiled by the Children's Services Division of the San Francisco Public Library and is reproduced with the permission of Grace Ruth, Children's Material Selection Specialist.

Abril Armenian Bookstore
415 E. Broadway, #102
Glendale, CA 91205-1029
tel. 323-467-9483

Arkipelago Philippine Books
953 Mission Street
San Francisco, CA 94103
tel. 415-371-8150
website: www.arkipelagobooks.com

The Bilingual Publications Company (Spanish)
270 Lafayette Street
New York, NY 10012
tel. 212-431-3500; fax 212-431-3567
Has approval plan
e-mail: lindagoodman@juno.com

The Book Cottage
(books from South Africa)
10 Harbour Road
Hermanus 7200 South Africa
tel. 0283-700834
fax 0283-70011

Books on Wings (Spanish)
973 Valencia Street
San Francisco, CA 94110 tel. 415 285-1145

Casalini Libri (Italian)
Via Benedetto da Maiano, 3 50014
Fiesole, Firenze, Italy
tel. 39-055-5018
fax 39-055-5018201
e-mail: gen@casalini.it
website: www.casalini.com

Croatian Book Shop
6313 St. Clair Avenue
Cleveland, OH 44103
tel. 216-391-5350

Cypress Book (US) Co., Inc.
(Chinese from People's Republic,
using simplified characters)
3450-3rd Street, #4B
San Francisco, CA 94124
tel. 415-821-3582

Daya Imports & Exports, Inc.
(Tamil, Hindi, Gujarati, Urdu)
Box 72031, Pine Valley Postal Outlet
7700 Pine Valley Drive, Woodbridge,
Ontario, Canada L4L 8N8
tel. 416-726-5311; fax 905-851-3494

Donars Spanish Books (Spanish)
Box 808, Lafayette, CO 80026-0808
tel. 303-666-9175
e-mail: donars@prolynx.com
website: www.concentric.net/~donars

Eastwind Books & Arts, Inc.
(Chinese from Hong Kong)
1435A Stockton Street
San Francisco, CA 94133
tel. 415-772-5877; fax 415-772-5885
e-mail: web@eastwindsf.com

European Book Company
(French, German)
925 Larkin Street
San Francisco, CA 94109
tel. 415-474-0626;
877-746-3666; fax 415-474-0630
e-mail: info@europeanbook.com

Far Eastern Books (Arabic, Bengali,
Greek, Gujarati, Hindi, Punjabi,
Tamil, Urdu, Vietnamese)
Box 846, Adelaide Street Station,
Toronto, Ontario, Canada M5C 2K1
tel. 905-477-2900, 800-291-8886;
fax 905-479-2988
e-mail: sales@febonline.com
website: www.febonline.com

G. L. S. Books (German)
Berlin office e-mail:
00074.1301@compuserve.com
Cambridge, MA, office:
tel. 617-497-0937
e-mail: glsbook@world.std.com
website: www.galda.com

**Harrassowitz, Booksellers &
Subscription Agents** (German)
65174 Wiesbaden
Germany

Hispanic Book Distributors
(Spanish)
1665 W. Grant Road
Tucson, AZ 85745
tel. 800-634-2124; fax 602 882-7696
e-mail: hbdus@cs.com
website: www.hispanicbooks.com

Irish Books & Media (Irish Gaelic)
1433 East Franklin Avenue
Minneapolis, MN 55404-2135
tel. 800-229-3505 or 612-871-3505;
fax 612-871-3358
e-mail: irishbook@aol.com
website: www.irishbook.com

Jeong Eum Sa Imports (Korean)
928 S. Western Avenue, #15
Los Angeles, CA 90006
tel. 213-387-0234

Kalamos Books (Greek)
725 Vermouth Avenue, #1
Mississauga, Ontario L5A 3X5
Canada   tel. 905-272-4841
e-mail: Kalamosbks@aol.com

**Ketabsara Persian Bookstore &
Publishers** (Persian)
1441 B Westwood Blvd.
Los Angeles, CA 90024
tel. 888-538-2272; fax 310-477-4546

**Kinokuniya Bookstores of America
Company, Ltd.** (Japanese)
1581 Webster Street
San Francisco, CA 94115
tel. 415 567-7625; fax 415-567-4109
Stores also in Seattle, New York, San
Jose, Los Angeles, Torrance, Costa
Mesa, CA

Lectorum Publications, Inc.
(Spanish)
111 Eighth Avenue
New York, NY 10011
tel. 800-345-5946
e-mail: lectorum@scholastic.com

Libros Sin Fronteras
(Spanish from Latin America)
Box 2085, Olympia, WA 98507-2085
tel. 800-454-2767
e-mail: info@librossinfronteras.com
website: www.librossinfronteras.com

Luso-Brazilian Books (Portuguese)
Box 170286, Brooklyn, NY 11217
tel. 800-727-LUSO (outside NYC);
718 624-4000; fax 718-858-0690
e-mail: info@lusobraz.com
website: www.lusobraz.com

**Mandarin Language & Cultural
Center** (Chinese, from Taiwan;
mail order only; requires knowledge
of Chinese language)
1630 Oakland Road, Suite A207
San Jose, CA 95131
tel. 408-441-9114; fax 408-441-9116

Mariuccia Iaconi Book Imports
(Spanish)
970 Tennessee Street
San Francisco, CA 94107
tel. 800-955-9577; 415-821-1216
fax 415-821-1596
e-mail: mibibook@ix.netcom.com
website: www.mibibook.com

MN Bilingual Publications
(Cambodian/Khmer, Korean, Lao-
tian, Vietnamese)
5300 La Fiesta
Yorba Linda, CA 92687-4009
tel. 714-692-2104

Mo Inc. (Vietnamese)
774 Geary Boulevard
San Francisco, CA 94109-7302
tel. 415 673-6836

Multi-Cultural Books and Videos
28880 Southfield Road, Suite 183
Lathrup Village, MI 48076
tel. 801-567-2220; fax 810-559-2465

e-mail: multicul@wincom.net
website: www.multiculbv.com

Multicultural Distributing Center
(Asian Language)
9440 Telstar Avenue, Suite #2
El Monte, CA 91731
tel. 800-537-4357; fax 626-527-9500
e-mail: info@greenshower.com

New Bayon Market (Cambodian)
1181 East 10th Street
Long Beach, CA 90813
tel. 562-599-3120; fax 562-599-2337
e-mail: newbayon1@aol.com

NoorArt (Arabic & Islamic)
31157 Plymouth Rd., #216
Livonia, MI 48150
tel. 734-266-9953; fax 425-969-6766
e-mail: Ammar@NoorArt.com

Pan Asian Publications (USA) Inc.
(Chinese, Vietnamese, Japanese,
Korean, Khmer, Lao, Hmong,
Spanish, Russian)
29564 Union City Blvd.
Union City, CA 94587
tel. 800-909-8088 (U.S. & Canada)
510-475-1185; fax 510-475-1489
e-mail: sales@panap.com
website: www.panap.com

Perma-Bound (Spanish)
617 East Vandalia Road
Jacksonville, IL 62650
tel. 800-637-6581; fax 800-551-1169
e-mail: perma-bound@
worldnet.att.net
website: www.perma-bound.com

**Philippine Expressions Mail
Order Bookshop**
2114 Trudie Drive
Rancho Palos Verdes, CA 90275-
2006
tel. 310 514-9139; fax 310 514-3485
e-mail: LindaNietes@earthlink.net

Polonia Bookstore
4738 N. Milwaukee Avenue
Chicago, IL 60630
tel. 773-481-6968
fax 773-481-6972
e-mail: books@polonia.com
website: www.polonia.com

Russian House, Ltd. (Russian)
253 Fifth Avenue
New York, NY 10016
tel. 212 685-1010; fax 212 685-1046
e-mail: russia@russianhouse.net
website: www.russianhouse.net

Schoenhof's Foreign Books
(many languages)
76A Mount Auburn Street
Cambridge, MA 02138
tel. 617-547-8855
fax 617-547-8551
e-mail: info@schoenhofs.com
website: www.schoenhofs.com

Shen's Books (Asian languages)
8625 Hubbard Road
Auburn, CA 95602-7815
tel. 530-888-6776, 800-456-6660;
fax 530 888-6763
e-mail: info@shens.com
website: www.shens.com

Siam Book Center
5178 Hollywood Blvd.
Los Angeles, CA 90027
tel. 323-665-4236
fax 323-665-0521

Sino-American Books & Arts
(Chinese/Taiwan, books & videos)
751 Jackson Street
San Francisco, CA 94133
tel. 415-421-3345

South Pacific Books, Ltd.
(Samoan, Tongan, Maori, etc.)
Library Supply 6 King Street
Grey Lynn, Box 3533
Auckland, New Zealand
tel. 09-376-2142; fax 09-376-2141
e-mail: Sales@southpacificbooks.
co.nz

Szwede Slavic Books
(Russian, Czech, Polish)
1629 Main Street
Redwood City, CA 94063
Box 1214, Palo Alto, CA 94302
tel. 650-780-0966
fax 650-780-0967

Toan Thu Bookstore
(Vietnamese speakers only, but e-
mail requests will receive help in
English; good source for A-V)
2115 Pedro Avenue
Milpitas, CA 95035
tel. 408-945-9959; fax 408-942-6600
e-mail: toanthu@aol.com

V & W Cultural Company
(Chinese; mail order only; requires
knowledge of Chinese language)
18850 Norwalk Blvd.
Artesia, CA 90701-5973
tel. 562-865-8882; fax 562-865-5542

Victor Kamkin Bookstore
(Russian)
4956 Boiling Brook Parkway
Rockville, MD 20852
tel. 301-881-5973; fax 301-881-1637
925 Broadway
New York, NY 10010
tel. 212673-0076
e-mail: kamkin@kamkin.com
website: www.kamkin.com

Author/Illustrator/Translator Index

Numbers indicate pages.

Abelove, Joan, 62
Ada, Alma Flor, 46, 61
Adler, Naomi, 271
Agard, John, 64, 225
Ahlberg, Allan, 226
Ajhar, Brian, 195
Akintola, Adelmola, 137, 253
Alarcon, Francisco X., 53
Alborough, Jez, 226
Alcantara, Ricardo, 216
Aldana, Patricia, 65
Alderson, Brian, 166
Alègrè, Hermès, 112
Aliki, 191
Allen, Thomas B., 49, 227
Allibone, Judith 237
Almond, David, 226
Alrawi, Karim, 118
Amado, Elisa, 45, 48
Ancona, George, 43, 47, 53, 54
Andersen, Hans Christian, 166
Anderson, James, 209, 210, 211
Anderson, Laurie Halse, 126
Anderson, Lena, 218
Andrew, Ian, 244, 258
Andrews, Jan, 69
Angelou, Maya, 129
Anholt, Catherine, 227
Anholt, Laurence, 227
Arcellana, Francisco, 112
Ardalan, Haydé, 168
Arrhenius, Peter, 218
Ashbé, Jeanne, 163
Ashforth, Camilla, 262
Atkins, Jeannine, 100
Axtel, David, 52

Axworthy, Anni, 100, 169
Ayliffe, Alex, 52
Ayto, Russell, 264

Baillie, Allan, 95, 138
Baker, Jeannie, 138
Balit, Christina, 228
Ballas, Toula, 171
Bancroft, Bronwyn, 142
Banks, Kate, 169, 170
Banks, Lynne Reid, 228
Bannatyne-Cugnet, Jo, 69
Barber, Antonio, 229
Barbour, Karen, 191
Barrett, Angela, 166, 249
Barth, Dominic, 170, 171
Bartlett, Alison, 240
Bash, Barbara, 100
Baskwill, Jane, 69
Bassède, Francine, 170
Bateson-Hill, Margaret, 97, 229
Bauer, Edith, 179
Baum, L. Frank, 162
Baumgart, Klaus, 179
Bawden, Nina, 191, 229, 230
Bayley, Nicola, 229
Beeler, Selby B., 271
Belafonte, Harry, 52
Bell, Anthea, 176, 184, 215
Bell, Don, 65
Bellwood, Shirley, 135
Belpré, Pura, 62
Bemelmans, Ludwig, 170
Ben-Ezer, Ehud, 119
Berkeley, John, 263
Berner, Susanne Rotraut, 181

Berry, Holly, 195
Binch, Caroline, 230, 244
Birchall, Mark 256
Bisson, Michel, 83
Björk, Christina, 219
Blackshaw, Anne, 131
Blake, Quentin, 230
Blandon, Hervé, 240
Bloom, Valerie, 52, 230
Blum, Robin, 200
Blythe, Gary, 247
Boeke, Wanda, 44, 204
Bogaerts, Gert, 177
Bognomo, Joel Eboueme, 124
Bond, Ruskin, 101
Boock, Paula, 157
Borton de Trevino, Elizabeth, 216
Bos, Burny, 202
Boudalika, Litsa, 121
Bowman, Leslie W., 60
Branford, Henrietta, 231
Breckler, Rosemary, 115
Brenner, Barbara, 104
Brewster, Hugh, 70
Brewster, Patience, 197
Brighton, Catherine, 231
Britton, Dorothy, 105
Brooks, Ron, 154
Browne, Anthony, 231, 232
Bruna, Dick, 203
Brusca, Maria Cristina, 64
Buchholz, Quint, 180
Buehner, Mark, 59
Bunting, Eve, 191, 195
Burchell, Chris, 127
Burgess, Lord, 52
Burgess, Melvin, 232, 233
Burr, Claudia, 54, 55
Butler, Geoff, 70
Butler, Nola, 171

Cameron, Ann, 49
Cann, Helen, 241
Carling, Amelie Lau, 49
Carmi, Daniella, 119

Carrier, Roch, 70
Carroll, Lewis, 162, 233, 234
Castañeda, Omar, 49, 50
Castillo, Ana, 55
Cecil, Laura, 234
Cencetti, Greta, 271
Cha, Chue, 111
Cha, Dia, 111
Cha, Nhia Thao, 111
Chan, Harvey, 78, 89
Chayka, Doug, 193
Chesworth, Michael, 217
Child, Lauren, 234
Chocolate, Debbi, 126
Choi, Yangsook, 104
Chow, Octavio, 61
Christopher, Peter, 70, 210
Claire, Elizabeth, 101
Clark, Emma Chichester, 234
Clarke, Judith, 139
Claverie, Jean, 176
Clement, Gary, 71
Clements, Andrew, 164
Coady, Chris, 136
Coburn, Jewell Reinhart, 95
Cockenpot, Marianne, 199
Cole, Babette, 234
Collicutt, Paul, 235
Colmer, David, 204
Coman, Carolyn, 130
Cooke, Trish, 235
Cooper, Floyd, 125
Cooper, Helen, 235
Cooper, Susan, 236
Copeland, Eric, 71
Coran, Pierre, 163
Corentin, Philippe, 171
Corpi, Lucha, 55
Corry, Frances, 219
Courtney-Clarke, Margaret, 129
Cowan, Catherine, 59
Cowley, Joy, 157, 158
Cox, David, 140
Craddock, Sonia, 180
Crampton, Patricia, 203, 219

Crawford, Elizabeth D., 183, 184
Creagh, Sean, 127
Cresp, Gael, 140
Crew, Gary, 140
Crosby-Jones, Michael, 209
Cross, Gillian, 236
Crossley-Holland, Kevin, 236
Czernecki, Stefan, 118

Dale, Penny, 261, 262
Daly, Jude, 132
Daly, Niki, 130, 131, 200
Dávalos, Felipe, 59, 272
Davenier, Christine, 171
Davis, Yvonne LeBrun, 114
de Beer, Hans, 202
de Thomasis, Antonio, 72
de Vries, Anke,
Dedieu, Thierry, 171, 172
Deetlefs, Rene, 131
Degens, T., 180
Delacre, Lulu, 64, 65
deMariscal, Blanca Lopez, 56
dePaola, Tomie, 58
DeSpain, Pleasant, 65
Dienes, Brian, 80
Doherty, Berlie, 236, 237
Dolphin, Ben, 119
Dolphin, Laurie, 119
Domi, 59
Dooling, Michael, 228
Doyle, Brian, 72
Doyle, Malachy, 237
Doyle, Roddy, 195
Drinker, Susan G., 98
Dubois, Claude K., 176
Dumas, Philippe, 172
Dunbar, James, 238
Dunrea, Olivier, 157
Duran, Diego, 54
Dyssegaard, Elisabeth Kallick, 218,
    220, 221

Eachus, Jennifer, 197, 262
Eagle, Ellen, 272

East, Stella, 83
Edwards, Michelle, 119
Egan, Ted, 141
Ekwensi, Cyprian, 135
Elgar, Susan, 141
Elivera, 66
Elling, Lars, 210, 211
Ellis, Deborah, 72
Ellis, Sarah, 73
Ellwand, David, 238
Emoe, Nicola, 197
Englebert, Victor, 45, 64
Enzensberger, Hans Magnus, 181
Erikson, Inga-Karin, 219
Eriksson, Eva, 221
Erlburch, Wolf, 181

Fanelli, Sara, 238, 239
Faría, Rosana, 44
Farjeon, Eleanor, 239
Farmer, Nancy, 134, 135
Fazzi, Maura, 223
Filipovic, Zlata, 269
Fine, Anne, 239
Fine, Edith Hope, 56
Fink, Galit, 121, 141
Finley,Carol, 73, 104, 136
Fischetto, Laura, 200
Fisher, Leonard Everett, 203
Fitzpatrick, Marie-Louise, 196
Flanigan, Caitlin, 228
Fleming, Candace, 200
Flores, Enrique, 56
Flotte, Eddie, 95
Fox, Mem, 142
Foxx, Jeffrey Jay, 59
Francia, Silvia, 172
Frankel, Lory, 171
Franklin, Kristine L., 50
Freeman, Milo, 205
French, Vivian, 240
Friesen, Gayle, 73
Frith, Michael, 249
Frost, Abigail, 254
Frost, Kristi, 77

Fuenmayor, Morella, 57

Gaarder, Jostein, 209
Gabar, Susan, 213
Gal, Laszlo, 77
Galassi, Jonathan, 200
Galli, Letizia, 200
Galloway, Priscilla, 192
Garay, Luis, 65, 66, 73, 74
Gardner, Sally, 209
Garland, Michael, 194
Garner, Alan, 240
Garrigue, Sheila, 74
Gay, Marie-Louise, 74, 75
Geeslin, Campbell, 56
Gelman, Rita Golden, 104
Geras, Adèle, 240
Germein, Katrina, 142
Gerrard, Roy, 240
Gershator, Phillis, 65, 173, 201
Gerstein, Mordicai, 173
Gibbie, Mike, 241
Gieth, Kinna, 218
Gilbert, Lyn, 131
Gilchrist, Cherry, 241
Gilliland, Judith Heide, 117, 122
Gillmore, Don, 75
Gleeson, Brian, 101
Gleich, Jacky, 120
Godard, Alex, 174
Godden, Rumer, 241
Godkin, Celia, 87
Gold, Alison Leslie, 105, 202
Gold, Caroline, 245
Goldthorpe, Peter, 149
Gollub, Matthew, 104, 105
Goodall, Jane, 241
Gorbachev, Valeri, 214
Gore, Leonid, 180
Graham, Bob, 143, 144
Gray, Nigel, 144
Greenwald, Roger, 222
Gregory, Nan, 75
Griff [Andrew Griffen], 242
Grimes, Nikki, 133

Gruber, Wilhelm, 182
Guarnieri, Paolo, 200
Guettier, Bénédicte, 163
Gukova, Julia, 214, 215
Gusti, 216
Guzmán, Eugenia, 59

Haeringen, Annemarie, 204
Hairs, Joya, 48
Hale, Christy, 134
Halkin, Hillel, 121
Hall, Amanda, 102, 247
Hallensleben, Georg, 169, 170
Halpern, Gina, 114
Hamanaka, Sheila, 182, 271
Hamlin, Janet, 210
Hänel, Wolfram, 182
Hanson, Regina, 52
Harris, Julie, 171
Harrison, Barbara, 192
Harrison, Ted, 82
Harshman, Marc, 272
Hart, Rebecca, 57
Haughton, Emma, 242
Hawkins, Jennifer, 221
Hays, Michael, 117
Hazelton, Hugh, 65
Heap, Sue, 242
Heide, Florence Parry, 117, 122
Heidenreich, Elke, 182
Heim, Michael Henry, 181
Heine, Helme, 182, 183
Henderson, Kathy, 242, 243
Hendry, Diana, 243
Heneghan, James, 76, 196
Henry, Marie H., 175
Heo, Yumi, 116
Heyne, Ulrike, 182
Hiçyilmaz, Gaye, 243, 269
Higa, Tomiko, 105
Highet, Alistair, 76
Hill, Anthony, 145
Hill, Trish, 69
Himler, Ronald, 78, 95
Hines, Sue, 145

Hirano, Cathy, 108
Ho, Minfong, 96, 113
Hoban, Russell
Hodge, Merle, 63
Hoffman, Mary, 244
Hofmeyr, Dianne
Hol, Coby, 203
Holeman, Linda, 76
Hollyer, Beatrice, 244, 272
Holt, Daniel D., 109
Holtwijk, Ineke, 44, 204
Holub, Josef, 183
Holubitsky, Katherine, 77
Holzwarth, Werner, 43, 183
Hom, Nancy, 97, 111
Homel, David, 82
Hooper, Meredith, 245
Horenstein, Henry, 64
Horowitz, Anthony, 245
Hort, Lenny, 201
Houghton, Eric, 245
Howard, Kim, 260
Howard, Paul, 226
Hu, Ying-Hwa, 98
Hughes, Monica, 66, 77
Hughes, Shirley, 245, 246
Hutchins, Pat, 246
Huynh, Quang Nhuong, 115

Ingpen, Robert, 141, 145, 257
Ingves, Gunilla, 219
Ingwersen, Faith, 209, 210
Inkpen, Mick, 246
Iribarren, Elena, 44
Isaacs, Anne, 164, 212
Isadora, Rachel, 66

Jabar, Cynthia, 64, 225
Jackson, Shelley, 134
Jaffe, Nina, 272
Jaffrey, Madhur, 102, 247
Jam, Teddy [Matt Cohen], 77, 78
James, J. Alison, 161, 184, 202
James, Simon, 247
Janisch, Heinz, 160

Jansson, Tove, 168
Jarmillo, Nelly Palacio, 66
Jarmillo, Raquel, 66
Jarvis, Robin, 247
Jay, Alison, 247
Jenkins, Debra Reid, 109
Jenkins, Lyll Becerra de, 46
Jeppson, Ann-Sofie, 219
Jiang, Ji Li, 97
Johnston, Tony, 47, 56, 57
Joos, Frédéric, 252
Jorg, Sabine, 184
Joseph, Lynn, 47, 63

Kaldhol, Marit, 209
Karas, G. Brian, 271
Karp, Cindy, 269
Katz, Welwyn Wilton, 78
Kazeroid, Sibylle, 203
Keller, Holly, 115
Kennaway, Adrienne, 137, 254
Kenneally, Thomas, 146
Kerins, Tony, 242
Kerner, Charlotte, 184
Keselman, Gabriela, 216
Kessler, Christina, 123, 129
Khan, Rukhsana, 77, 95
King, Thomas, 79
King-Smith, Dick, 248
Kitamura, Satoshi, 248
Kitsao, Jay, 127
Kleven, Elisa, 56, 67
Klinting, Lars, 220
Knight, Christopher G., 57
Kraan, Hanna, 204
Krischanitz, Raoul, 160
Kroll, Virginia, 105
Kruusval, Catarina, 219
Kuckreja, Madhovi, 96
Kühner, Peter, 223
Kuklin, Susan, 106
Kurelek, William, 79
Kurtz, Jane, 125, 126

Laird, Elizabeth, 249

Lally, Soinbhe, 197
Lambora, Frances, 221
Lamo-Jiminez, Mario, 65
Landis, Alison, 121
Landmann, Bímba, 200, 201
Landström, Lena, 220
Landström, Olof, 220, 221
Lankford, Mary D., 273
Lanning, Rosemary, 160, 175, 182,
    223, 224
Laroche, Giles, 275
Lasky, Kathryn, 57
Laukel, Hans Gerold, 220
Launko, Okinaba, 136
Laurabeatriz, 44
Lauture, Denizé, 51
Lee, Cynthia Chin, 116
Legge, David, 154
Lehmann, Christian, 174
Leiber, Heinrich, 207
Lemieux, Michèle, 79
Lessac, Frane, 128
Lester, Alison, 146
Levine, Ellen, 166
Levy, Janice, 57
Lewin, Betsy, 133
Lewin, Ted, 48, 102, 122, 123
Lewington, Anna, 44, 249
Lewis, E. B., 125, 134
Lewis, Kim, 237, 249
Lewis, Naomi, 166
Lewis, Paul, 80
Lia, Simone, 250
Libura, Krystyna, 54, 55
Liersch, Anne, 184
Ligasan, Darryl, 95
Lindgren, Astrid, 220
Lindgren, Barbro, 220
Littlechild, George, 80, 84
Litty, Julie, 241
Llanque, Carlos, 43, 183
Lobel, Anita, 212
Lodge, Katherine, 250
London, Jonathan, 123
Lorbiecki, Marybeth, 270

Lottridge, Celia Barker, 80
Low, Mei-Yim, 136
Loya, Olgo, 66
Lozardo-Rivera, Carmen, 67
Luciani, Brigitte, 175
Lunelli, Guilano, 176
Lunn, Janet, 80, 81
Lützen, Hanna, 167

MacDonald, Margaret Read, 113
MacGrory, Yvonne, 197
Machado, Ana, 44
Machalek, Jan, 164
Madrigal, Antonio Hernandez, 58
Maeno, Itoko, 193
Maggs, Catherine, 209
Magombe, Paulinos Vincent, 136
Magyar, Sabina, 181
Mah, Adeline Yen, 98
Mahy, Margaret, 158, 273
Malone, Peter, 236
Manning, Mick, 222
Manson, Ainslie, 81
Marchetta, Melina, 148
Marijanovic, Stanislav, 192
Marsden, John, 148, 149
Marshak, Samuel, 214
Martinez, Alejandro Cruz, 58
Marx, Trish, 269
Masurel, Claire, 175
Mathenge, Wanjiku, 127
Mathers, Petra, 56
Matje, Martin, 173, 177
Mattingley, Christobel, 150
Mattotti, Lorenzo, 196
Mazer, Anne, 273
McAllister, Angela, 250
McAllister, Margaret, 250
McBratney, Sam, 197
McCaughrean, Geraldine, 251
McClure, Gillian, 251
McCully, Emily Arnold, 97
McDonnell, Flora, 252
McGirr, Nancy, 50
McKay, Lawrence, 95

McKee, Tim, 131
McKenna, Laura, 43, 174, 186, 216
McLoone, Margo, 274
McMahon, Patricia, 98
McNaughton, Colin, 252
Mead, Alice, 271
Meade, Holly, 113
Medlicott, Mary, 137, 253
Micklethwait, Lucy, 253
Milone, Karen, 273
Mistry, Nilesh, 256
Mockford, Caroline, 253
Moeyaert, Bart, 204, 205
Mollel, Tololwa M., 134
Monkman, Kent, 79
Montserrat, Pep, 216
Moodie, Fiona, 131
Moore, Inga, 254
Moore, Yvette, 69
Moreno, Rene King, 56
Morgenstern, Susie, 175
Mori, Kyoko, 106
Morimoto, Junko, 150
Moroz, Georges, 177
Moss, Miriam, 137, 254
Moss, Sally, 150
Mulherin, Jennifer, 254
Mullins, Patricia, 150
Munduruku, Daniel, 44
Muñoz, Claudio, 254
Murray, Steven T., 219

Nascimbeni, Barbara, 241
Navasky, Bruno, 106
Neugebauer, Charise, 184
Neumeyer, Peter F., 180
Newsome, Jill, 254
Newth, Mette, 209, 210
Nichols, Grace, 64, 225
Nicholson, William, 255
Nieuwenhuisen, John, 127, 206
Nieuwsma, Milton J., 212
Nikly, Michelle, 176
Nix, Garth, 151
Njeng, Pierre Yves, 124

Norac, Carl, 176
Nye, Naomi Shihab, 58, 120
Nygren, Tord, 219
Nyman, Ingrid, 220

Obrist, Jürg, 224
Olaleye, Issac, 128
Oliver, Narelle, 151
Olivera, Fernando, 58
Onyefulu, Ifeoma, 128
Oporto, Freddy, 43, 183
Oppel, Kenneth, 81
Oppenheim, Shulamith, 117, 193
Oram, Hiawyn, 255, 256
Orgel, Doris, 160, 182
Orlev, Uri, 120
Orozco, Jose-Luis, 67
Orozco, Rebecca, 61
Orr, Wendy, 152
Otani, June, 104
Overend, Jenni, 152
Oxenbury, Helen, 230
Oyen, Wenche, 209

Pacovská, Kveta, 164
Padt, Maartje, 205
Pallandt, Nicolas van, 205
Parillo, Tony, 200
Park, Eung Won, 110
Park, Frances, 109, 110
Park, Ginger, 109, 110
Park, Linda Sue, 110
Parker, Edward, 249
Paul, Korky, 256
Paz, Octavio, 59
Pelgrom, Els, 206, 217
Pelizzoli, Francesca, 97, 229
Pelletier, Gilles, 70
Penney, Ian, 256
Perrault, Charles, 176
Peterson, Ingela, 218
Pevear, Richard, 219
Pevsner, Stella, 116
Pfister, Marcus, 224
Pinkney, Brian, 120, 126

Pinto, Venantius J., 100
Pirotta, Saviour, 256
Pohl, Peter, 218
Pohrt, Tom, 47
Polacco, Patricia, 176
Pollack, Pamela, 120
Potter, Giselle, 200
Pow, Tom, 257
Pratt, Pierre, 82
Preiss, Byron, 274
Pressler, Mirjam, 184
Price, Susan, 257
Prins, Johanna H., 206
Prins, Johanna W., 206
Prokofiev, Sergei, 215
Propp, Vera W., 206
Pullman, Philip, 257

Qu, Sha-liu, 97, 229
Quan, Shiu Wong, 97
Quintana, Anton, 127, 206

Rabinovici, Schoschana, 185
Radin, Ruth Yaffe, 210
Rahaman, Vashanti, 63
Rana, Indi, 102
Rascal, 177
Raulinson, Hayden, 59
Ray, Deborah Kogan, 115
Reichstein, Alexander, 161, 184
Reiper-Bastian, Marlies, 182
Reisberg, Mira, 76
Reiser, Lynn, 67
Remphry, Martin, 238
Rennison, Louise, 157
Repchuck, Caroline, 257
Rich, Susan, 181
Riddell, Chris, 166
Riddle, Tohby, 153
Riggio, Anita, 114
Rinaldi, Angelo, 242
Roberts, Mark, 201
Robinson, Roland
Roca, François, 76
Rodarmor, William, 174

Rohmer, Harriet, 58, 61
Ros, Saphan, 96
Rosen, Billi, 193, 258
Rosenberry, Vera, 101, 102
Rosenthal, Marc, 142, 214
Rosner, Gill, 175
Ross, Tony, 259, 265
Roundtree, Ruth, 105
Rowe, Gavin, 263
Rowe, John, 161, 259
Rowling, J. K., 260
Ruaro, Alfonso, 45
Rubalcaba, Jill, 117
Rubin, Susan Goldman, 165
Ruepp, Krista, 186
Ruffins, Reynold, 51
Russell, Ching Yeung
Russell, Lynne, 244
Ryan, Stephen, 146

Sacré, Marie-José, 163
Sanchez, Enrique O., 50
Sandin, Joan, 220
Sandoval, Dolores, 129
Sanroman, Susana, 59
Sansone, Adele, 161
Sanvoisin, Eric, 177
Saport, Linda, 63
Savadier, Elivia, 142
Say, Allen, 107
Schami, Rafik, 186
Schecter, David, 58
Scheffler, Ursel, 186, 187
Scheidl, Gerda Marie, 176
Schneider, Antonie, 188
Schubert, Dieter, 207
Schubert, Ingrid, 207
Schur, Maxine, 120, 126
Schwartz, David M., 45, 64
Scuderi, Lucia, 201
Segerberg, Ebba, 222
Semel, Nava, 121
Serrano, Francisco, 59
Service, Robert W., 82
Sha'ban, Mervet Akram, 121

Sharratt, Nick, 260
Shea, Pegi Deitz, 114
Shepard, Aaron, 102
Sherman, Whitney, 272
Shulevitz, Uri, 118
Siegal, Aranka, 195
Siegel, Alice, 274
Sierra, F. John, 57
Silverman, Erica, 213
Simard, Rémy, 82
Simmons, Lesley Ann, 274
Simmons, Steven J., 260
Sís, Peter, 114, 165
Sisulu, Elinor Batezat, 132
Skarmeta, Antonio, 45
Skurzynski, Gloria, 177
Sofilas, Mark, 145
Sola, Michele, 59
Solheim, James, 275
Sortland, Bjørn, 210
Souhami, Jessica, 260
Spagnoli, Cathy, 97, 111
Speidel, Sandra, 63
Spetter, Jung-Hee, 203, 207
Springer, Jane, 44
Spudvilas, Ann, 140
Stanley, Sanna, 124, 125
Staples, Suzanne Fisher, 103, 112
Stark, Ulf, 222
Sterling, Shirley, 82
Stevenson, Harvey, 52
Stevenson, Robert Lewis, 261
Stewart, Dianne, 132
Stinchecum, Amanda, 108
Stock, Catherine, 52
Stojic, Manya, 261
Stone, Kazuko G., 105
Sturges, Philemon, 275
Sturtevant, Katherine, 261
Stuve-Bodeen, Stephanie, 134
Sutcliff, Rosemary, 261

Tabor, Nancy Maria Grande, 60
Takao, Yuko, 108
Takashima, Shizuye, 83

Takaya, Julia, 104
Talbott, Hudson, 208
Talley, Linda, 193
Tan, Shaun, 140
Tang, Fay, 116
Tauss, Herbert, 270
Taylor, Alice, 197
Taylor, William, 158
Temple, Frances, 48, 51
Testa, Fulvio, 201
Tharlet, Eve, 175
Thomas, Meredith, 150
Thomas, Valerie, 256
Thompson, Carol, 243
Thompson, Colin, 153
Thompson, Kate, 198
Tola, Erlini, 43, 183
Tompert, Ann, 198
Torres, Leyla, 46
Trenter, Anna, 215
Treviño, Elizabeth Borton de, 60, 216
Trivizas, Eugene, 194
Trottier, Maxine, 83
Tseng, Jean, 96, 110
Tseng, Mou-sien, 96, 110
Tsubakiyama, Margaret Holloway, 98

Uhlig, Elizabeth, 216
Ungerer, Tomi, 178
Unzer, Christa, 184
Urrutia, Maria Cristina, 54, 55, 61

Valgardson, W. D., 83, 84
Van Camp, Richard, 84
Van der Merwe, Anita, 126
Van Wright, Cornelius, 98
vanKampen, Vlasta, 84
Vargo, Kurt, 101
Varley, Susan, 255
Vathanaprida, Supaporn, 113
Vendrell, Carme Solé, 217
Vincent, Gabrielle, 164
Visconti, Guido, 201
Voake, Charlotte, 239

Waboose, Jan Bourdeau, 85
Waddell, Martin, 262
Wahl, Mats, 223
Waite, Judy, 263
Waldman, Neil, 121
Walgren, Judy, 133
Walker, Kate, 153
Wallace, Ian, 84, 85
Wallace, Karen, 263
Walters, Eric, 86
Wan, Manyee, 97, 229
Ward, John, 126
Wassiljewa, Tatjana, 215
Watkins, Yoko Kawashima, 111
Watts, Bernadette, 263
Watts, Irene N., 86
Weigelt, Udo, 189
Weiler, Diana, 86
Wells, Ruth, 108
Wen, George, 174
Weninger, Brigitte, 161
Whelan, Gloria, 103
White, Kathryn, 264
Whitesel, Cheryl Aylward, 115
Whybrow, Ian, 264, 265
Wiencirz, Gerlinde, 215
Wild, Margaret, 154
Willey, Bee, 245
Williams, Karen Lynn, 52
Williams, Marcia, 265
Williams, Richard, 229
Willis, Jeanne, 265
Wilson, Sharon, 132, 235
Wilson, Tona, 64
Wilson-Max, Ken, 127, 266
Winch, John, 155

Winter, Kathryn, 216
Winton, Tim, 155
Withrow, Sarah, 87
Wolf, Bernard, 61, 122
Woods, Shirley, 87
Wormell, Christopher, 266
Wormell, Mary, 248, 266
Wright, Cliff, 264
Wynne-Jones, Tim, 87, 88

Xiong, Blia, 111
Xiong, Gu, 88

Yagyu, Genichiro, 108
Yang, You, 114
Yee, Paul, 88
Yen, Clara, 99
Yerxa, Leo, 89
Yorinks, Adrienne, 275
Yorinks, Arthur, 275
Yoshi, 108
Young, Selina, 158
Yumoto, Kazumi, 108

Zägwyn, Deborah Turney, 89, 90
Zak, Drahos, 141
Zeitlin, Steve
Zeman, Ludmilla, 90
Zemser, Amy Bronwen, 128
Zhang, Ange, 77
Zhang, Christopher Zhang-Yuan, 110
Zhang, Hao Yu, 91, 99
Zhang, Song Nan, 69, 90, 01, 99, 116
Zubizarreta, Rosalma, 58, 61
Zwerger, Lisbeth, 160, 162, 239

Title Index

Numbers indicate pages.

A Is for Africa, 128
A Is for Asia, 116
A to Zen, 108
Aani and the Tree Huggers, 100
Abel's Moon, 245
Aboriginal Art of Australia, 141
Abracadabra, 207
The Absentminded Fellow, 214
Abuela's Weave, 50
The Acorn Eaters, 206, 217
Adem's Cross, 271
Adventures of Marco and Polo, 189
Albert & Lila, 186
Alfie's ABC, 246
Alfred's Party, 238
Ali, Child of the Desert, 123
Alice-by-Accident, 228
Alice in Wonderland, 162, 234
Alice's Adventures in Wonderland, 233
All about Scabs, 108
All Mixed-Up: A Mixed-Up Matching
    Book, 214
All the Way to Morning, 273
All-Weather Friends, 189
Alone at Ninety Foot, 77
The Alphabet Atlas, 276
The Amber Spyglass, 257
Among the Volcanoes, 50
Anastasia's Album, 70, 214
And if the Moon Could Talk, 169
Andi's War, 193, 258
Andrei's Search, 221
Angela Weaves a Dream: The Story of
    a Young Maya Artist, 59
Angkat: The Cambodian Cinderella, 95

Angus, Thongs, and Full-Frontal
    Snogging, 258
Anna's Art Adventure, 210
Anne Frank: A Hidden Life, 184
Anni's Diary of France, 169
Anni's India Diary, 100
Antonio's Rain Forest, 44, 249
Apple Batter, 89
The Art of African Masks, 136
Art of Japan, 104
Art of the Far North, 73
Asphalt Angels, 44, 204
At the Sign of the Star, 261
Atlantis: The Legend of a Lost City, 228

Baboon, 169
The Baboon King, 127, 206
The Baby Dances, 242
Back Soon, 243
Bare Hands, 204
Barrilete: a Kite for the Day of the
    Dead, 48
Baseball in the Barrios, 64
Bat Summer, 87
Be Brave, Little Lion!, 186
Be Patient Abdul, 129
Bear's Eggs, 207
Beautiful Warrior: The Legend of the
    Nun's Kung Fu, 97
Beauty and the Beast, 251
Bedtime Ba-a-alk, 78
A Bedtime Story, 142
Beetle Bedlam, 84
Beneath the Stone, 61
Benny: An Adventure Story, 143

Benny's Had Enough! 221
Beowulf, 78
The Best Beak in Boonaroo Bay, 151
The Best Children's Books in World, 275
The Best-Loved Plays of Shakespeare,
   254
Beyond the Mango Tree, 128
The Big Big Sea, 262
Big Boy, 134
A Big Day for Little Jack, 254
Big Rain Coming, 142
Billy and the Big New School, 227
Binya's Blue Umbrella, 101
The Birth of the Moon, 203
Black Nell: The Adventure of a
   Coyote, 87
The Blackbirch Kid's Almanac of
   Geography, 275
The Blue Lawn, 158
Blue Rabbit and Friends, 266
Blueprint, 184
The Boggart, 236
Boo and Baa in Windy Weather, 220
The Book of Changes, 87
A Book of Promises, 249
The Boxer and Princess, 182
The Boy in the Attic, 88
A Boy Named Giotto, 200
Boy of the Deeps, 85
The Boy Who Ate Words, 171
The Boy Who Lost His Belly Button,
   265
The Boy on the Beach, 130
The Bravest Ever Bear, 226
Bravo, Mr. William Shakespeare! 265
Bravo, Zan Angelo! 130, 200
Breakaway, 88
Bright Star, 140
Broken Shields, 54
The Brothers Gruesome, 141
Bruno the Baker, 220
The Burnt Stick, 145
The Butterfly, 176

Caged Eagles, 86

A Calendar of Festivals, 241
The Calypso Alphabet, 225
Can You Spot the Spotted Dog? 259
Can You Whistle, Johanna? 222
Caravan, 95
Caribbean Dream, 66
Carnaval, 43
A Carp for Kimiko, 105
Celeste Sails to Spain, 146
Charlotte, 80
Charro: The Mexican Cowboy, 53
Checkers, 148
Chibi: A True Story from Japan, 104
Chicken Man, 119
A Child in Prison Camp, 83
The Children of China, 90, 99
A Child's Book of Art, 253
A Child's Treasury of Irish Rhymes,
   197
Chinese Cinderella, 98
Cinco de May: Yesterday and Today,
   61
Clarice Bean, That's Me, 234
The Clay Marble, 96
The Clever Cowboy, 250
Clown, 230
The Collector of Moments, 180
The Color of My Words, 47
The Composition, 45
Cool Melons-Turn to Frogs! 104
Copper Treasure, 232
The Cow of No Color: Riddle Stories
   and Justice Tales from around the
   World, 273
Cowboy Baby, 242
Cowboy on the Steppes, 91, 99
A Coyote Columbus Story, 79
The Crooked Apple Tree, 245
Cuban Kids, 47

Dare Truth or Promise, 157
The Dark Light, 209
The Dark Portal, 247
Darkness over Denmark, 166
A Day, a Dog, 164

The Day Gogo Went to Vote, 132
The Day of Ahmed's Secret, 117
A Day with the Bellyflops, 170
Days Like This: A Collection of Small
    Poems, 247
Days of the Dead, 57
The Dead of Night, 148
Dear Diary, 238
The Deep, 155
The Desert Fox Family Book, 224
The Devil and His Boy, 245
The Devil in Vienna, 160
Dia's Story Cloth, 111
Diez Deditos: Ten Little Fingers &
    Other Plays, 67
The Distant Talking Drum: Poems
    from Nigeria, 128
The Divorced Kids Club and Other
    Stories, 83
Do You Know Me? 134
Do You Know Pippi Longstocking?
    220
Dog and Cat, 216
A Dog Came, Too, 81
Don't Read This! And Other Tales of
    the Unnatural, 274
Dr. White, 241
The Dreamkeeper, 145
Dreamstones, 83
The Drover's Boy, 141
Duck in the Truck, 226

The Ear, the Eye, and the Arm, 135
El Guëro: A True Adventure Story, 60
The Elf's Hat, 161
Elizabeti's Doll, 134
Elsie Piddock Skips in Her Sleep, 239
The Emerald Lizard: Fifteen Latin
    American Tales, 65
The Emperor's New Clothes, 166
Erandi's Braids, 58
Escape to the Forest, 213
The Eternal Spring of Mr. Ito, 74
Eugenio, 199
Eva's Summer Vacation, 164

The Fabulous Fantoras, Book Two,
    237
The Fabulous Song, 75
Family Tree, 163
A Farm, 172
The Father Who Had 10 Children, 163
Festival in My Heart: Poems by
    Japanese Children, 106
Fiesta Fireworks, 53
Fire, Bed, & Bone, 231
Fireflies in the Dark, 165
Firefly Summer, 62
The First Red Maple Leaf, 90
A Fish Tale, 89
The Fishing Summer, 77
Flying, 164
Flying Lessons, 121
For the Life of Laetitia, 63
Forging Freedom, 208
The Forgotten Garden, 258
The Fossil Girl, 231
Frances, 83
Freya on the Wall, 180
Friends, 183
From Far and Wide: A Canadian
    Citizenship, 69
From the Bellybutton of the Moon and
    Other Summer, 53
Fruits: A Caribbean Counting Poem,
    52, 230
Full House, 144
Furaha Means Happy: A Book of
    Swahili Words, 127, 266

Gabriella's Song, 200
Garbage Creek and Other Stories, 83
The Genius of Leonardo, 201
George's Store at the Shore, 170
Ghost Train, 89
The Gift, 216
Gift of the Sun: A Tale from South
    Africa, 132
The Giggler Treatment, 195
A Girl Named Disaster, 135
The Girl Who Lost Her Smile, 118

The Girl Who Wore Too Much, 113
The Girl with White Flag, 105
Go and Come Back, 62
Good Night! 175
Good-bye Marianne: A Story of
    Growing Up in Nazi Germany, 86
Goodbye Rune, 209
Good-Bye, Vivi! 188
Grab Hands and Run, 48
The Grandad Tree, 235
Grandfather's Dream, 116
Grandfather's Laika, 223
Grandmother's Nursery Rhymes, 66
Grandpa's Amazing Computer, 187
The Grave, 76, 196
The Great Escape from City Zoo, 153
The Great Poochini, 71
Growing Frogs, 240

Habibi, 120
Hair in Funny Places: A Book about
    Puberty, 234
Hairy Tuesday, 120
Halinka, 185
Hamadi and the Stolen Cattle, 127
A Handful of Seeds, 66
The Hangashore, 70
The Happy Hedgehog, 224
A Happy New Year's Day, 70
Harlequin and the Green Dress, 200
Harry Potter and the Sorcerer's Stone,
    260
Harry's Home, 227
The Harvest Birds, 56
Harvey Hare, Postman
    Extraordinaire, 263
Haveli, 112
Having a Wonderful Time, 275
Hello? Is Anybody There? 209
Here Comes Pontus! 219
The Hidden Forest, 138
Hiding Horatio, 189
A Hive for the Honeybee, 197
Hold My Hand and Run, 250
The Hollow Tree, 81

Homeless Bird, 103
The Honorable Prison, 46
Hopscotch around the World, 274
Hornet's Nest, 205
Horses in the Fog, 186
Hosni the Dreamer, 118
Hostage to War, 215
Hound without Howl, 90
A House is Not a Home, 184
The House of Wisdom, 118
How Smudge Came, 75
How Will We Get to the Beach? 175
The Hundredth Name, 117
The Hunt, 151
Hunting For Fur, 172

I Dream of Peace, 269
I Have an Olive Tree, 191
I, Juan de Pareja, 216
I Love Animals, 252
I Love Boats, 252
I Love You So Much, 176
I Miss You, I Miss You, 222
I Spy a Freight Train: Transportation
    in Art, 253
I Want To Be, 259
Ian Penney's ABC, 256
The Idle Bear, 146
Idora, 174
If I Forget Thee, O Jerusalem, 122
If You Could Be My Friend, 121
I'm José and I'm Okay, 183
I'm Sorry, 197
Imagine, 147
In the Heart of the Village, 100
In Wibbly's Garden, 246
The Ink Drinker, 177
The Ink-Keeper's Apprentice, 107
The Invisible Hunters, 61
Is It Far to Zanzibar? 133
Island in the Sun, 52
It's Disgusting and We Ate It! 276

Jade and Iron: Latin American Tales
    from Two Cultures, 65, 73

Jamela's Dress, 131
Janey's Girl, 73
Jody's Beans, 237
Jon's Moon, 217
Judge Rabbit and the Tree Spirit, 97
Jump Up Time: A Trinidad Carnival
    Story, 63
Just Stay Put, 71

Katarína, 216
Kente Colors, 126
The Killick, 70
Kinderlager, 212
Kinderdike, 203
King Forever! 135
Kiss it Better, 255
Kite, 232
The Kite Fighters, 110
Kit's Wilderness, 226
Kodomo: Children of Japan, 106

The Land I Lost: Adventures of a Boy
    in Vietnam, 115
Lao-Lao of Dragon Mountain, 97, 229
Las Navidades: Popular Songs from
    Latin America, 64
Laura's Star, 179
Leon and Albertine, 171
Leona: A Love Story, 60
Lily and Trooper's Spring, 207
Little Brother, 95, 138
The Little Brown Jay, 101
Little Calf, 249
The Little Green Goose, 161
A Little Salmon for Witness, 63
A Little Tiger in the Chinese Night,
    91, 99
Little Wolf's Book of Badness, 264
Lizzy and Skunk, 196
The Long March, 196
The Long Road, 74
Looking for Alibrandi, 148
Looking for X, 72
The Lost Boys of Natinga, 133
The Lost Day, 139

Lost in Time, 181
Luke the Lionhearted, 188
Lumberjack, 79

Madeline, 170
Madoulina, 124
The Maestro, 88
The Magic Maguey, 56
The Magic Saddle, 150
Mama and Papa Have a Store, 49
Mama, Across the Sea, 174
Ma'mi, 136
A Man Called Raven, 84
A Manual of House Monsters, 192
Many Stones, 130
Mariathe's Story: Spoken Memories,
    191
Market Day, 195
Mary Anning and the Sea Dragon, 228
Masada, 121
The Mats, 112
Max, 143
Max and Molly and the Mystery of the
    Missing Honey, 224
Mayeros: A Yucatec Maya Family, 54
McHeshi Goes on a Journey, 127
Me and My Cat? 248
Meet Kofi, Maria & Sunita: Family
    Life in Ghana, Peru & India, 275
Meet the Molesons, 202
Mei-Mei Loves the Morning, 98
Melinda and Nock and the Magic
    Spell, 188
Memorial, 140
Mercy's Birds, 76
Michaelangelo's Surprise, 201
Miffy in the Hospital, 203
Milton, 168
Milton, My Father's Dog, 71
Mina and the Bear, 184
Mister Once-Upon-A-Time, 82
Momento Magicos/Magic Moments,
    66
Monkey Sunday, 124
Monkey Trouble, 259

The Montreal of My Childhood, 72
Moomin, Mymble, and Little My, 168
Morning on the Lake, 85
The Most Beautiful Place in World, 49
The Mousehole Cat, 229
Mr. Kalogo's Factory, 136
Mrs. Meyer the Bird, 181
My Daughter, My Son, the Eagle, the Dove, 55
My Farm, 147
My Freedom Trip, 109
My Life with the Wave, 59
My Map Book, 259
My Mexico/Mexico mio, 57
My Name Is Seepeetza, 82
My Painted House, My Friendly Chicken, and Me, 129
My Palace of Leaves in Sarajevo, 270
My Shadow, 261

Nabulela, 131
Ndito Runs, 126
Ned Kelly & the City of the Bees, 146
Nero Corleone: A Cat's Story, 182
Neve Shalom/Wahat al-Salam: Oasis of Peace, 119
Night Train, 139
The Night Worker, 170
Nilo and the Tortoise, 48
Nina Bonita, 44
Nine-in-One, Grr! Grr! 111
No Condition is Permanent, 129
No Dinner! The Story of the Old Woman and the Pumpkin, 260
No Hickory, No Dickory, No Dock, 64, 225
No More Strangers Now, 131
No Pretty Pictures: A Child of War, 212
Noah and the Space Ark, 234
Noah's Ark, 160
Nobody Likes Me! 160
Norton's Hut, 149
The Number Devil: A Mathematical Adventure, 181

Off the Road, 229
Old Pig, 154
An Old Shell: Poems of the Galapagos, 47
The Old Woman Who Loved to Read, 155
On My Island, 74
On Ramon's Farm, 56
On the Pampas, 43
On the Wings of Peace: In Memory of Hiroshima and Nagasaki, 272
One Boy from Kosovo, 270
One Night: A Story from the Desert, 123
Only a Pigeon, 125
Our Lady of Guadalupe, 59
Out of the Dump: Writings and Photographs by Children of Guatemala, 50
Out of the Shadows, 145

Pablo Remembers: The Fiesta of the Day of the Dead, 54
Painted Dreams, 52
Papa! 171
Pa's Harvest, 69
Patakin: World Tales of Drums and Drummers, 273
Peeling the Onion, 152
The Penguin Quartet, 218
Percy to the Rescue, 260
The Perfume of Memory, 176
Peter, 153
Peter and the Wolf, 215
Peter's Painting, 150
Peter's Picture, 214
Picture This, 247
Piggy's Birthday Dream, 203
Pippi's Extraordinary Ordinary Day, 220
The Pirate's Son, 251
Plato's Journey, 193
Play Me a Story, 272
A Prairie Alphabet, 69
Prayer for the Twenty-First Century, 149

Premlata and the Festival of Lights, 241
Prince Norodom Sihanouk, 96
Princess Chamomile's Garden, 255
Pulling the Lion's Tail, 125
Pumpkin Soup, 235
Puss in Boots, 176

Quacky, Quack-Quack, 264
Queenie, One of the Family, 143
The Quicksand Pony, 147

Rain, 261
The Rains are Coming, 125
Rainy Day, 242
Raisel's Riddle, 213
RanVan: The Defender, 86
The Real Plato Jones, 191, 230
Rebel: A Tibetan Odyssey, 115
Red Scarf Girl: A Memory of the Cultural Revolution, 97
The Red Woolen Blanket, 144
Red's Great Chase, 250
Rescue at Sea! 182
Rice Is Life, 104
Rice Without Rain, 113
River Story, 245
The River That Went to the Sky, 137, 253
The Robber and Me, 183
Roberta's Vacation, 172
Robi Dobi: The Marvelous Adventures of an Indian Elephant, 102, 247
Rocking Horse Land & Other Classic Tales, 249
The Roller Birds of Rampur, 102
The Roman Twins, 240
Rosa Moves to Town, 221
The Roses in My Carpet, 78, 95
Rosie and Tortoise, 154
Rosie's Babies, 262
The Royal Bee, 110
Running the Road to ABC, 51
The Rusty, Trusty, Tractor, 157

Sabriel, 151
Sacred Places, 276
Sacred River, 102
Saint Patrick, 198
Salsa Stories, 65
Sami and the Time of the Troubles, 122
Samir and Yonatan, 119
Sammy and the Dinosaurs, 265
Sarah and the People of Sand River, 84
Saturday Sancocho, 46
Savitri: A Tale of Acient India, 102
Scarlette Beane, 263
Secret Letters from 0 to 10, 175
The Secret of Ruby Ring, 197
Seesaw Girl, 110
Selkie, 251
Senora Reganona, 59
Shabanu: Daughter of the Wind, 112
Shadow, 254
Shanti, 205
Shark-Mad Stanley, 242
Sheep in Wolves' Clothing, 248
Shiva's Fire, 103
Shizuko's Daughter, 106
The Shooting of Dan McGrew, 82
Silverwing, 81
Since Dad Left, 230
Sing For Your Father, Su Phan, 116
Six Words, Many Turtles, & Three Days in Hong Kong, 98
Skellig, 227
SkySisters, 85
Sleeping Boy, 180
Smack, 233
Small Brown Dog's Bad Remembering Day, 241
A Small Tall Tale from the Far Far North, 165
Smiling for Strangers, 243, 269
Snake Dreamer, 192
The Snake-Stone, 236
So Far from the Bamboo Grove, 111
Socrates, 177

Somewhere, 69
The Song of Six Birds, 131
Sophie and the New Baby, 227
A South African Night, 130
Special Delivery, 161
A Special Fate, 104, 202
Spider's Voice, 177
Spirit of Hope, 144
*The Spirit of Tio Fernando /Es
   espiritu de tío Fernando*, 57
Split Ends, 260
The Spotty Pig, 248
The Spring Tone, 108
The Spy in the Attic, 187
Starbright and the Dream Eater, 158
Starring Grace, 244
Stella: Star of the Sea, 75
Stephen Fair, 88
The Sterkarm Handshake, 257
The Stoneboat, 77
The Stones are Hatching, 251
The Storm, 243
Storm Boy, 80
Stormy Night, 79
The Story of Rosy Dock, 138
The Story of Search for Story, 210
The Storyteller's Beads, 126
The Storytellers, 122
The Straight Line Wonder, 142
The Stray Kitten, 263
Street Child, 237
A Summery Saturday Morning, 158
Susan Laughs, 265
The Swan's Stories, 166
Sweet Dried Apples, 115
Sweet, Sweet Fig Banana, 65
Switchers, 198
Sword Song, 261

The Tale of Gilbert Alexander Pig, 140
Tales of the Amazon, 44
The Tangerine Tree, 52
*Taste of Salt: A Story of Modern
   Haiti*, 51
A Taste of the Mexican Market, 60

Tea for Ten, 218
Tea with Milk, 107
Ten Red Apples, 246
Thanks to My Mother, 185
Theo, 192
There's a Hole in my Bucket, 207
This Is the Tree, 254
This Land is My Land, 80
This Train, 235
This Tree is Older Than You Are, 58
The Three Golden Keys, 165
*The Three Little Wolves and Big Bad
   Pig*, 194
Three Wise Women, 244
Throw Your Tooth on the Roof, 272
Tibet through the Red Box, 114
Tick-Tock, 218
The Tiger and the Brahmin, 101
Tigers, Frogs and Rice Cakes, 109
Tightrope, 236
A Time of Golden Dragons, 91, 99
To Cross a Line, 185
To Fly, 201
*To Pluto and Back: A Voyage in the
   Milky Way*, 219
Tom Goes to Kindergarten, 154
Tomi: A Childhood Under the Nazis,
   178
Tommy's New Sister, 187
Tonight by Sea, 51
Torn Thread, 164, 212
*Tortillas and Lullabies/ Tortillas y
   Cancioncitas*, 67
The Transformation, 210
Travel Tales, 171
Tree of Cranes, 107
Troll's Search for Summer, 205
ttuM, 78
The Tulip Touch, 239
Turtle Bay, 256
Turtle Spring, 90
The Two Brothers, 96
The Two Bullies, 150

Ultimate Game, 174

Uncle Ronald, 72
Under the Lemon Moon, 56
Under the Royal Palms: A Childhood in Cuba, 46
Unknown, 153
Upon the Head of the Goat: A Childhood in Hungary, 195
The Upside-Down Reader, 182

Vacation in the Village, 124
Vendela in Venice, 219
Victor, 173
Vlad the Undead, 167
Voices in the Park, 231

The Wadjet Eye, 117
Wake Up, World! 244, 273
A Walk in My World: International Short Stories about Youth, 274
Walk the Dark Streets, 179
Welcome with Love, 152
The Well of the Wind, 240
We're Going on a Lion Hunt, 228
What a Viking! 222
What Have You Done, Davy? 162
What's Inside? 163
What's the Most Beautiful Thing You Know about Horses? 84
What's This? 253
When I Left My Village, 120, 126
When I Was Young, 238
When It Starts to Snow, 173
When Jaguars Ate the Moon and Other Stories, 64
When the Soldiers Were Gone, 206
When the Viceroy Came, 55
When They Fight, 264

Where Fireflies Dance / Ahi, donde bailan las luciérnagas, 55
Where Is Tibet? 114
The Whispering Cloth, 114
Who Do You Love? 262
Who Is the World For? 257
Why Not? 266
Why Rat Comes First: A Story of the Chinese Zodiac, 99
The Wicked Witch Is at It Again, 204
The Wild Boy, 173
Willa and Old Miss Annie, 237
Willy the Dreamer, 232
Willy's Pictures, 232
The Wind Singer, 255
Wings to Fly, 80
Winnie Flies Again, 256
A Winter Concert, 108
Wish Me Luck, 76
Wish You Were Here (and I Wasn't), 252
The Wizard of Oz, 162
Wolf, 239
The Woman Who Outshone Sun, 58
The World of King Arthur and His Court, 236
The Wrong Overcoat, 256

Yanni Rubbish, 193
Yanomami: People of the Amazon, 45, 64
The Yellow Train, 76
The Young Writer's Companion, 73

Zlata's Diary: A Child's Life in Sarajevo, 269

Subject Guide

Numbers indicate book entry.

Adoption
360, 574

Alphabet books
81, 208, 231, 268, 536, 644

Anthropology
60, 267

Art and artists
27, 95, 194, 202, 271, 289, 304, 330, 405, 408, 495, 503, 507, 510, 517, 632, 633

Babies
284, 433, 543, 595, 496

Beaches
271, 348, 388, 395

Bears
317, 421, 488, 537

Bedtime
114, 305, 383, 396, 515, 595

Bilingual books
39, 49, 78, 68, 209, 222, 224, 549

Birthdays
284, 474, 511, 522

Boats and boating
85, 86, 361, 629

Books and reading
232, 236, 414, 496

Circus and clowns
462, 522, 531, 553

Cloth and clothing
260, 642

Courage and heroism
113, 140, 286, 309, 331, 430, 444, 586, 588

Cowboys and ranch life
1, 32, 128, 158, 595, 622

Death
35, 86, 108, 144, 214, 315, 340, 434, 528, 539

Deserts
218, 250, 251, 296

Diaries and writing
94, 181, 347, 547, 581, 649

Disabilities
85, 335, 347, 404, 675

Dragons
100, 113, 160

Ecology and the environment
180, 295, 296, 332, 618

Emigration and immigration
20, 26, 98, 122, 149, 286, 440, 442, 550

Future societies
286, 550

Family life
14, 39, 172, 183, 230, 285, 310, 312, 479, 483

Family relationships
Fathers
16, 25, 30, 90, 140, 290, 361, 378, 397, 419, 594, 688

Grandfathers
138, 227, 249, 346, 393, 431, 442,
529, 530, 533, 539, 542, 569
Grandmothers
11, 19, 41, 64, 76, 393, 434, 542
Mothers
38, 47, 79, 96, 200, 252, 287, 290,
315, 393, 524, 547, 572, 574
Parents and children
276, 511, 353, 552, 646, 669
Siblings
14, 63, 101, 254, 282, 414, 433, 543,
586, 607, 623
Stepmothers
173, 255, 623

Fathers
See Family relationships

Farms and farm life
31, 40, 42, 80, 111, 240, 321, 346,
387, 542, 619

Folklore
59, 68, 71, 72, 89, 185, 222, 235, 292,
549, 686

Friendship
50, 105, 112, 144, 238, 239, 245, 258,
388, 397, 402, 408, 418, 438, 474,
478, 509, 515, 540, 560, 570, 576,
582, 584, 600, 677

Gay/lesbian identity
315, 339, 345, 349

Grandparents
See Family relationships

Holidays and festivals
33, 35, 43, 45, 69, 87, 98, 204, 328

Holocaust
142, 195, 244, 349, 352, 371, 401,
406, 424, 426, 427, 450, 484, 490,
497, 498, 499, 508

Homelessness
93, 109, 575

Horses
136, 322, 328, 428

Hospitals
238, 324, 592

Imagination
118, 320, 330, 505, 524, 613, 644

Internment camps
99, 129, 141

Kites
18, 212

Language
384, 676

Markets
11, 54, 451

Mothers
See Family relationships

Moon
476, 513, 606

Moving
149, 312, 576

Mysteries
84, 112, 322, 432, 481, 533

Oceans
50, 86, 124, 295, 320, 329

Opera
89, 154

Orphans
109, 173, 281, 390, 391, 402, 419,
420, 444, 508, 575, 576, 604

Parents
See Family relationships

Plants and gardening
73, 109, 296, 534, 577, 667

Poetry
15, 28, 31, 38, 44, 49, 201, 260, 327,
554, 611, 630, 646, 681

Poverty
23, 25, 107, 150, 211, 290, 483

Prejudice and discrimination
111, 150, 258, 429, 509, 582

Refugees
98, 115, 163, 165, 195, 214, 215, 223, 245, 281, 599

Schools and classrooms
22, 24, 62, 112, 199, 342, 425, 440, 541, 655

Seasons
61, 139, 285, 348, 389, 423, 482, 489, 543

Siblings
See Family relationships

Stepmothers
See Family relationships

Suicide
62, 108, 200

Theater
263, 272, 464, 604, 661

Toys
317, 355, 553, 595, 609, 620, 672

Travel
104, 181, 375, 382, 517, 518, 565, 630, 695

Trees
30, 41, 99, 168, 180, 182, 204, 301, 442, 636

Twins
166, 347, 528, 533, 588, 639

War
56, 105, 122, 123, 129, 165, 195, 197, 238, 248, 255, 281, 288, 301, 307, 325, 371, 394, 409, 427, 437, 444, 488, 490, 551, 597, 651, 679, 681, 682, 684

Weather
255, 307, 437, 488, 597

Women and women's rights
180, 217, 269, 398, 601

Zoos
337, 435

About the Editor

Susan Stan is an assistant professor of English at Central Michigan University, where she teaches courses in children's literature, including one devoted to international literature for children and young adults. An active member of the United States Board on Books for Young People, she has served on that organization's executive board and has attended numerous world congresses of the International Board on Books for Young People.